GEGE AKUTAMI

That's good, that's good.
Aaaaaand stop!

GEGE AKUTAMI published a few short
works before starting *Jujutsu Kaisen*, which began
serialization in *Weekly Shonen Jump* in 2018.

JUJUTSU KAISEN

VOLUME 8
SHONEN JUMP MANGA EDITION

BY GEGE AKUTAMI

TRANSLATION Stefan Koza
TOUCH-UP ART & LETTERING Snir Aharon
DESIGN Joy Zhang
EDITOR John Bae
CONSULTING EDITOR Erika Onabe

JUJUTSU KAISEN © 2018 by Gege Akutami
All rights reserved.
First published in Japan in 2018 by SHUEISHA Inc., Tokyo.
English translation rights arranged by SHUEISHA Inc.

The stories, characters and incidents mentioned
in this publication are entirely fictional.

Printed in Italy

Published by VIZ Media, LLC
P.O. Box 77010
San Francisco, CA 94107

10 9 8 7 6 5
First printing, February 2021
Fifth printing, August 2021

PARENTAL ADVISORY
JUJUTSU KAISEN is rated T+ for Older Teen
and is recommended for ages 16 and up. This
volume contains fantasy violence.

viz.com

JUJUTSU KAISEN

8

HIDDEN INVENTORY

STORY AND ART BY GEGE AKUTAMI

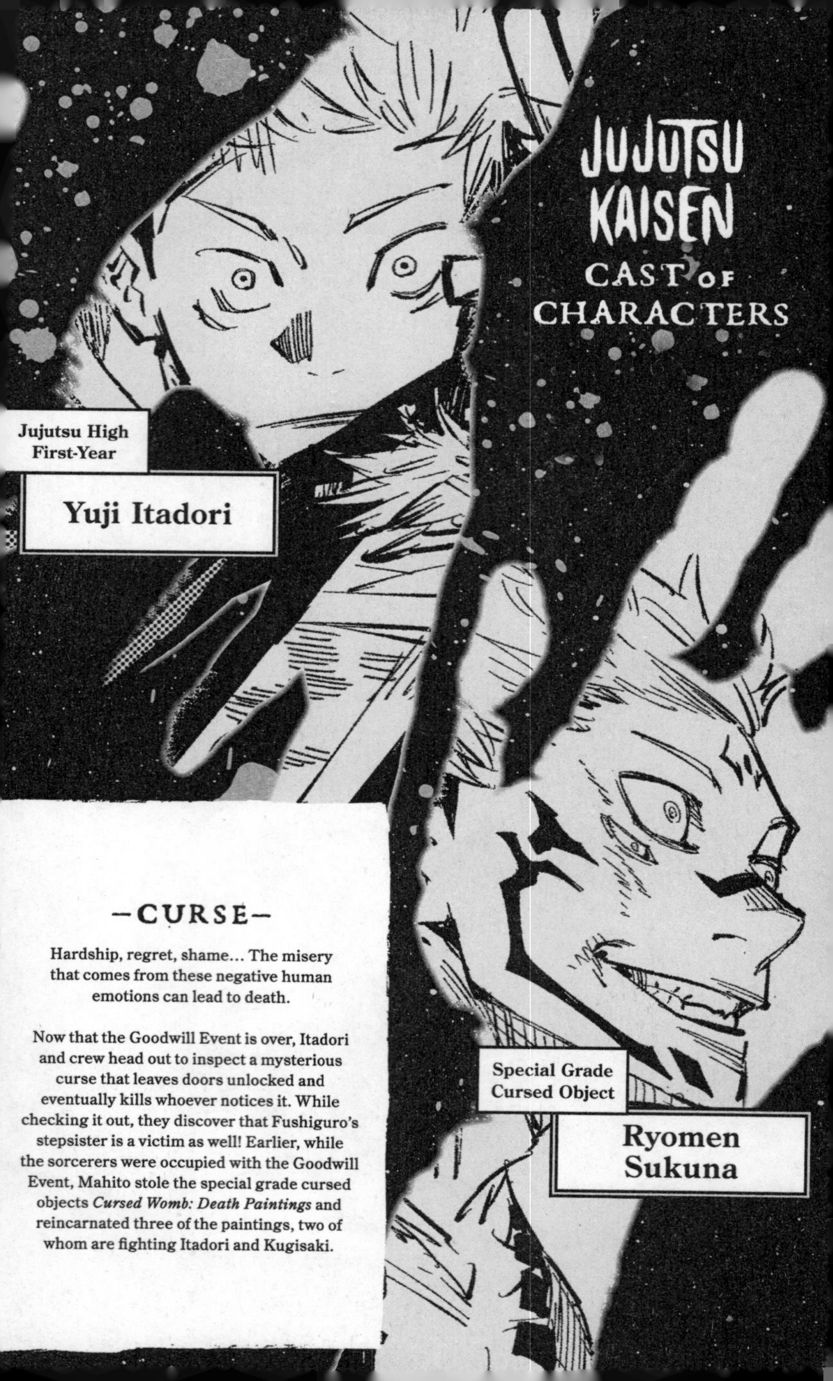
JUJUTSU KAISEN
CAST OF CHARACTERS
Special Grade Cursed Object
Ryomen Sukuna
Jujutsu High First-Year
Yuji Itadori

—CURSE—

Hardship, regret, shame… The misery that comes from these negative human emotions can lead to death.

Now that the Goodwill Event is over, Itadori and crew head out to inspect a mysterious curse that leaves doors unlocked and eventually kills whoever notices it. While checking it out, they discover that Fushiguro's stepsister is a victim as well! Earlier, while the sorcerers were occupied with the Goodwill Event, Mahito stole the special grade cursed objects *Cursed Womb: Death Paintings* and reincarnated three of the paintings, two of whom are fighting Itadori and Kugisaki.

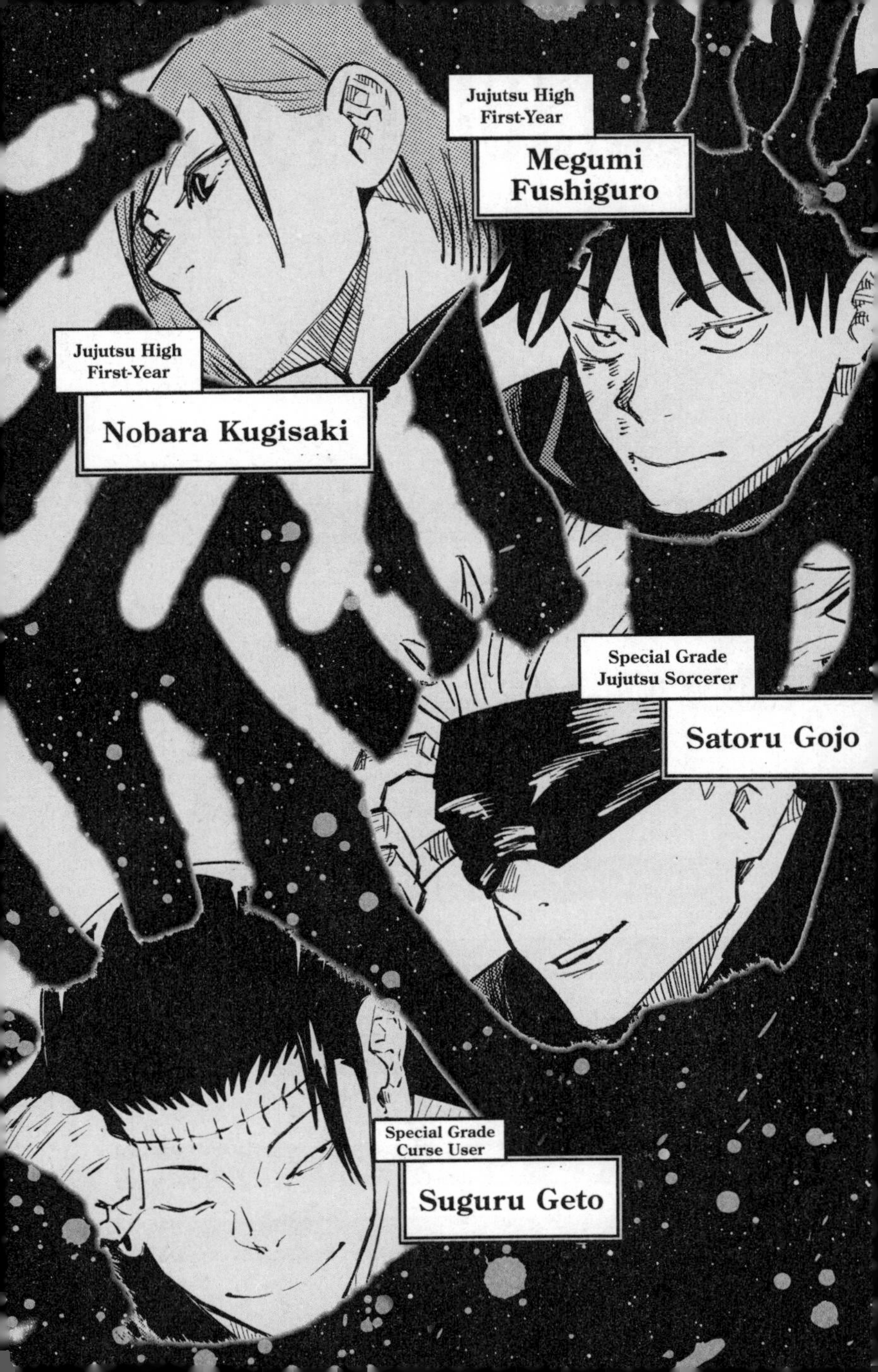
Jujutsu High First-Year
Megumi Fushiguro
Jujutsu High First-Year
Nobara Kugisaki
Special Grade Jujutsu Sorcerer
Satoru Gojo
Special Grade Curse User
Suguru Geto

JUJUTSU KAISEN

8

HIDDEN INVENTORY

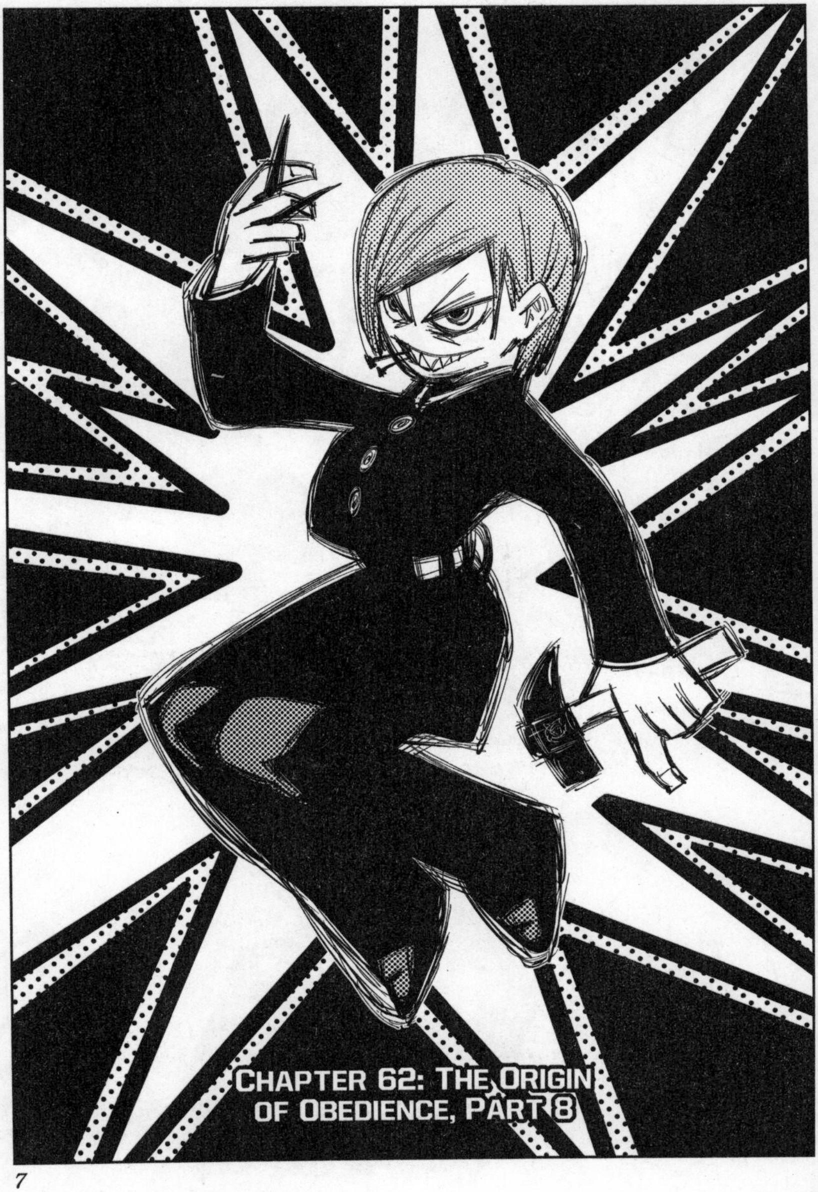
CHAPTER 62: THE ORIGIN
OF OBEDIENCE, PART 8

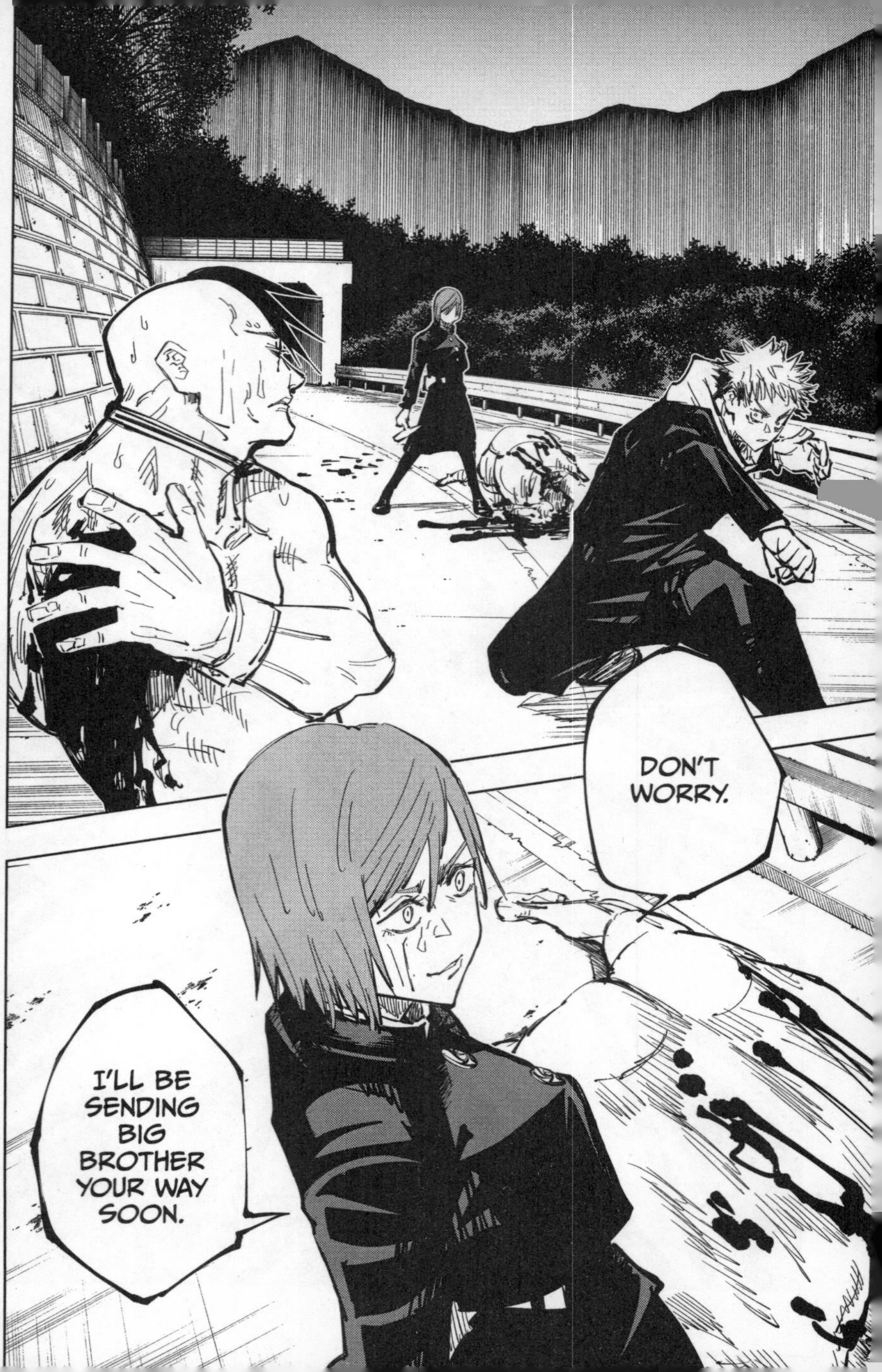
DON'T WORRY.
I'LL BE SENDING BIG BROTHER YOUR WAY SOON.

WE THREE ARE ONE.

KECHIZU...

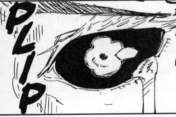

I'M SORRY, BIG BROTHER. EVEN THOUGH I WAS HERE, I WASN'T ABLE TO PROTECT HIM.

PLIP

TEARS OF AFFECTION...

BECAUSE OF THIS SURPRISING DISPLAY OF EMOTION, ITADORI DIDN'T FINISH HIM OFF.

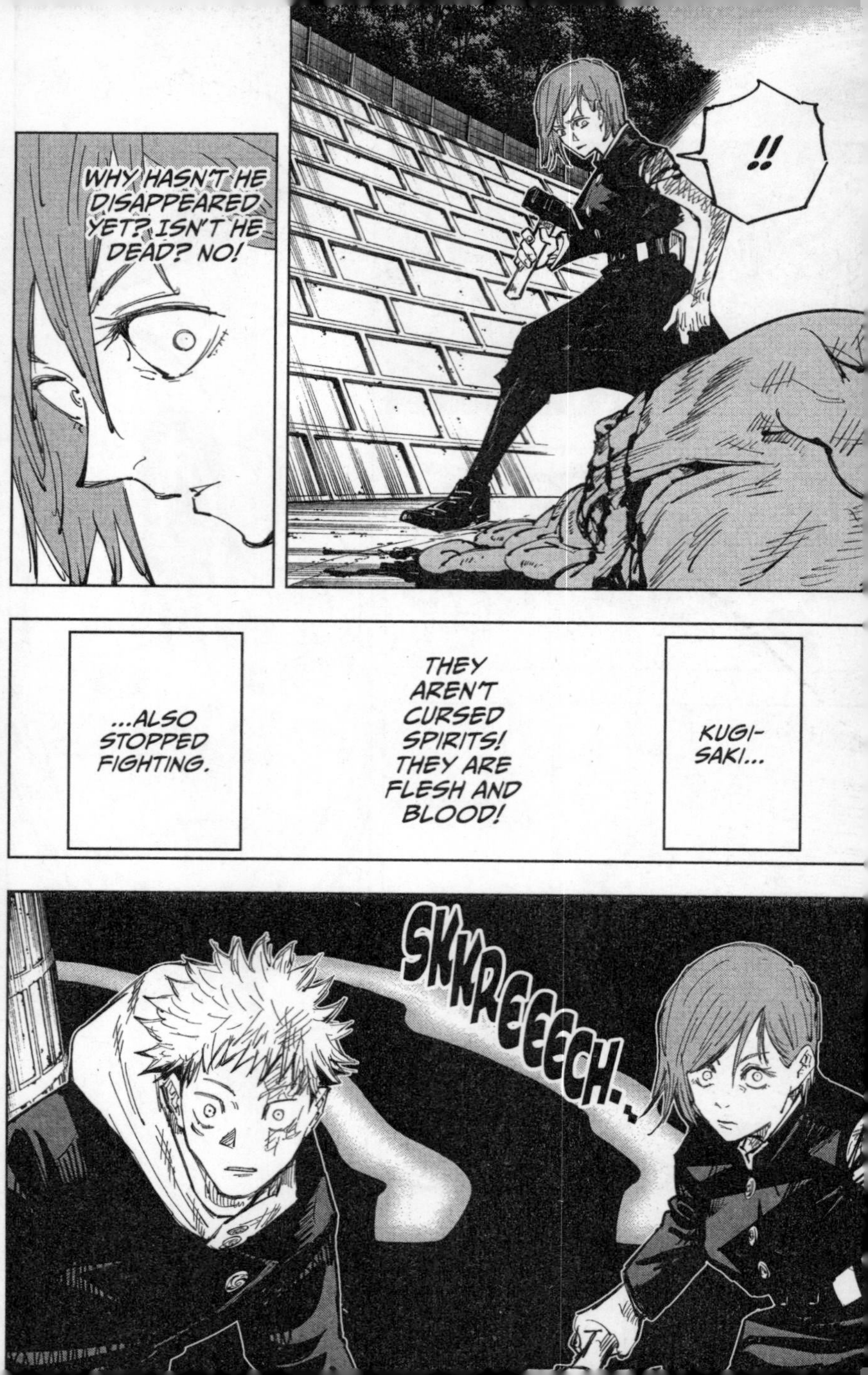
!!
WHY HASN'T HE DISAPPEARED YET? ISN'T HE DEAD? NO!
KUGI-SAKI...
THEY AREN'T CURSED SPIRITS! THEY ARE FLESH AND BLOOD!
...ALSO STOPPED FIGHTING.
SKKREEEECH..

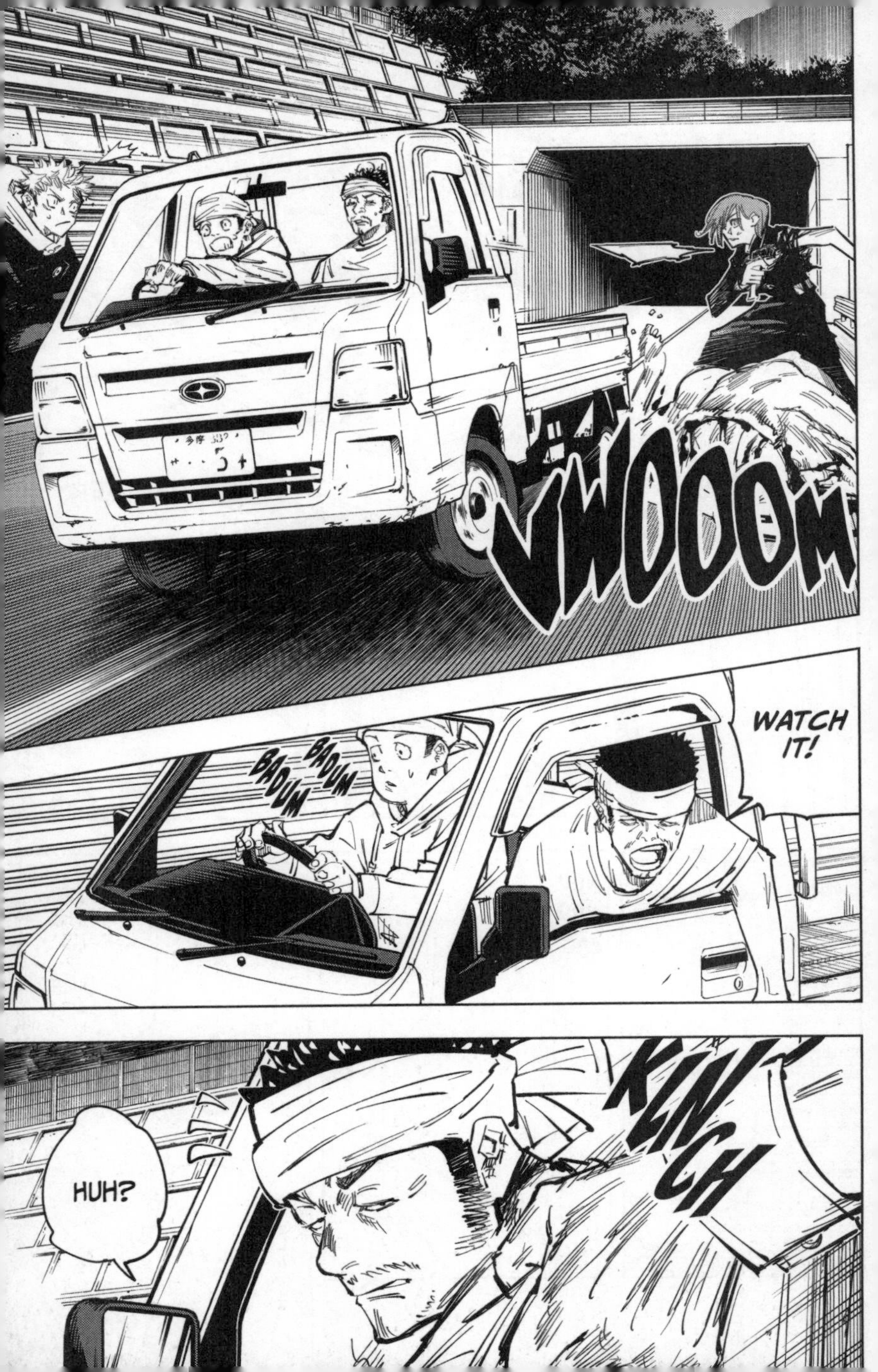
VWOOOM
WATCH IT!
BADUM BADUM
KLINCH
HUH?

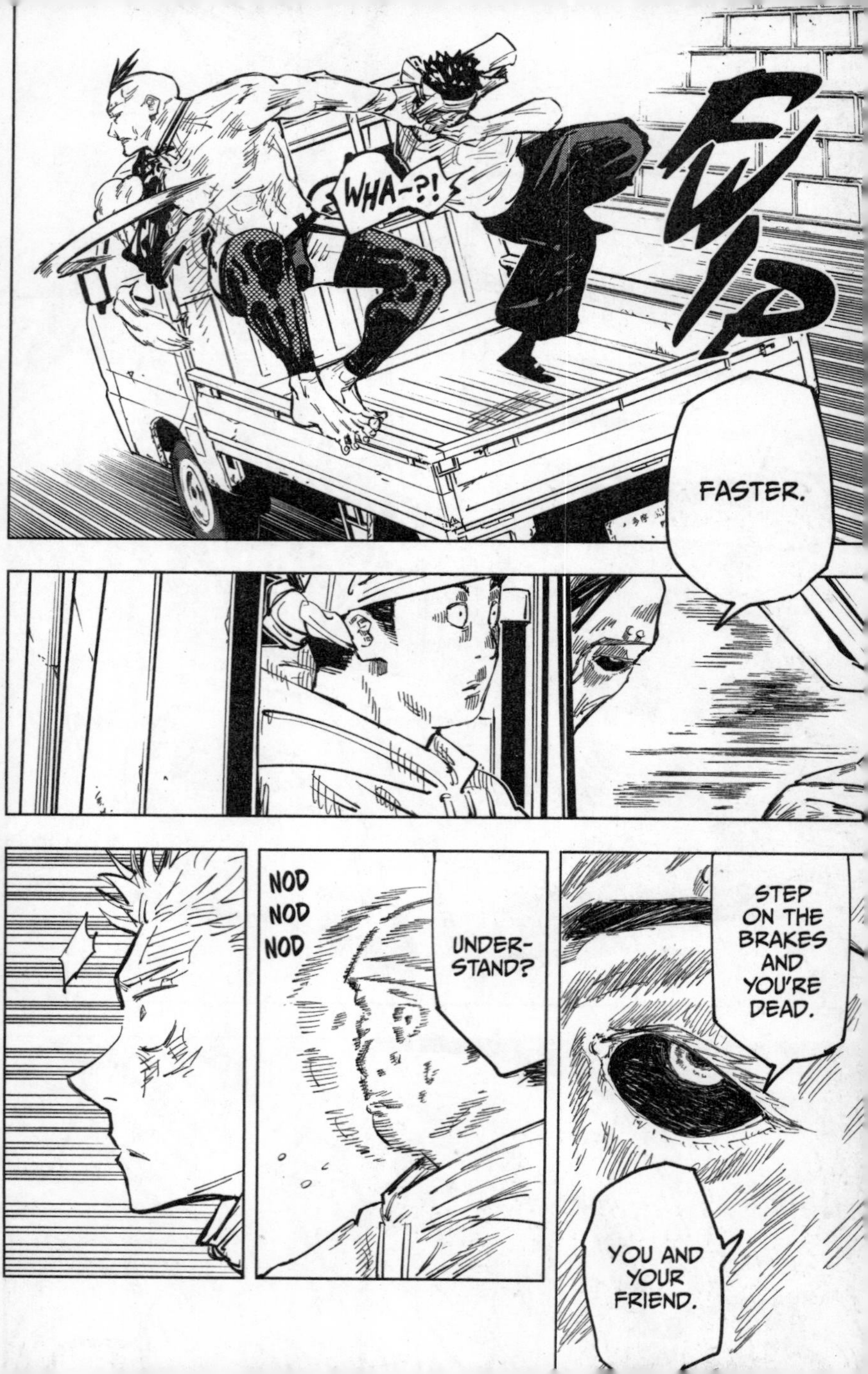
FWIP
WHA-?!
FASTER.
STEP ON THE BRAKES AND YOU'RE DEAD.
YOU AND YOUR FRIEND.
UNDER-STAND?
NOD NOD NOD

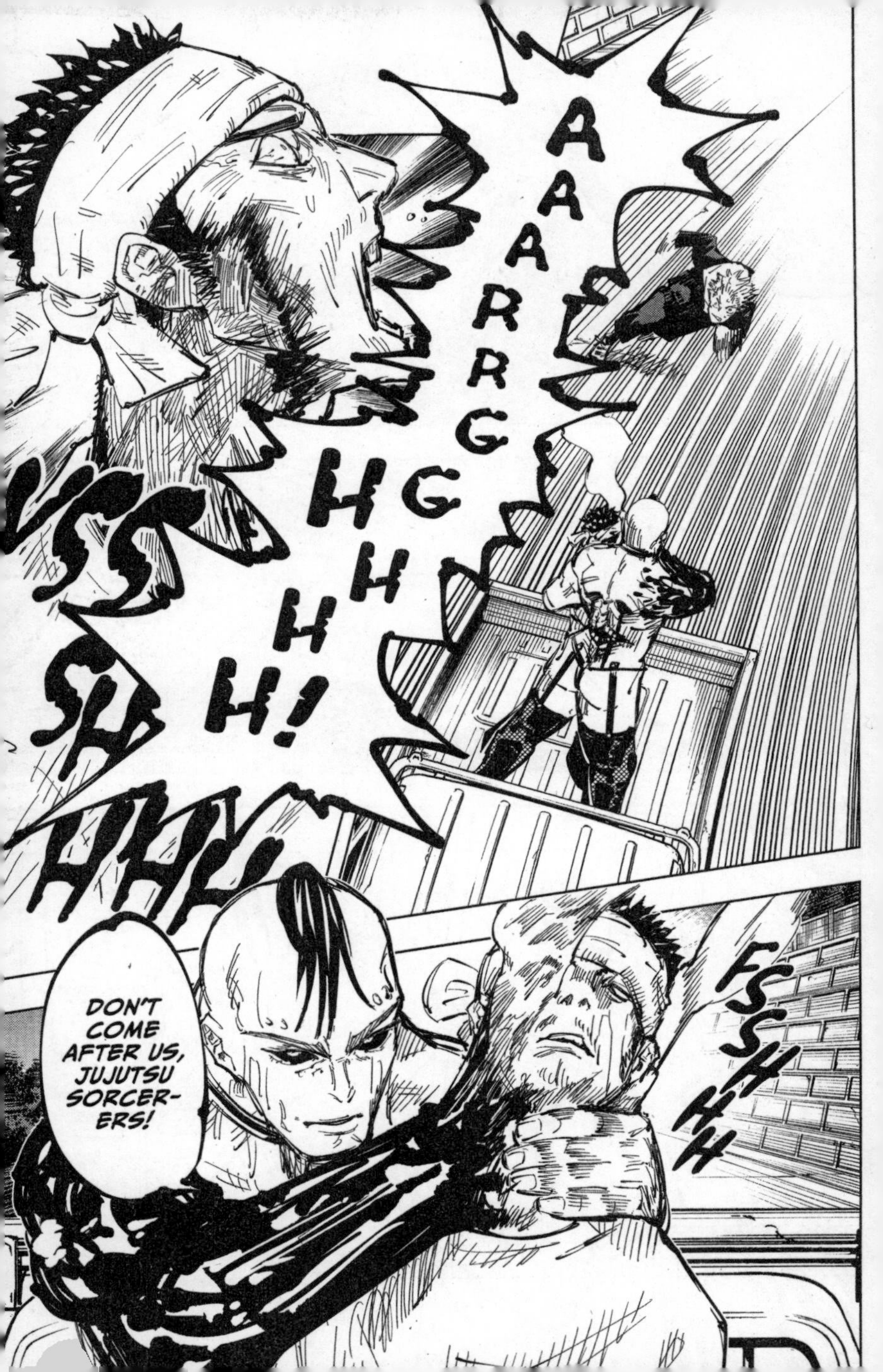
AAARRGGHHHH!
FSSHHH
DON'T COME AFTER US, JUJUTSU SORCERERS!

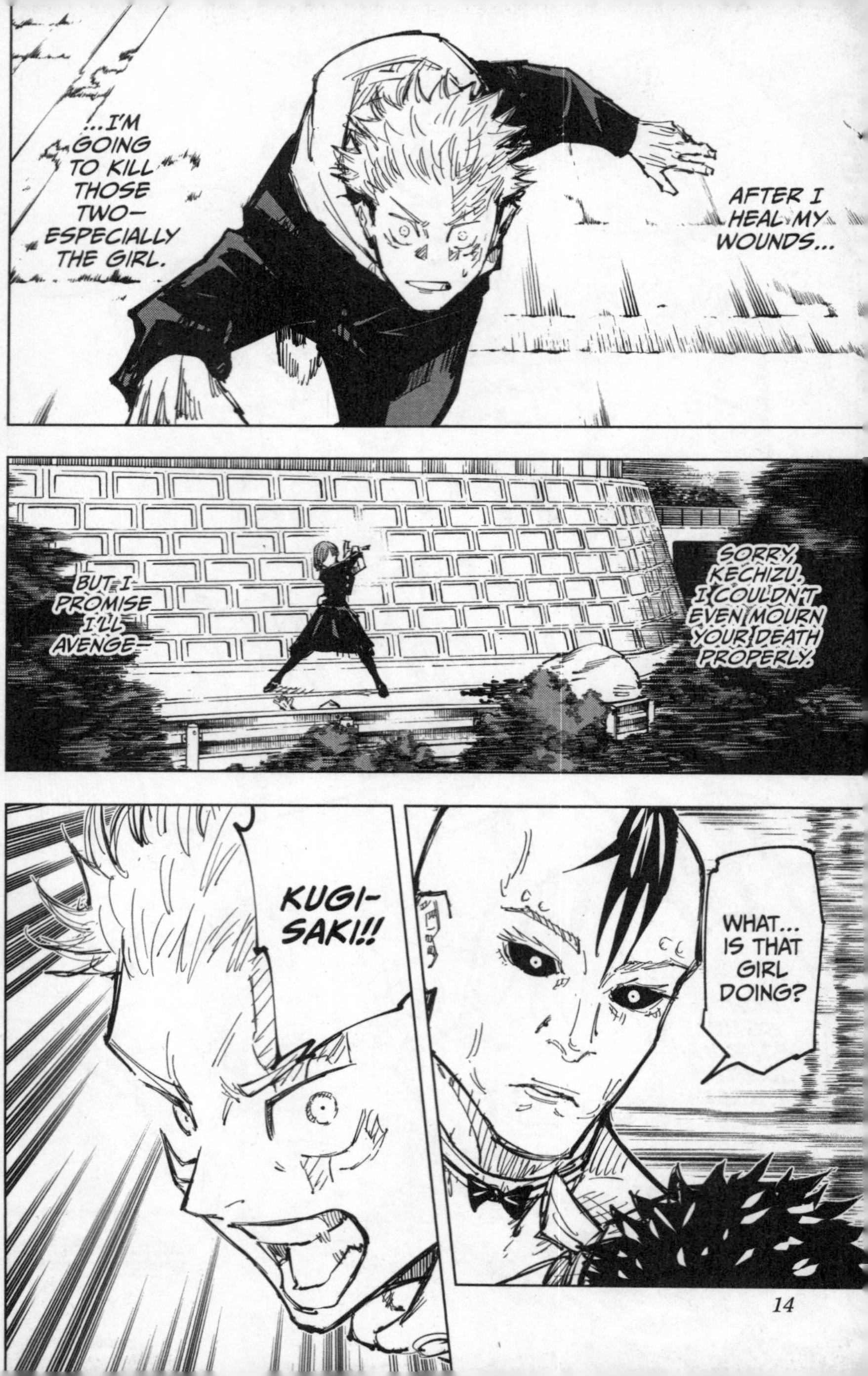
AFTER I HEAL MY WOUNDS...
...I'M GOING TO KILL THOSE TWO— ESPECIALLY THE GIRL.
SORRY, KECHIZU. I COULDN'T EVEN MOURN YOUR DEATH PROPERLY.
BUT I PROMISE I'LL AVENGE—
WHAT... IS THAT GIRL DOING?
KUGI-SAKI!!

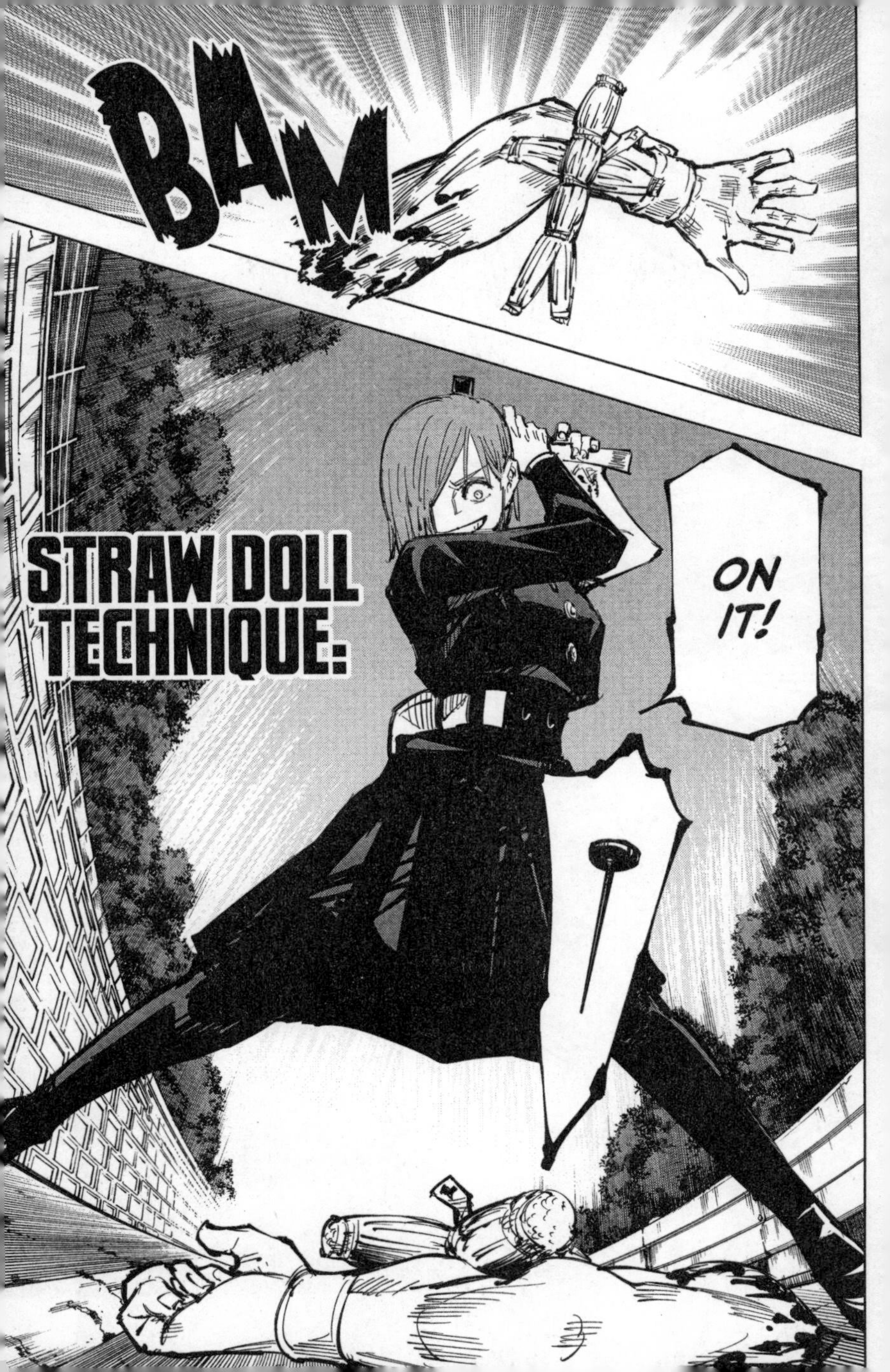
BAM
ON IT!
STRAW DOLL TECHNIQUE.

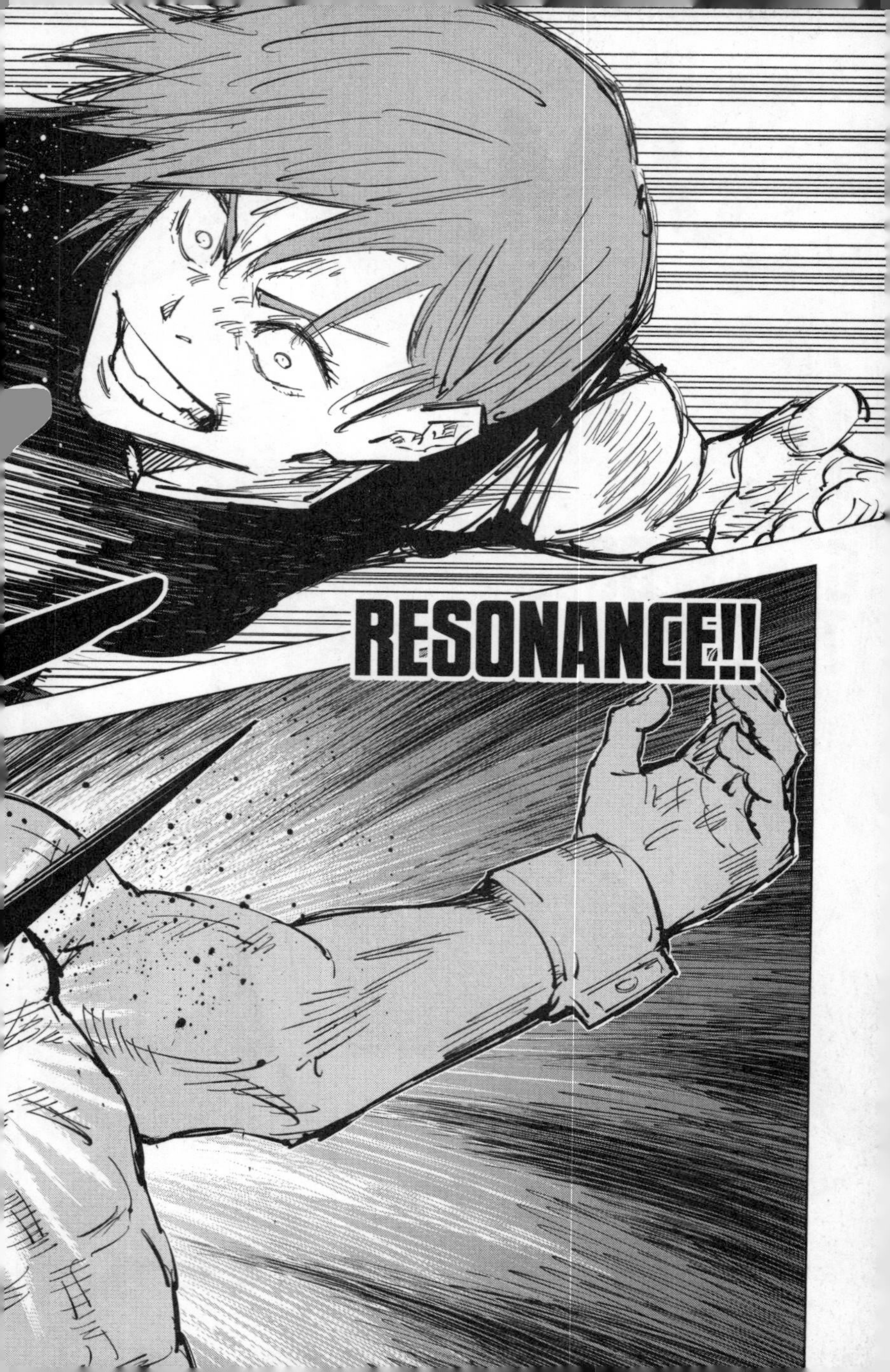
RESONANCE!!

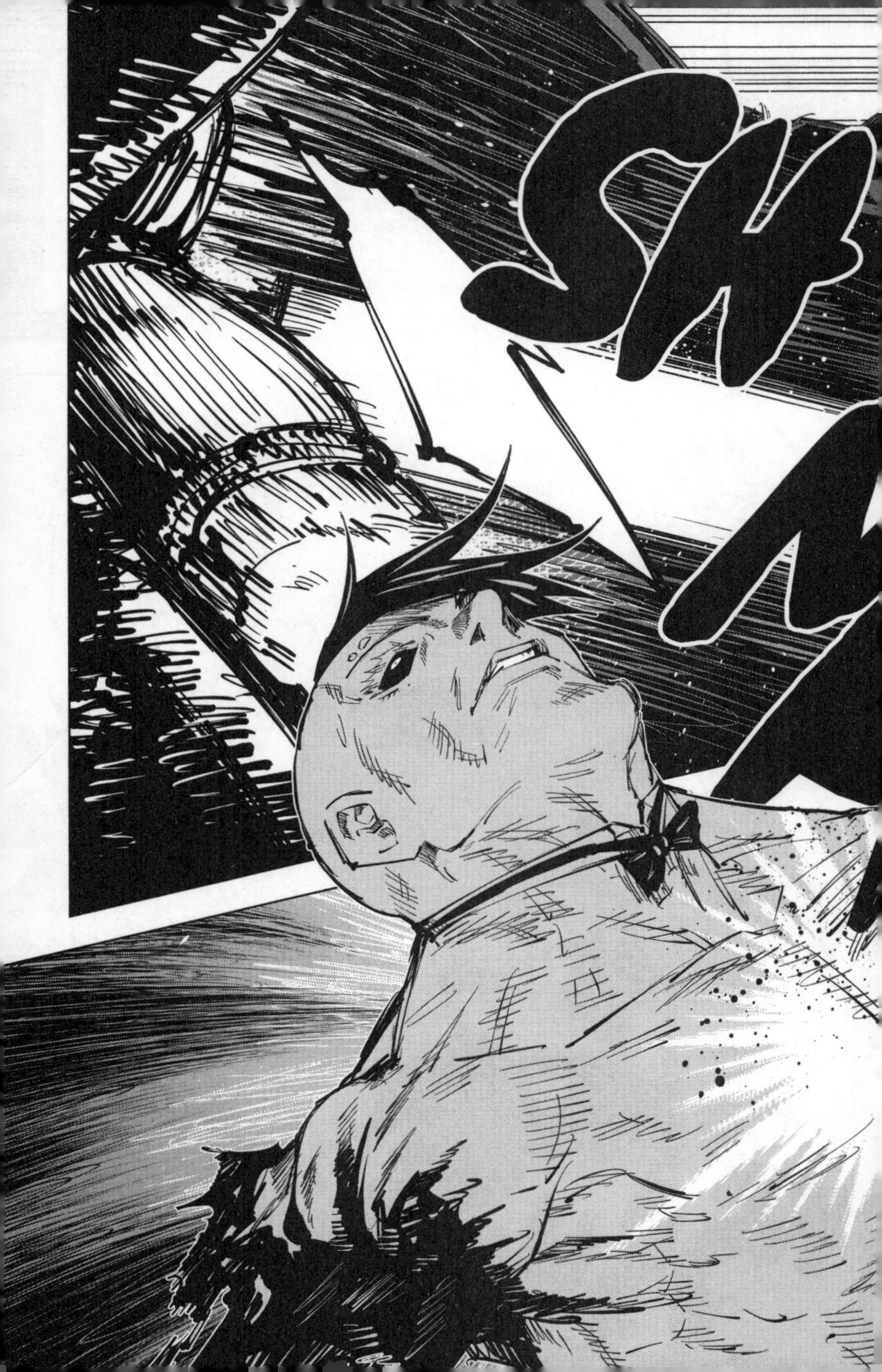
SH

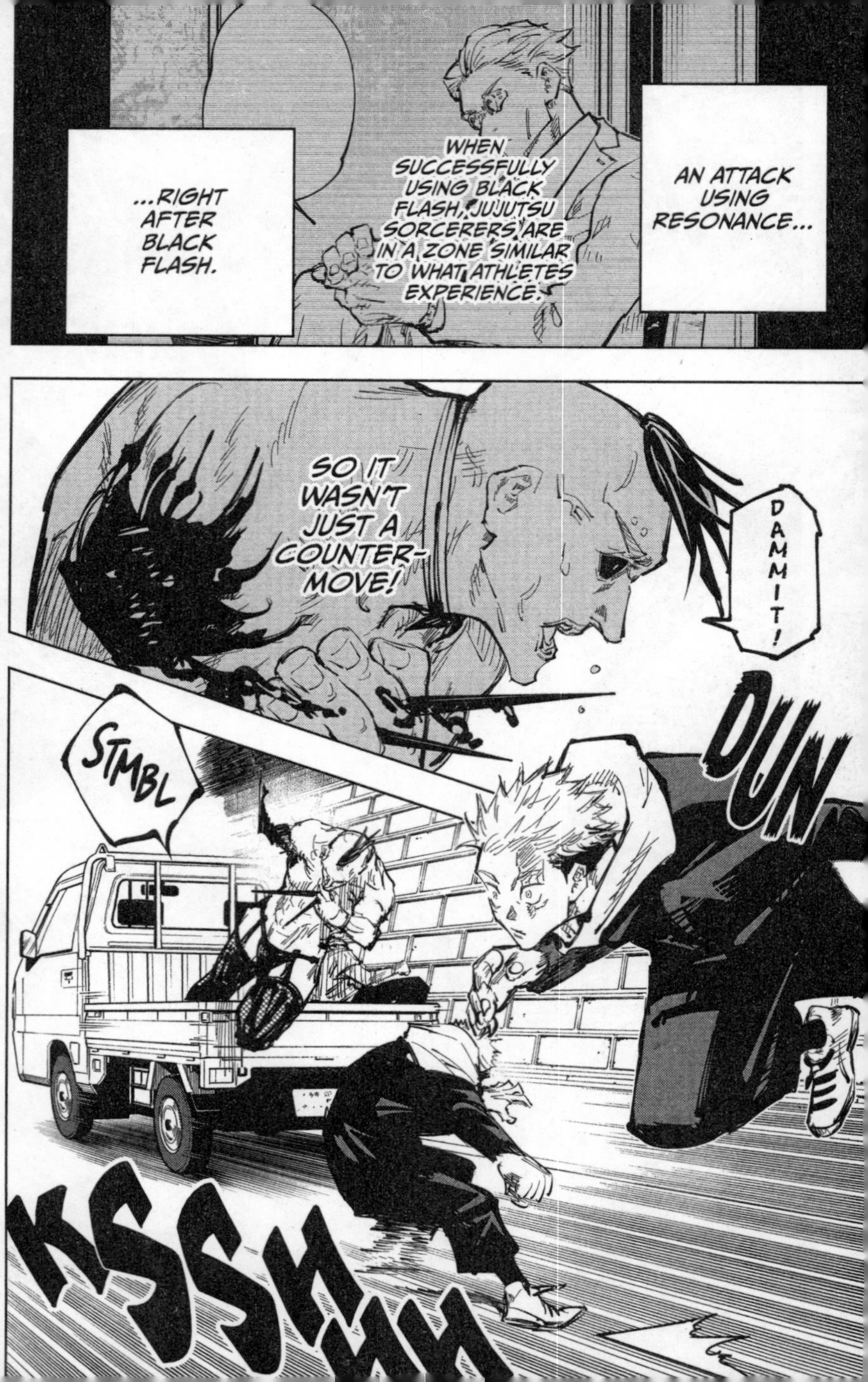
AN ATTACK USING RESONANCE...
WHEN SUCCESSFULLY USING BLACK FLASH, JUJUTSU SORCERERS ARE IN A ZONE SIMILAR TO WHAT ATHLETES EXPERIENCE.
...RIGHT AFTER BLACK FLASH.
DAMMIT!
SO IT WASN'T JUST A COUNTER-MOVE!
DUN
STMBL
KSSHHH

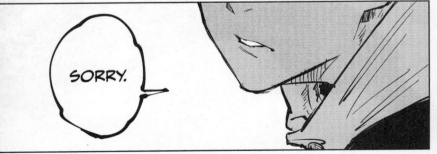

SORRY.

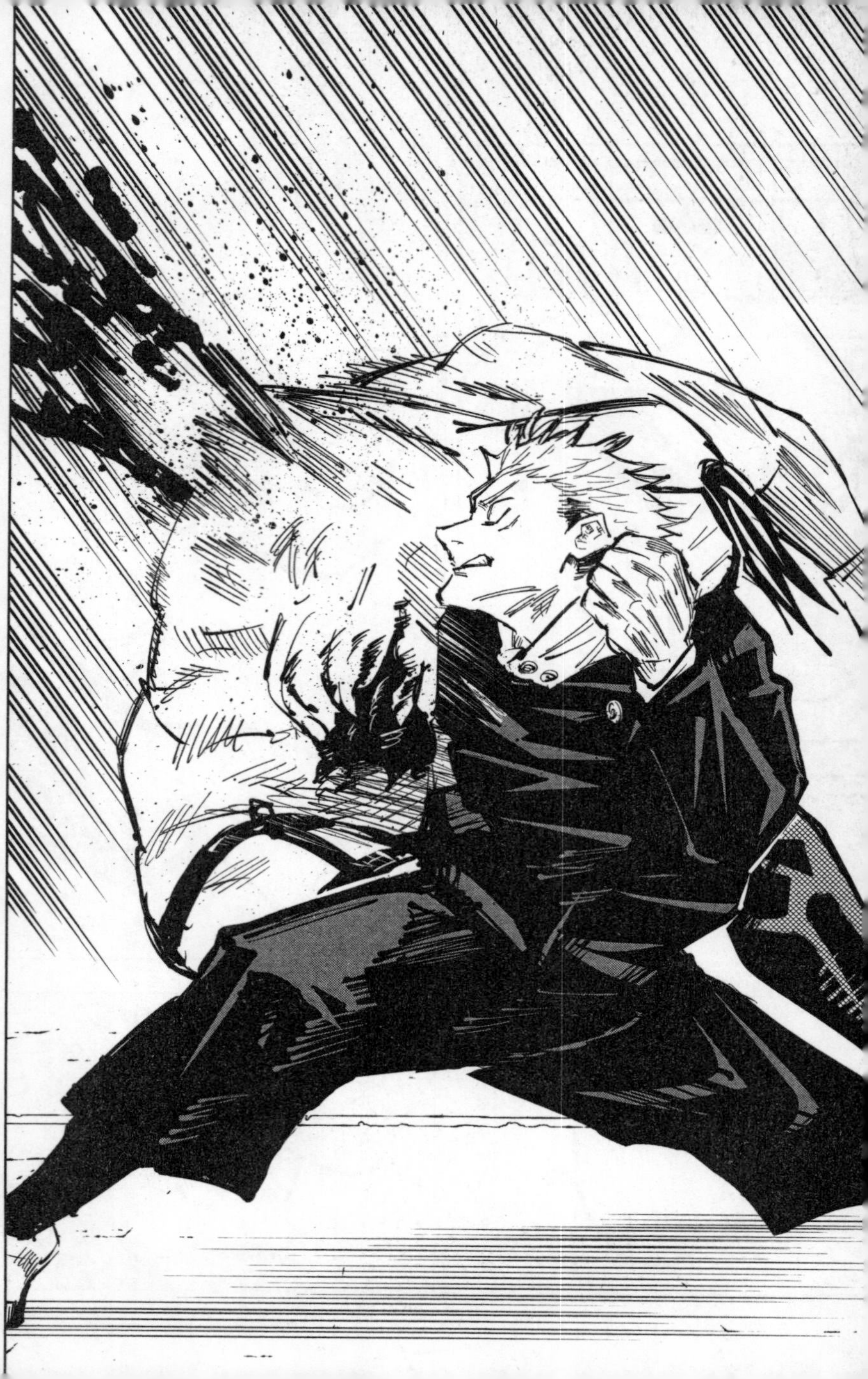

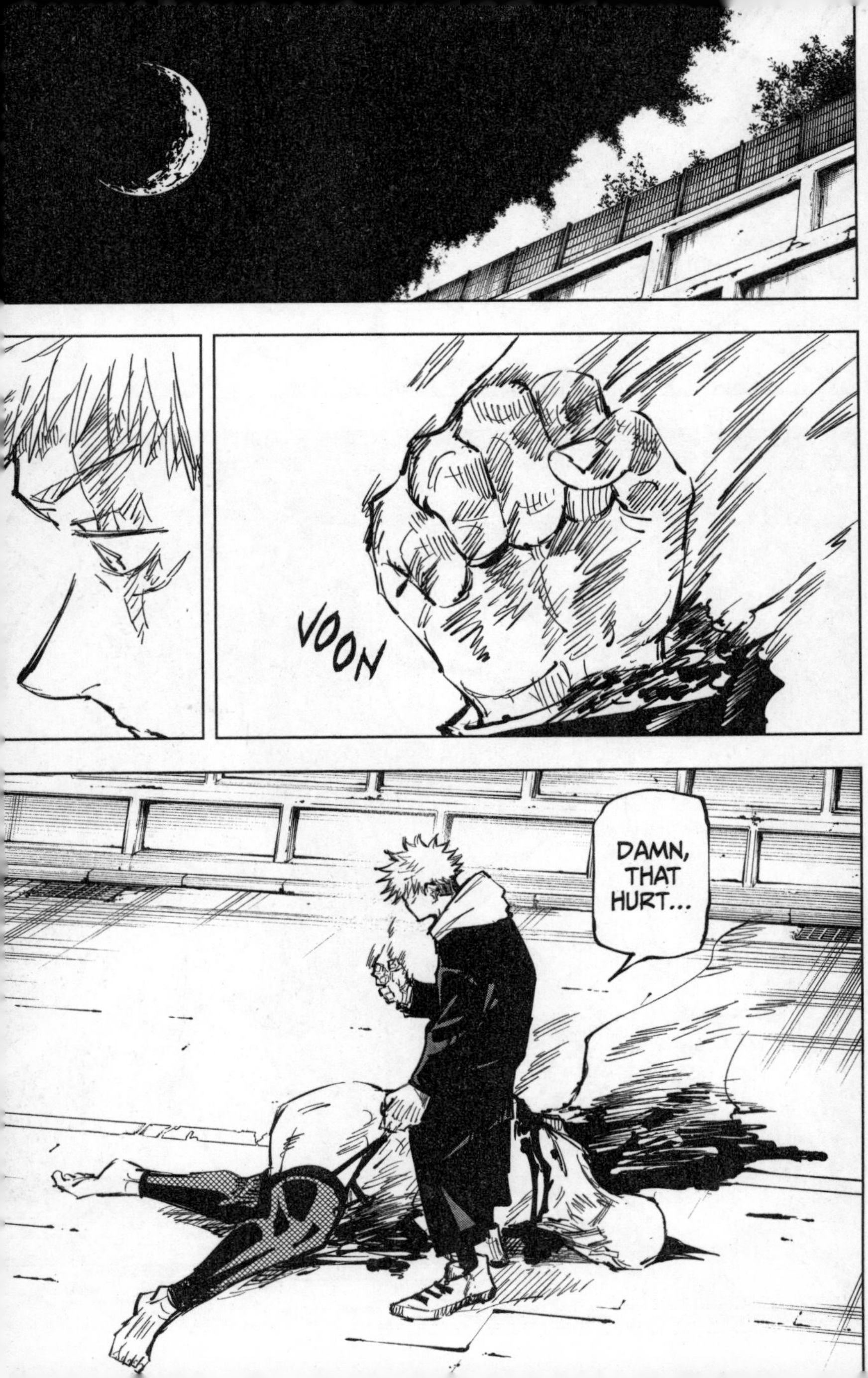
VOON
DAMN, THAT HURT...

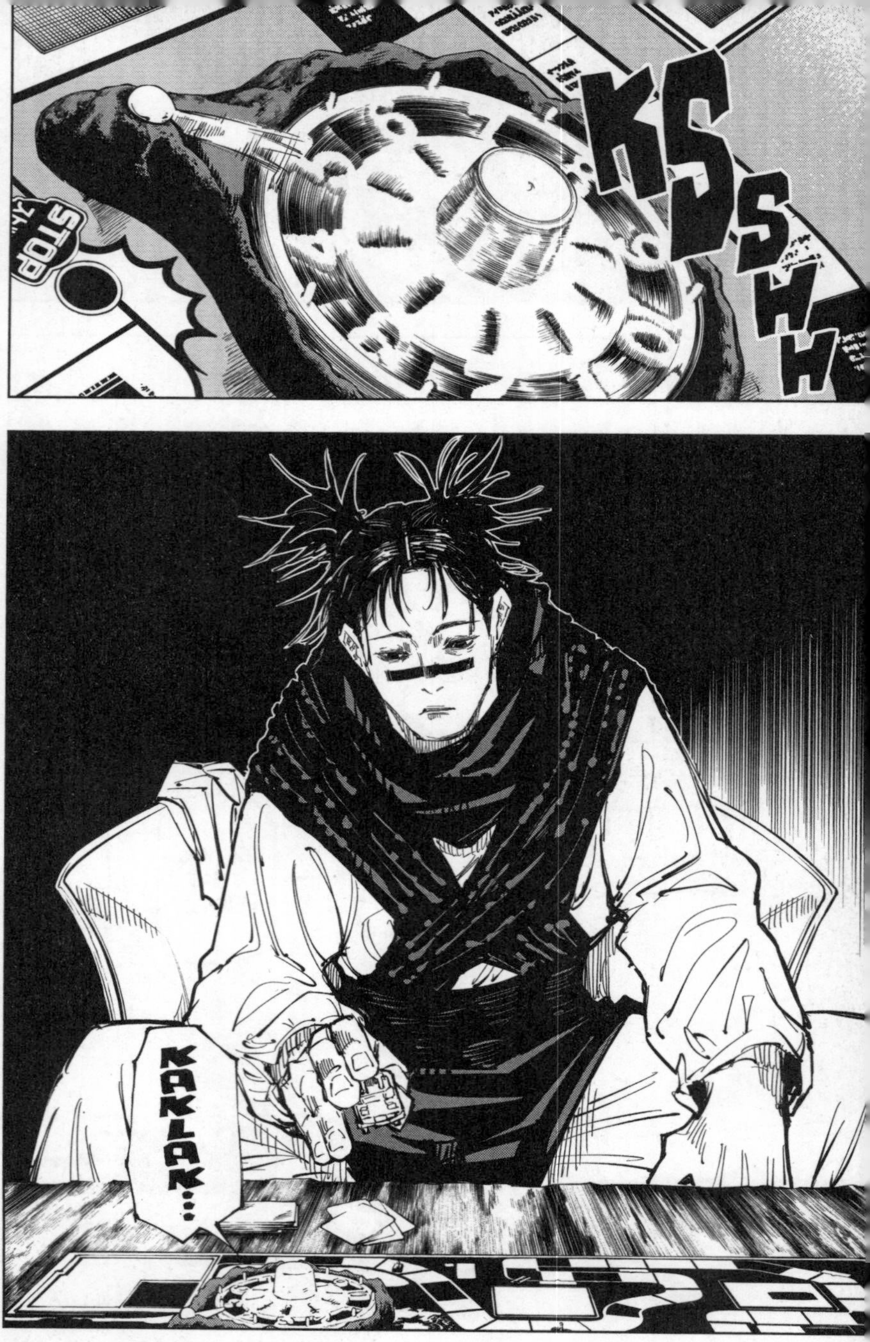
KSSHH
STOP
KAKLAK...

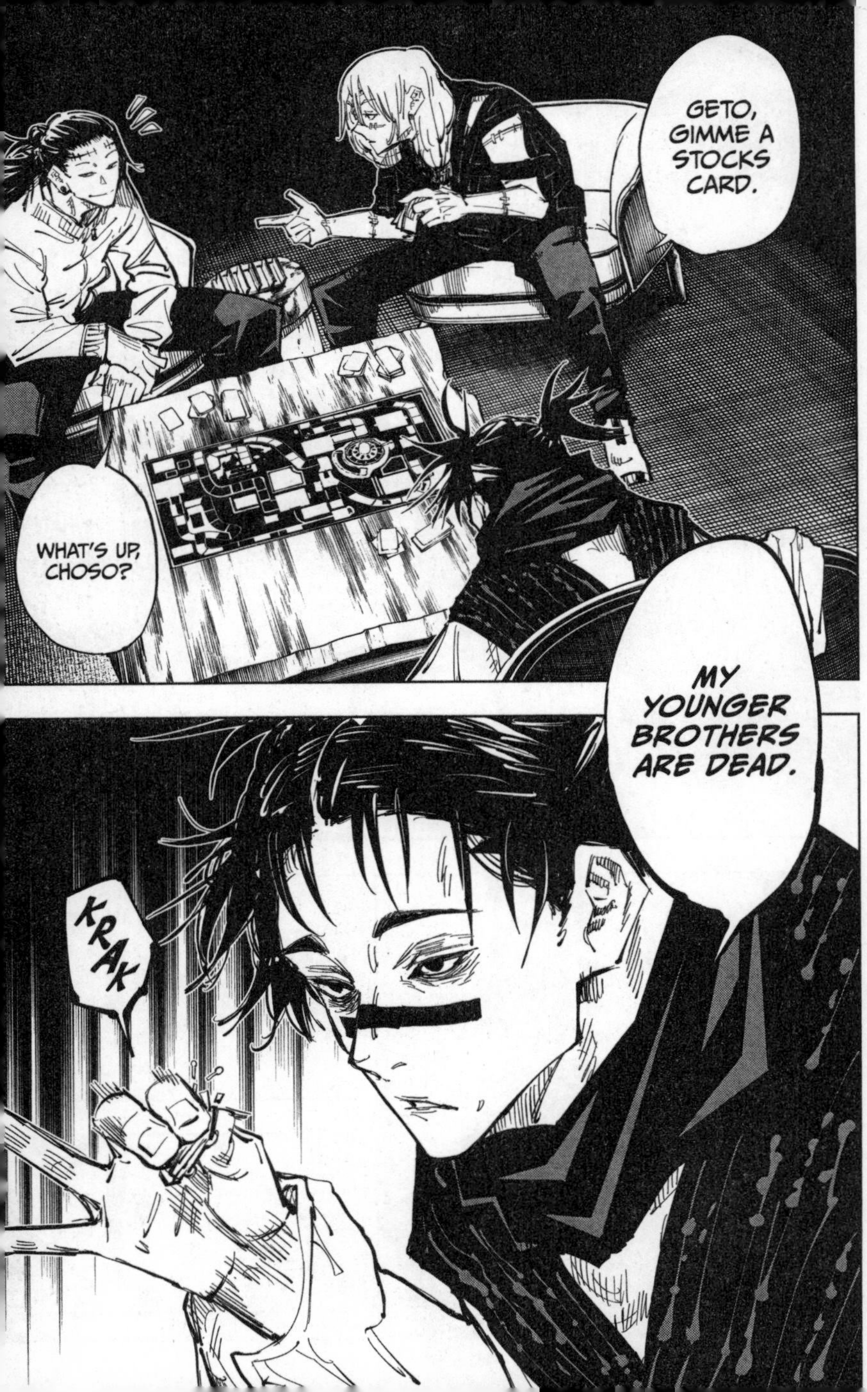
GETO, GIMME A STOCKS CARD.
WHAT'S UP, CHOSO?
MY YOUNGER BROTHERS ARE DEAD.
KRAK

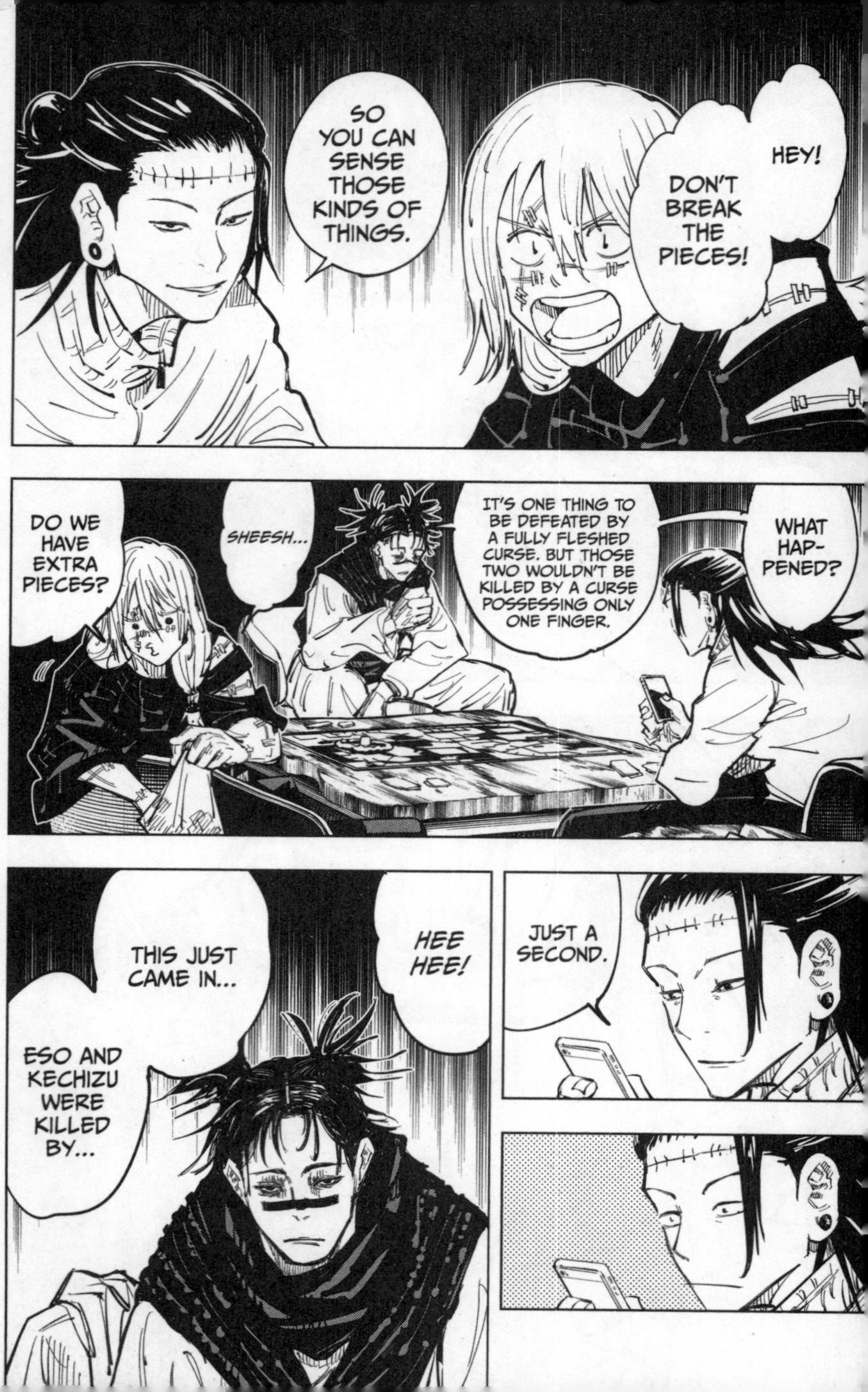
HEY!
DON'T BREAK THE PIECES!
SO YOU CAN SENSE THOSE KINDS OF THINGS.
WHAT HAP-PENED?
IT'S ONE THING TO BE DEFEATED BY A FULLY FLESHED CURSE. BUT THOSE TWO WOULDN'T BE KILLED BY A CURSE POSSESSING ONLY ONE FINGER.
SHEESH...
DO WE HAVE EXTRA PIECES?
JUST A SECOND.
HEE HEE!
THIS JUST CAME IN...
ESO AND KECHIZU WERE KILLED BY...

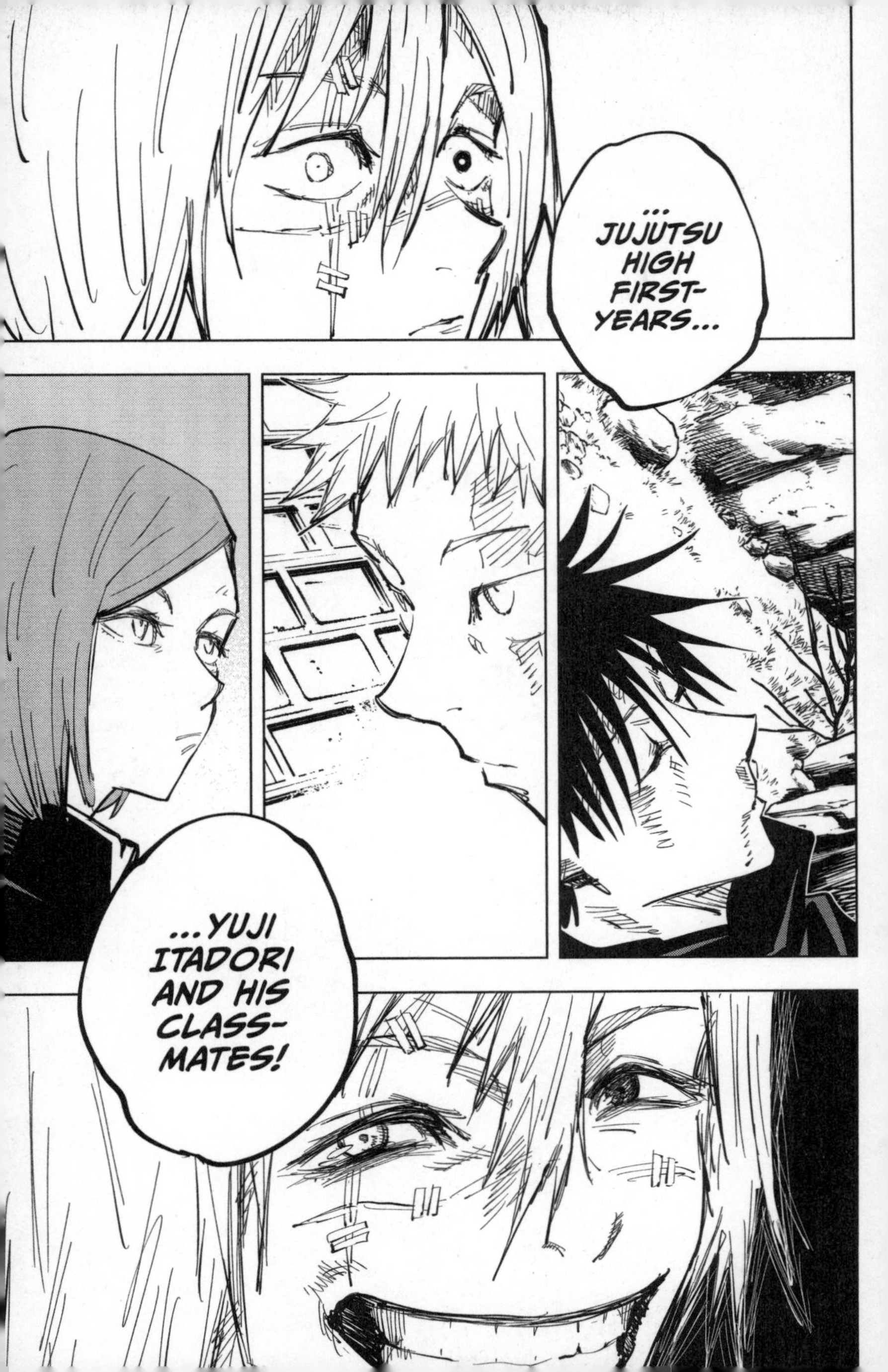
...JUJUTSU HIGH FIRST-YEARS...
...YUJI ITADORI AND HIS CLASS-MATES!

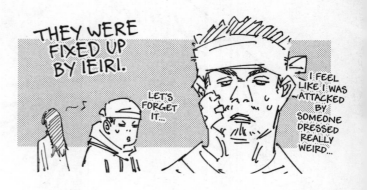

THEY WERE FIXED UP BY IEIRI.
I FEEL LIKE I WAS ATTACKED BY SOMEONE DRESSED REALLY WEIRD...
LET'S FORGET IT...

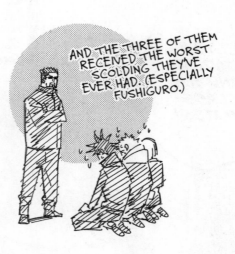

AND THE THREE OF THEM RECEIVED THE WORST SCOLDING THEY'VE EVER HAD. (ESPECIALLY FUSHIGURO.)

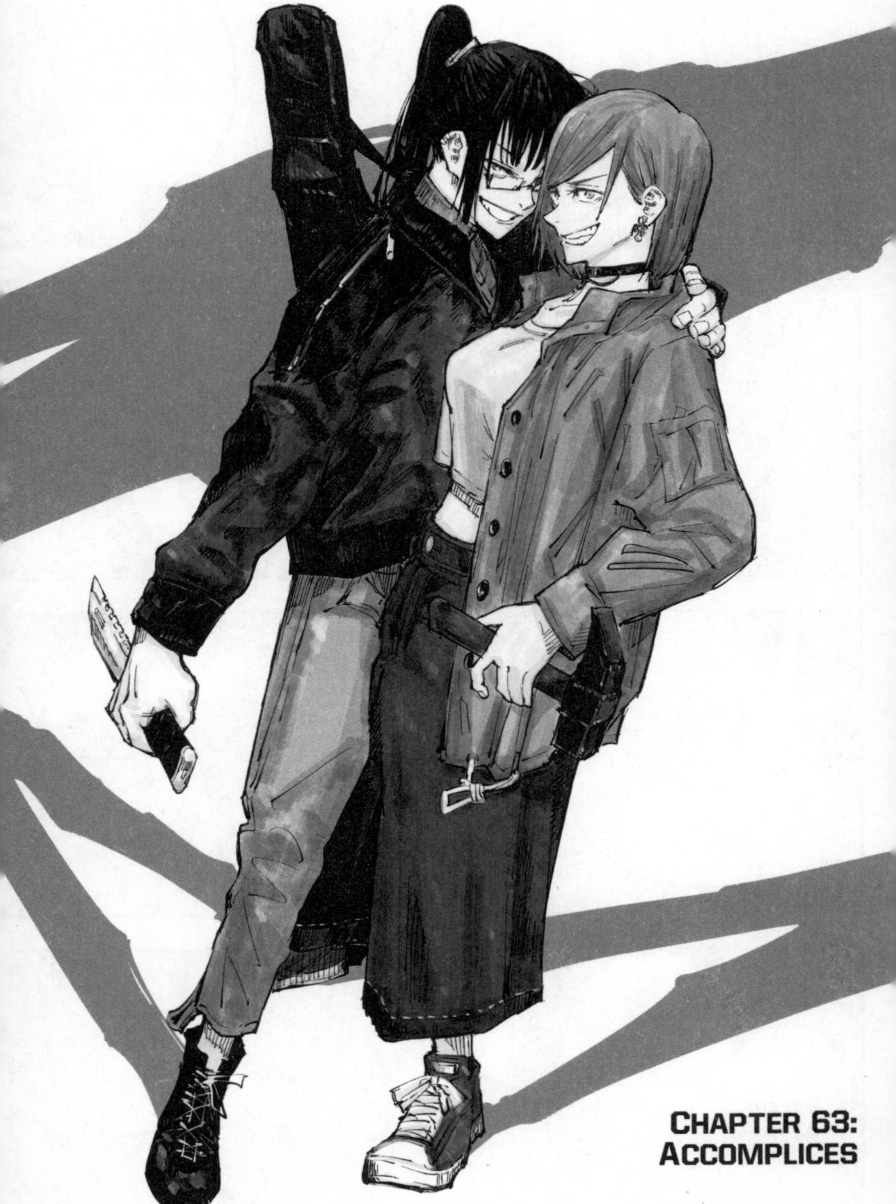

CHAPTER 63: ACCOMPLICES

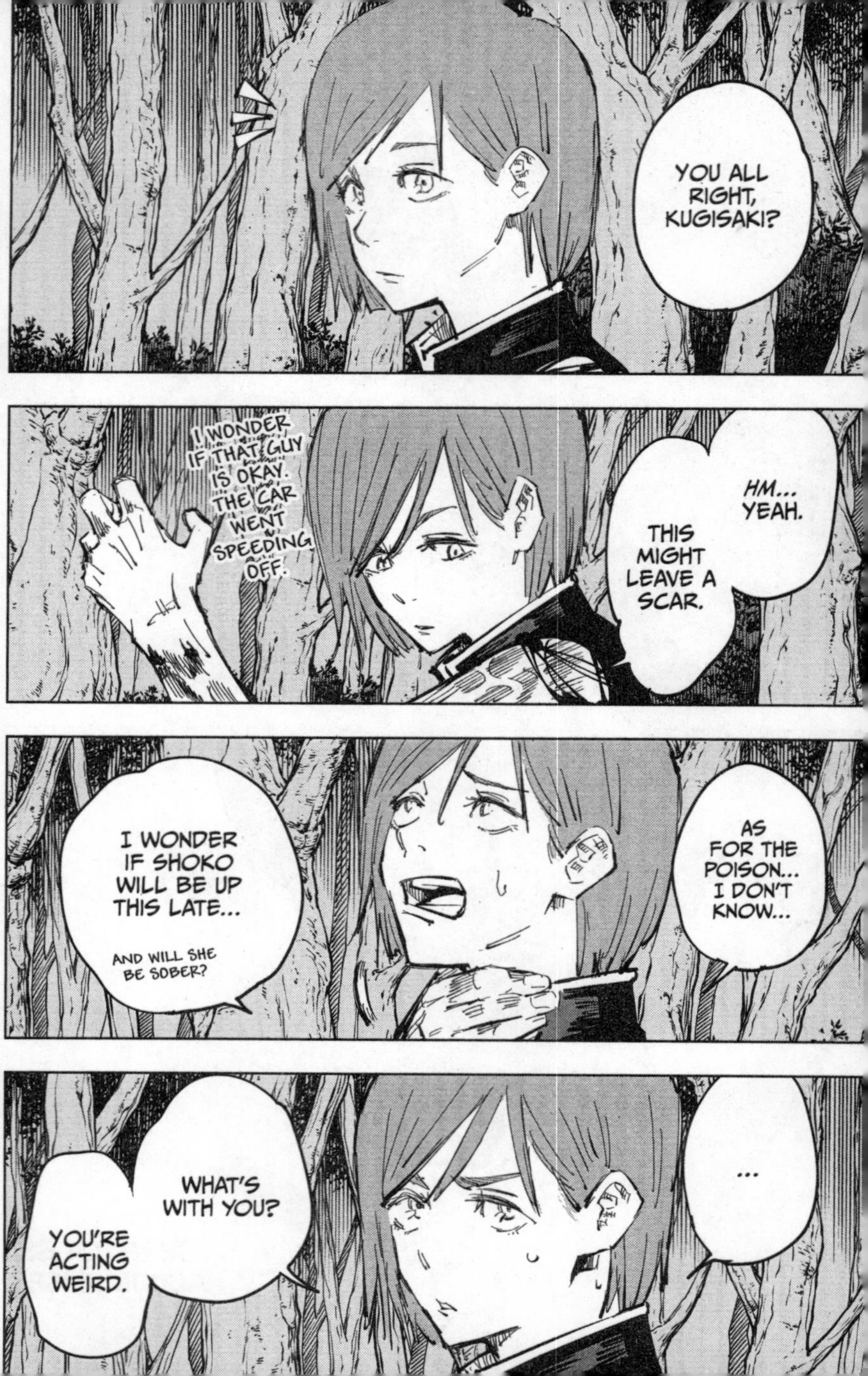
YOU ALL RIGHT, KUGISAKI?
HM... YEAH.
THIS MIGHT LEAVE A SCAR.
I WONDER IF THAT GUY IS OKAY. THE CAR WENT SPEEDING OFF.
AS FOR THE POISON... I DON'T KNOW...
I WONDER IF SHOKO WILL BE UP THIS LATE...
AND WILL SHE BE SOBER?
...
WHAT'S WITH YOU?
YOU'RE ACTING WEIRD.

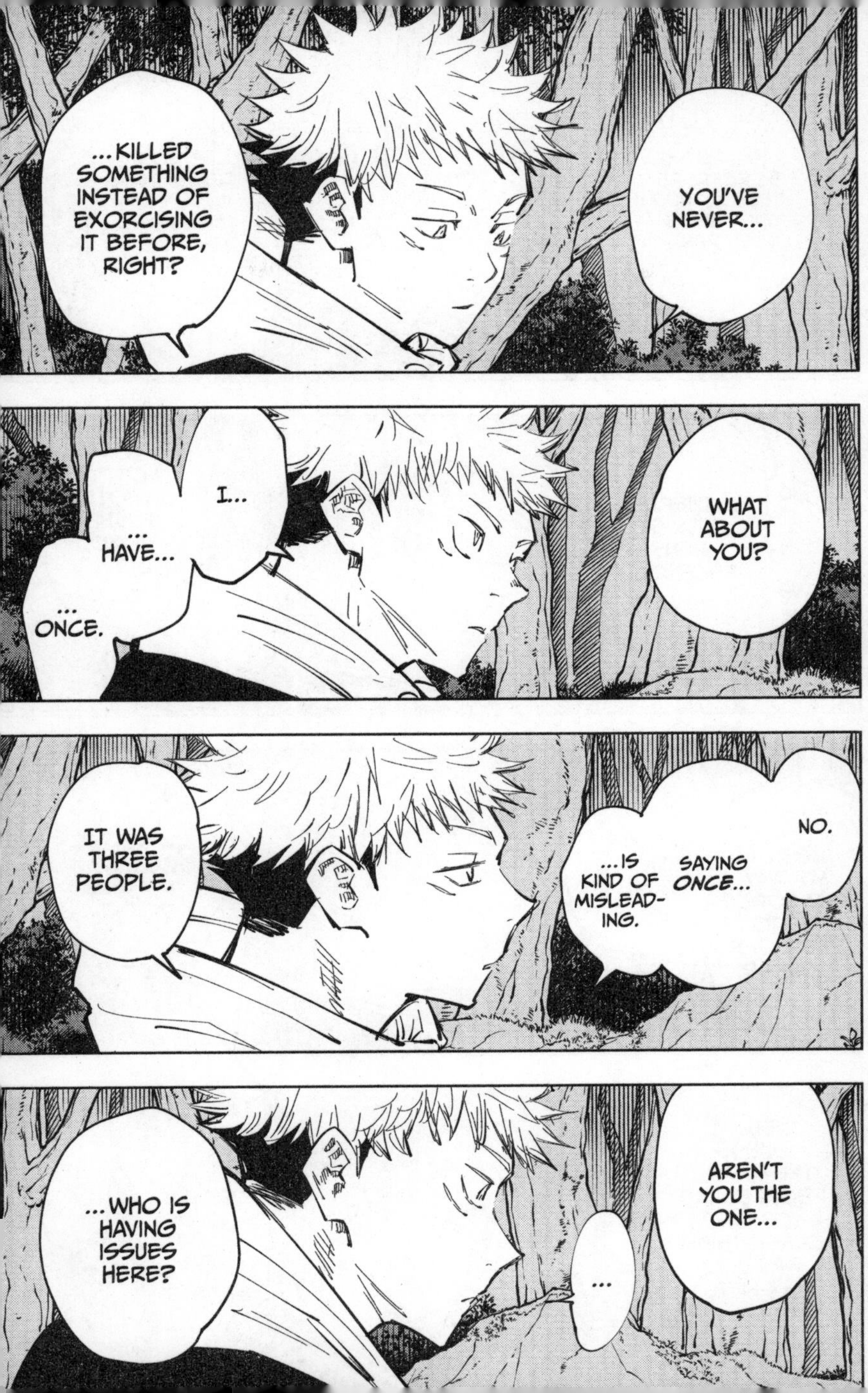
YOU'VE NEVER...
...KILLED SOMETHING INSTEAD OF EXORCISING IT BEFORE, RIGHT?
WHAT ABOUT YOU?
I...
...HAVE...
...ONCE.
NO.
SAYING *ONCE*...
...IS KIND OF MISLEAD-ING.
IT WAS THREE PEOPLE.
AREN'T YOU THE ONE...
...
...WHO IS HAVING ISSUES HERE?

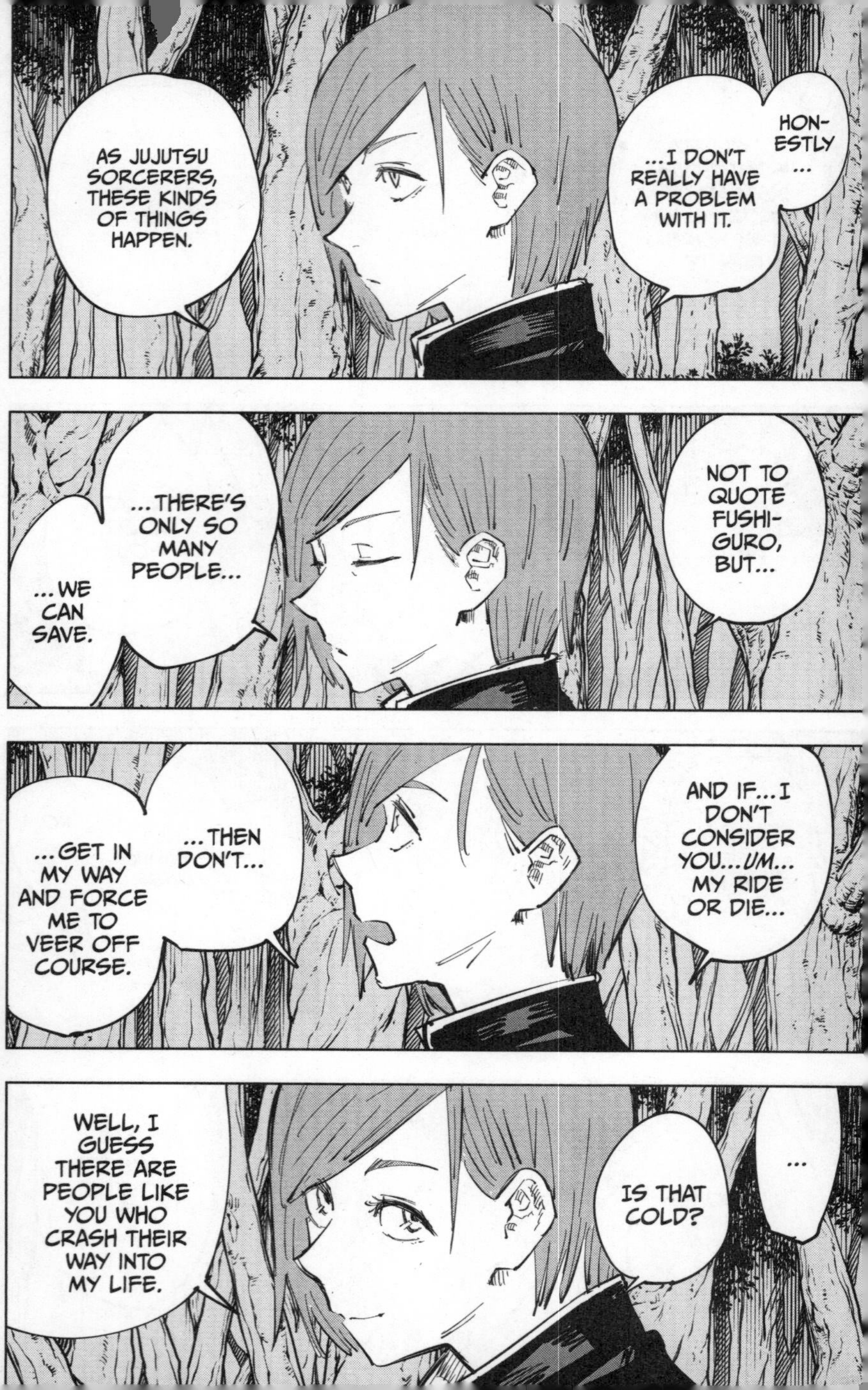
HON-ESTLY...
...I DON'T REALLY HAVE A PROBLEM WITH IT.
AS JUJUTSU SORCERERS, THESE KINDS OF THINGS HAPPEN.
NOT TO QUOTE FUSHIGURO, BUT...
...THERE'S ONLY SO MANY PEOPLE...
...WE CAN SAVE.
AND IF...I DON'T CONSIDER YOU...*UM*... MY RIDE OR DIE...
...THEN DON'T...
...GET IN MY WAY AND FORCE ME TO VEER OFF COURSE.
...
IS THAT COLD?
WELL, I GUESS THERE ARE PEOPLE LIKE YOU WHO CRASH THEIR WAY INTO MY LIFE.

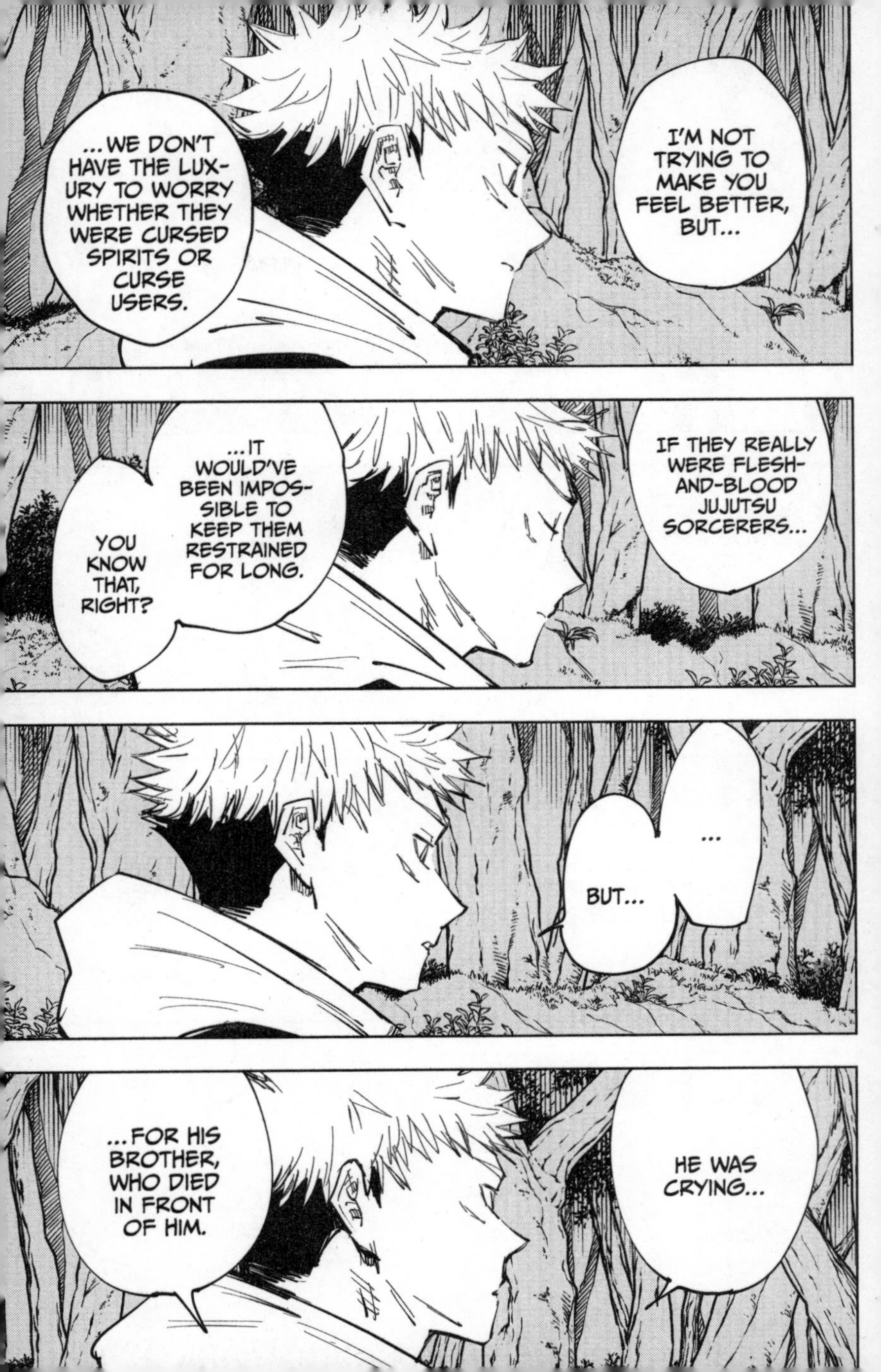
I'M NOT TRYING TO MAKE YOU FEEL BETTER, BUT...
...WE DON'T HAVE THE LUXURY TO WORRY WHETHER THEY WERE CURSED SPIRITS OR CURSE USERS.
IF THEY REALLY WERE FLESH-AND-BLOOD JUJUTSU SORCERERS...
...IT WOULD'VE BEEN IMPOSSIBLE TO KEEP THEM RESTRAINED FOR LONG.
YOU KNOW THAT, RIGHT?
...
BUT...
HE WAS CRYING...
...FOR HIS BROTHER, WHO DIED IN FRONT OF HIM.

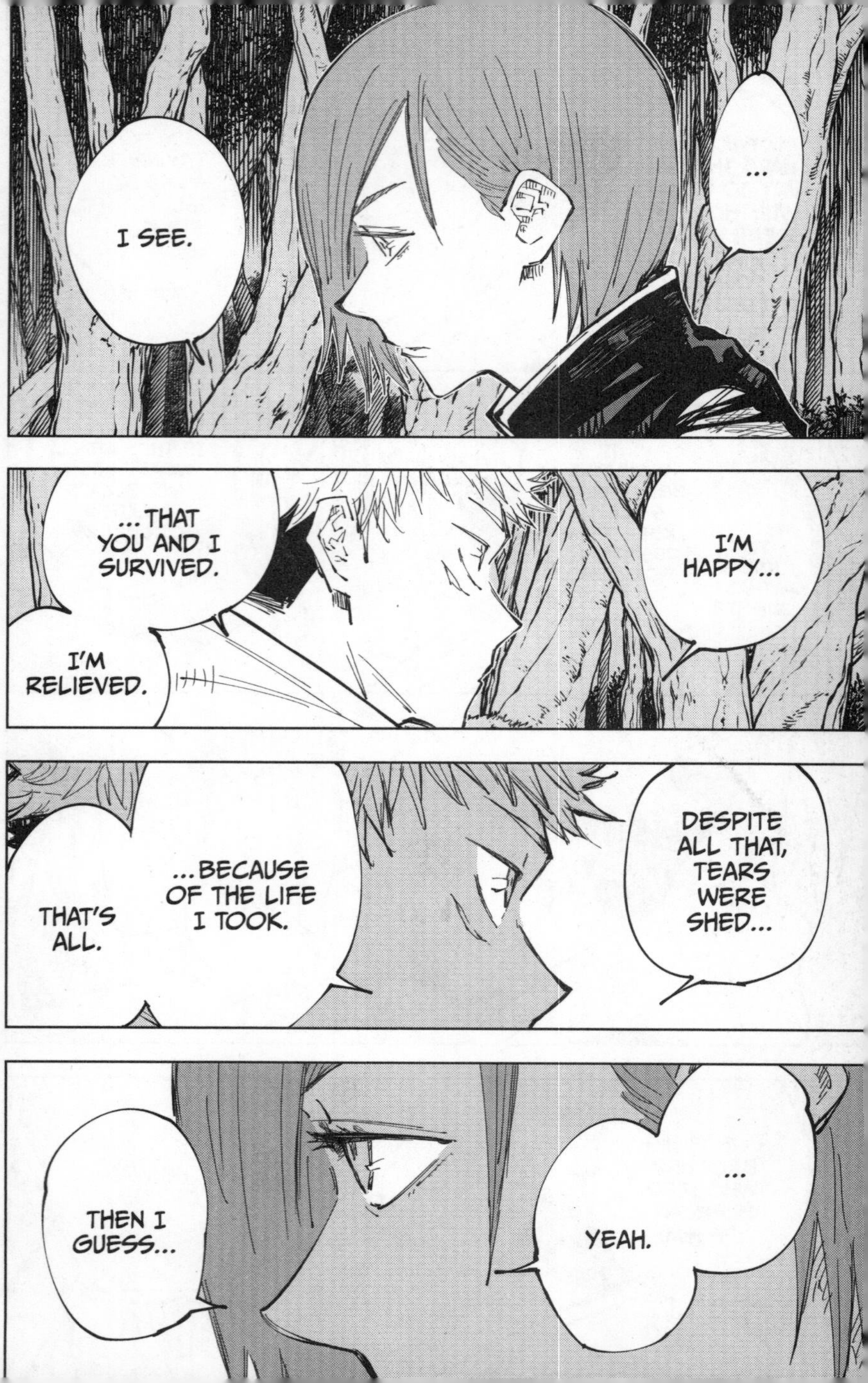
...
I SEE.
I'M HAPPY...
...THAT YOU AND I SURVIVED.
I'M RELIEVED.
DESPITE ALL THAT, TEARS WERE SHED...
...BECAUSE OF THE LIFE I TOOK.
THAT'S ALL.
... YEAH.
THEN I GUESS...

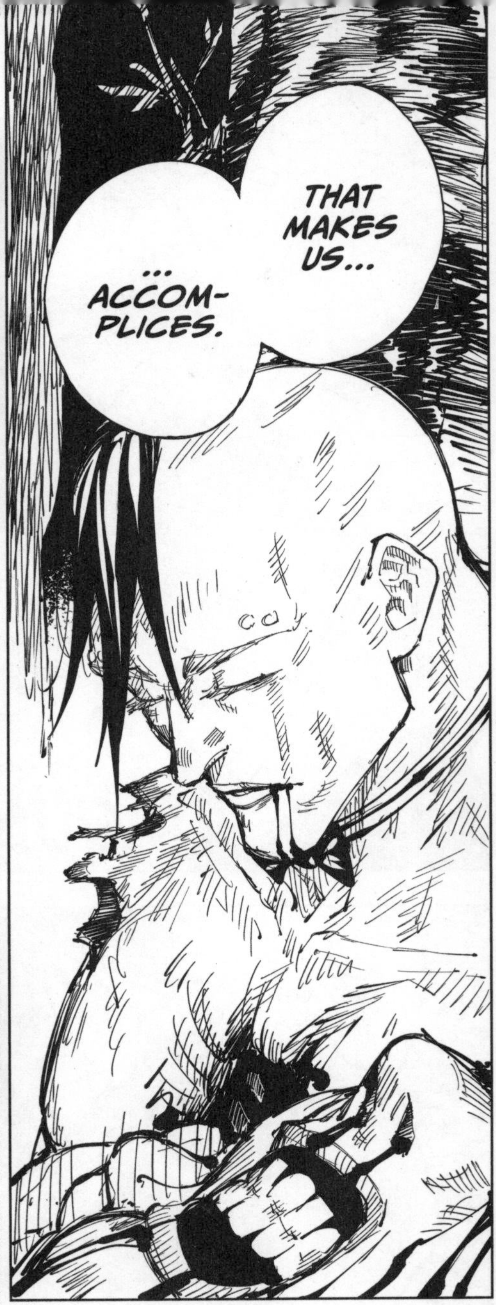
THAT MAKES US...
... ACCOM-PLICES.
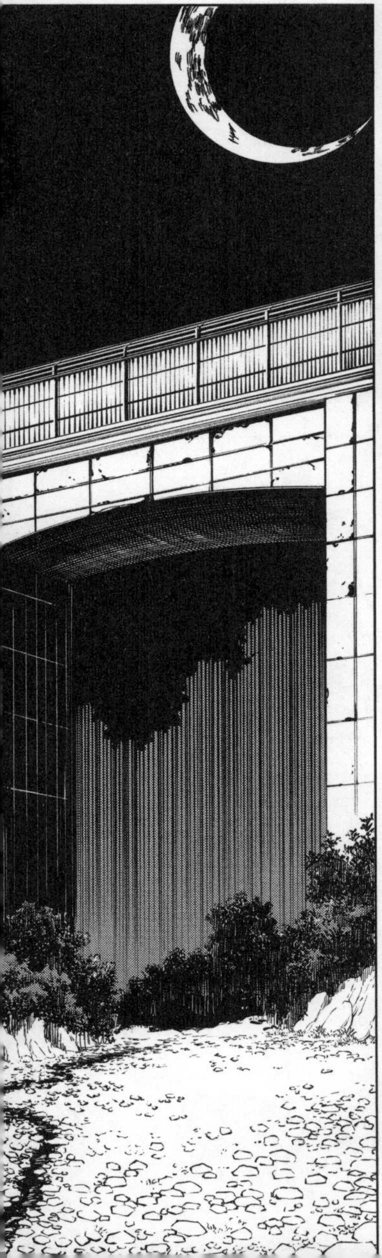

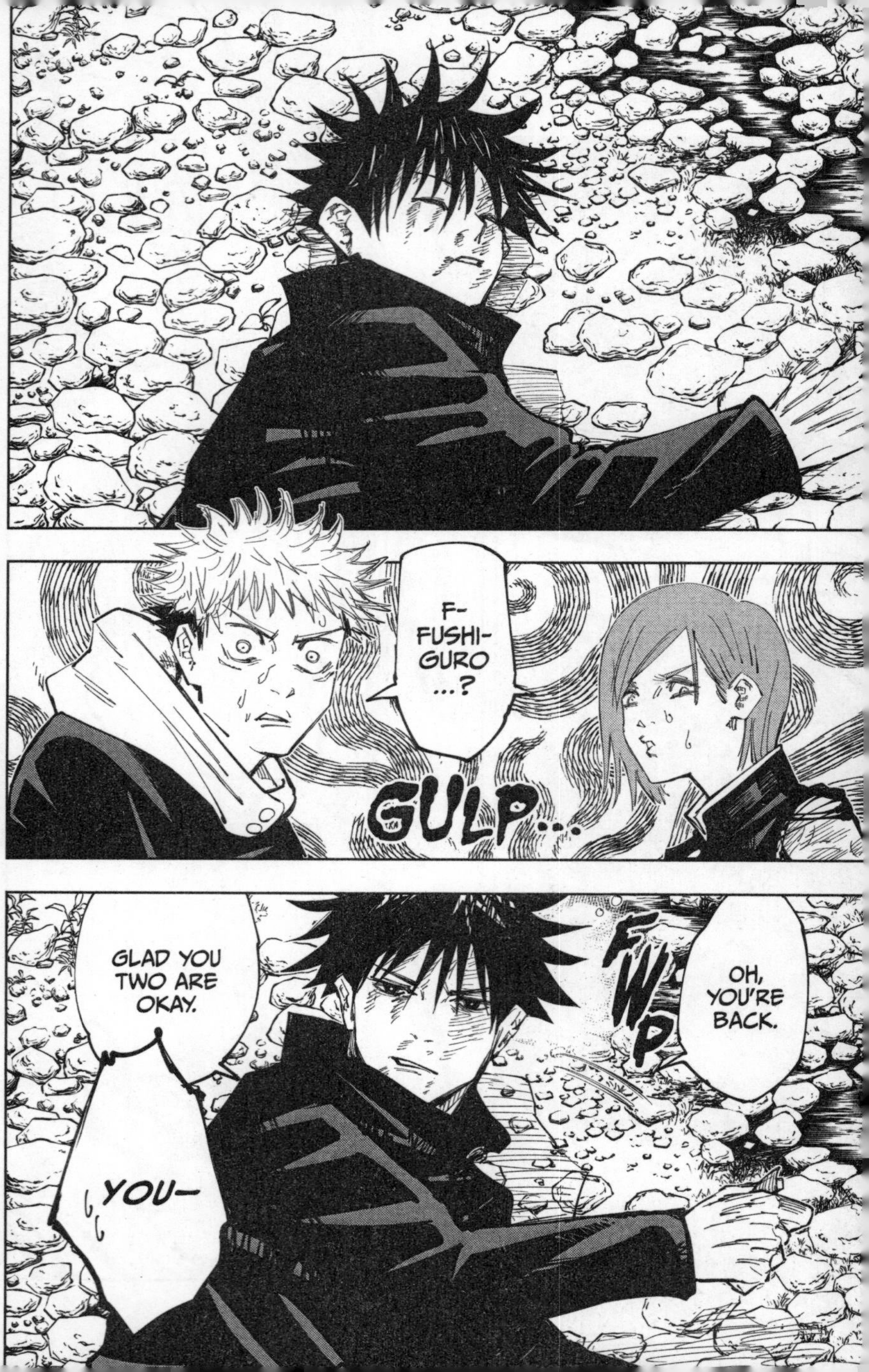
F-FUSHI-GURO ...?
GULP...
OH, YOU'RE BACK.
FWP
GLAD YOU TWO ARE OKAY.
YOU—

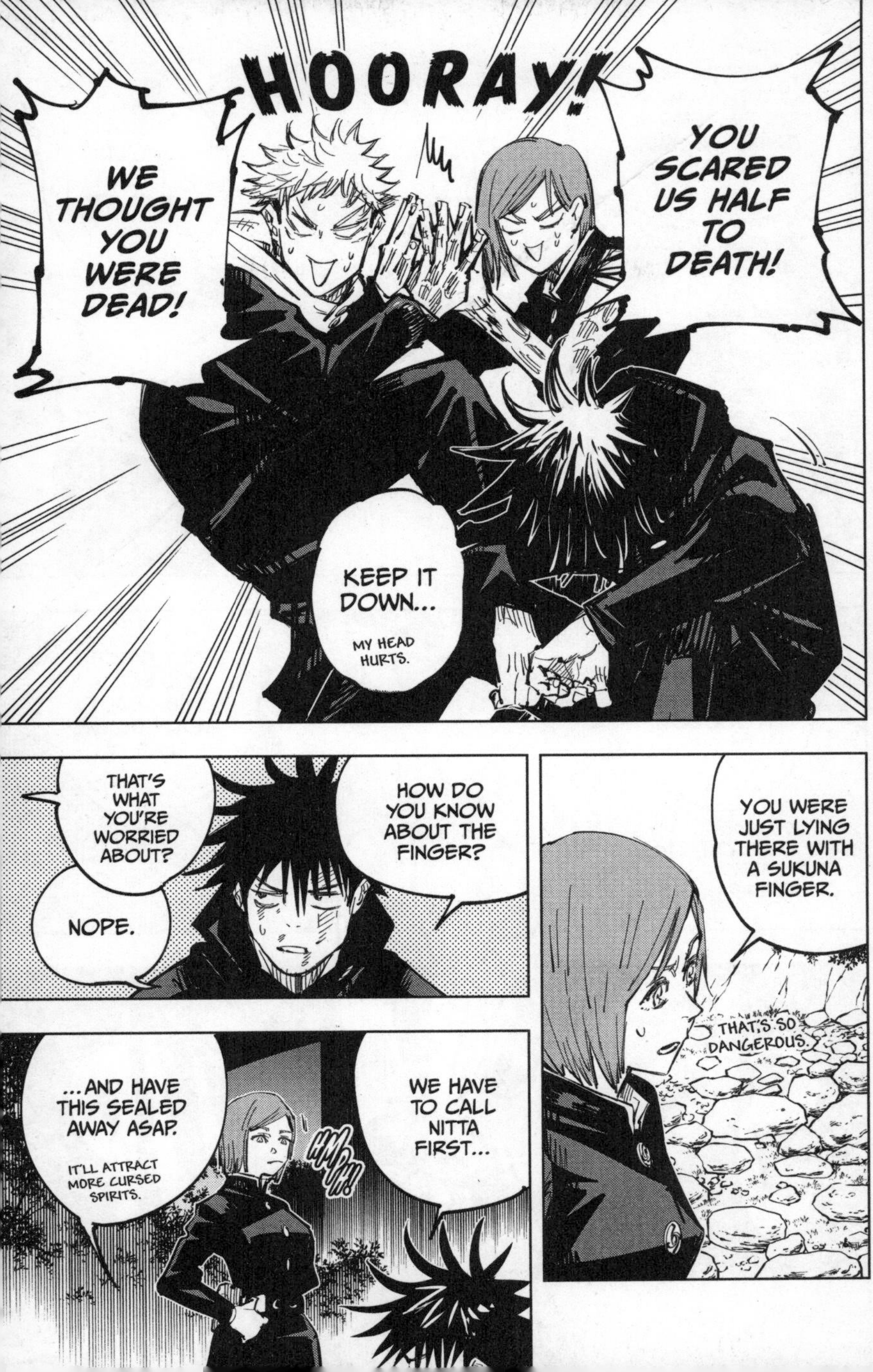
YOU SCARED US HALF TO DEATH!
HOORAY!
WE THOUGHT YOU WERE DEAD!
KEEP IT DOWN...
MY HEAD HURTS.
YOU WERE JUST LYING THERE WITH A SUKUNA FINGER.
THAT'S SO DANGEROUS.
HOW DO YOU KNOW ABOUT THE FINGER?
THAT'S WHAT YOU'RE WORRIED ABOUT?
NOPE.
WE HAVE TO CALL NITTA FIRST...
HMPH!
...AND HAVE THIS SEALED AWAY ASAP.
IT'LL ATTRACT MORE CURSED SPIRITS.

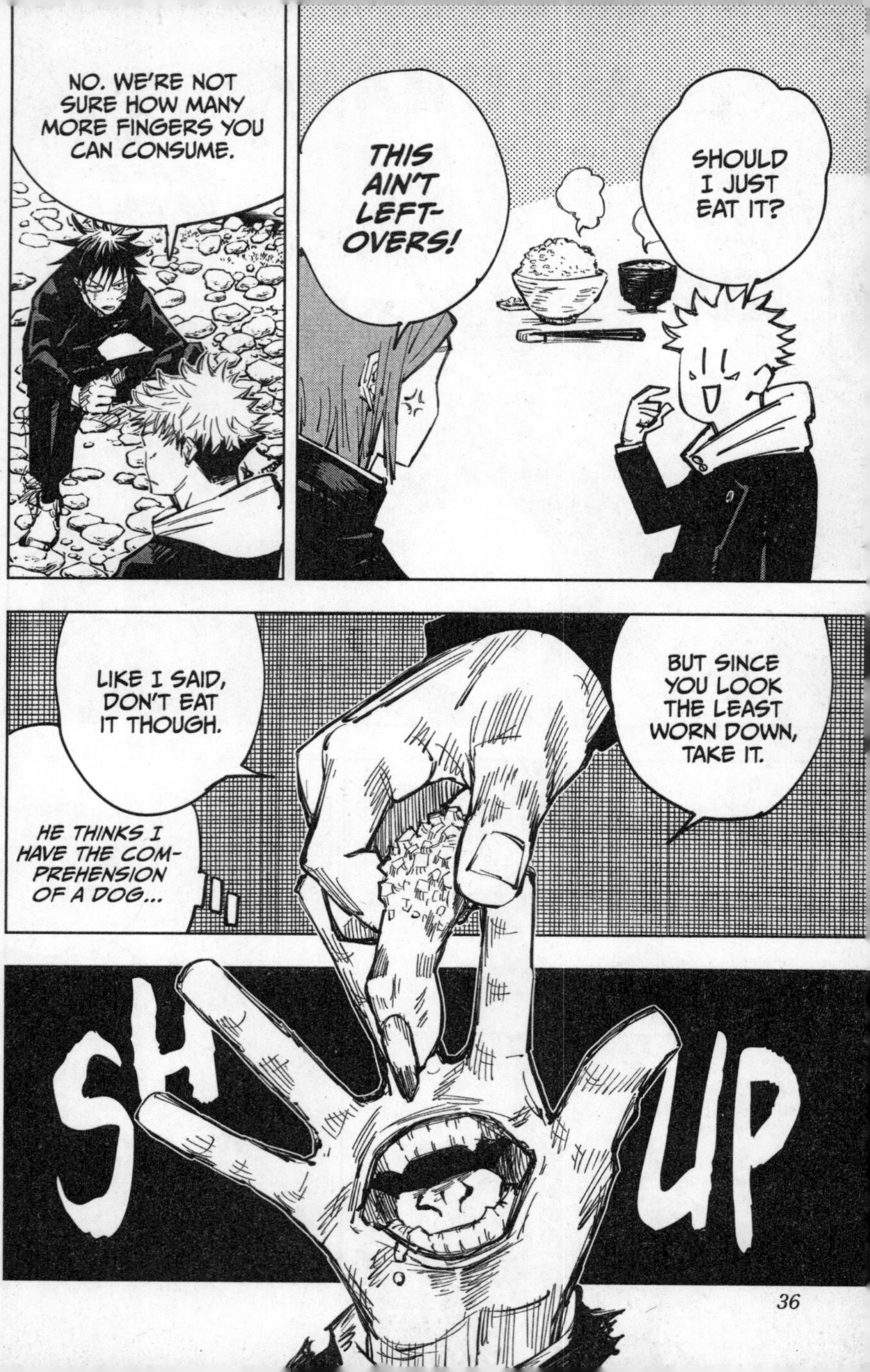
SHOULD I JUST EAT IT?
THIS AIN'T LEFT-OVERS!
NO. WE'RE NOT SURE HOW MANY MORE FINGERS YOU CAN CONSUME.
BUT SINCE YOU LOOK THE LEAST WORN DOWN, TAKE IT.
LIKE I SAID, DON'T EAT IT THOUGH.
HE THINKS I HAVE THE COM-PREHENSION OF A DOG...
SH UP

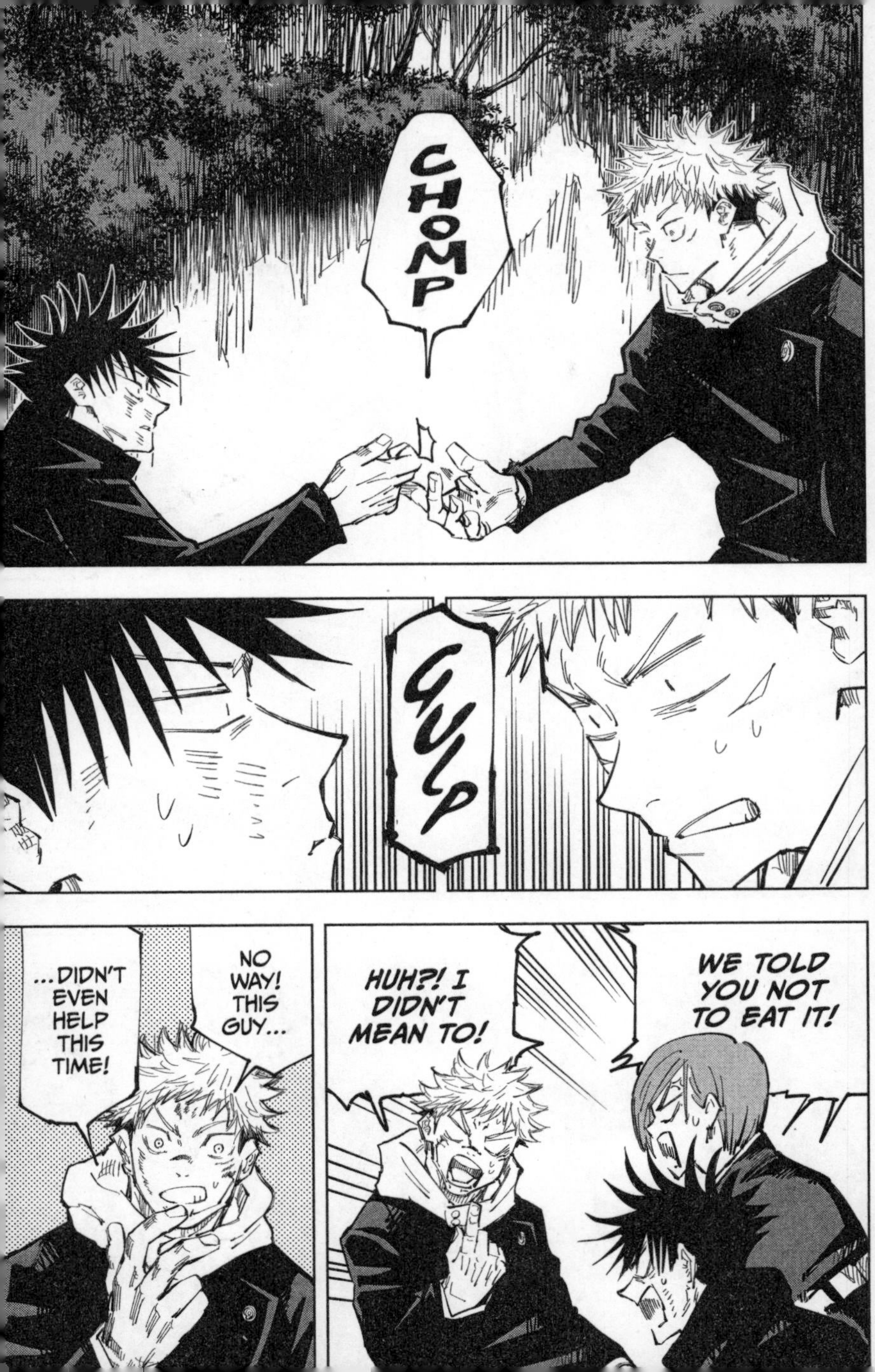
CHOMP
GULP
WE TOLD YOU NOT TO EAT IT!
HUH?! I DIDN'T MEAN TO!
NO WAY! THIS GUY...
...DIDN'T EVEN HELP THIS TIME!

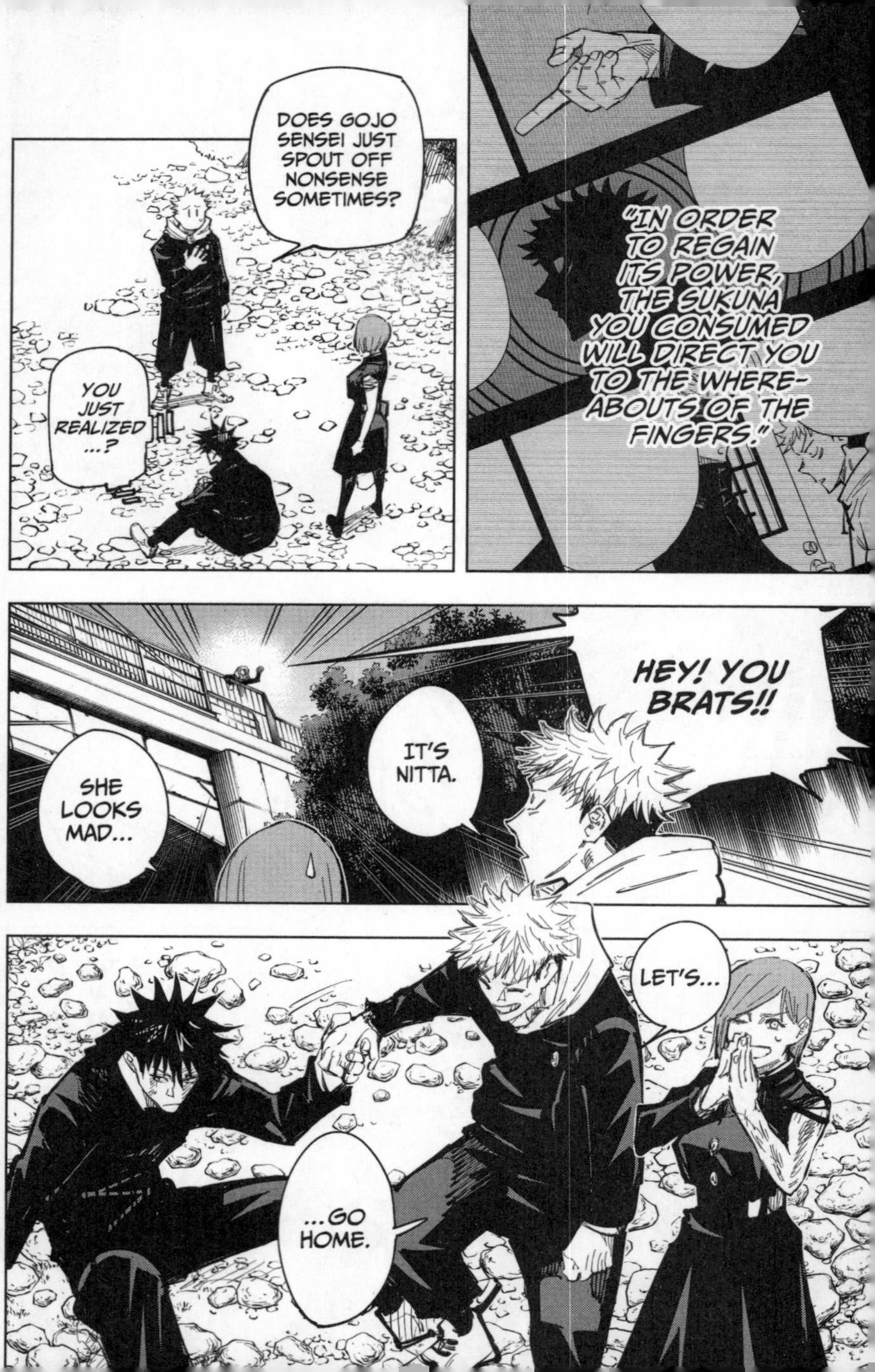
"IN ORDER TO REGAIN ITS POWER, THE SUKUNA YOU CONSUMED WILL DIRECT YOU TO THE WHERE-ABOUTS OF THE FINGERS."
DOES GOJO SENSEI JUST SPOUT OFF NONSENSE SOMETIMES?
YOU JUST REALIZED ...?
HEY! YOU BRATS!!
IT'S NITTA.
SHE LOOKS MAD...
LET'S...
...GO HOME.

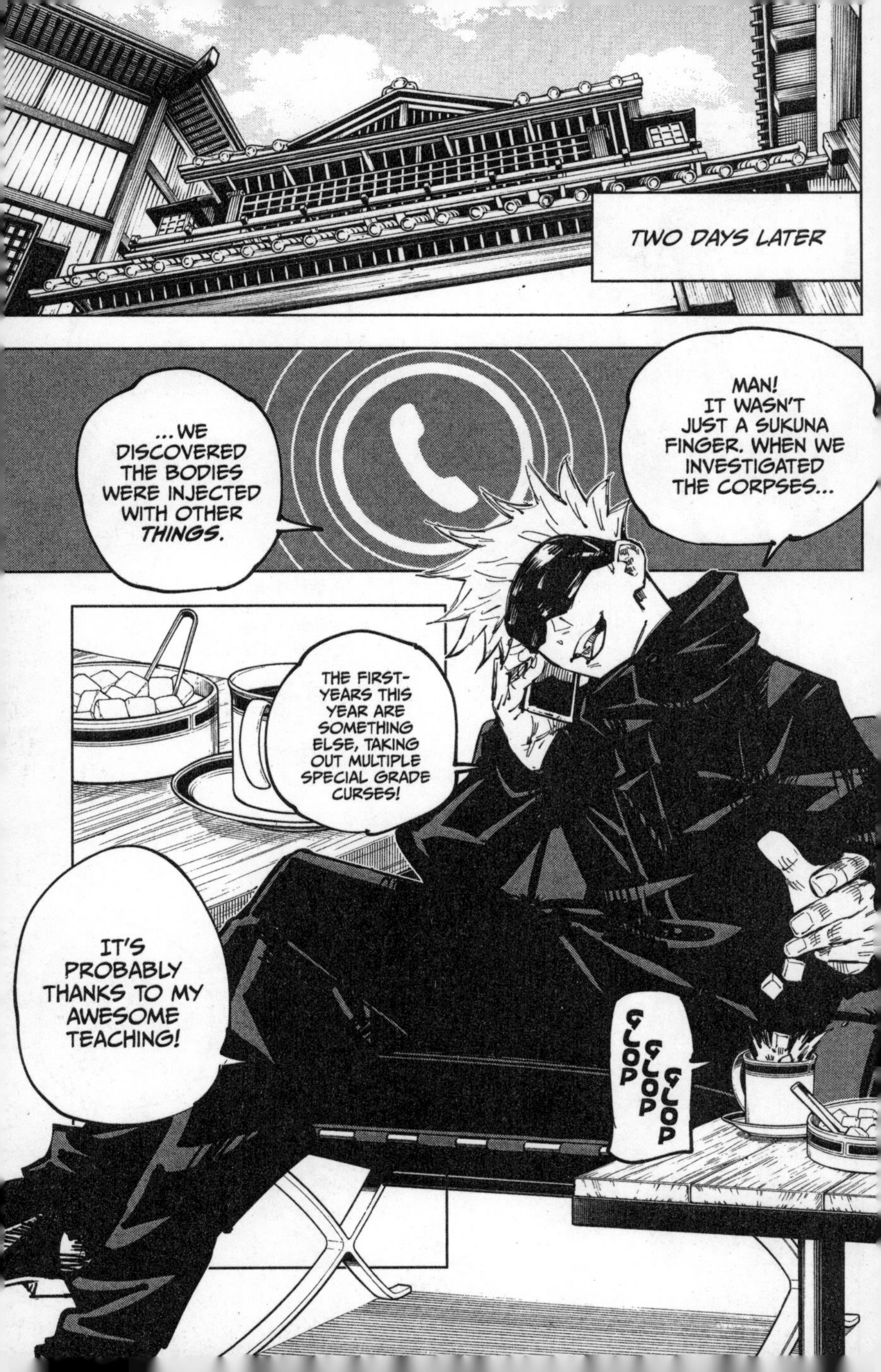
TWO DAYS LATER
MAN! IT WASN'T JUST A SUKUNA FINGER. WHEN WE INVESTIGATED THE CORPSES...
...WE DISCOVERED THE BODIES WERE INJECTED WITH OTHER *THINGS*.
THE FIRST-YEARS THIS YEAR ARE SOMETHING ELSE, TAKING OUT MULTIPLE SPECIAL GRADE CURSES!
GLOP GLOP GLOP
IT'S PROBABLY THANKS TO MY AWESOME TEACHING!

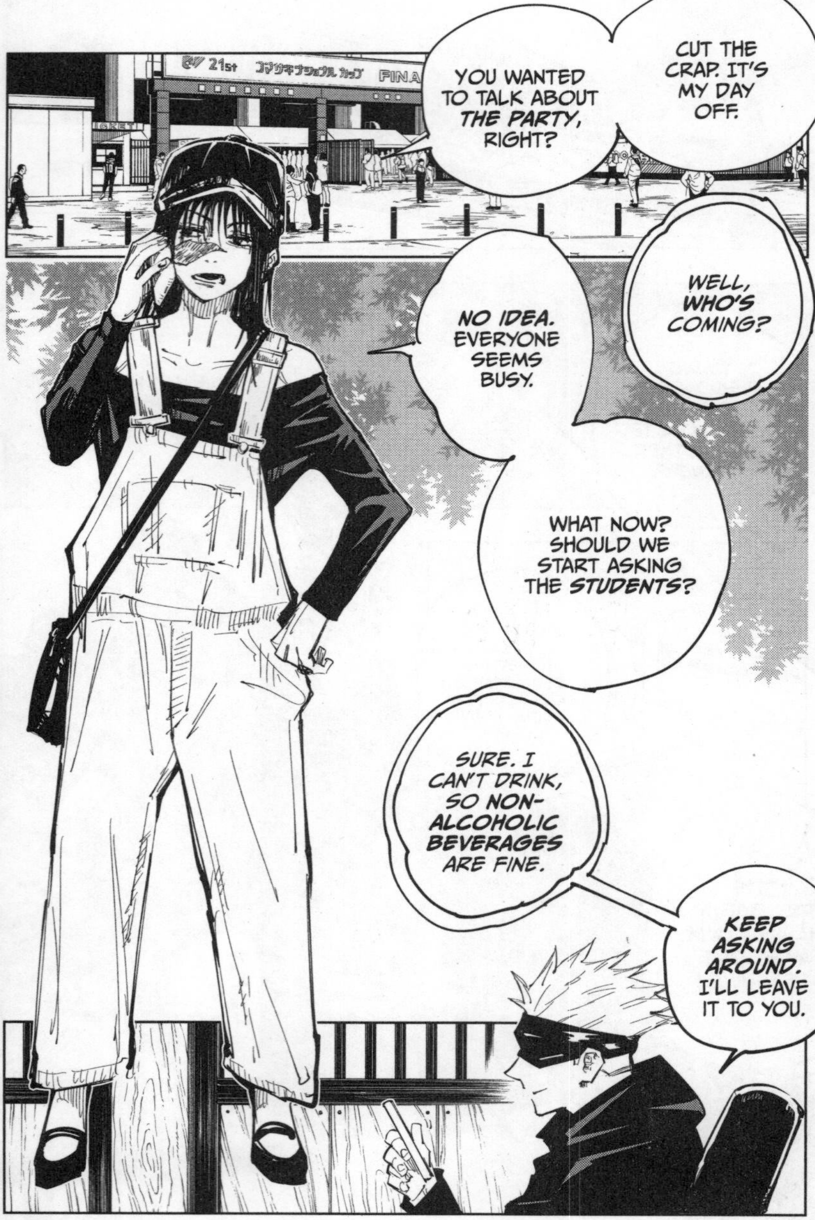
CUT THE CRAP. IT'S MY DAY OFF.
YOU WANTED TO TALK ABOUT THE PARTY, RIGHT?
WELL, WHO'S COMING?
NO IDEA. EVERYONE SEEMS BUSY.
WHAT NOW? SHOULD WE START ASKING THE STUDENTS?
SURE. I CAN'T DRINK, SO NON-ALCOHOLIC BEVERAGES ARE FINE.
KEEP ASKING AROUND. I'LL LEAVE IT TO YOU.

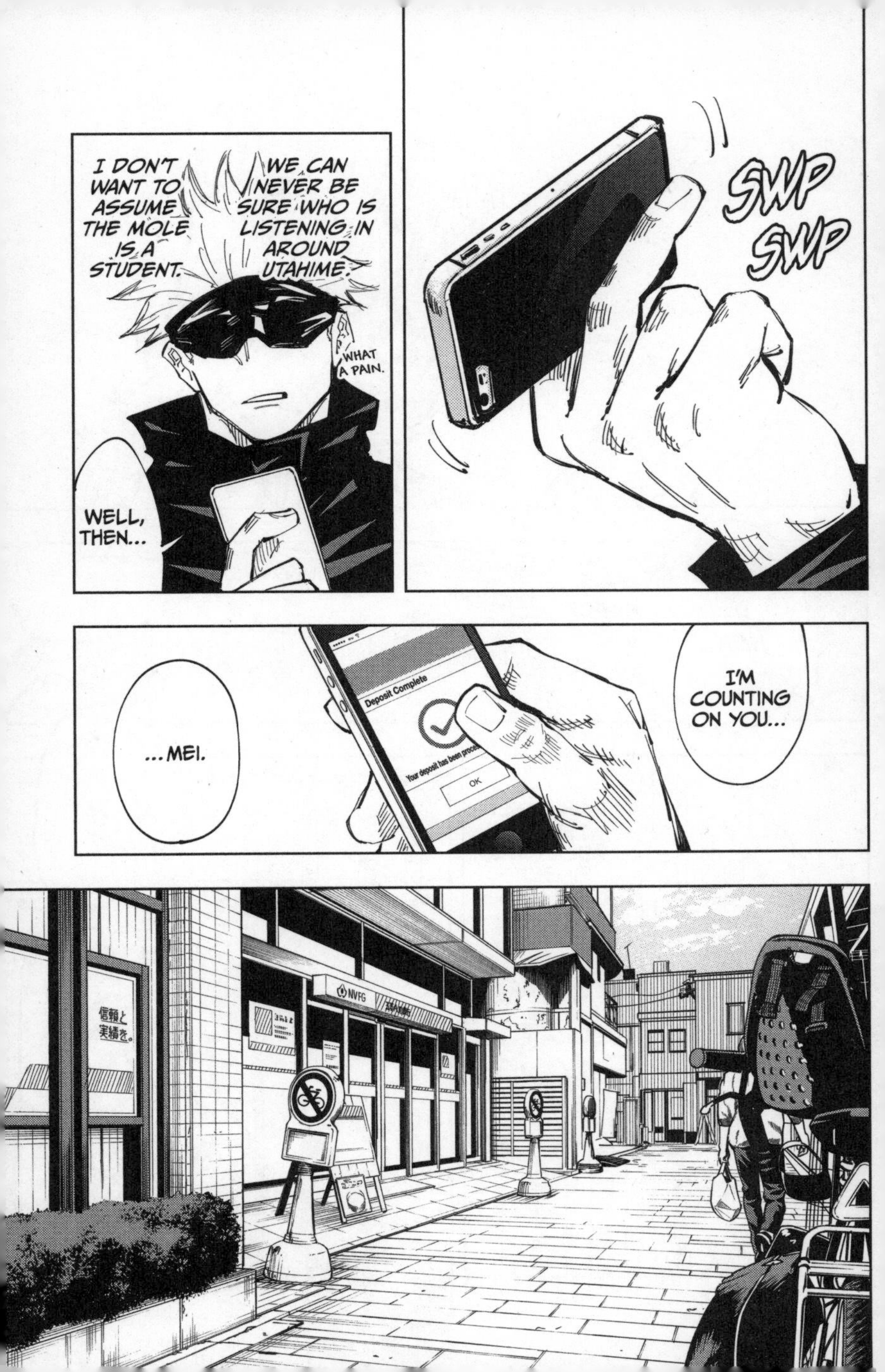
SWP SWP
WE CAN NEVER BE SURE WHO IS LISTENING IN AROUND UTAHIME.
I DON'T WANT TO ASSUME THE MOLE IS A STUDENT.
WHAT A PAIN.
WELL, THEN...
I'M COUNTING ON YOU...
Deposit Complete
OK
...MEI.
NVFG
信頼と実績を。

HEH
HEH...

ANSFER	SATO ACCOUNTING	¥6,200,000		
ANSFER	NOGI FIRM	¥3,500,000		¥240,00
ARD		¥25,000		¥250,0
DEPOSIT	SATORU GOJO		¥10,000,000	

DON'T TELL ITADORI ABOUT THE FINGERS RESONATING.

?

HA HA HA!

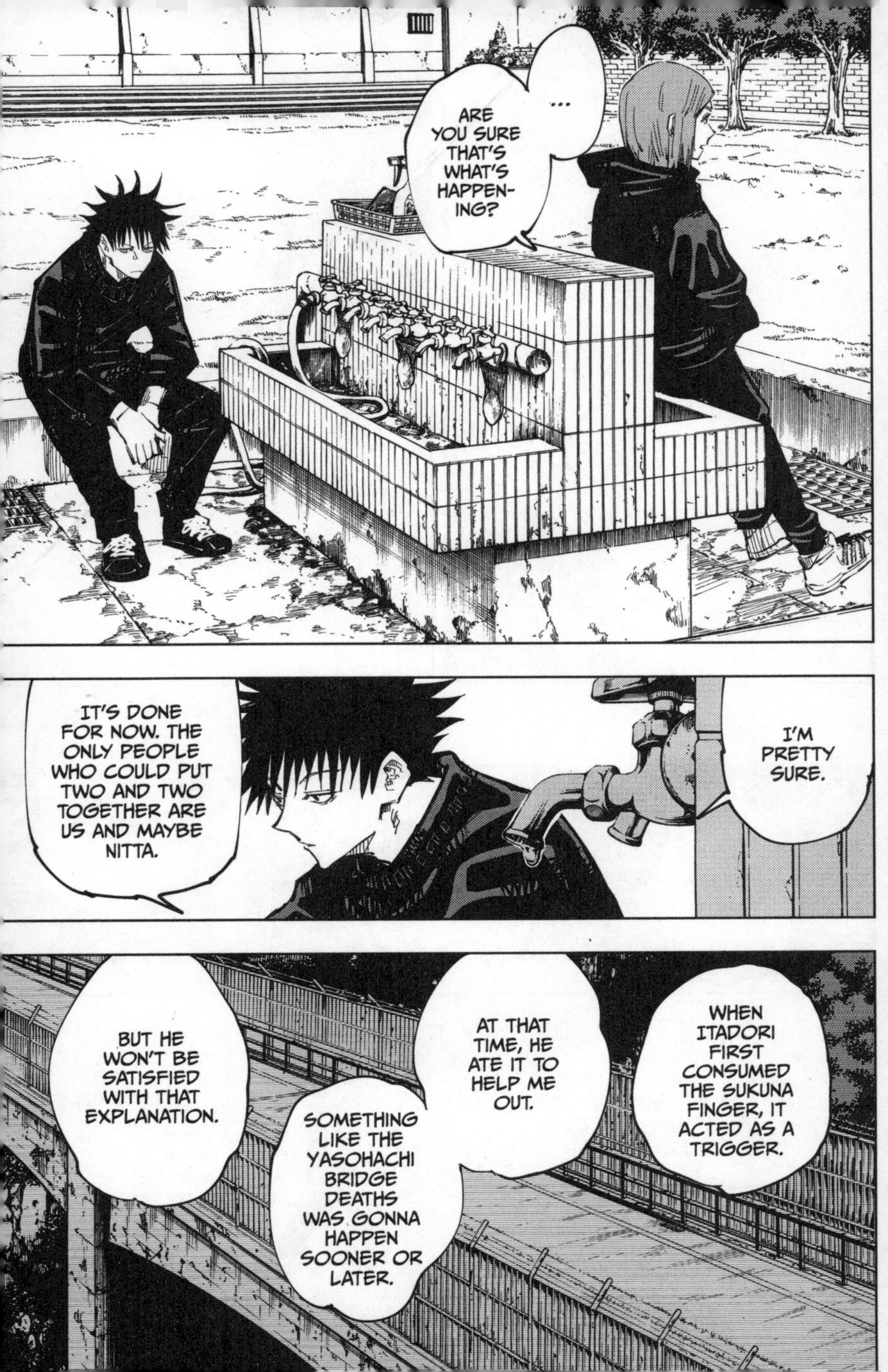
...
ARE YOU SURE THAT'S WHAT'S HAPPENING?
I'M PRETTY SURE.
IT'S DONE FOR NOW. THE ONLY PEOPLE WHO COULD PUT TWO AND TWO TOGETHER ARE US AND MAYBE NITTA.
WHEN ITADORI FIRST CONSUMED THE SUKUNA FINGER, IT ACTED AS A TRIGGER.
AT THAT TIME, HE ATE IT TO HELP ME OUT.
SOMETHING LIKE THE YASOHACHI BRIDGE DEATHS WAS GONNA HAPPEN SOONER OR LATER.
BUT HE WON'T BE SATISFIED WITH THAT EXPLANATION.

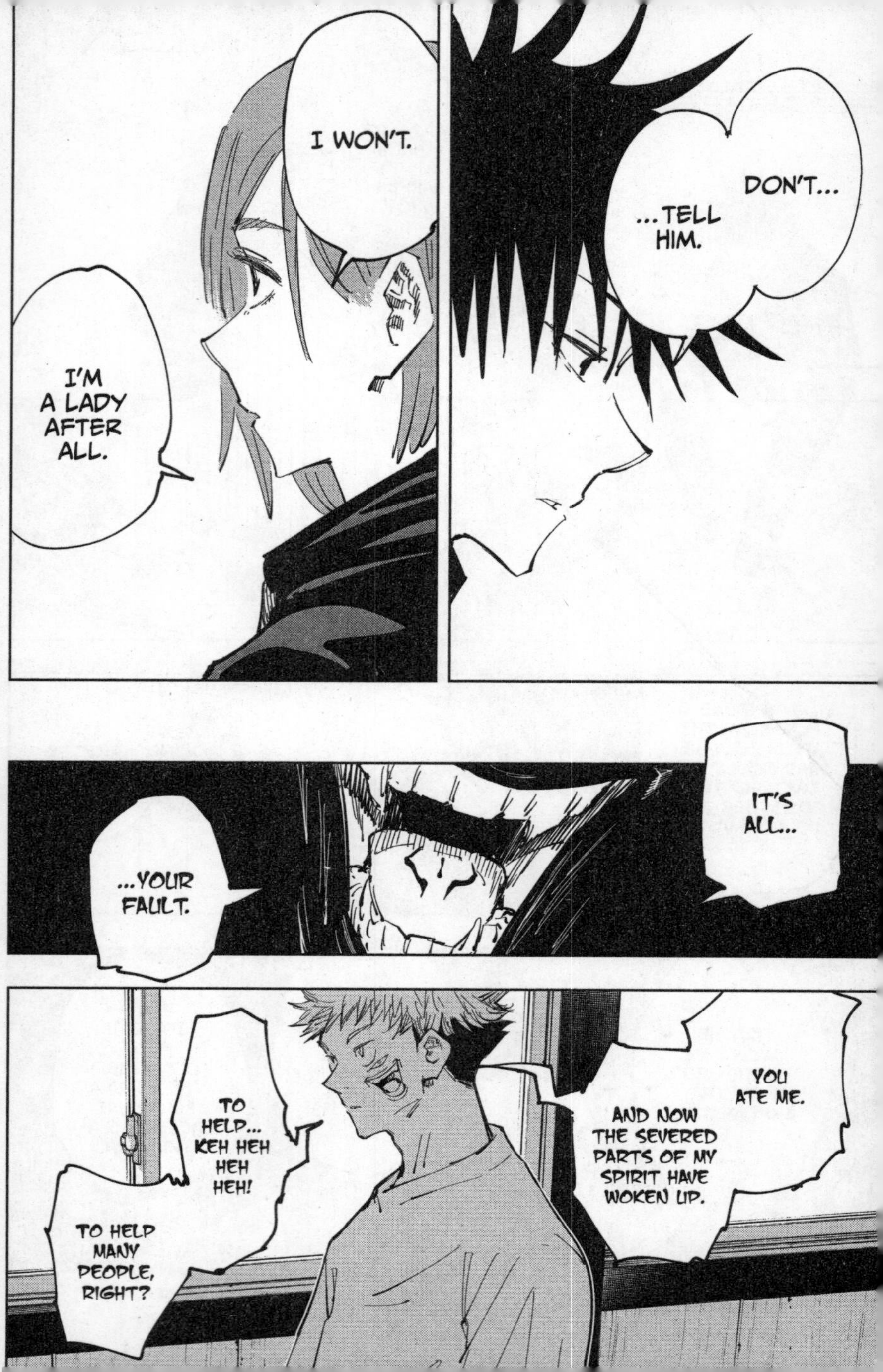
DON'T...
...TELL HIM.
I WON'T.
I'M A LADY AFTER ALL.
IT'S ALL...
...YOUR FAULT.
YOU ATE ME.
AND NOW THE SEVERED PARTS OF MY SPIRIT HAVE WOKEN UP.
TO HELP... KEH HEH HEH HEH!
TO HELP MANY PEOPLE, RIGHT?

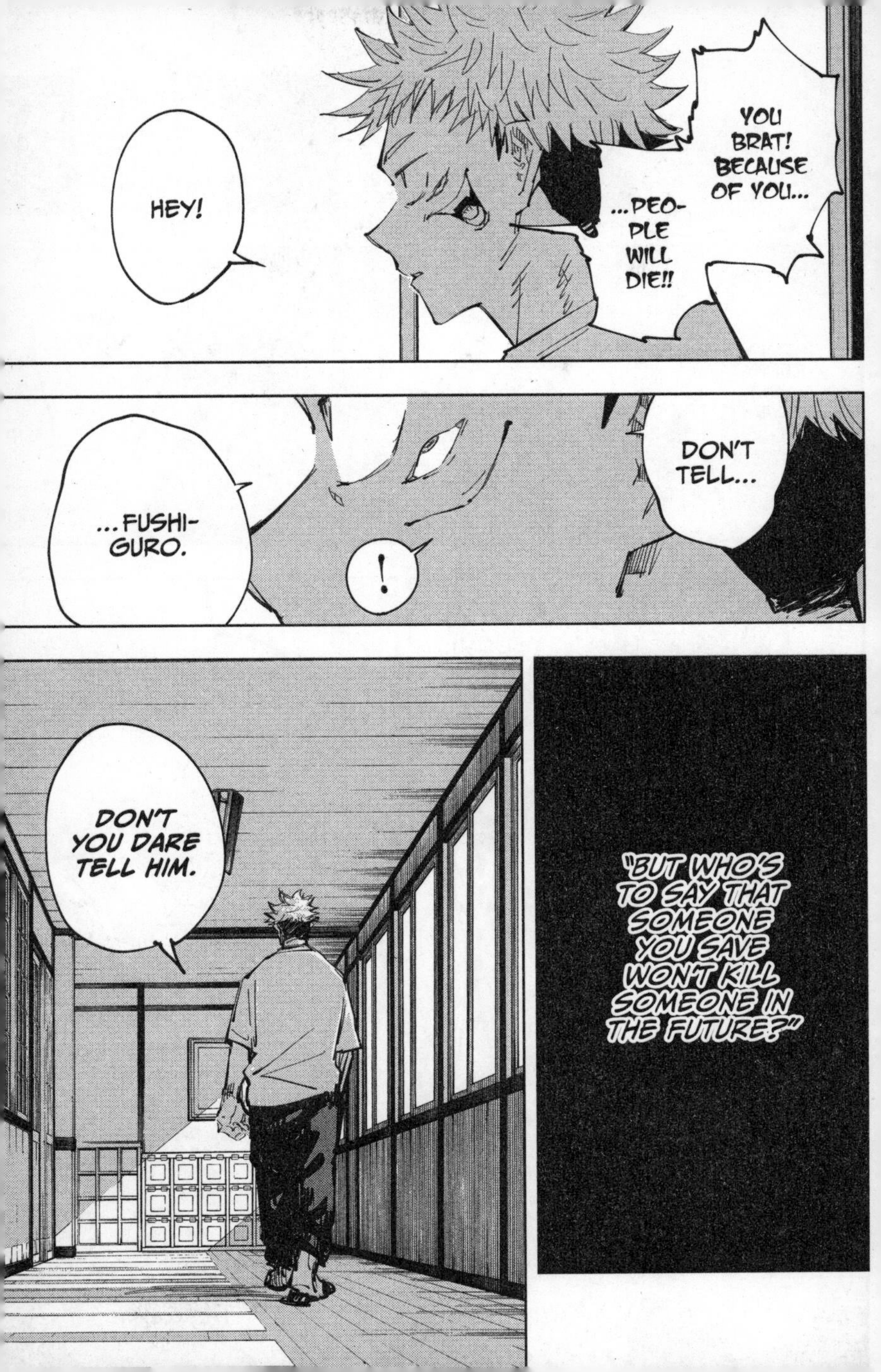
YOU BRAT! BECAUSE OF YOU...
...PEO-PLE WILL DIE!!
HEY!
DON'T TELL...
!
...FUSHI-GURO.
"BUT WHO'S TO SAY THAT SOMEONE YOU SAVE WON'T KILL SOMEONE IN THE FUTURE?"
DON'T YOU DARE TELL HIM.

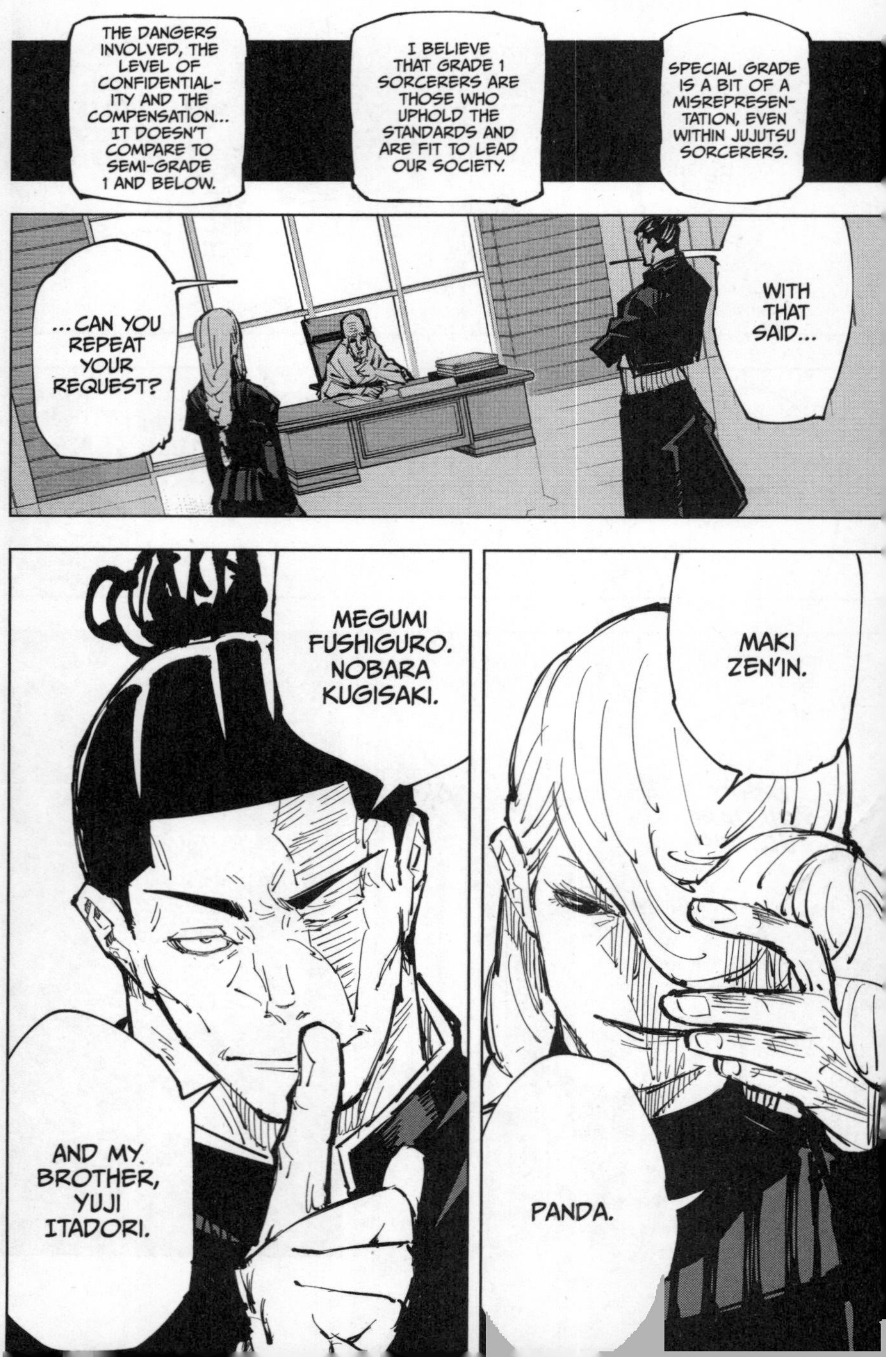
SPECIAL GRADE IS A BIT OF A MISREPRESENTATION, EVEN WITHIN JUJUTSU SORCERERS.
I BELIEVE THAT GRADE 1 SORCERERS ARE THOSE WHO UPHOLD THE STANDARDS AND ARE FIT TO LEAD OUR SOCIETY.
THE DANGERS INVOLVED, THE LEVEL OF CONFIDENTIALITY AND THE COMPENSATION... IT DOESN'T COMPARE TO SEMI-GRADE 1 AND BELOW.
WITH THAT SAID...
...CAN YOU REPEAT YOUR REQUEST?
MAKI ZEN'IN.
PANDA.
MEGUMI FUSHIGURO. NOBARA KUGISAKI.
AND MY BROTHER, YUJI ITADORI.

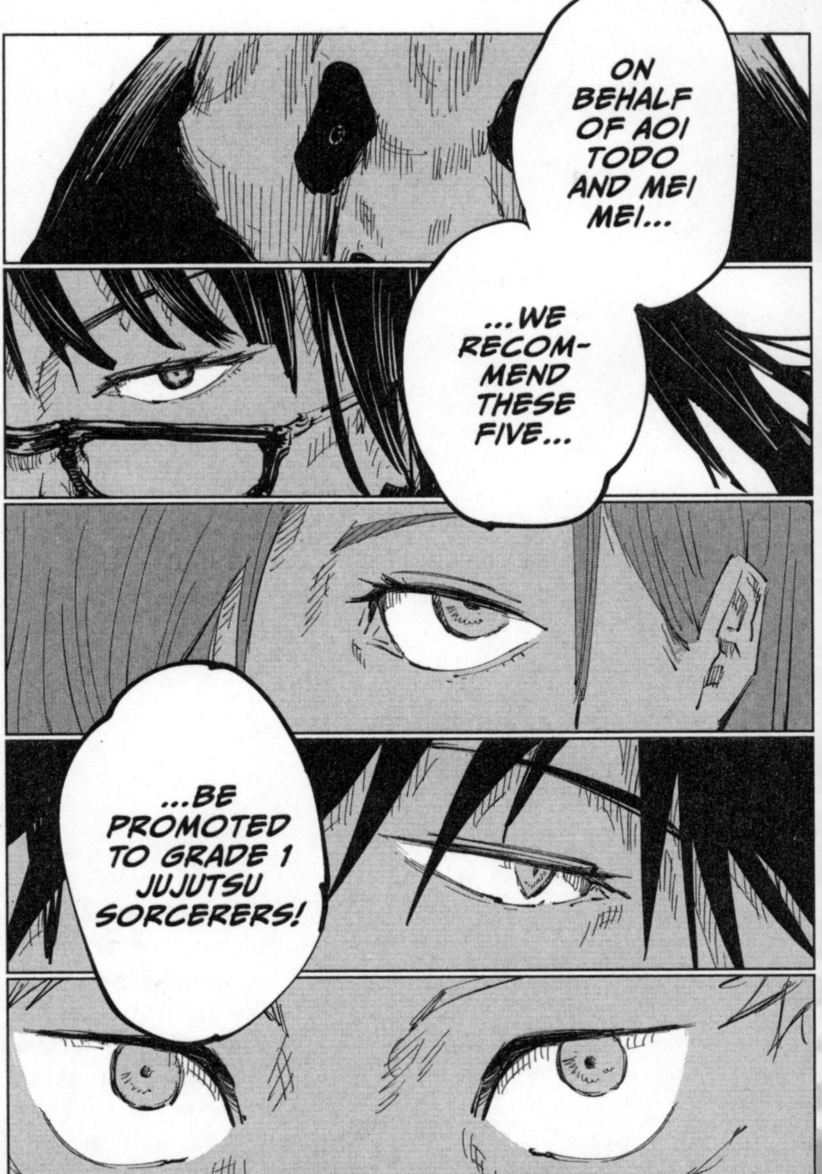
ON BEHALF OF AOI TODO AND MEI MEI...
...WE RECOMMEND THESE FIVE...
...BE PROMOTED TO GRADE 1 JUJUTSU SORCERERS!

	TRANSFER	SATO ACCOUNTING	+620000	
	TRANSFER	NOGI FIRM	+3500000	
	CARD		+25000	+3460
	DEPOSIT	SATORU GOJO	+10000000	+350

Mei is a rare case of a jujutsu sorcerer who works independently, so she doesn't have an issue with getting money from Gojo. Plus, she makes up the stuff she does for work anyway.

CHAPTER 64: IT'S LIKE THAT

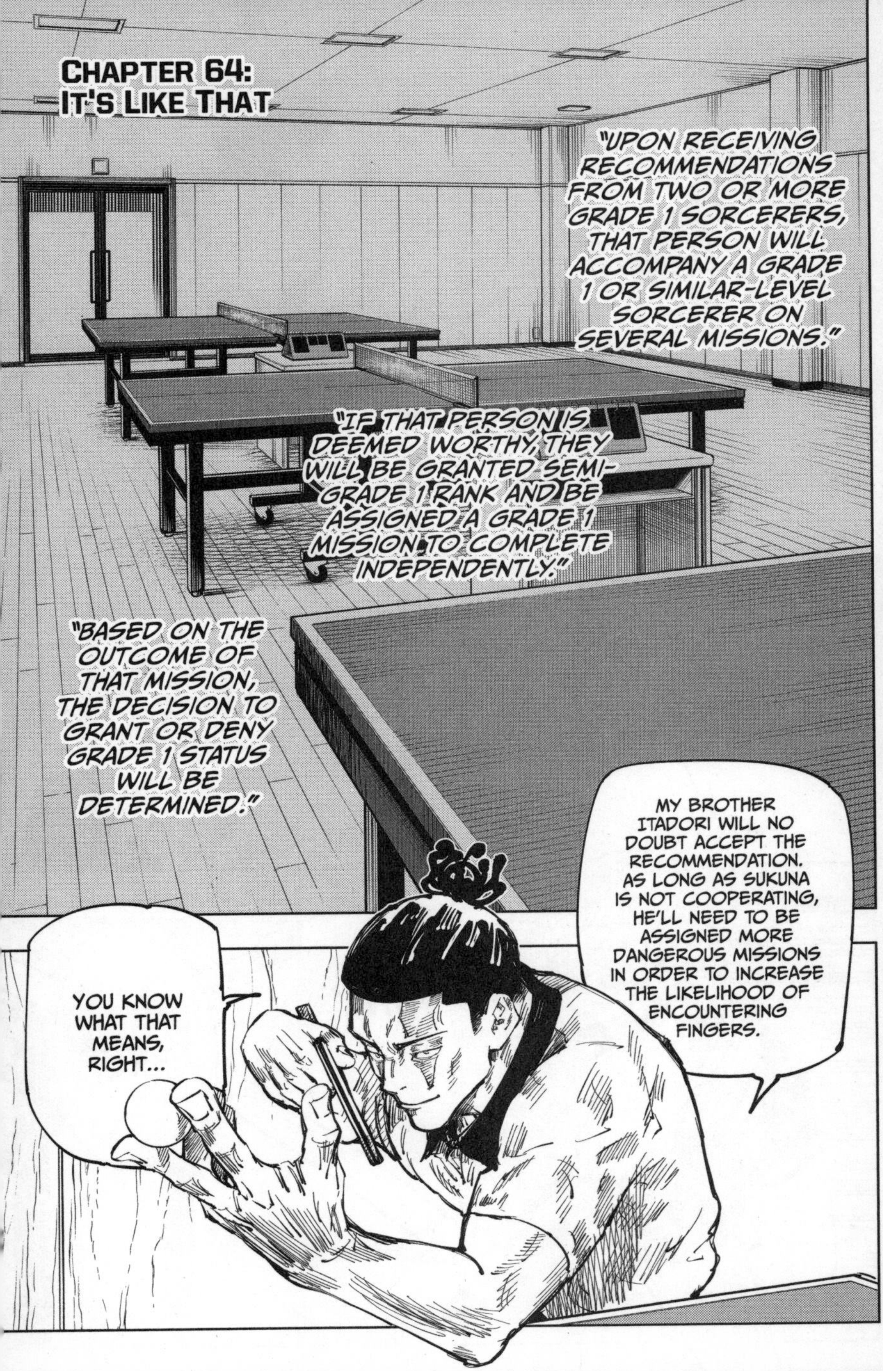
"UPON RECEIVING RECOMMENDATIONS FROM TWO OR MORE GRADE 1 SORCERERS, THAT PERSON WILL ACCOMPANY A GRADE 1 OR SIMILAR-LEVEL SORCERER ON SEVERAL MISSIONS."
"IF THAT PERSON IS DEEMED WORTHY, THEY WILL BE GRANTED SEMI-GRADE 1 RANK AND BE ASSIGNED A GRADE 1 MISSION TO COMPLETE INDEPENDENTLY."
"BASED ON THE OUTCOME OF THAT MISSION, THE DECISION TO GRANT OR DENY GRADE 1 STATUS WILL BE DETERMINED."
MY BROTHER ITADORI WILL NO DOUBT ACCEPT THE RECOMMENDATION. AS LONG AS SUKUNA IS NOT COOPERATING, HE'LL NEED TO BE ASSIGNED MORE DANGEROUS MISSIONS IN ORDER TO INCREASE THE LIKELIHOOD OF ENCOUNTERING FINGERS.
YOU KNOW WHAT THAT MEANS, RIGHT...

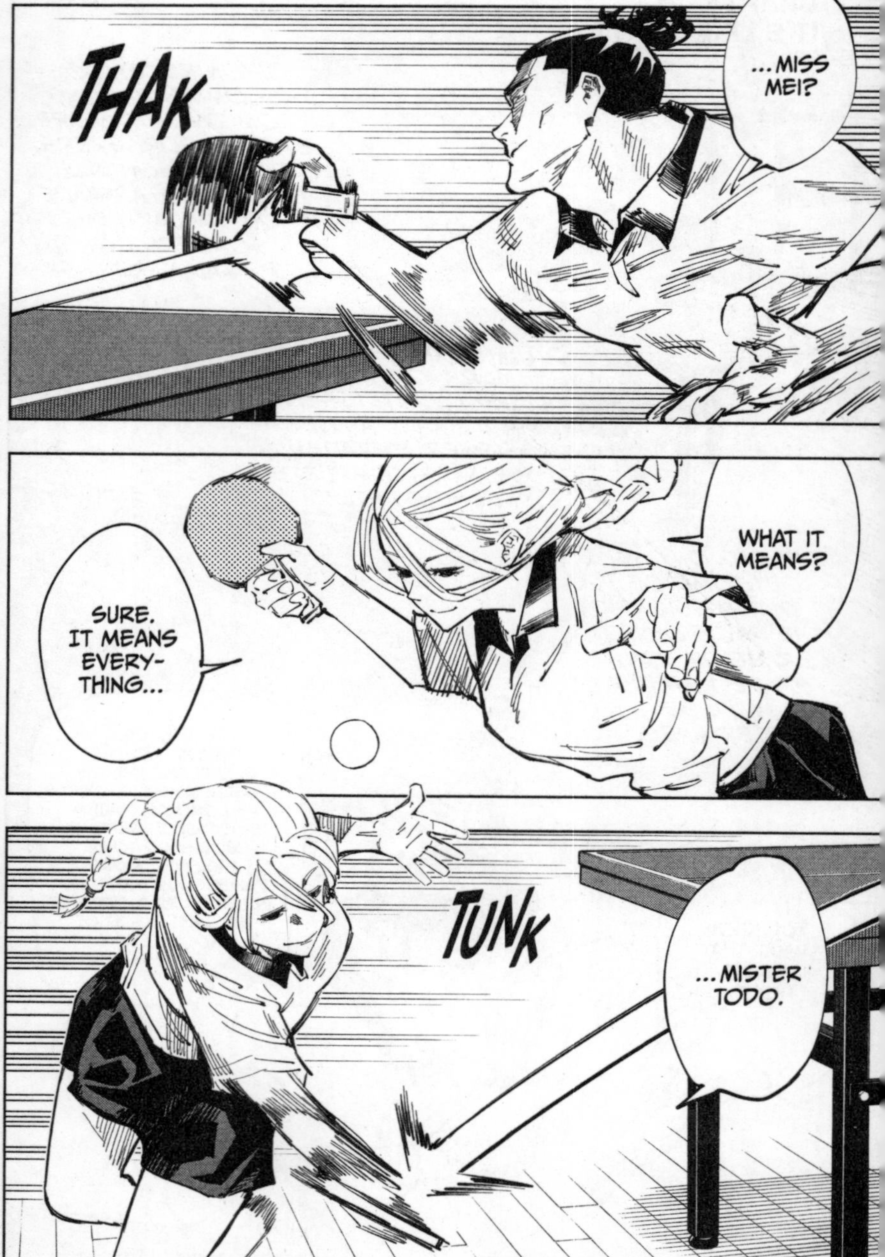
...MISS MEI?
THAK
WHAT IT MEANS?
SURE. IT MEANS EVERY-THING...
...MISTER TODO.
TUNK

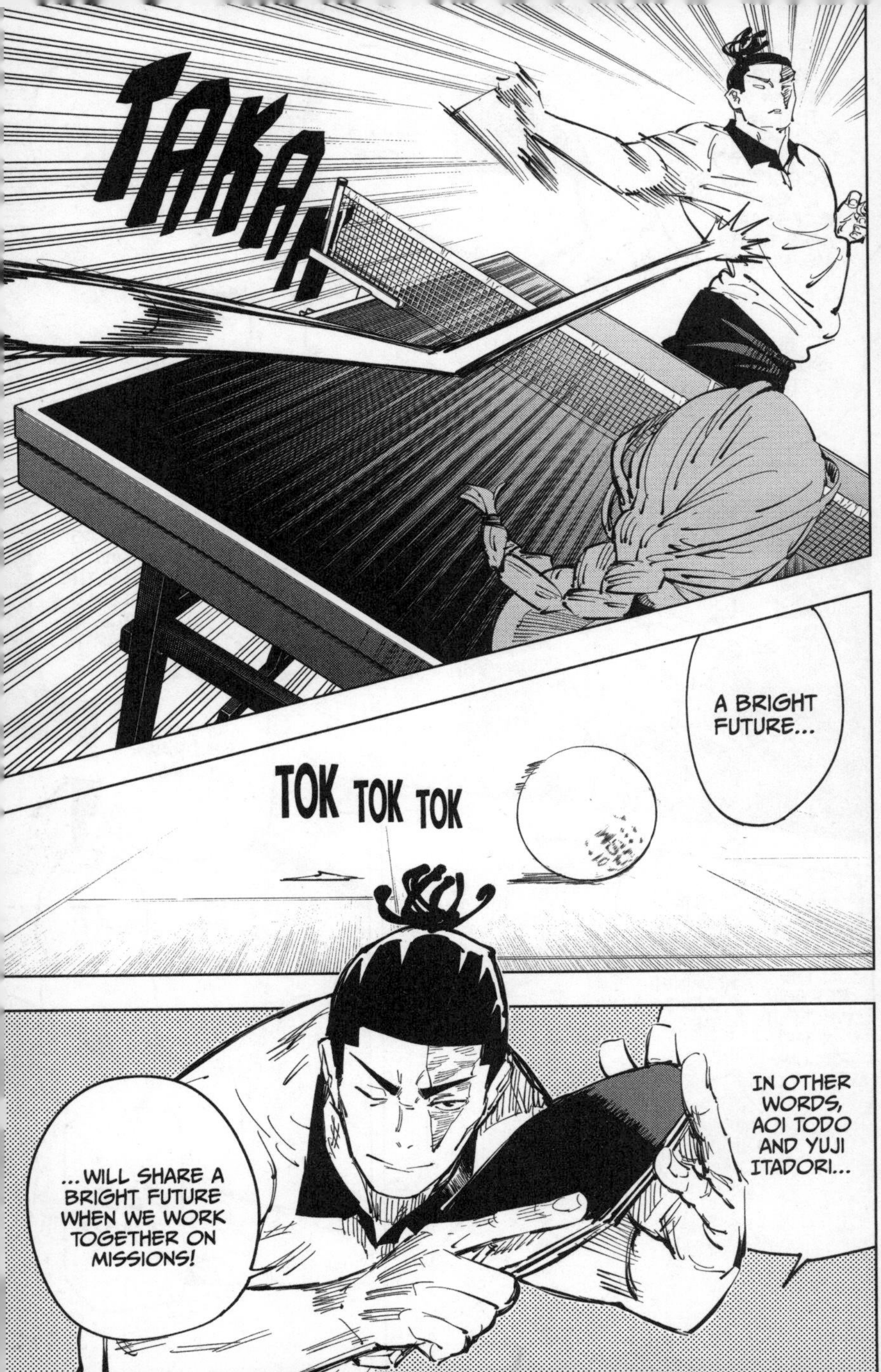
TAKA!!
A BRIGHT FUTURE...
TOK TOK TOK
IN OTHER WORDS, AOI TODO AND YUJI ITADORI...
...WILL SHARE A BRIGHT FUTURE WHEN WE WORK TOGETHER ON MISSIONS!

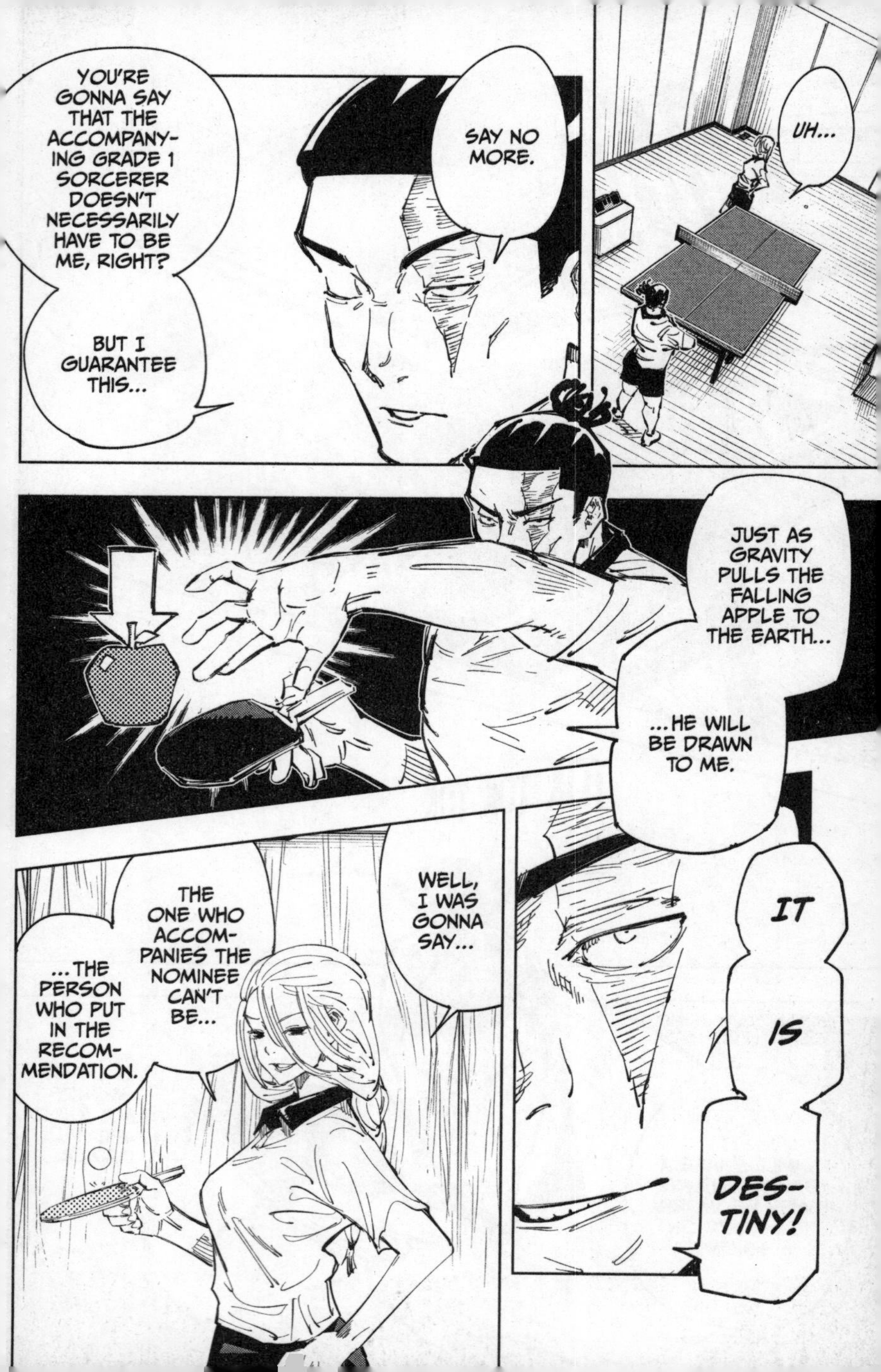
UH...
SAY NO MORE.
YOU'RE GONNA SAY THAT THE ACCOMPANYING GRADE 1 SORCERER DOESN'T NECESSARILY HAVE TO BE ME, RIGHT?
BUT I GUARANTEE THIS...
JUST AS GRAVITY PULLS THE FALLING APPLE TO THE EARTH...
...HE WILL BE DRAWN TO ME.
IT IS DESTINY!
WELL, I WAS GONNA SAY...
THE ONE WHO ACCOMPANIES THE NOMINEE CAN'T BE...
...THE PERSON WHO PUT IN THE RECOMMENDATION.

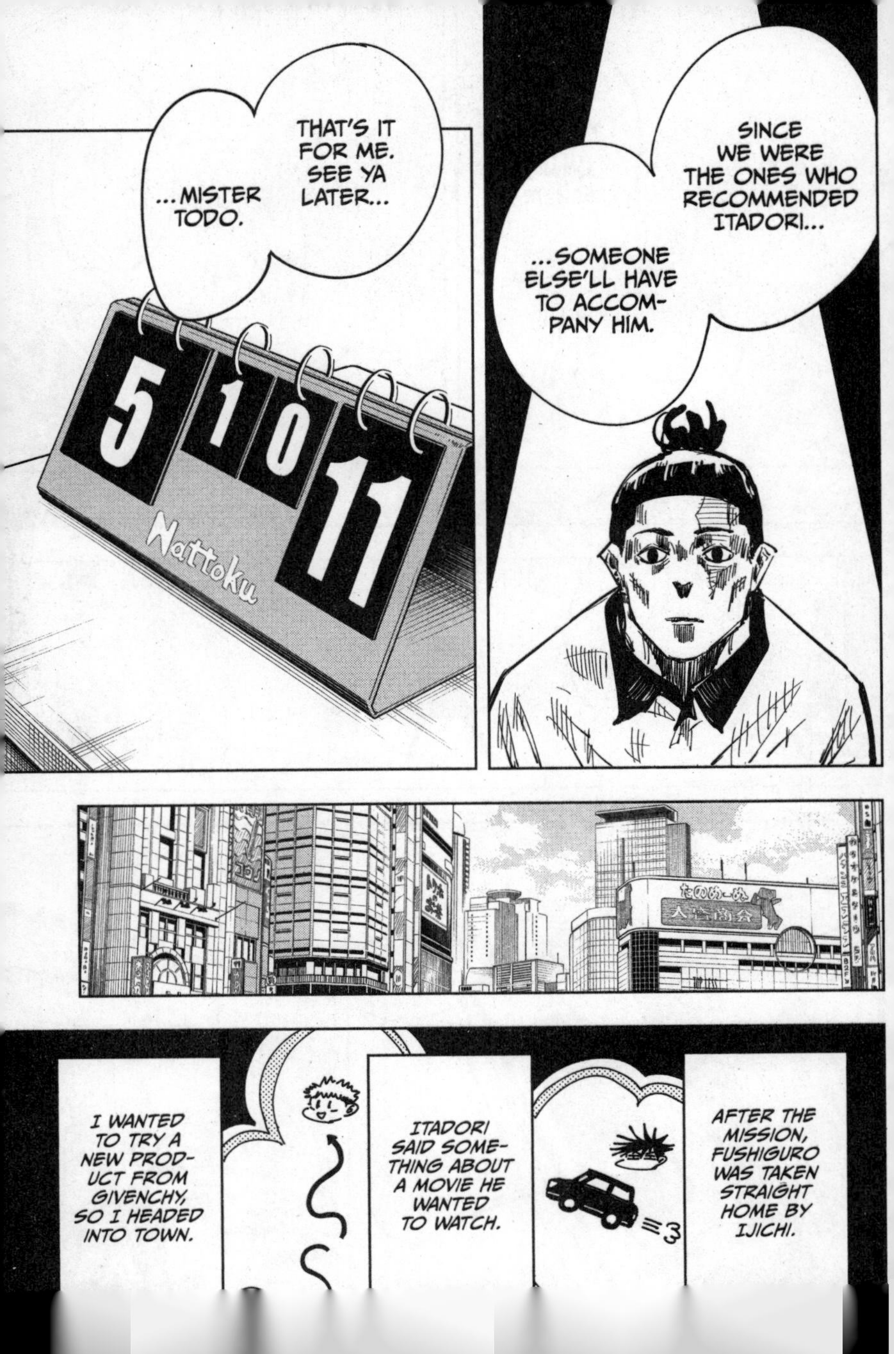
SINCE WE WERE THE ONES WHO RECOMMENDED ITADORI...
...SOMEONE ELSE'LL HAVE TO ACCOMPANY HIM.
THAT'S IT FOR ME. SEE YA LATER...
...MISTER TODO.
5 10 11
Nattoku
AFTER THE MISSION, FUSHIGURO WAS TAKEN STRAIGHT HOME BY IJICHI.
=3
ITADORI SAID SOMETHING ABOUT A MOVIE HE WANTED TO WATCH.
I WANTED TO TRY A NEW PRODUCT FROM GIVENCHY, SO I HEADED INTO TOWN.

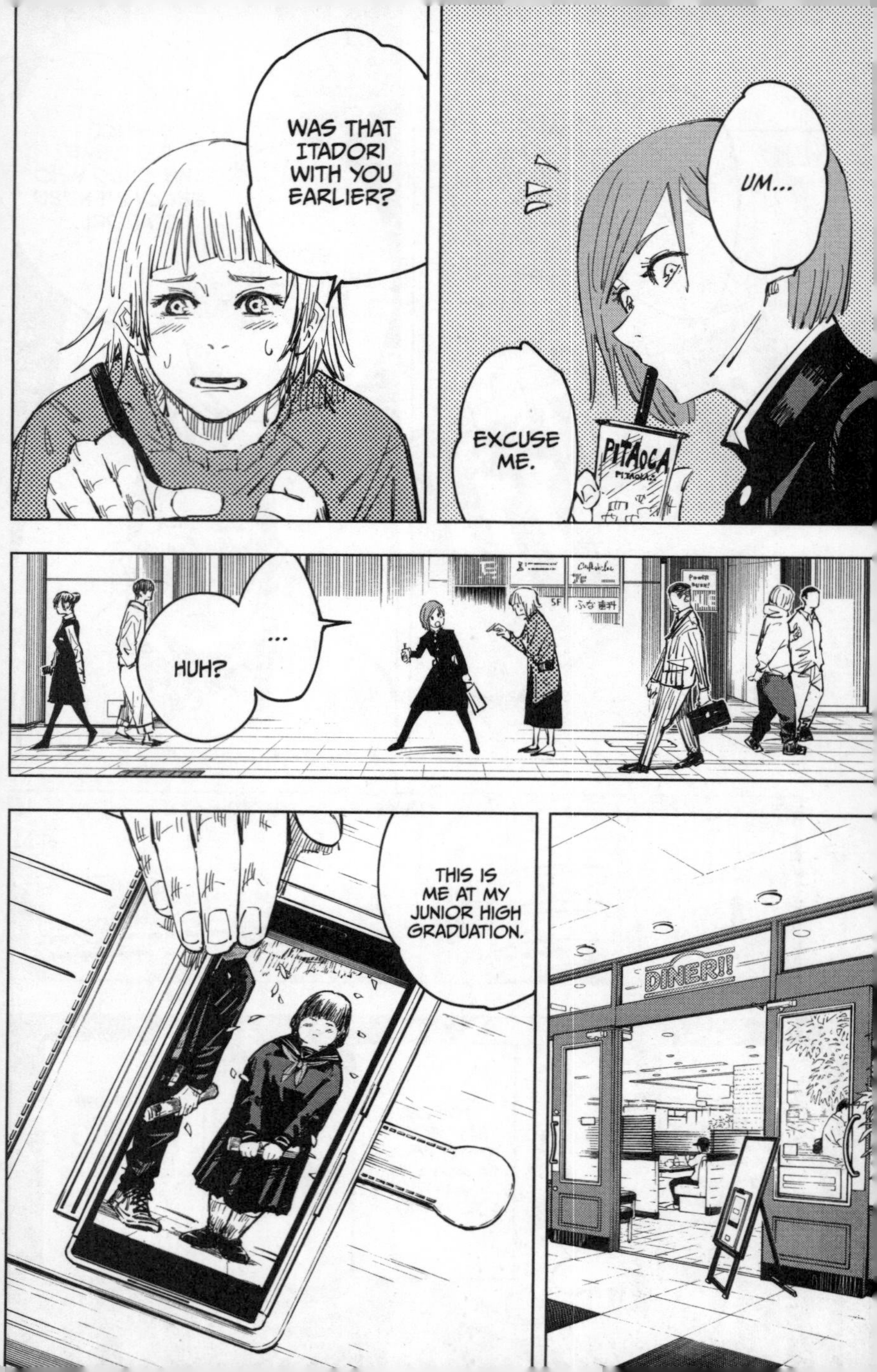
UM...
PITAOCA
EXCUSE ME.
WAS THAT ITADORI WITH YOU EARLIER?
...
HUH?
DINER!!
THIS IS ME AT MY JUNIOR HIGH GRADUATION.

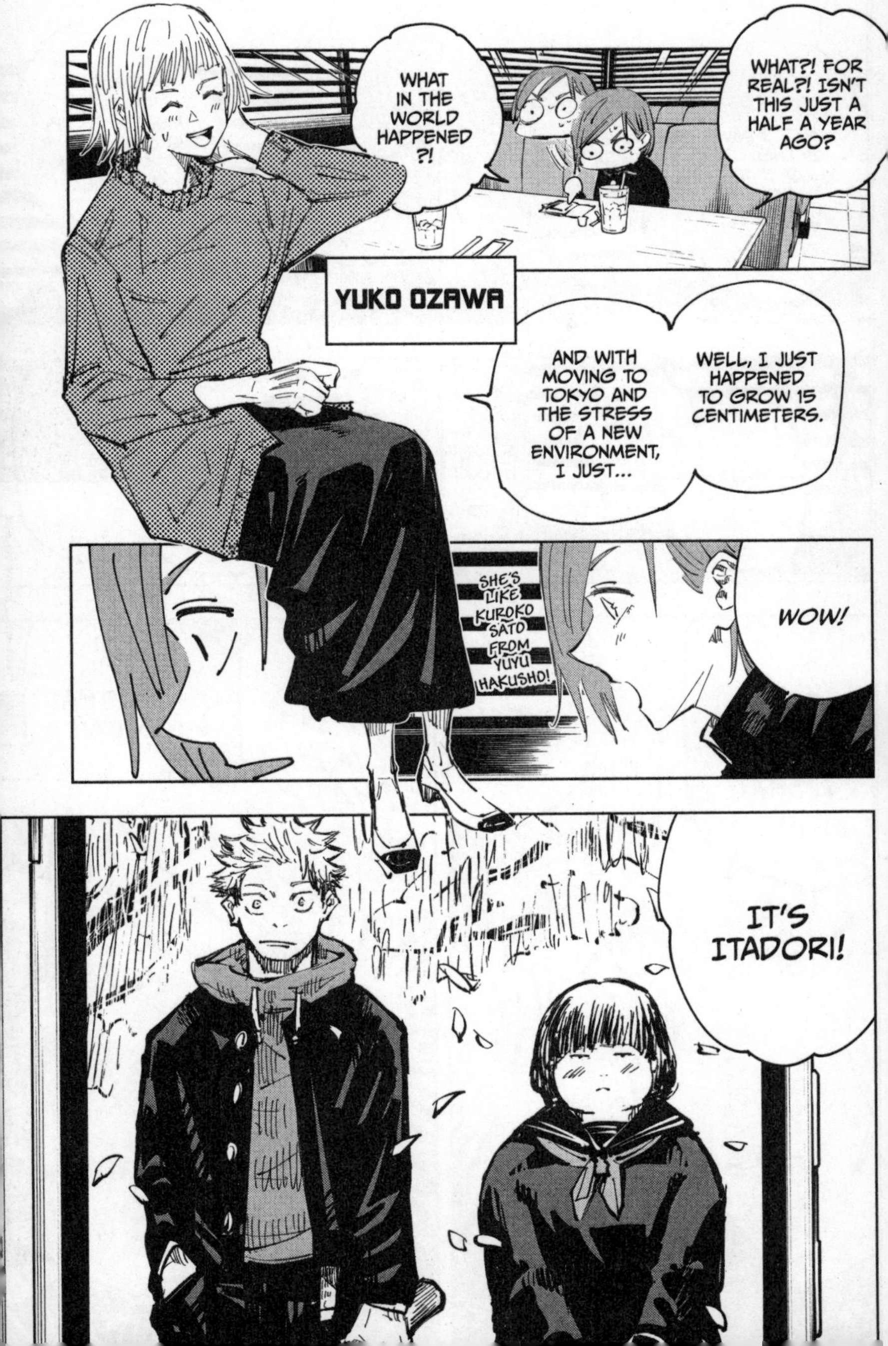
WHAT?! FOR REAL?! ISN'T THIS JUST A HALF A YEAR AGO?
WHAT IN THE WORLD HAPPENED ?!
YUKO OZAWA
WELL, I JUST HAPPENED TO GROW 15 CENTIMETERS.
AND WITH MOVING TO TOKYO AND THE STRESS OF A NEW ENVIRONMENT, I JUST...
WOW!
SHE'S LIKE KUROKO SATO FROM YUYU HAKUSHO!
IT'S ITADORI!

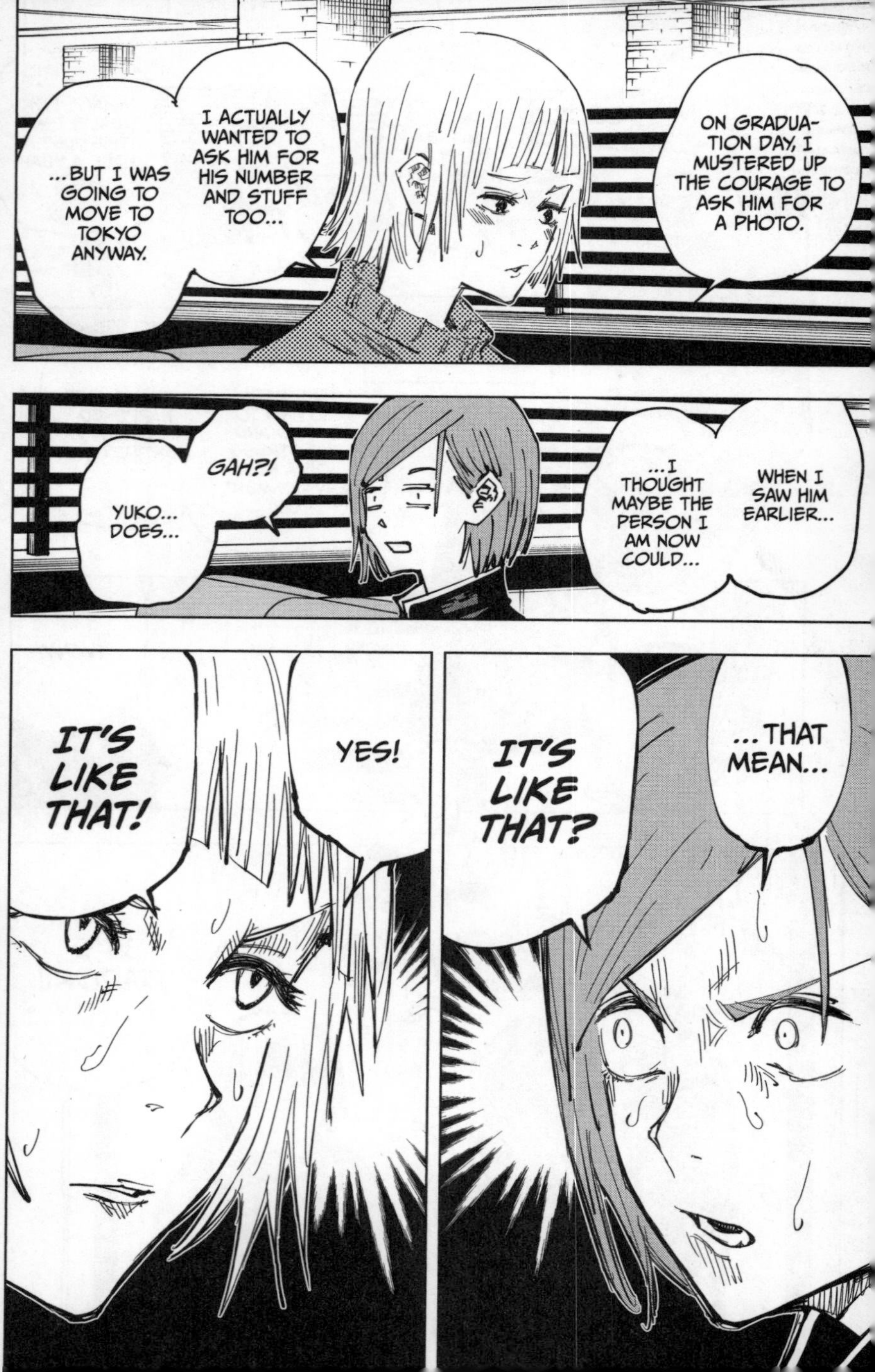
ON GRADUATION DAY, I MUSTERED UP THE COURAGE TO ASK HIM FOR A PHOTO.
I ACTUALLY WANTED TO ASK HIM FOR HIS NUMBER AND STUFF TOO...
...BUT I WAS GOING TO MOVE TO TOKYO ANYWAY.
WHEN I SAW HIM EARLIER...
...I THOUGHT MAYBE THE PERSON I AM NOW COULD...
GAH?!
YUKO... DOES...
...THAT MEAN...
IT'S LIKE THAT?
YES!
IT'S LIKE THAT!

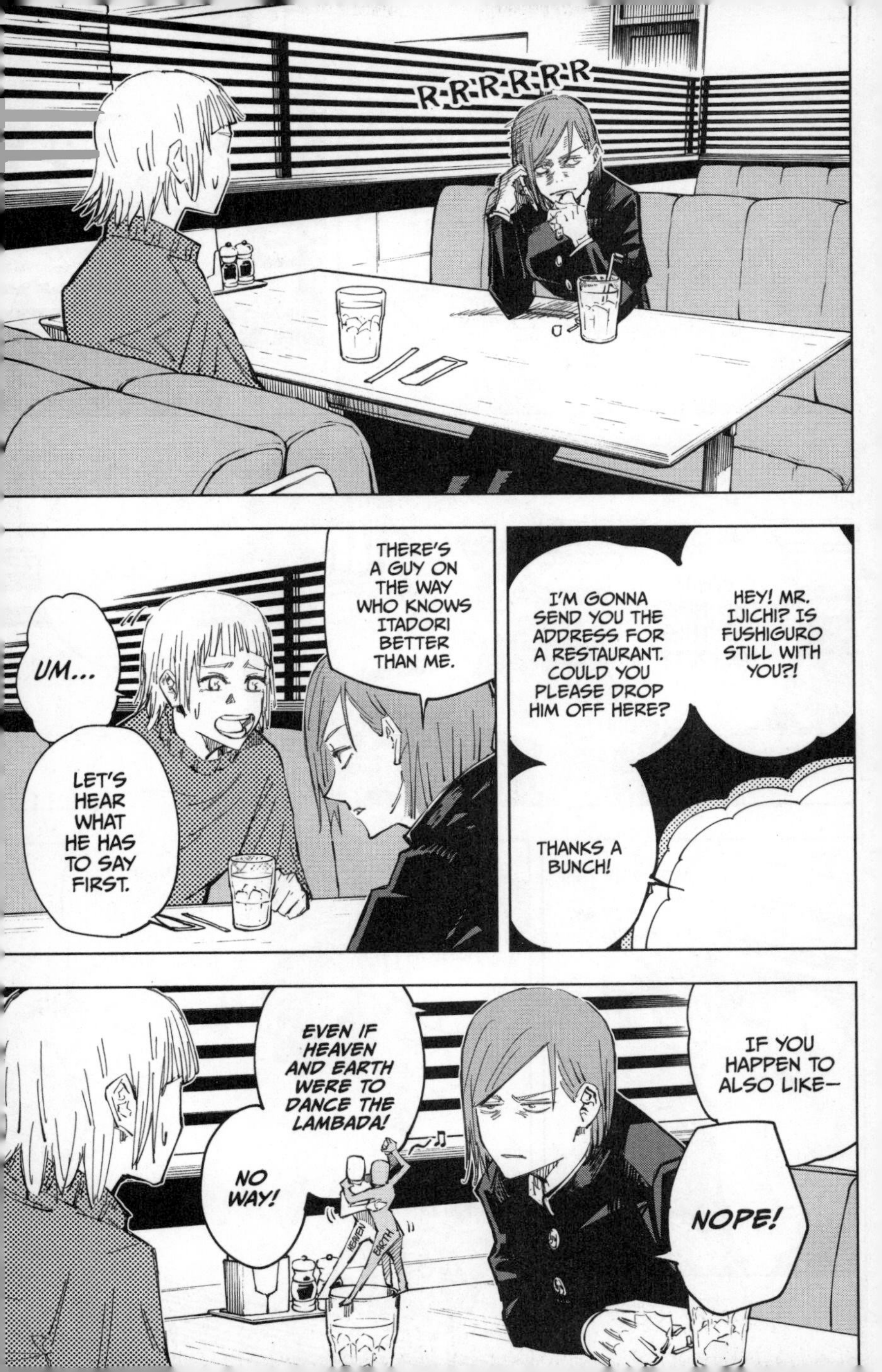
R-R-R-R-R-R
HEY! MR. IJICHI? IS FUSHIGURO STILL WITH YOU?!
I'M GONNA SEND YOU THE ADDRESS FOR A RESTAURANT. COULD YOU PLEASE DROP HIM OFF HERE?
THANKS A BUNCH!
THERE'S A GUY ON THE WAY WHO KNOWS ITADORI BETTER THAN ME.
UM...
LET'S HEAR WHAT HE HAS TO SAY FIRST.
IF YOU HAPPEN TO ALSO LIKE—
NOPE!
EVEN IF HEAVEN AND EARTH WERE TO DANCE THE LAMBADA!
NO WAY!
HEAVEN
EARTH

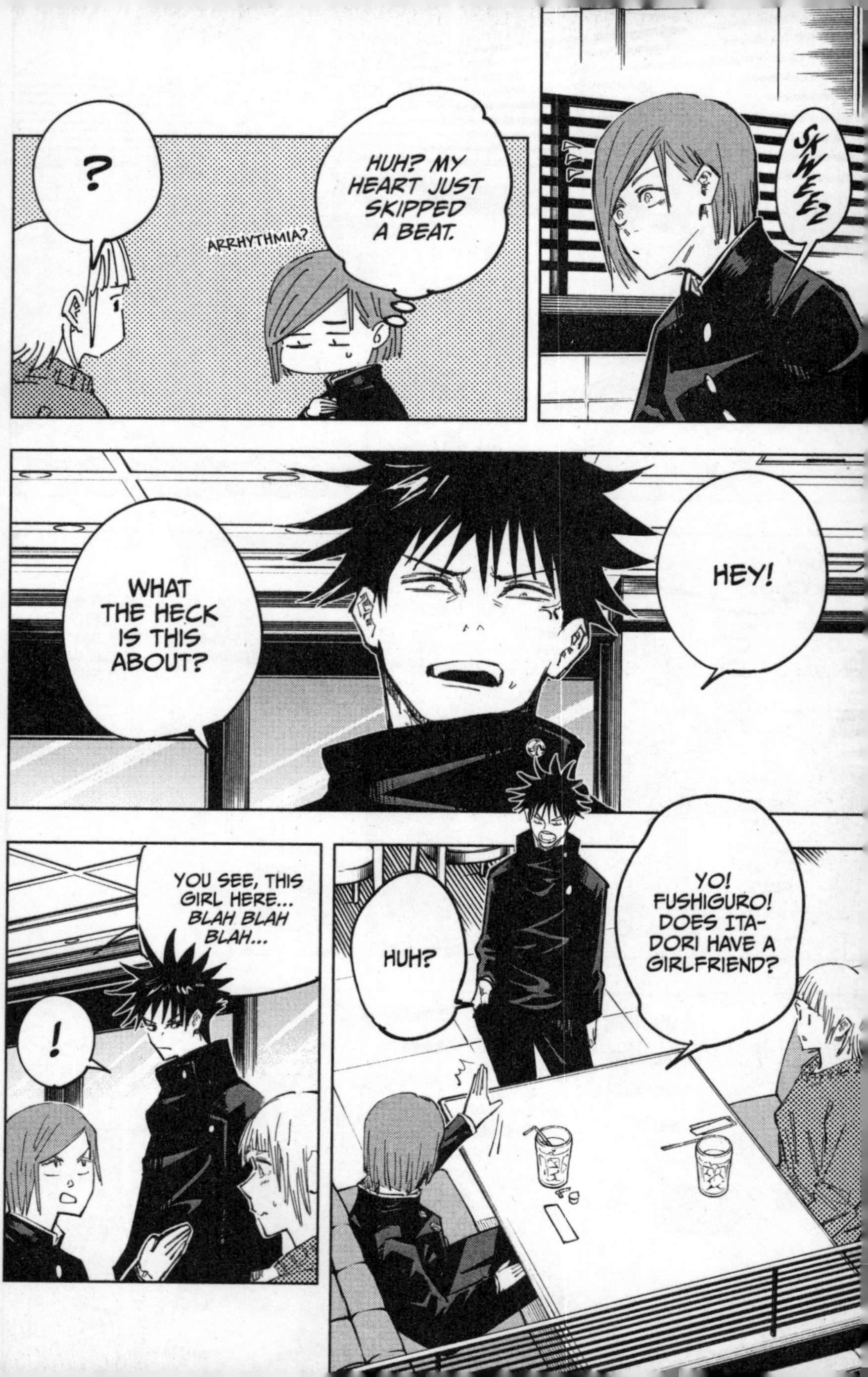
SKWEEZ
HUH? MY HEART JUST SKIPPED A BEAT.
ARRHYTHMIA?
?
HEY!
WHAT THE HECK IS THIS ABOUT?
YO! FUSHIGURO! DOES ITA-DORI HAVE A GIRLFRIEND?
HUH?
YOU SEE, THIS GIRL HERE... BLAH BLAH BLAH...
!

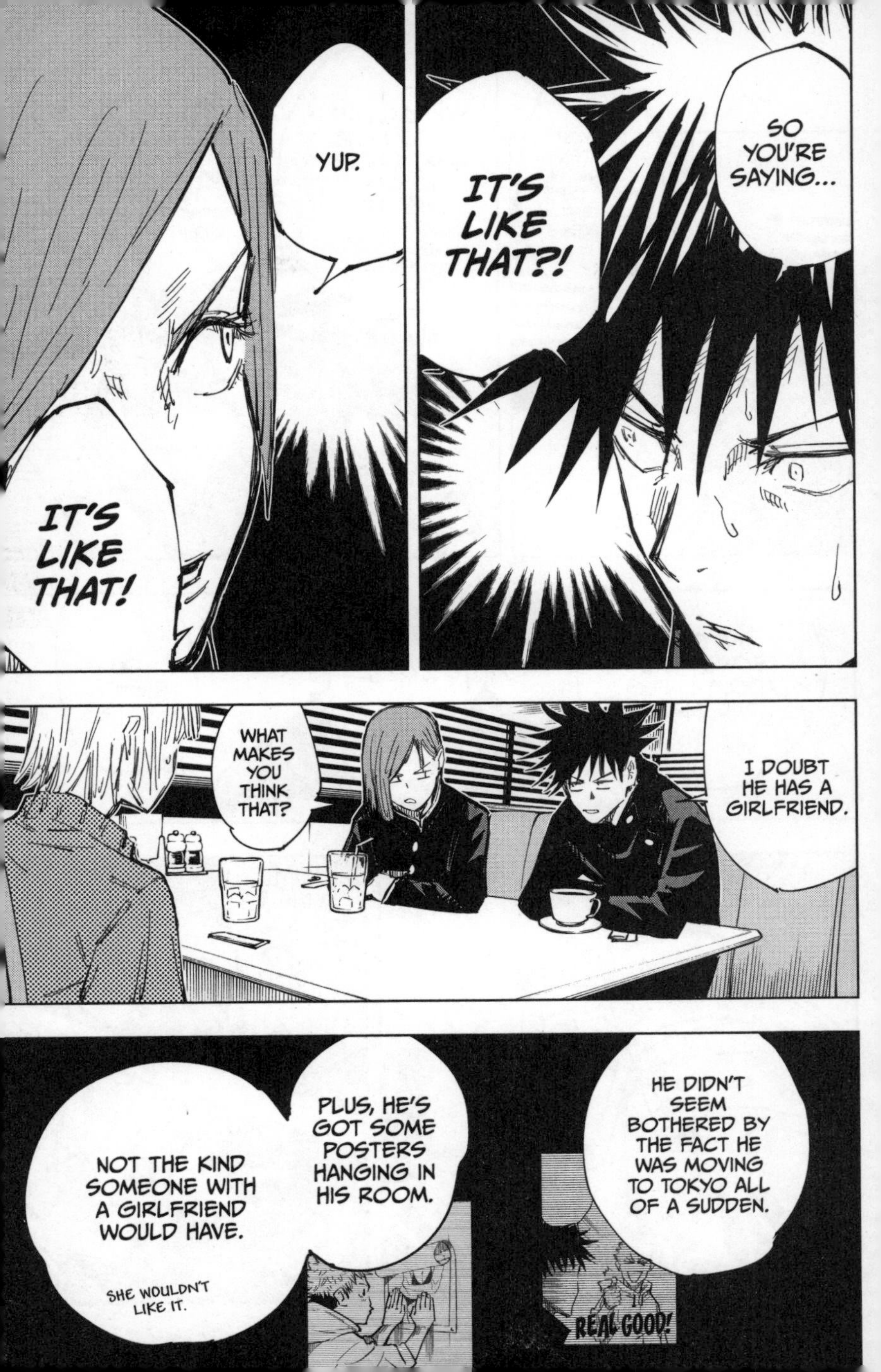
SO YOU'RE SAYING...
IT'S LIKE THAT?!
YUP.
IT'S LIKE THAT!
I DOUBT HE HAS A GIRLFRIEND.
WHAT MAKES YOU THINK THAT?
HE DIDN'T SEEM BOTHERED BY THE FACT HE WAS MOVING TO TOKYO ALL OF A SUDDEN.
REAL GOOD!
PLUS, HE'S GOT SOME POSTERS HANGING IN HIS ROOM.
NOT THE KIND SOMEONE WITH A GIRLFRIEND WOULD HAVE.
SHE WOULDN'T LIKE IT.

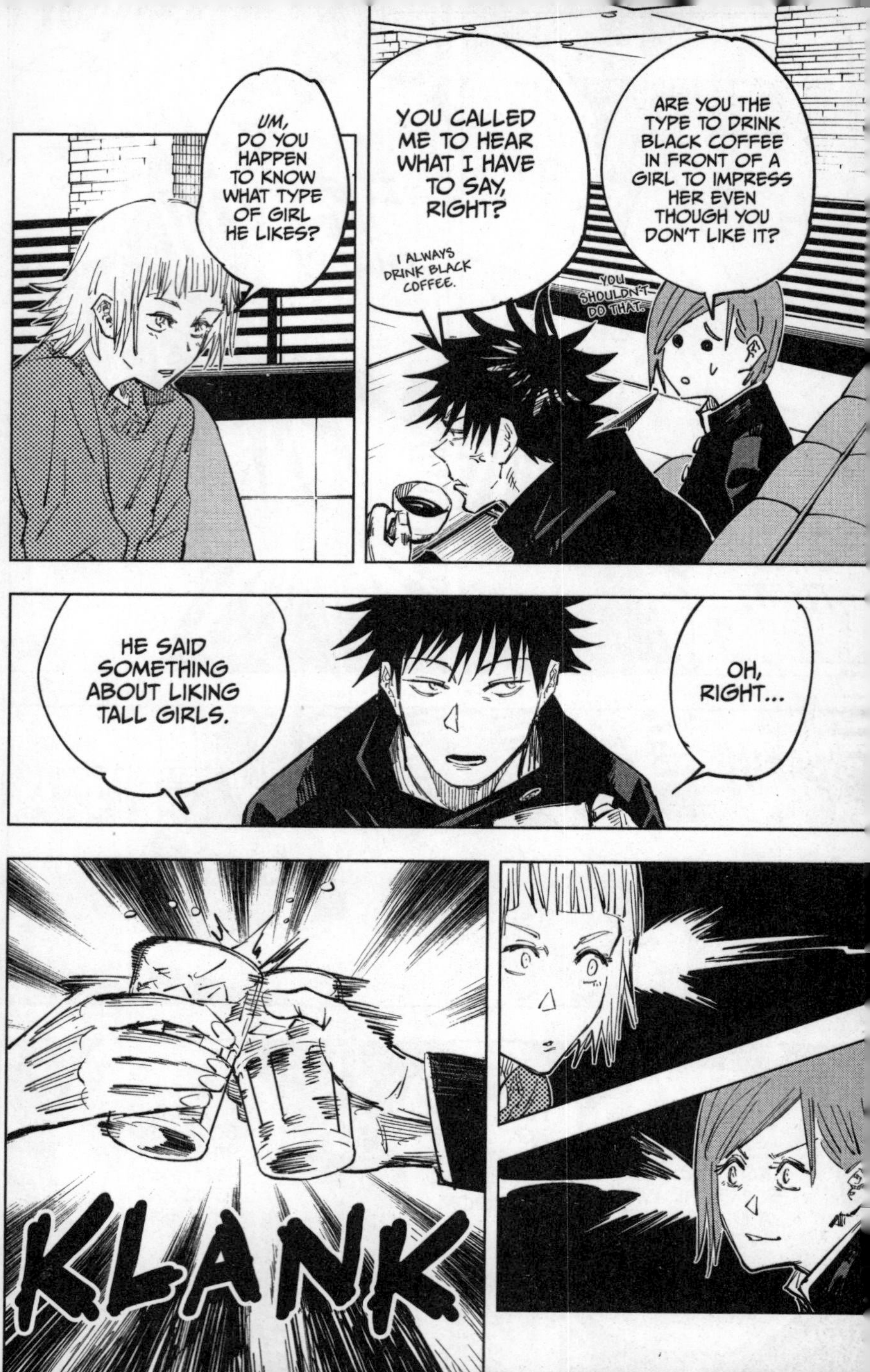
ARE YOU THE TYPE TO DRINK BLACK COFFEE IN FRONT OF A GIRL TO IMPRESS HER EVEN THOUGH YOU DON'T LIKE IT?
YOU CALLED ME TO HEAR WHAT I HAVE TO SAY, RIGHT?
YOU SHOULDN'T DO THAT.
I ALWAYS DRINK BLACK COFFEE.
UM, DO YOU HAPPEN TO KNOW WHAT TYPE OF GIRL HE LIKES?
OH, RIGHT...
HE SAID SOMETHING ABOUT LIKING TALL GIRLS.
KLANK

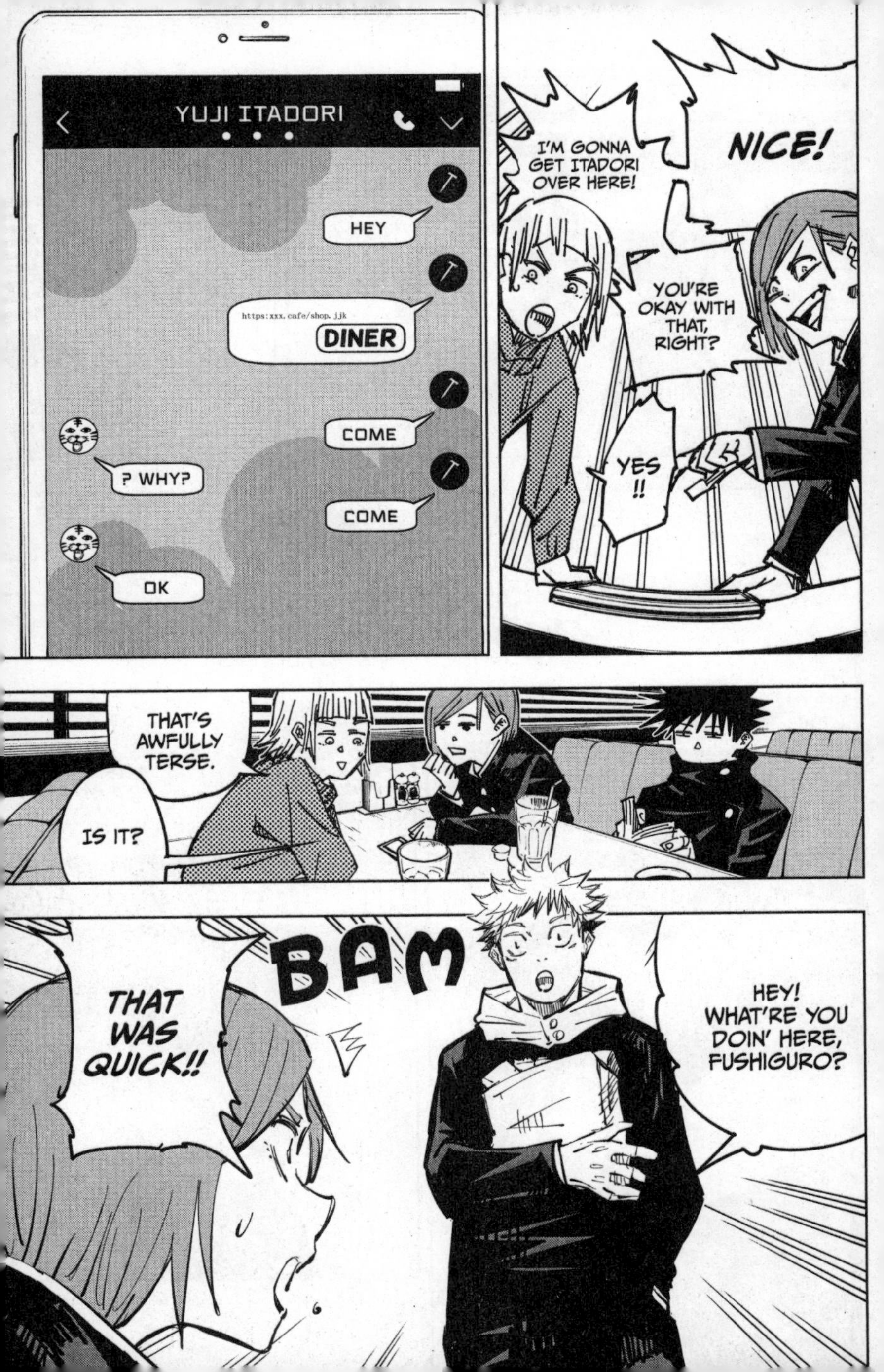
I'M GONNA GET ITADORI OVER HERE!
NICE!
YOU'RE OKAY WITH THAT, RIGHT?
YES !!
YUJI ITADORI
HEY
https:xxx.cafe/shop.jjk
DINER
COME
? WHY?
COME
OK
THAT'S AWFULLY TERSE.
IS IT?
HEY! WHAT'RE YOU DOIN' HERE, FUSHIGURO?
BAM
THAT WAS QUICK!!

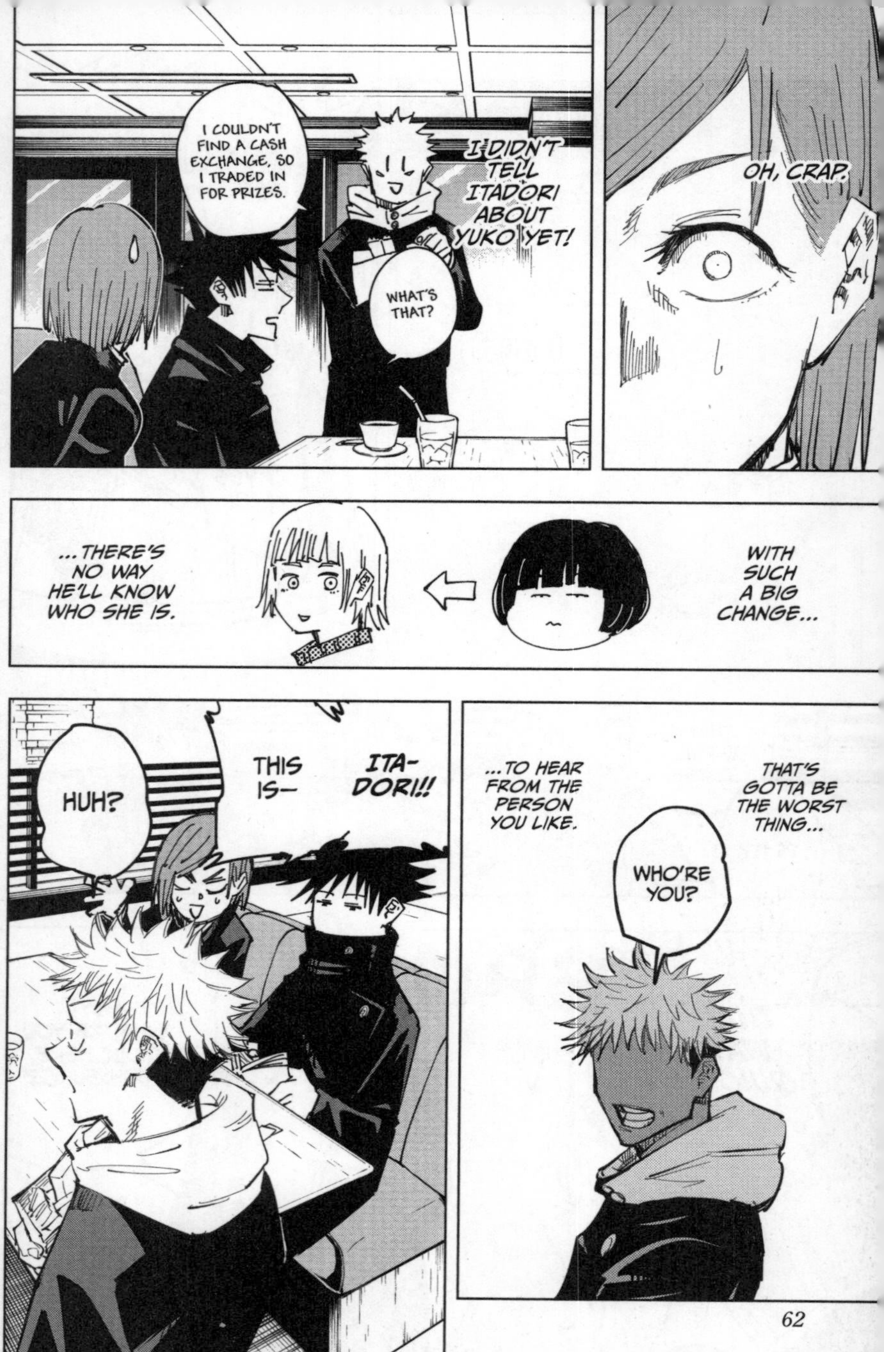
OH, CRAP.
I DIDN'T TELL ITADORI ABOUT YUKO YET!
I COULDN'T FIND A CASH EXCHANGE, SO I TRADED IN FOR PRIZES.
WHAT'S THAT?
WITH SUCH A BIG CHANGE...
...THERE'S NO WAY HE'LL KNOW WHO SHE IS.
THAT'S GOTTA BE THE WORST THING...
...TO HEAR FROM THE PERSON YOU LIKE.
WHO'RE YOU?
ITA-DORI!!
THIS IS—
HUH?

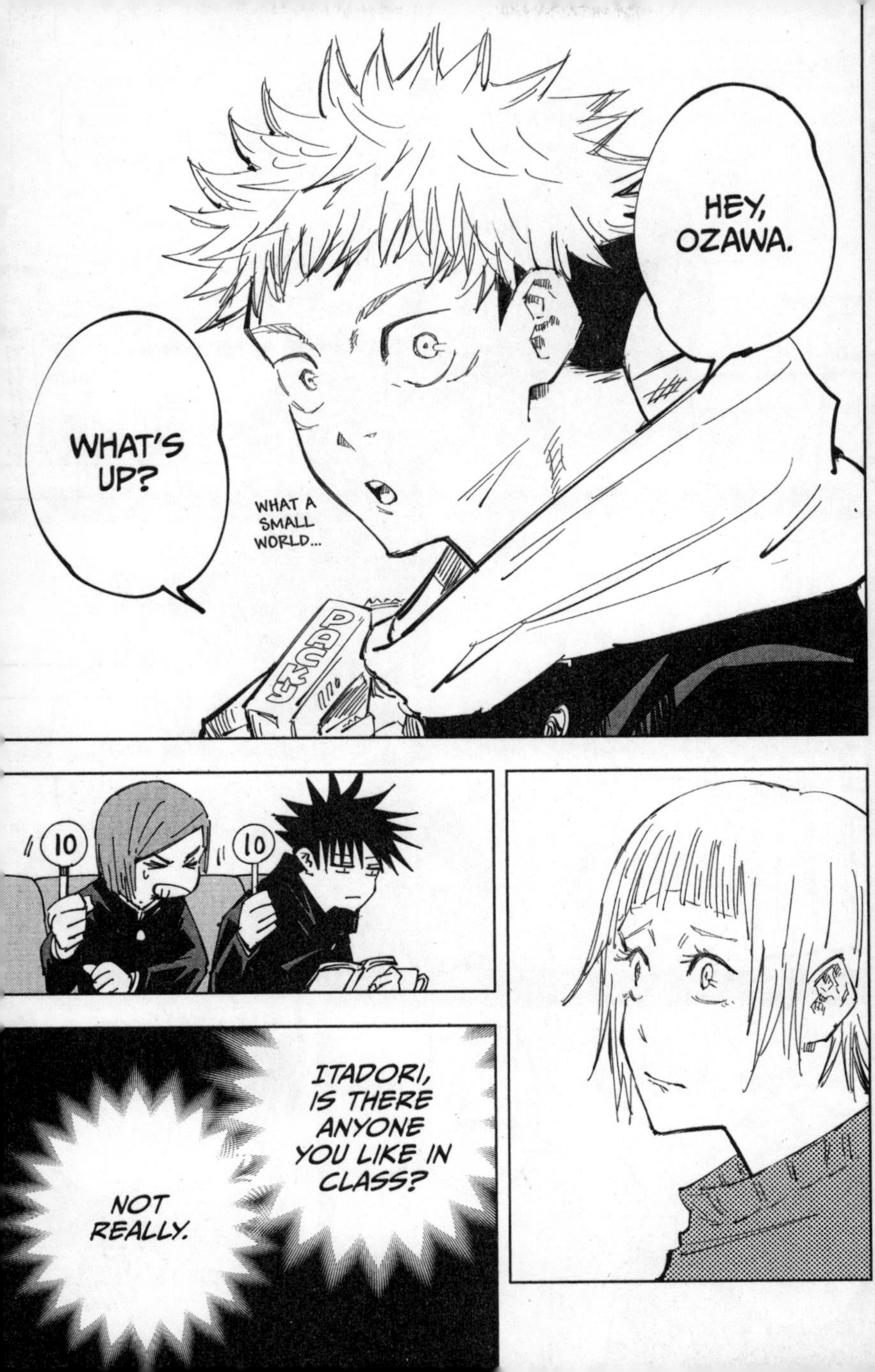
HEY, OZAWA.
WHAT'S UP?
WHAT A SMALL WORLD...
PACKY
10
10
ITADORI, IS THERE ANYONE YOU LIKE IN CLASS?
NOT REALLY.

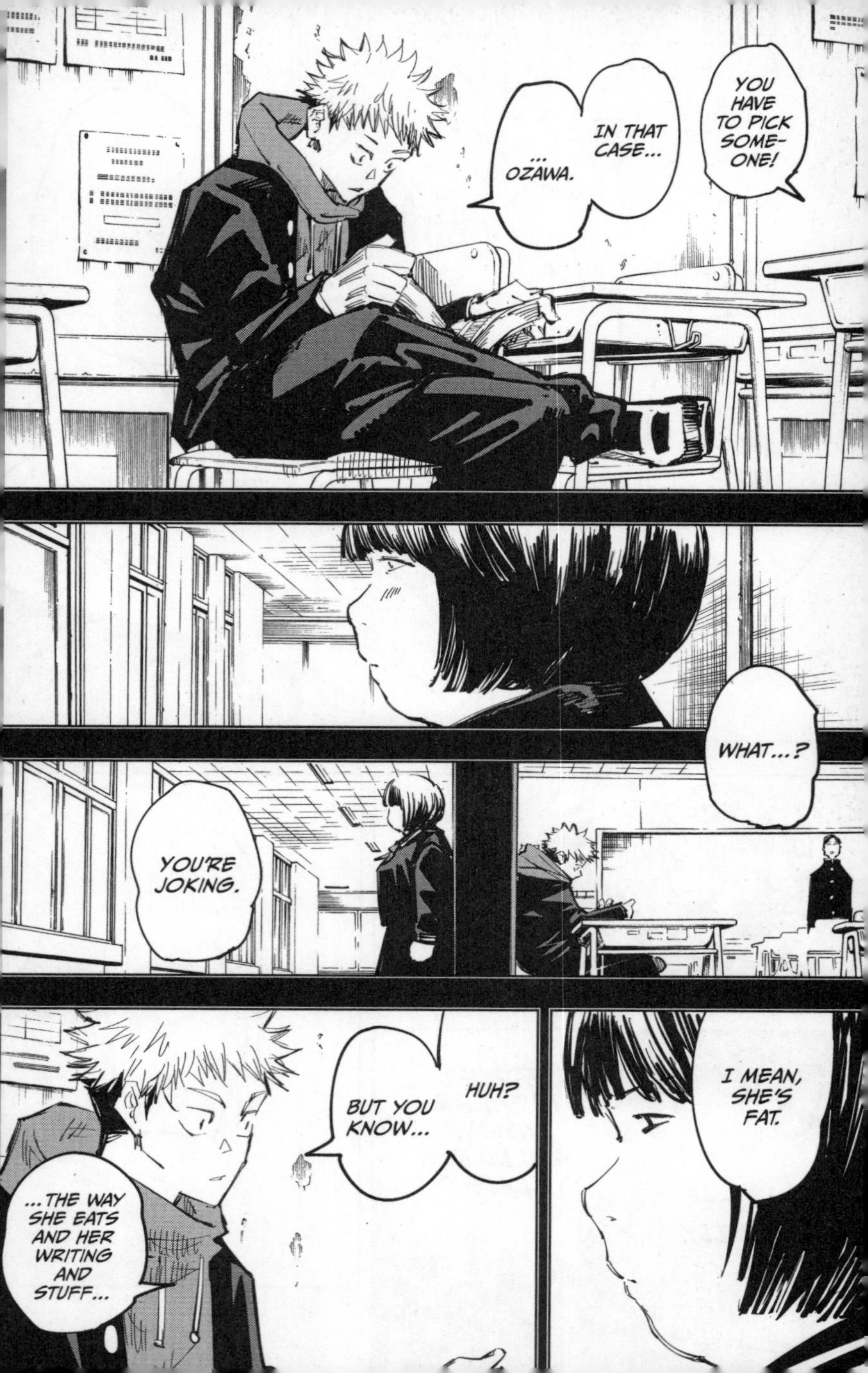
YOU HAVE TO PICK SOME-ONE!
IN THAT CASE...
...OZAWA.
WHAT...?
YOU'RE JOKING.
I MEAN, SHE'S FAT.
HUH?
BUT YOU KNOW...
...THE WAY SHE EATS AND HER WRITING AND STUFF...

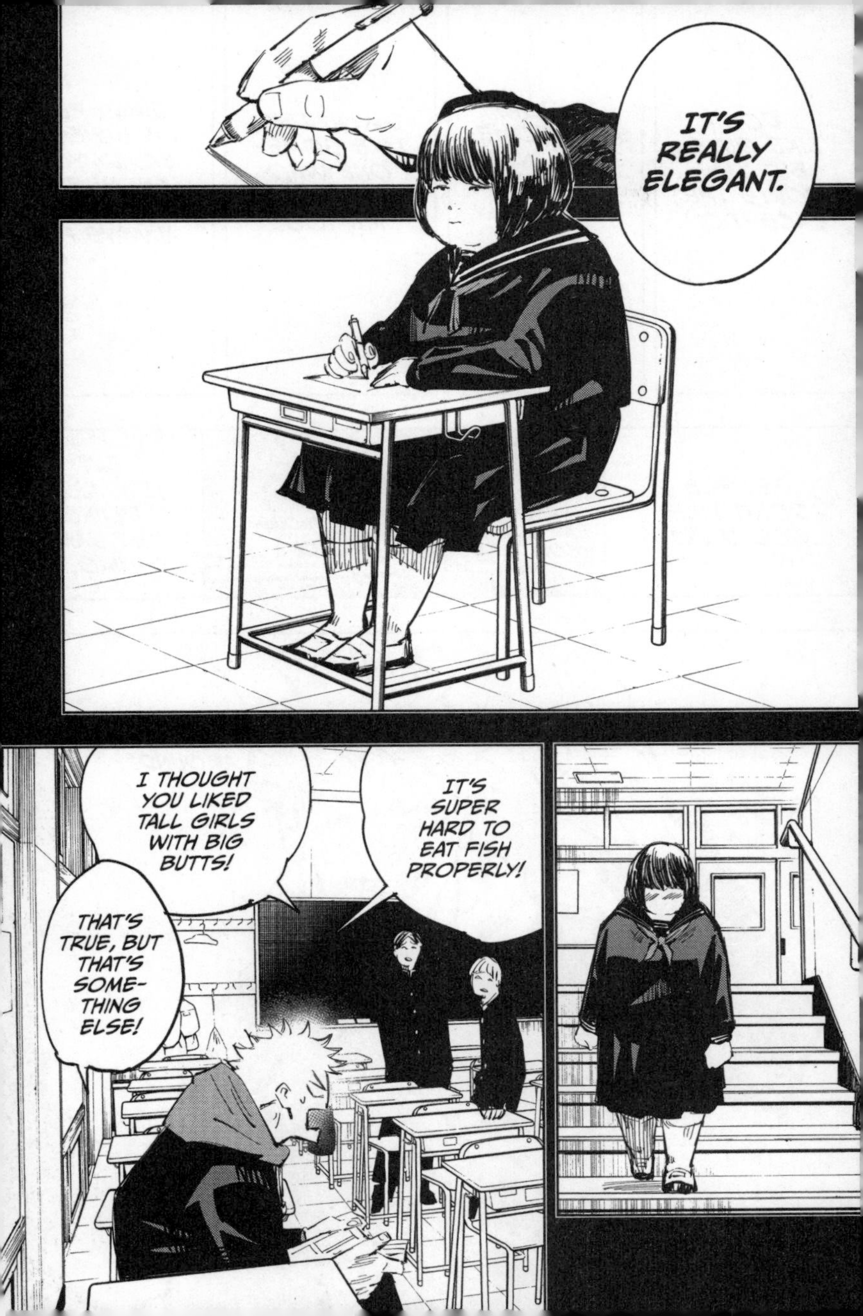
IT'S REALLY ELEGANT.
IT'S SUPER HARD TO EAT FISH PROPERLY!
I THOUGHT YOU LIKED TALL GIRLS WITH BIG BUTTS!
THAT'S TRUE, BUT THAT'S SOME-THING ELSE!

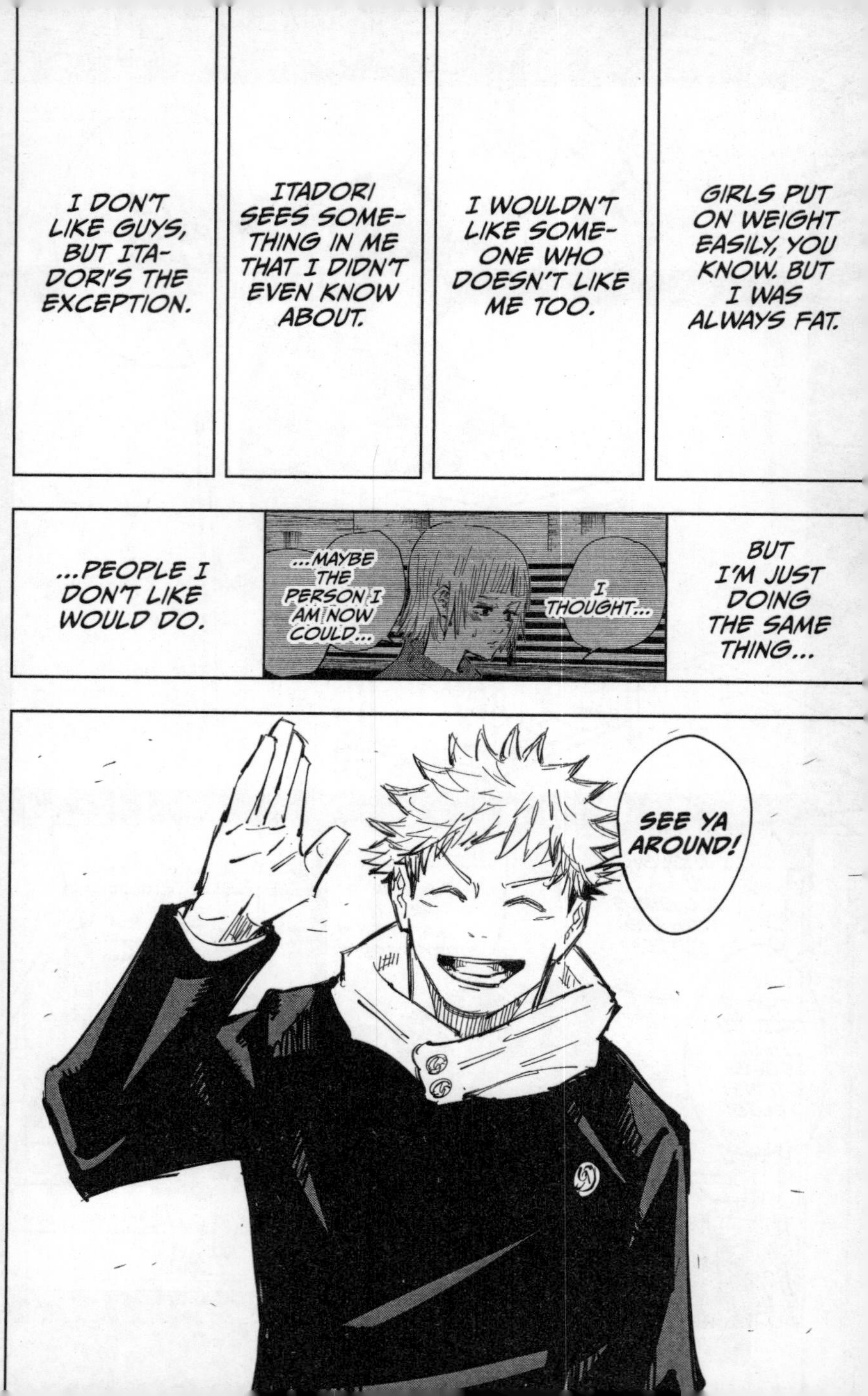
GIRLS PUT ON WEIGHT EASILY, YOU KNOW. BUT I WAS ALWAYS FAT.
I WOULDN'T LIKE SOMEONE WHO DOESN'T LIKE ME TOO.
ITADORI SEES SOMETHING IN ME THAT I DIDN'T EVEN KNOW ABOUT.
I DON'T LIKE GUYS, BUT ITADORI'S THE EXCEPTION.
BUT I'M JUST DOING THE SAME THING...
I THOUGHT...
...MAYBE THE PERSON I AM NOW COULD...
...PEOPLE I DON'T LIKE WOULD DO.
SEE YA AROUND!

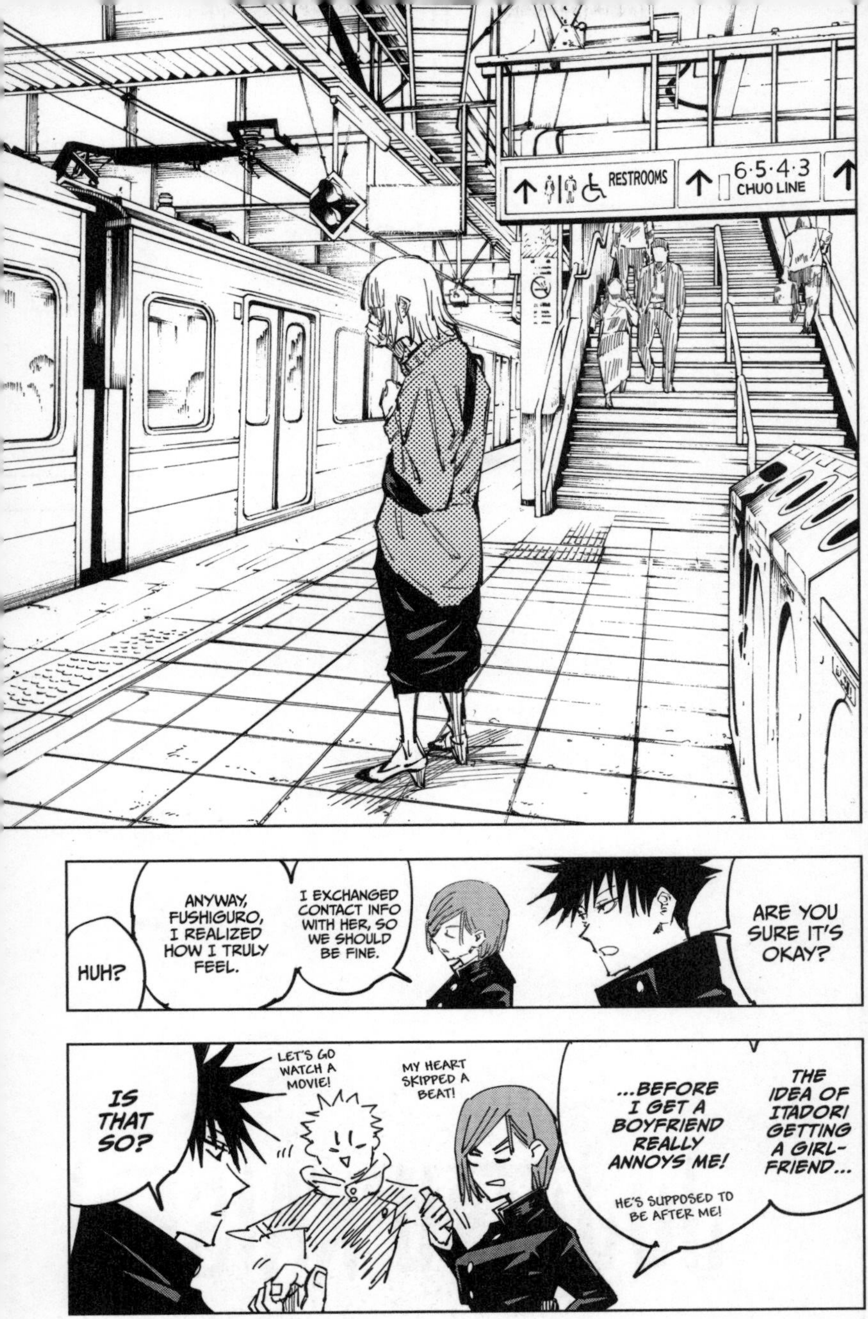
RESTROOMS
6·5·4·3
CHUO LINE
ARE YOU SURE IT'S OKAY?
I EXCHANGED CONTACT INFO WITH HER, SO WE SHOULD BE FINE.
ANYWAY, FUSHIGURO, I REALIZED HOW I TRULY FEEL.
HUH?
THE IDEA OF ITADORI GETTING A GIRL-FRIEND...
...BEFORE I GET A BOYFRIEND REALLY ANNOYS ME!
HE'S SUPPOSED TO BE AFTER ME!
MY HEART SKIPPED A BEAT!
LET'S GO WATCH A MOVIE!
IS THAT SO?

JUJUTSU KAISEN

CHAPTER 65: HIDDEN INVENTORY

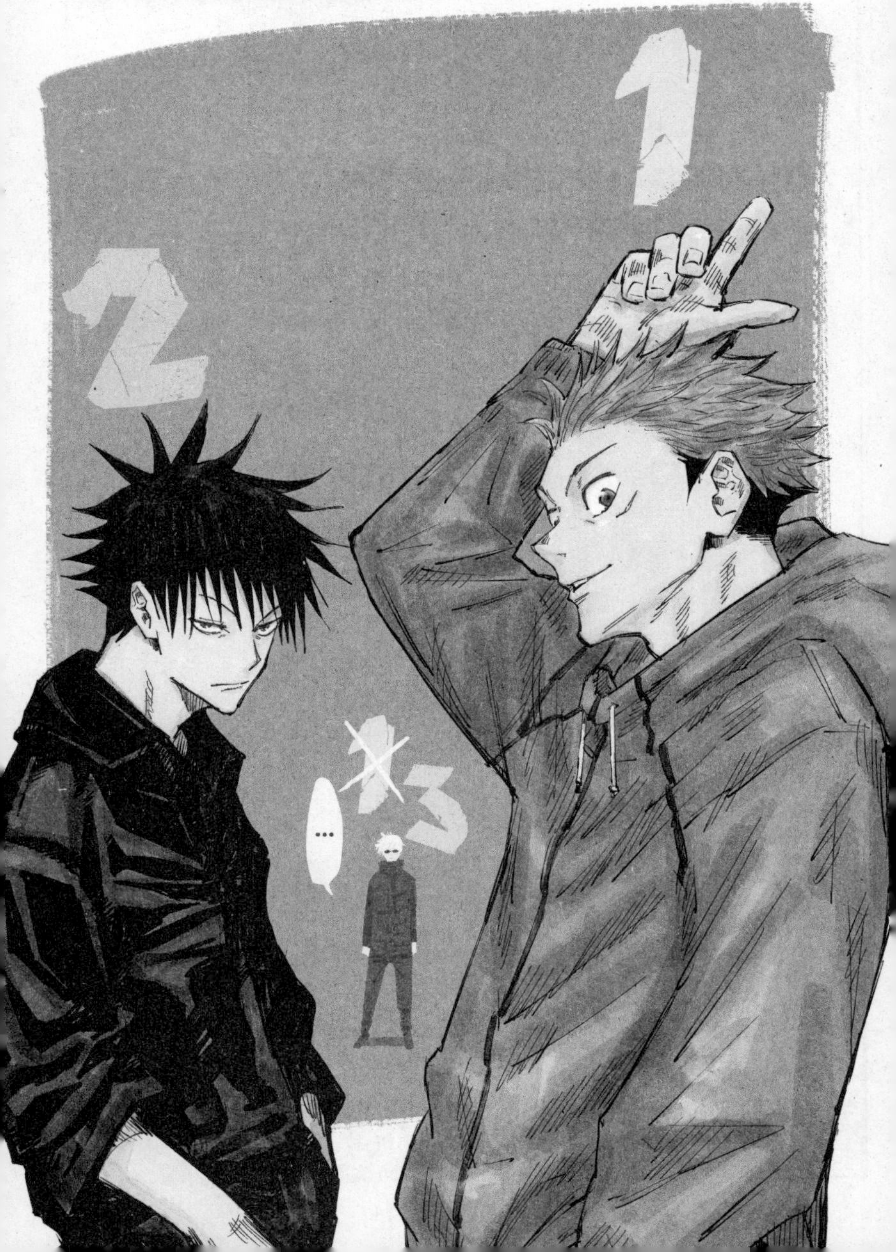
1
2
3
...

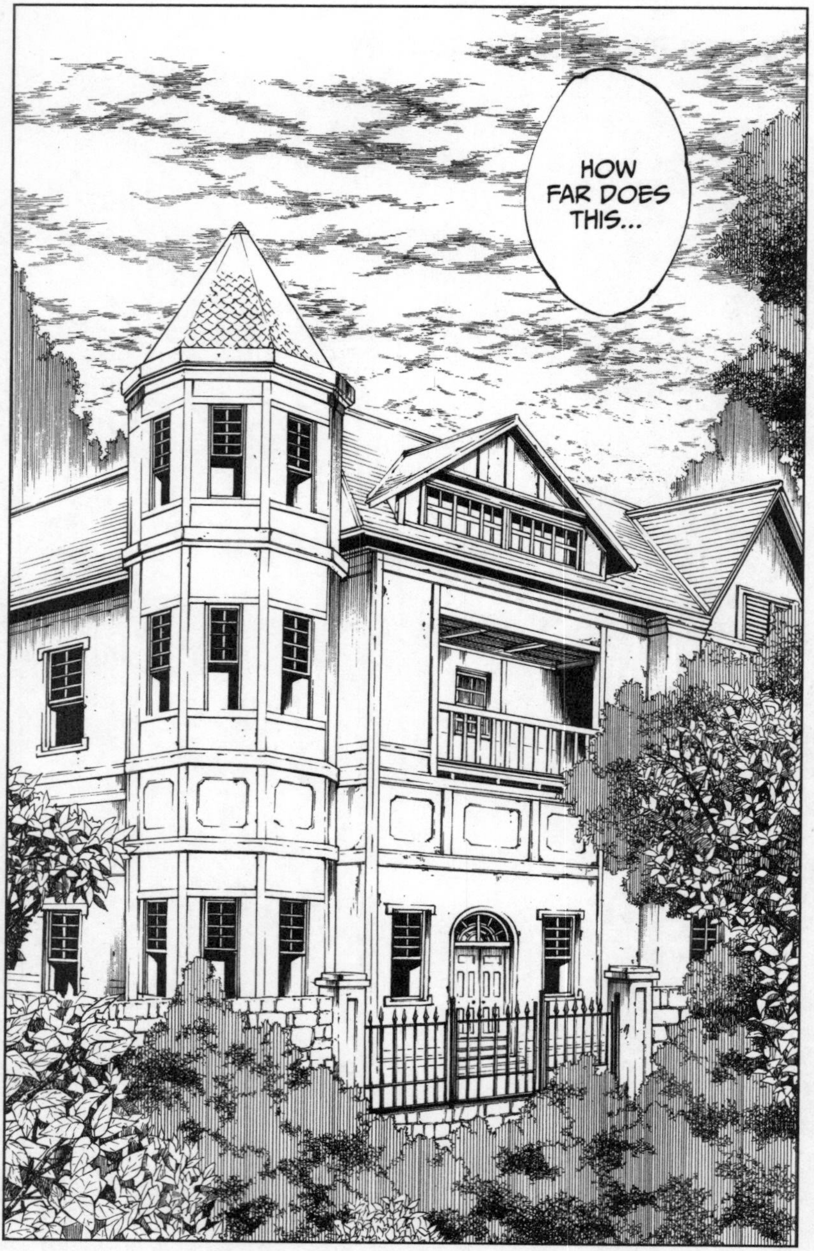
HOW FAR DOES THIS...

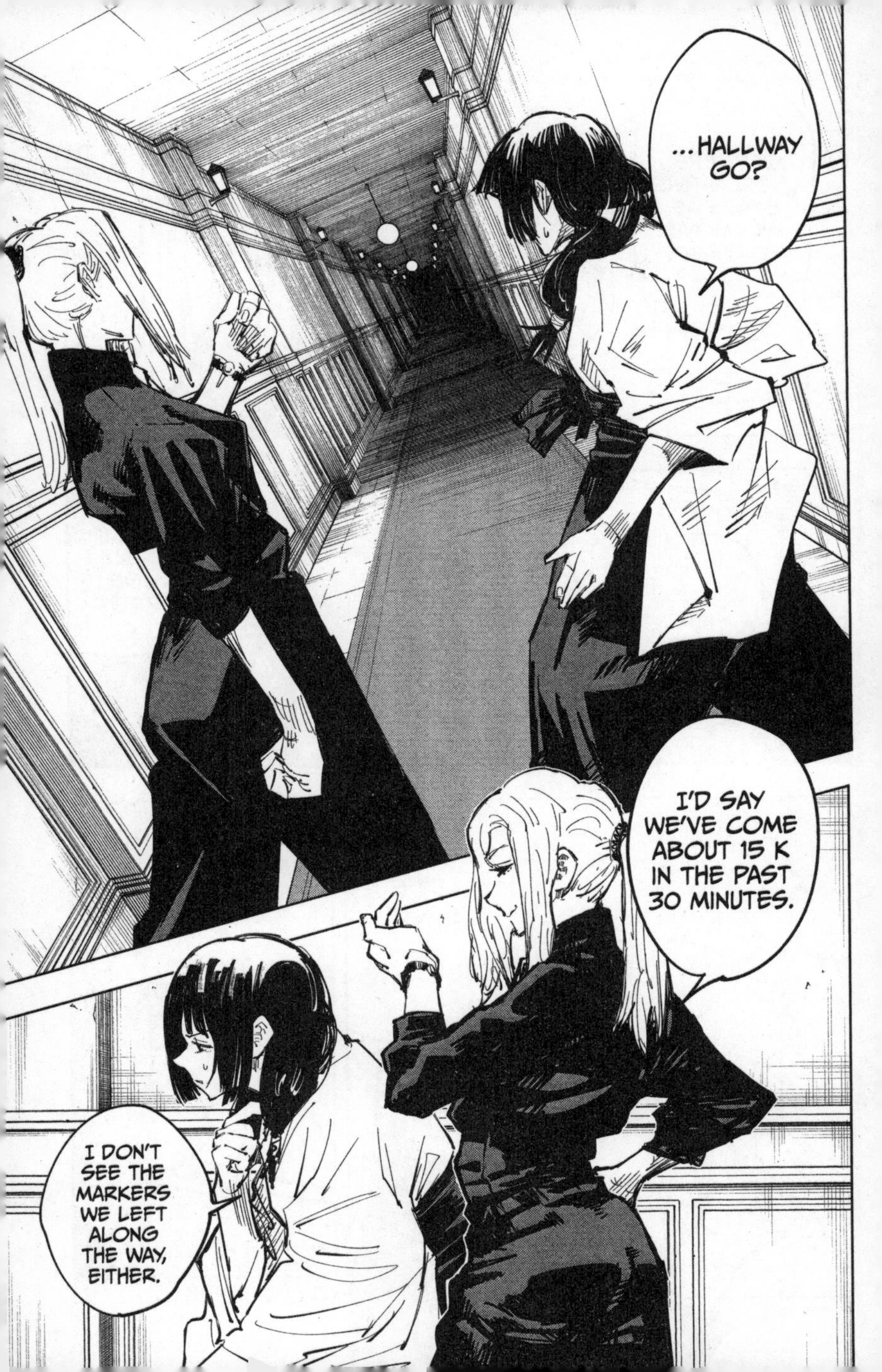
...HALLWAY GO?
I'D SAY WE'VE COME ABOUT 15 K IN THE PAST 30 MINUTES.
I DON'T SEE THE MARKERS WE LEFT ALONG THE WAY, EITHER.

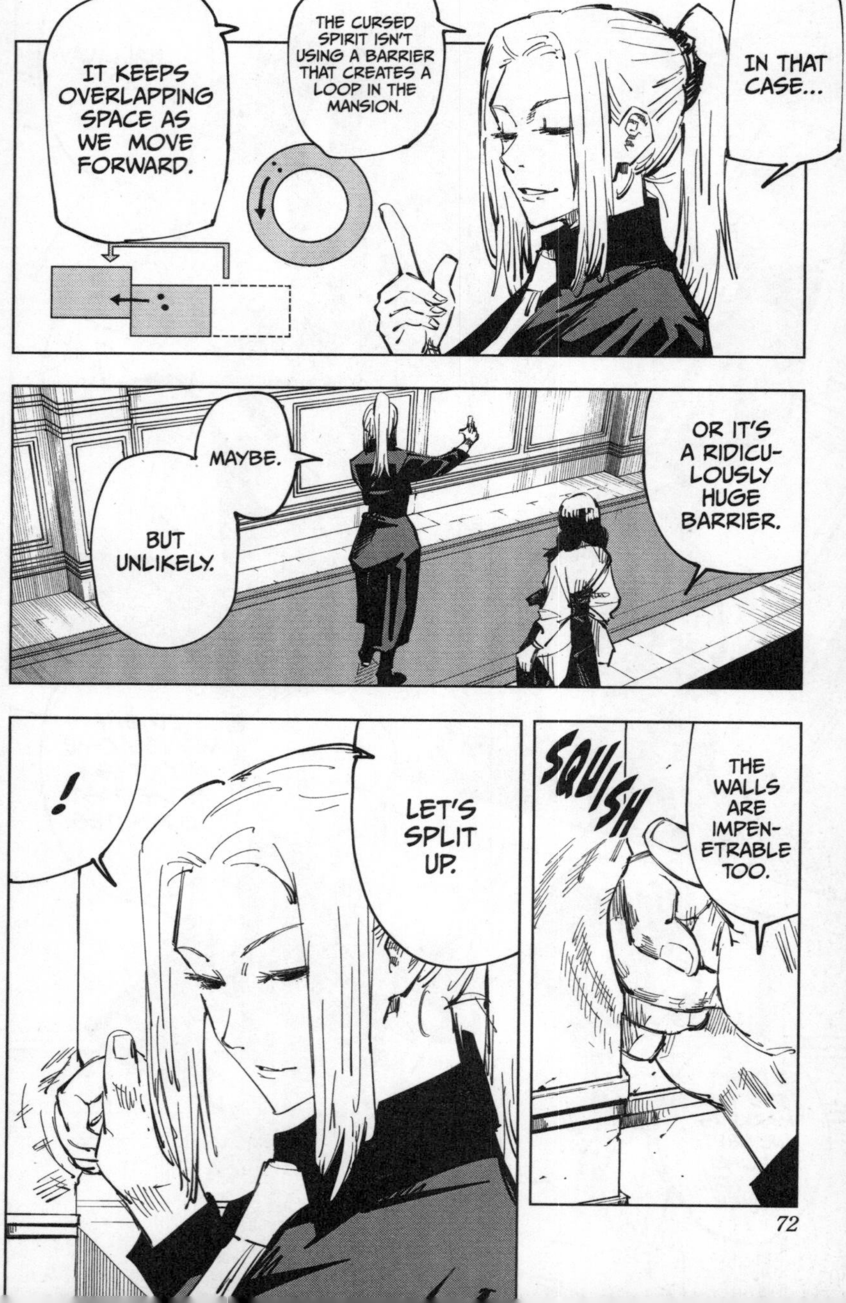
IN THAT CASE...
THE CURSED SPIRIT ISN'T USING A BARRIER THAT CREATES A LOOP IN THE MANSION.
IT KEEPS OVERLAPPING SPACE AS WE MOVE FORWARD.
OR IT'S A RIDICU-LOUSLY HUGE BARRIER.
MAYBE.
BUT UNLIKELY.
SQUISH
THE WALLS ARE IMPEN-ETRABLE TOO.
LET'S SPLIT UP.
!

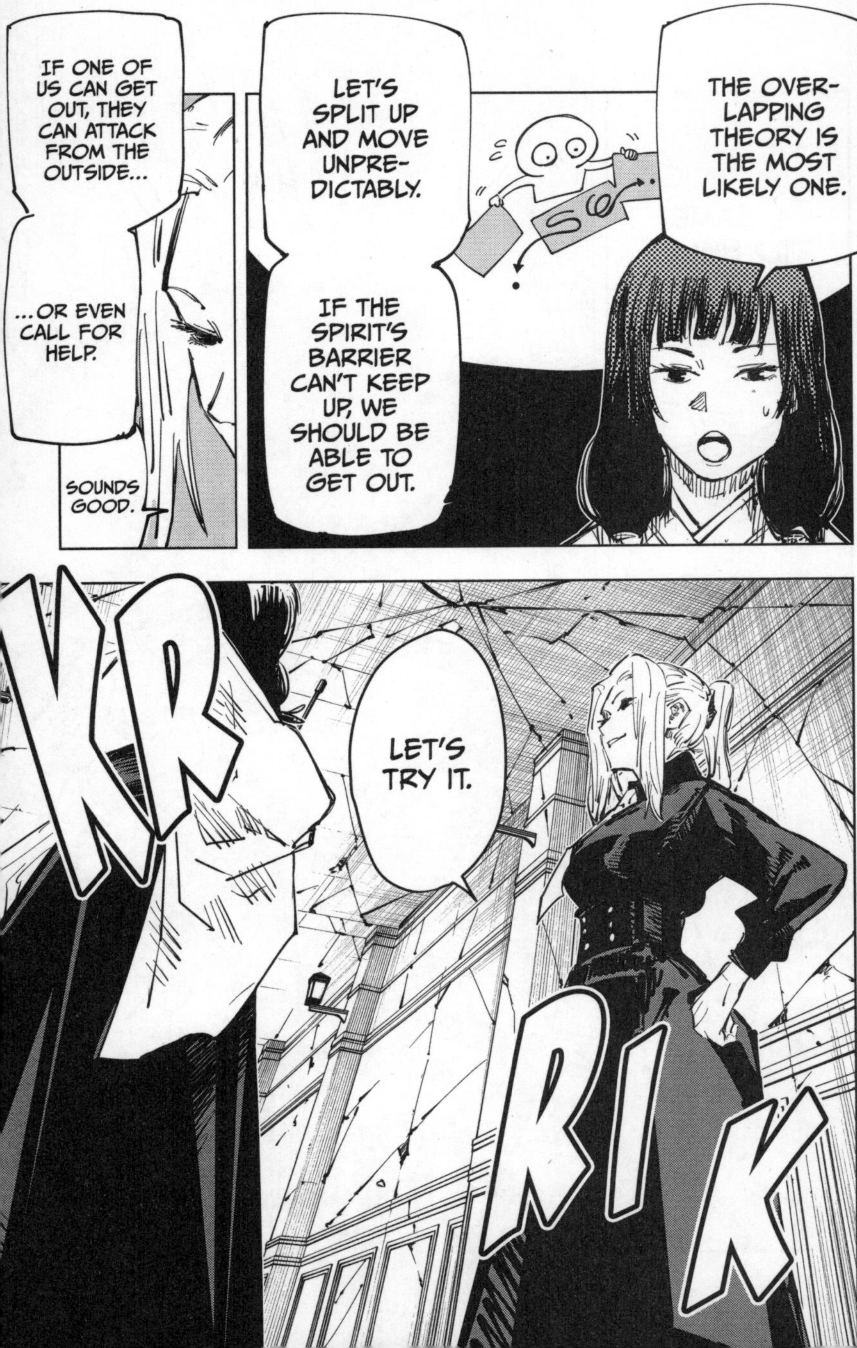
THE OVER-LAPPING THEORY IS THE MOST LIKELY ONE.
LET'S SPLIT UP AND MOVE UNPRE-DICTABLY.
IF THE SPIRIT'S BARRIER CAN'T KEEP UP, WE SHOULD BE ABLE TO GET OUT.
IF ONE OF US CAN GET OUT, THEY CAN ATTACK FROM THE OUTSIDE...
...OR EVEN CALL FOR HELP.
SOUNDS GOOD.
LET'S TRY IT.
KR
RIK

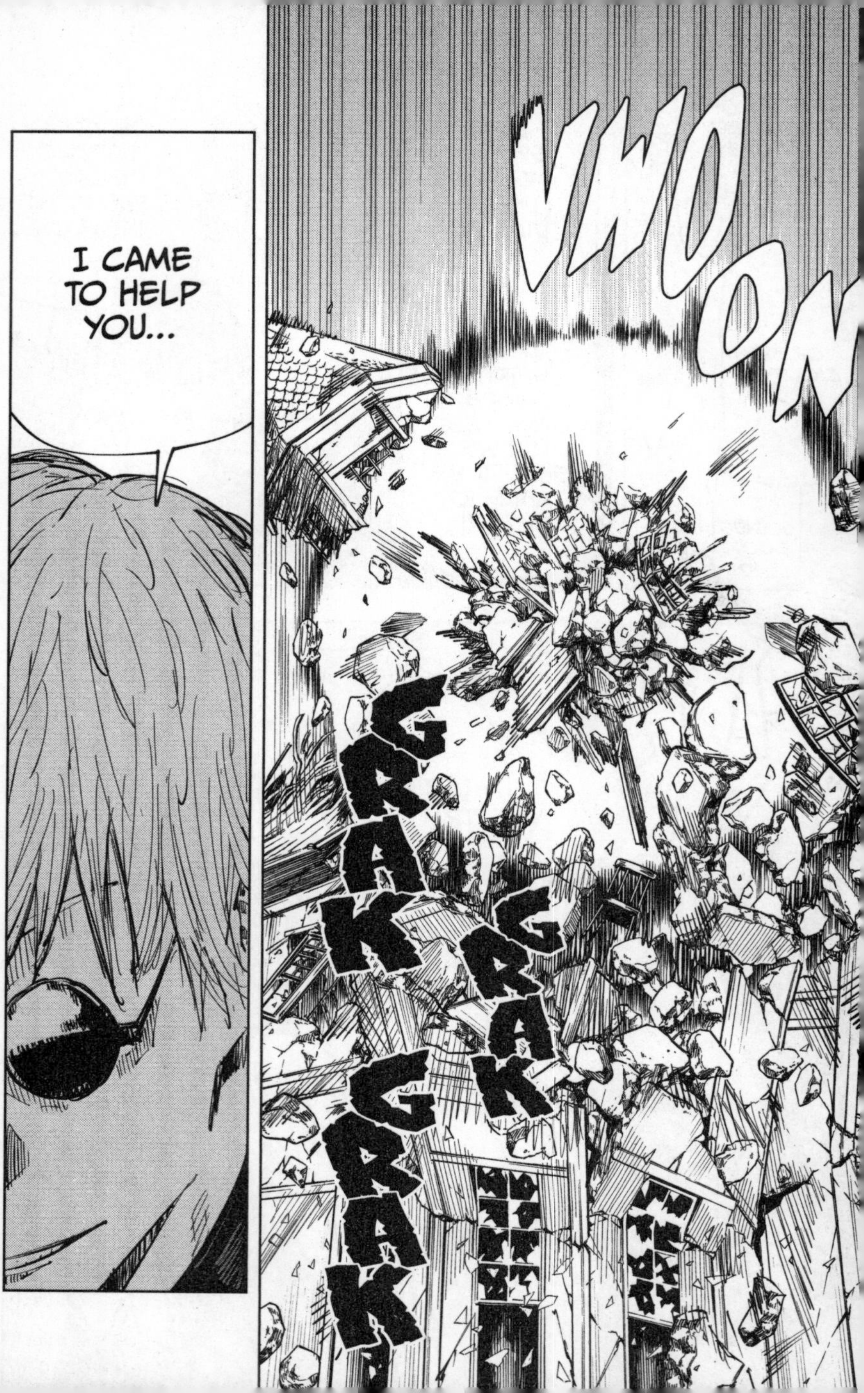
VWOON
GRAK
GRAK
GRAK
I CAME TO HELP YOU...

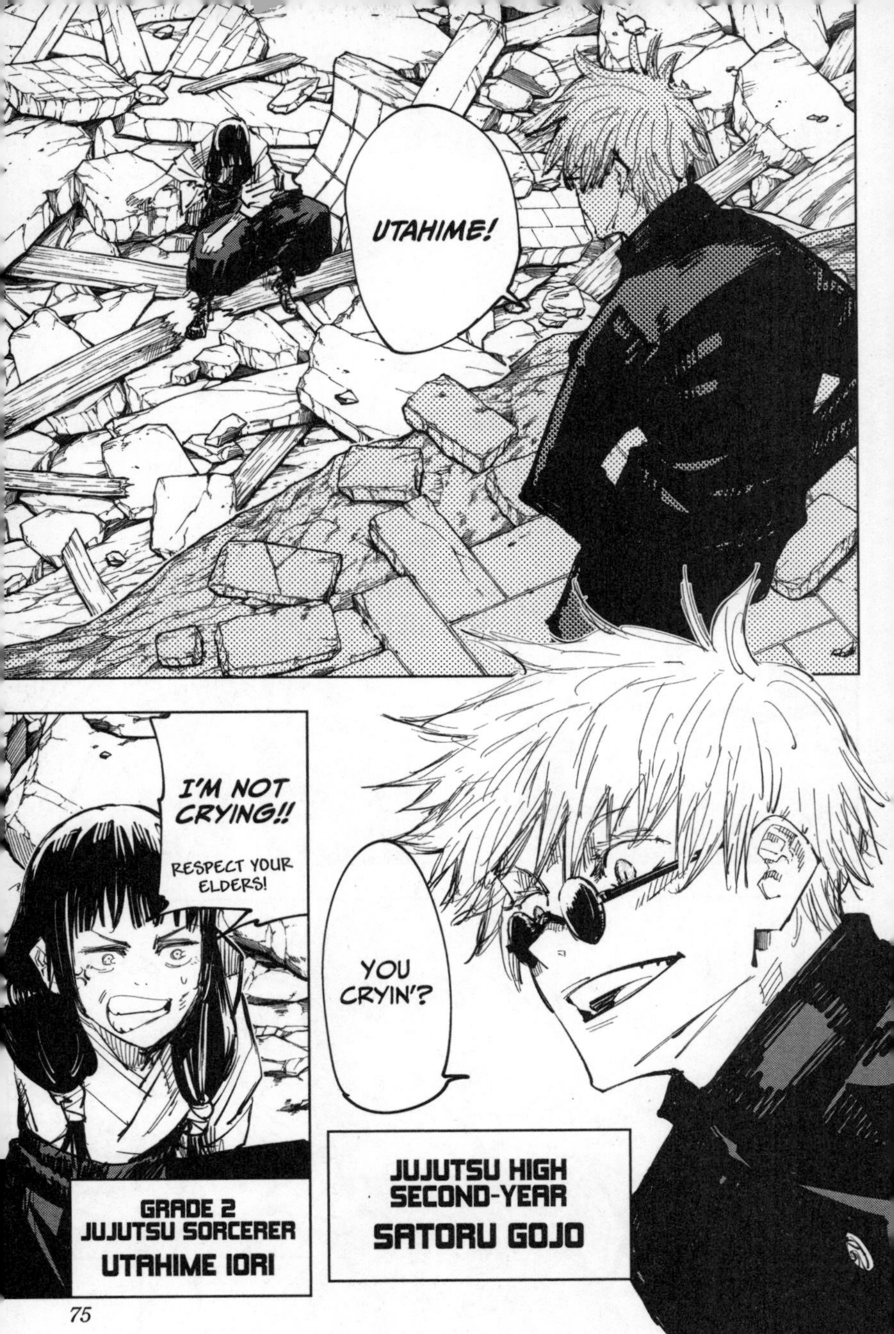
UTAHIME!
YOU CRYIN'?
JUJUTSU HIGH SECOND-YEAR SATORU GOJO
I'M NOT CRYING!! RESPECT YOUR ELDERS!
GRADE 2 JUJUTSU SORCERER UTAHIME IORI

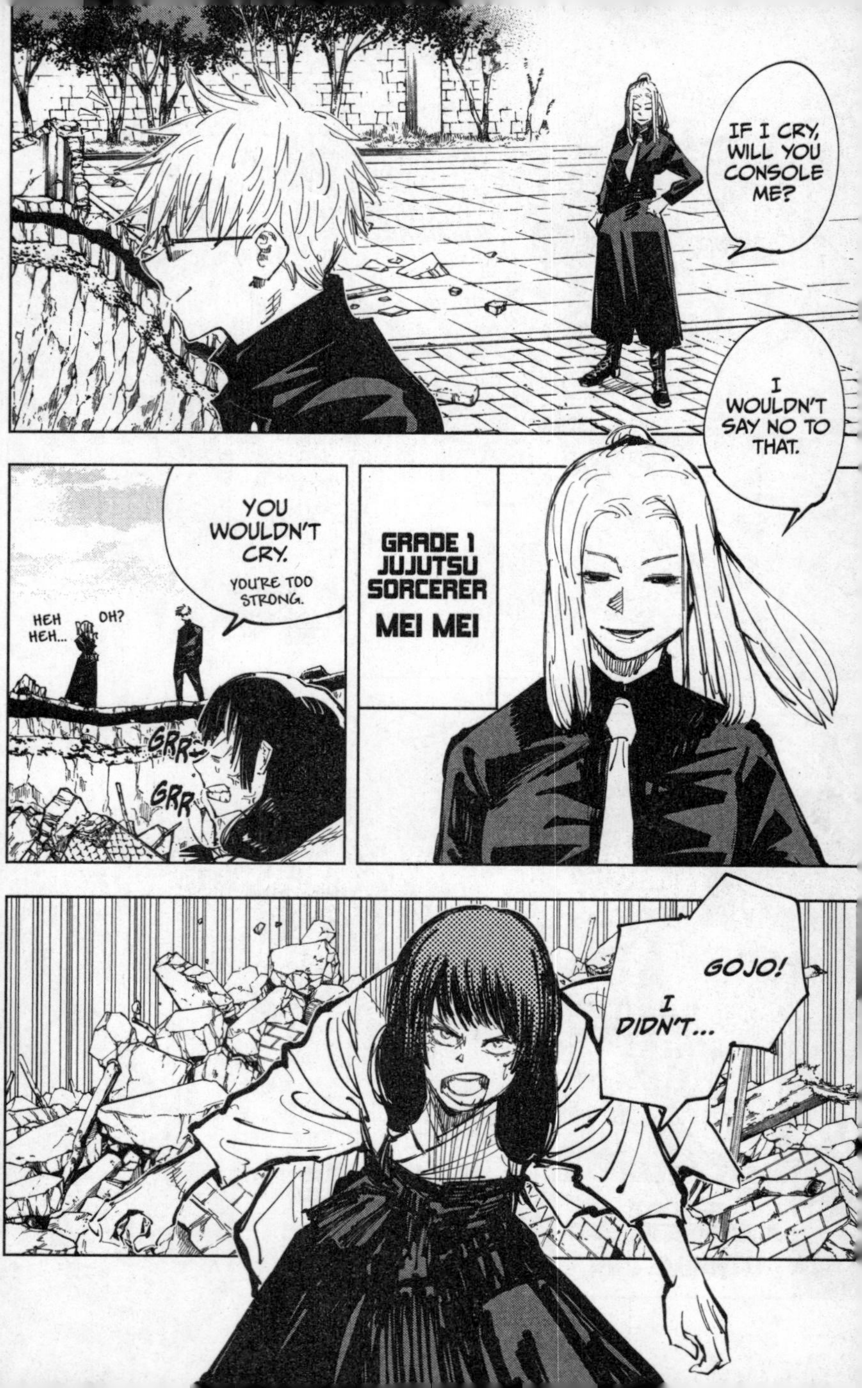
IF I CRY, WILL YOU CONSOLE ME?
I WOULDN'T SAY NO TO THAT.
GRADE 1 JUJUTSU SORCERER
MEI MEI
YOU WOULDN'T CRY.
YOU'RE TOO STRONG.
OH?
HEH HEH...
GRR
GRR
GOJO!
I DIDN'T...

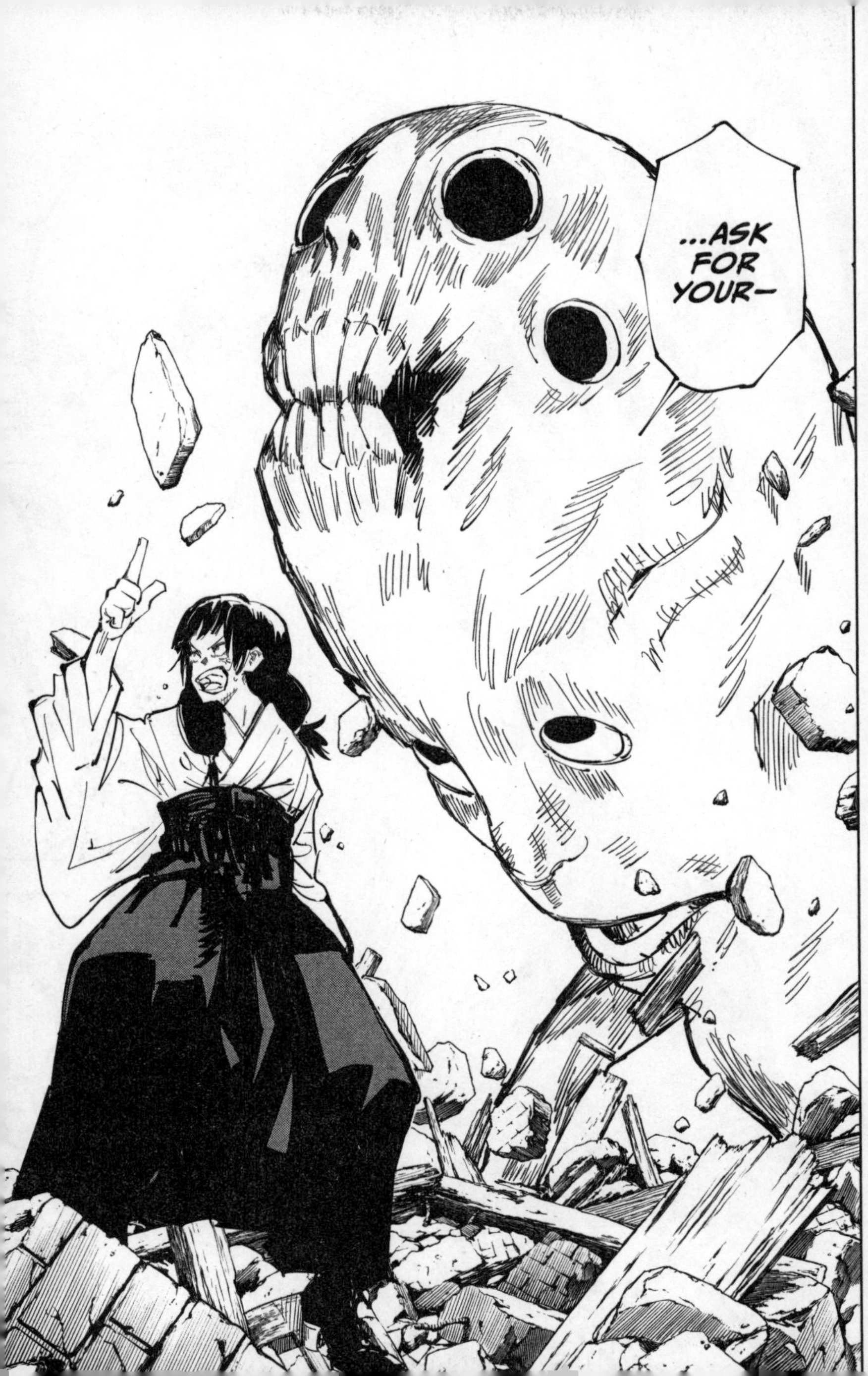
...ASK FOR YOUR—

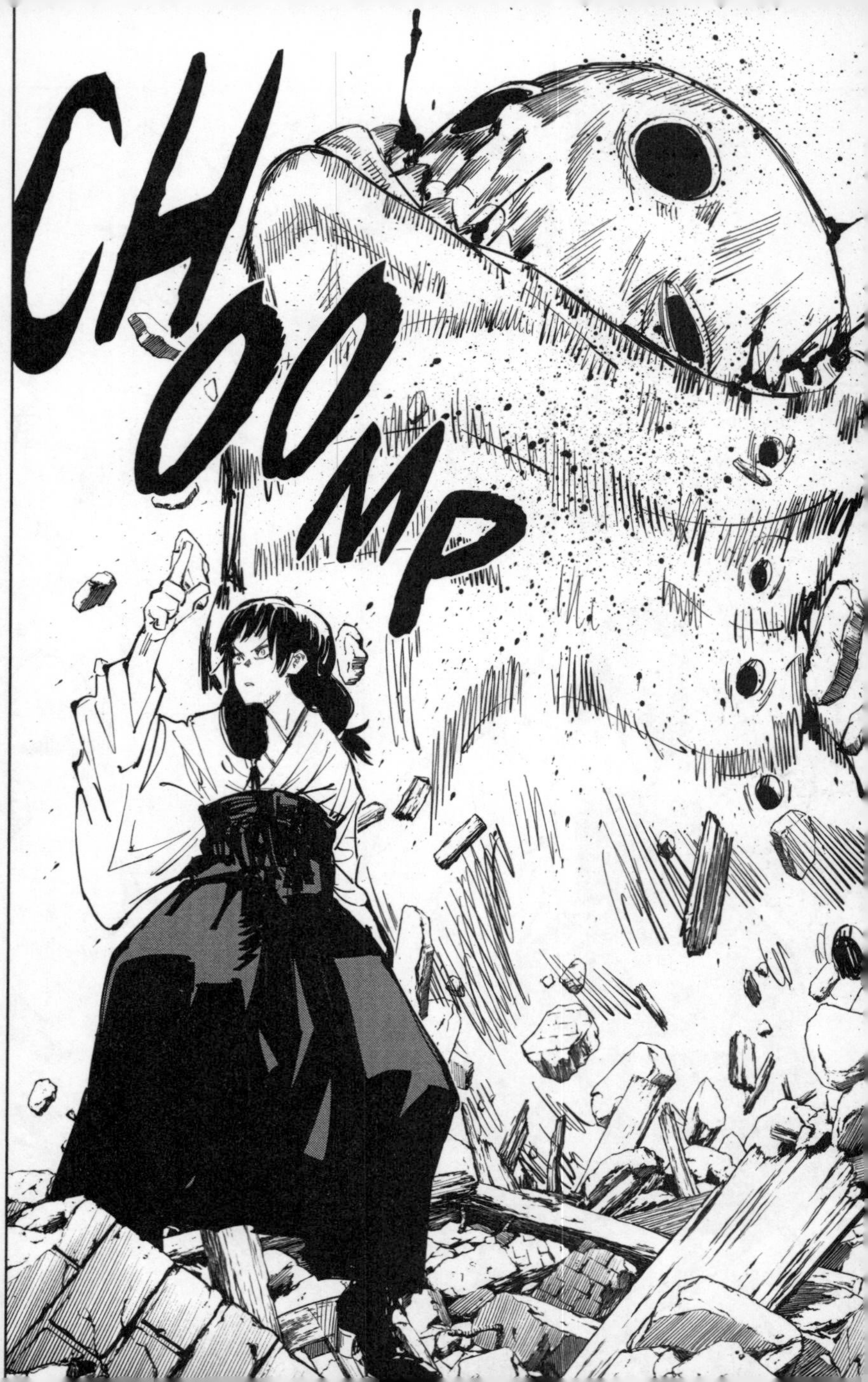
CHOOMP

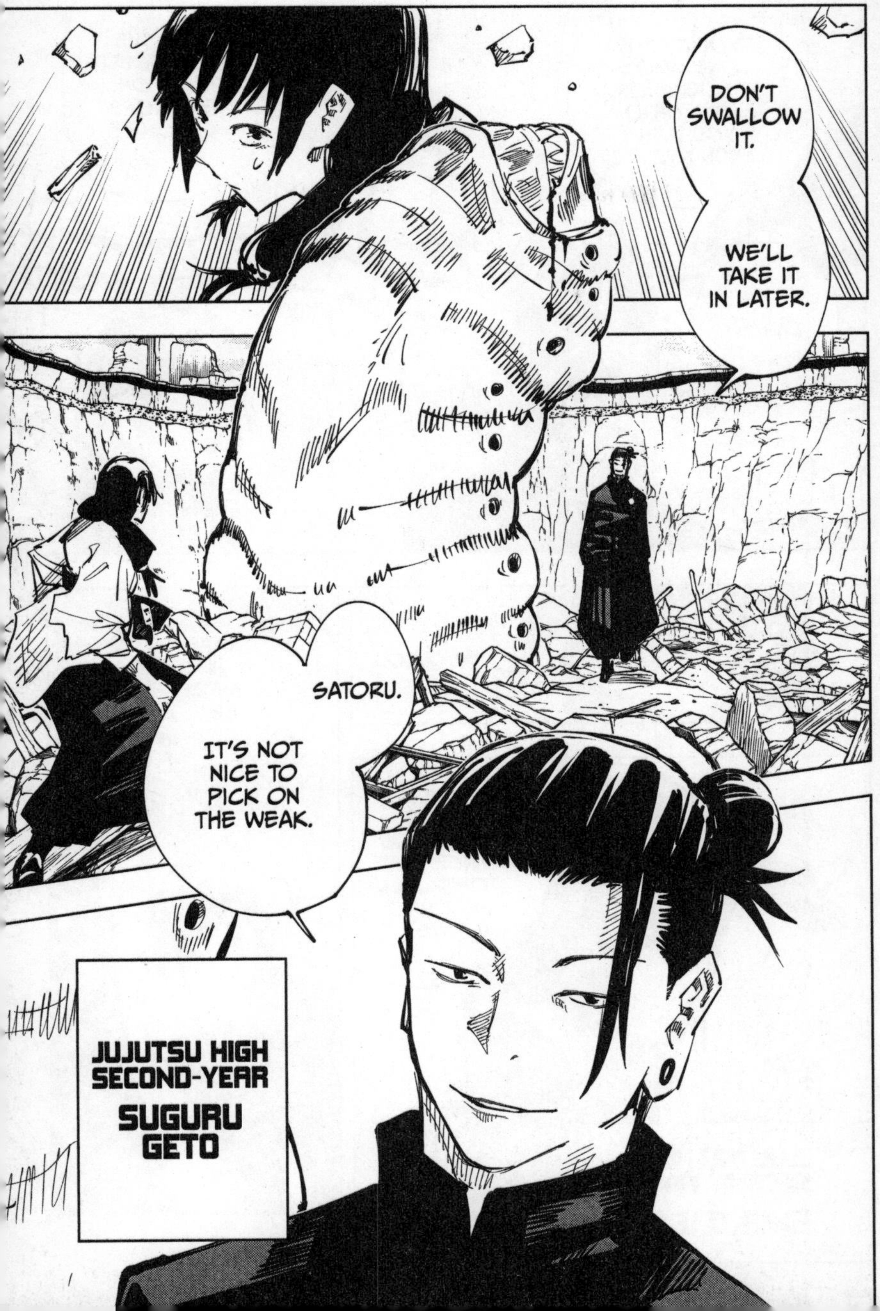
DON'T SWALLOW IT.
WE'LL TAKE IT IN LATER.
SATORU.
IT'S NOT NICE TO PICK ON THE WEAK.
JUJUTSU HIGH SECOND-YEAR
SUGURU GETO

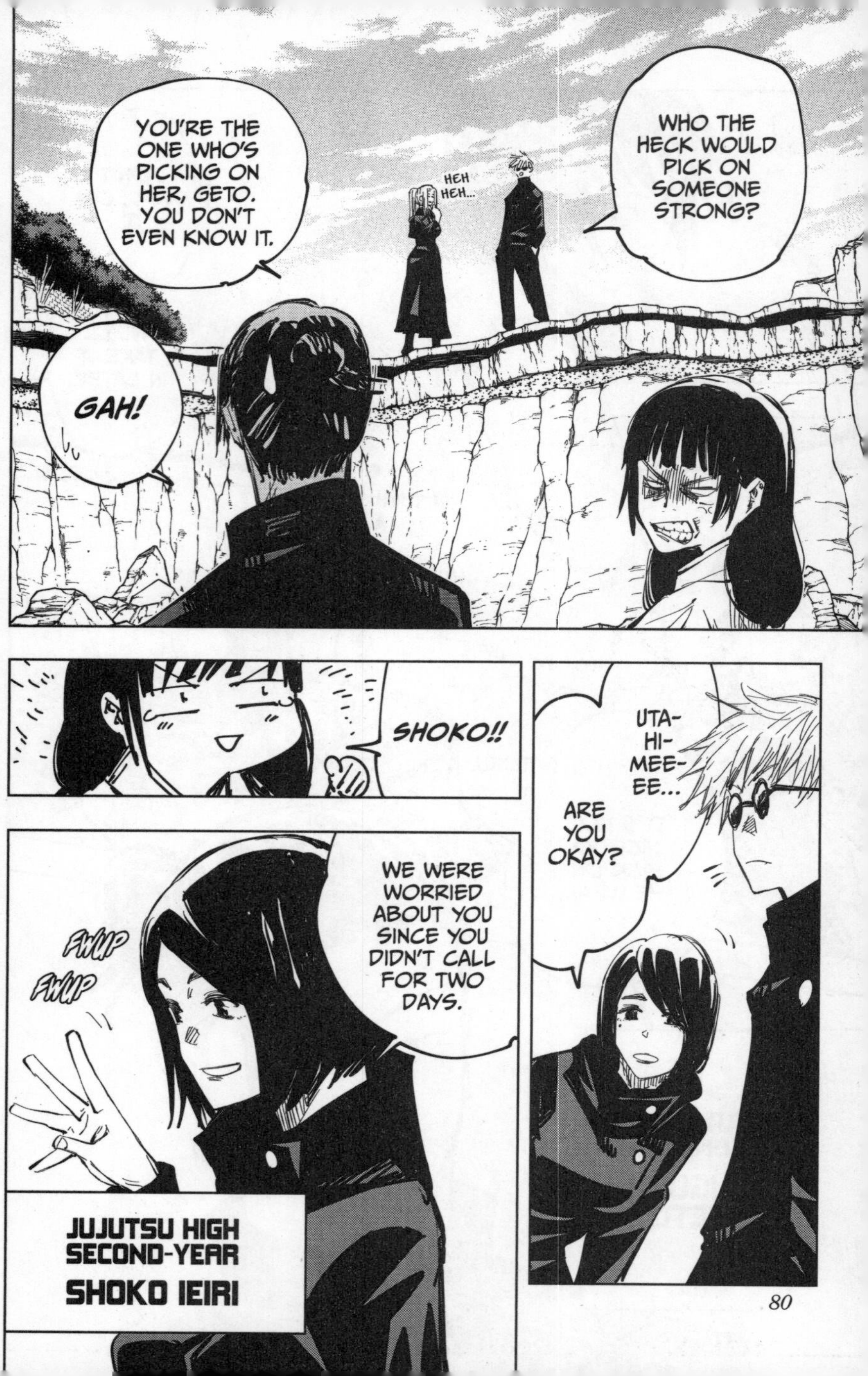
WHO THE HECK WOULD PICK ON SOMEONE STRONG?
HEH HEH...
YOU'RE THE ONE WHO'S PICKING ON HER, GETO. YOU DON'T EVEN KNOW IT.
GAH!
UTA-HI-MEEE-EE... ARE YOU OKAY?
SHOKO!!
WE WERE WORRIED ABOUT YOU SINCE YOU DIDN'T CALL FOR TWO DAYS.
FWUP
FWUP
JUJUTSU HIGH SECOND-YEAR
SHOKO IEIRI

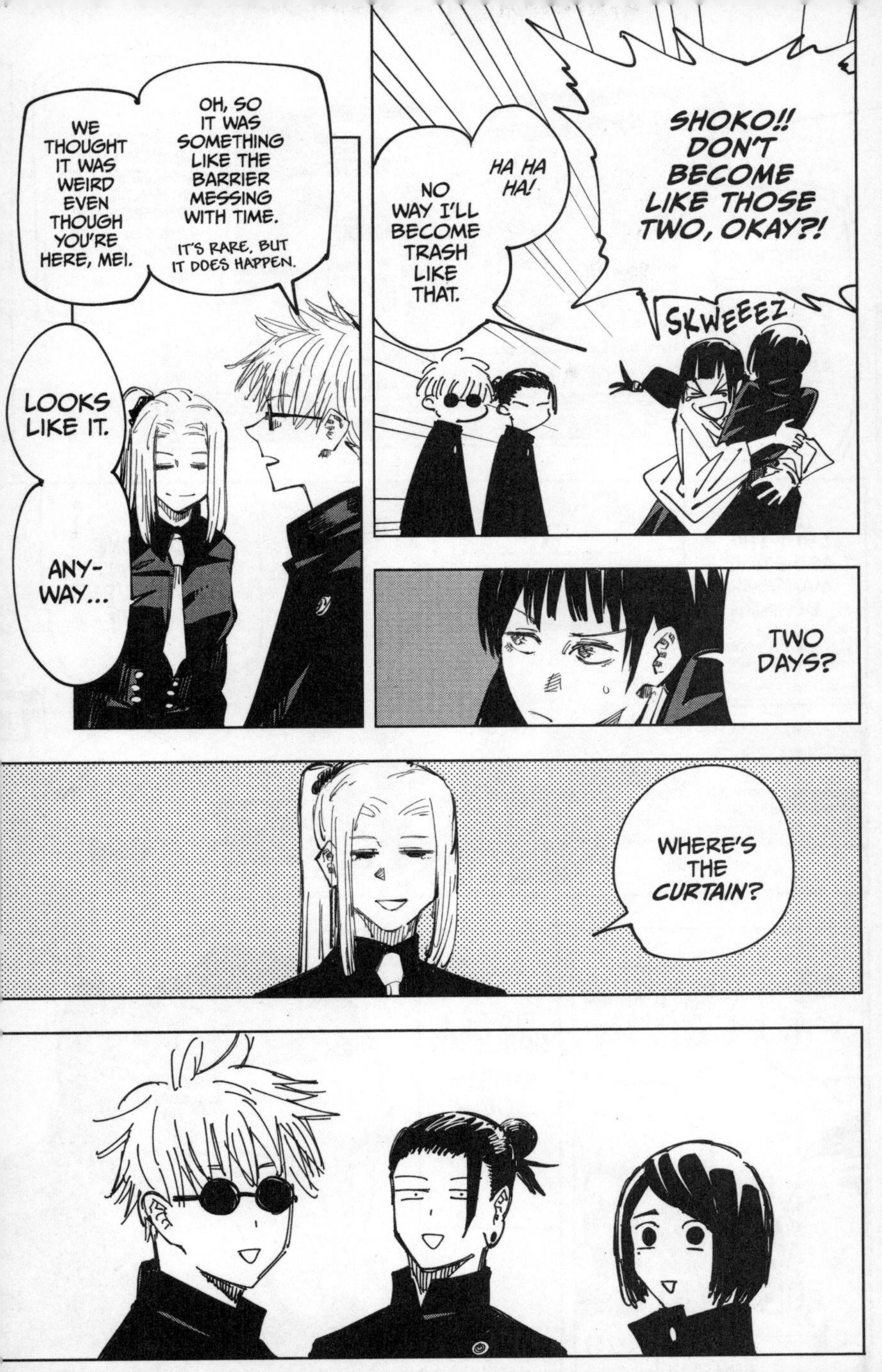
SHOKO!! DON'T BECOME LIKE THOSE TWO, OKAY?!
HA HA HA!
NO WAY I'LL BECOME TRASH LIKE THAT.
SKWEEEZ
TWO DAYS?
OH, SO IT WAS SOMETHING LIKE THE BARRIER MESSING WITH TIME.
IT'S RARE, BUT IT DOES HAPPEN.
WE THOUGHT IT WAS WEIRD EVEN THOUGH YOU'RE HERE, MEI.
LOOKS LIKE IT.
ANY-WAY...
WHERE'S THE CURTAIN?

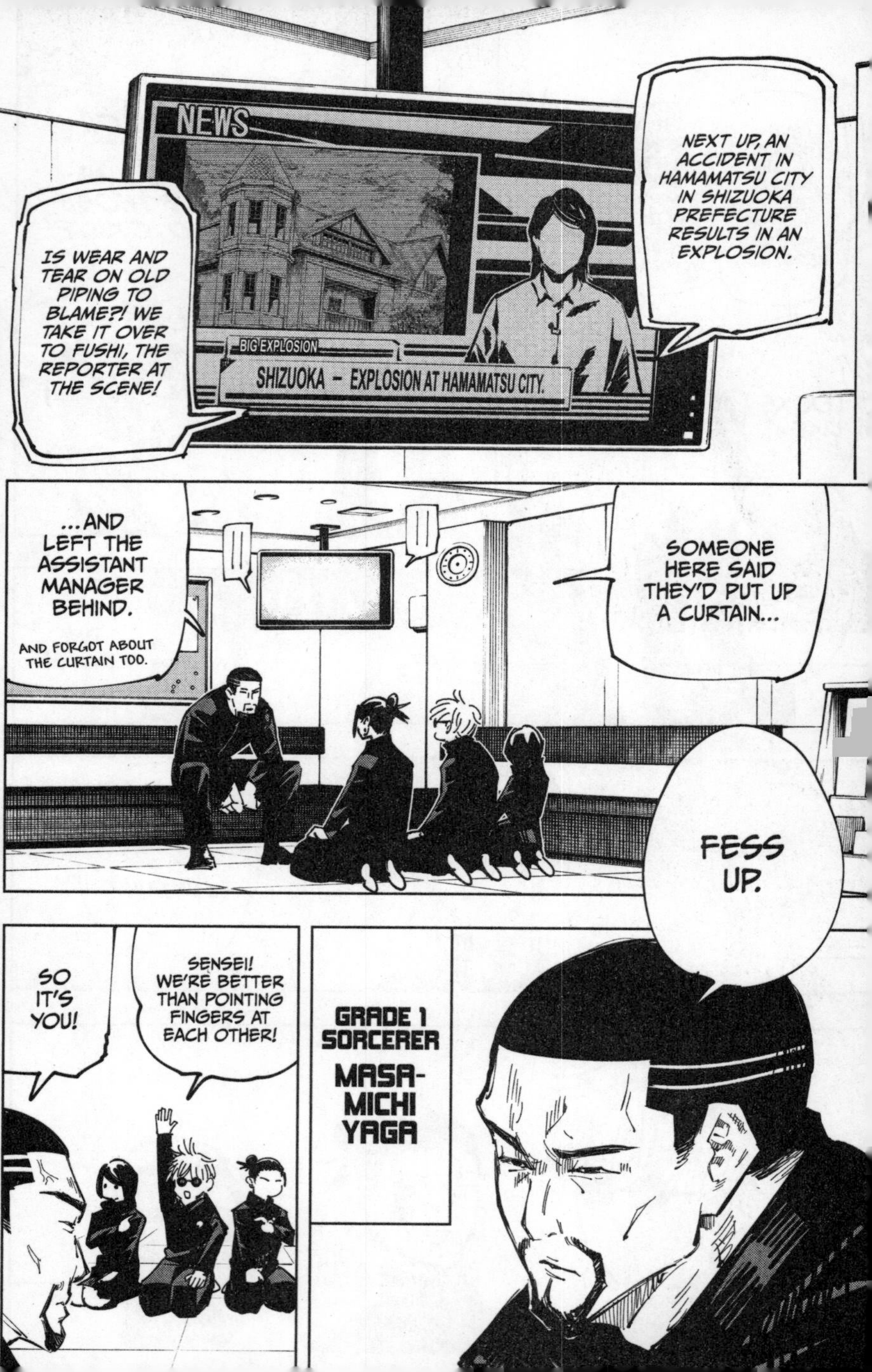
NEWS
NEXT UP, AN ACCIDENT IN HAMAMATSU CITY IN SHIZUOKA PREFECTURE RESULTS IN AN EXPLOSION.
BIG EXPLOSION
SHIZUOKA – EXPLOSION AT HAMAMATSU CITY.
IS WEAR AND TEAR ON OLD PIPING TO BLAME?! WE TAKE IT OVER TO FUSHI, THE REPORTER AT THE SCENE!
SOMEONE HERE SAID THEY'D PUT UP A CURTAIN...
...AND LEFT THE ASSISTANT MANAGER BEHIND.
AND FORGOT ABOUT THE CURTAIN TOO.
FESS UP.
GRADE 1 SORCERER
MASA-MICHI YAGA
SENSEI! WE'RE BETTER THAN POINTING FINGERS AT EACH OTHER!
SO IT'S YOU!

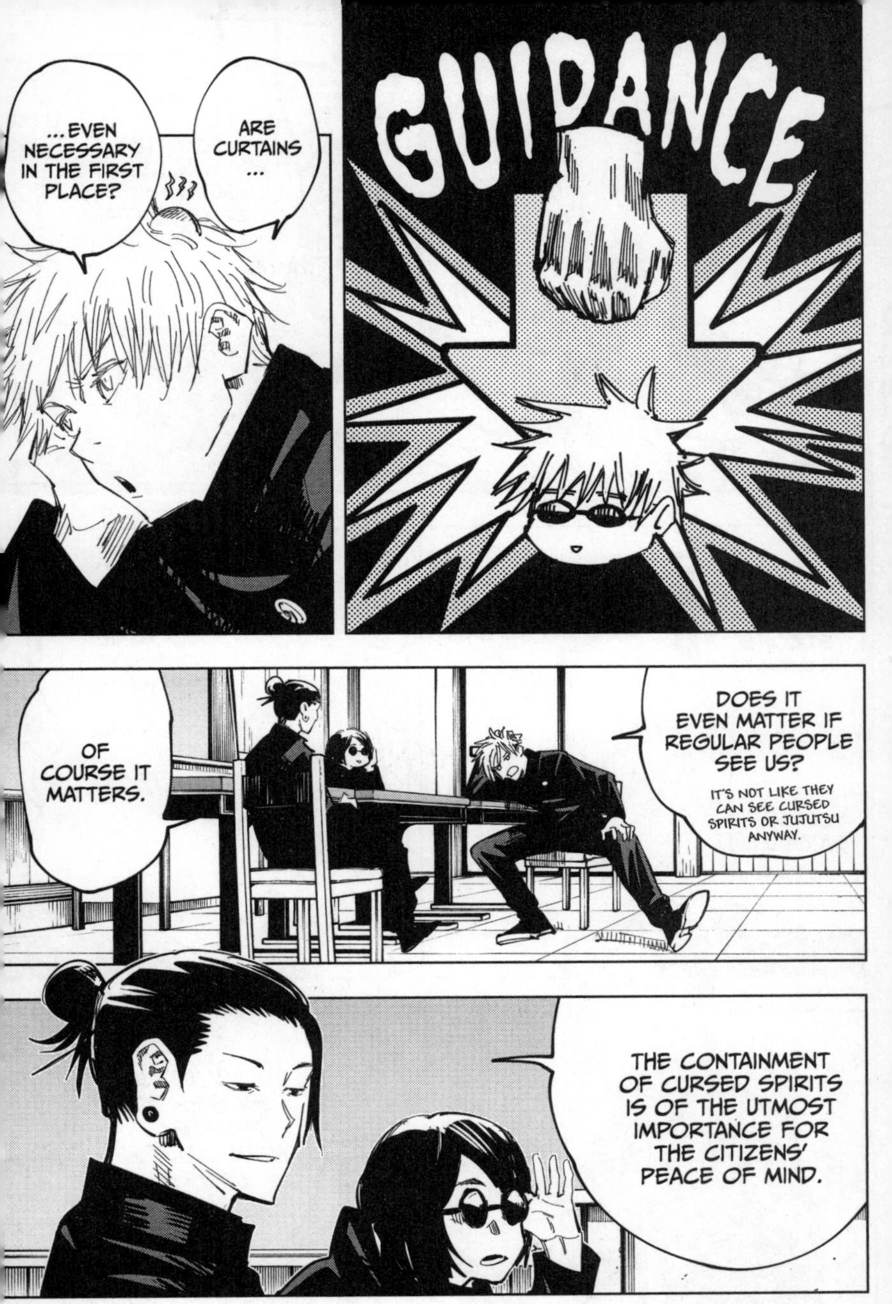
GUIDANCE
ARE CURTAINS ...
...EVEN NECESSARY IN THE FIRST PLACE?
DOES IT EVEN MATTER IF REGULAR PEOPLE SEE US?
IT'S NOT LIKE THEY CAN SEE CURSED SPIRITS OR JUJUTSU ANYWAY.
OF COURSE IT MATTERS.
THE CONTAINMENT OF CURSED SPIRITS IS OF THE UTMOST IMPORTANCE FOR THE CITIZENS' PEACE OF MIND.

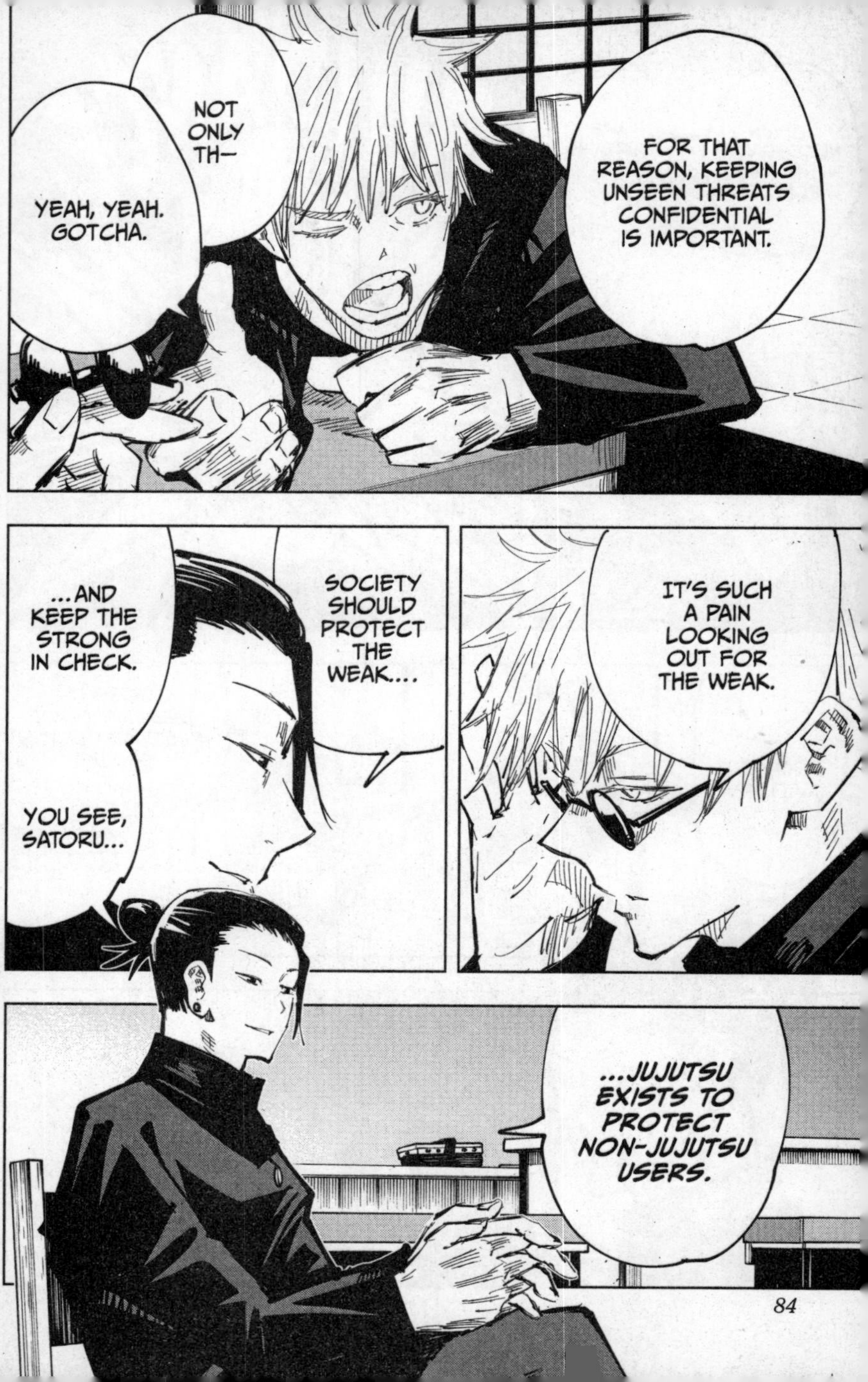
FOR THAT REASON, KEEPING UNSEEN THREATS CONFIDENTIAL IS IMPORTANT.
NOT ONLY TH—
YEAH, YEAH. GOTCHA.
IT'S SUCH A PAIN LOOKING OUT FOR THE WEAK.
SOCIETY SHOULD PROTECT THE WEAK....
...AND KEEP THE STRONG IN CHECK.
YOU SEE, SATORU...
...JUJUTSU EXISTS TO PROTECT NON-JUJUTSU USERS.

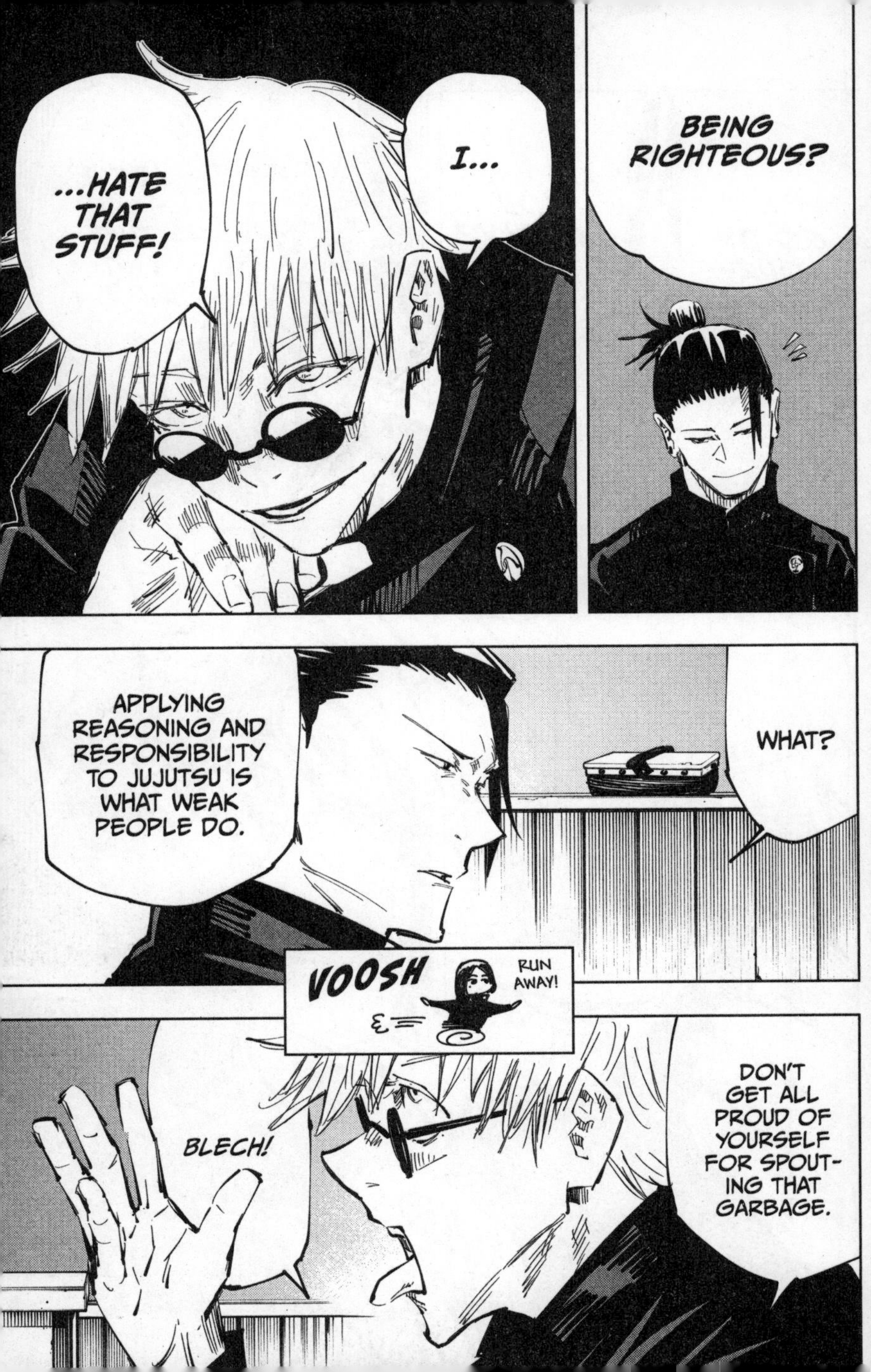
BEING RIGHTEOUS?
I...
...HATE THAT STUFF!
WHAT?
APPLYING REASONING AND RESPONSIBILITY TO JUJUTSU IS WHAT WEAK PEOPLE DO.
VOOSH
RUN AWAY!
DON'T GET ALL PROUD OF YOURSELF FOR SPOUT-ING THAT GARBAGE.
BLECH!

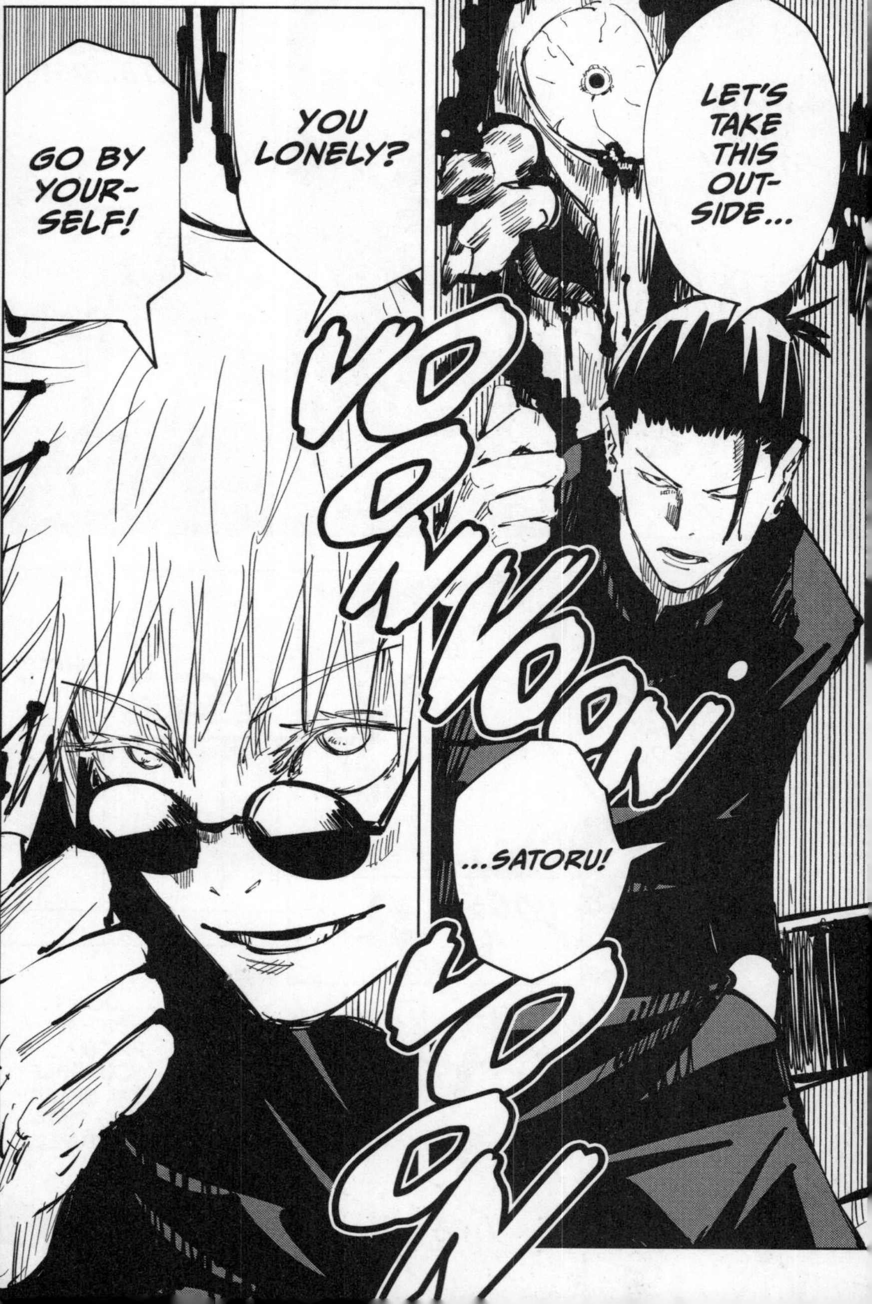
LET'S TAKE THIS OUT-SIDE...
...SATORU!
YOU LONELY?
GO BY YOUR-SELF!

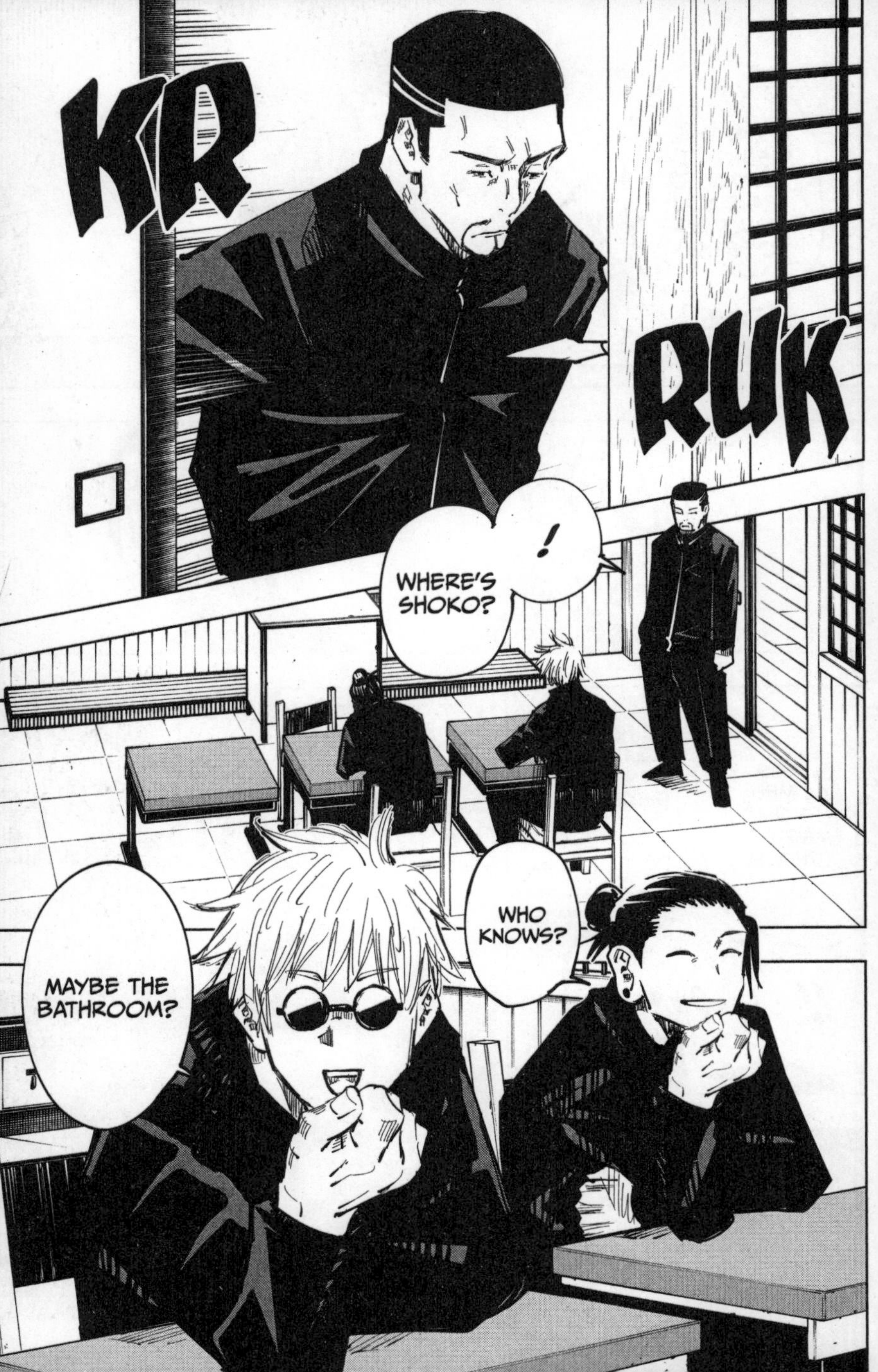
KR
RUK
!
WHERE'S SHOKO?
WHO KNOWS?
MAYBE THE BATHROOM?

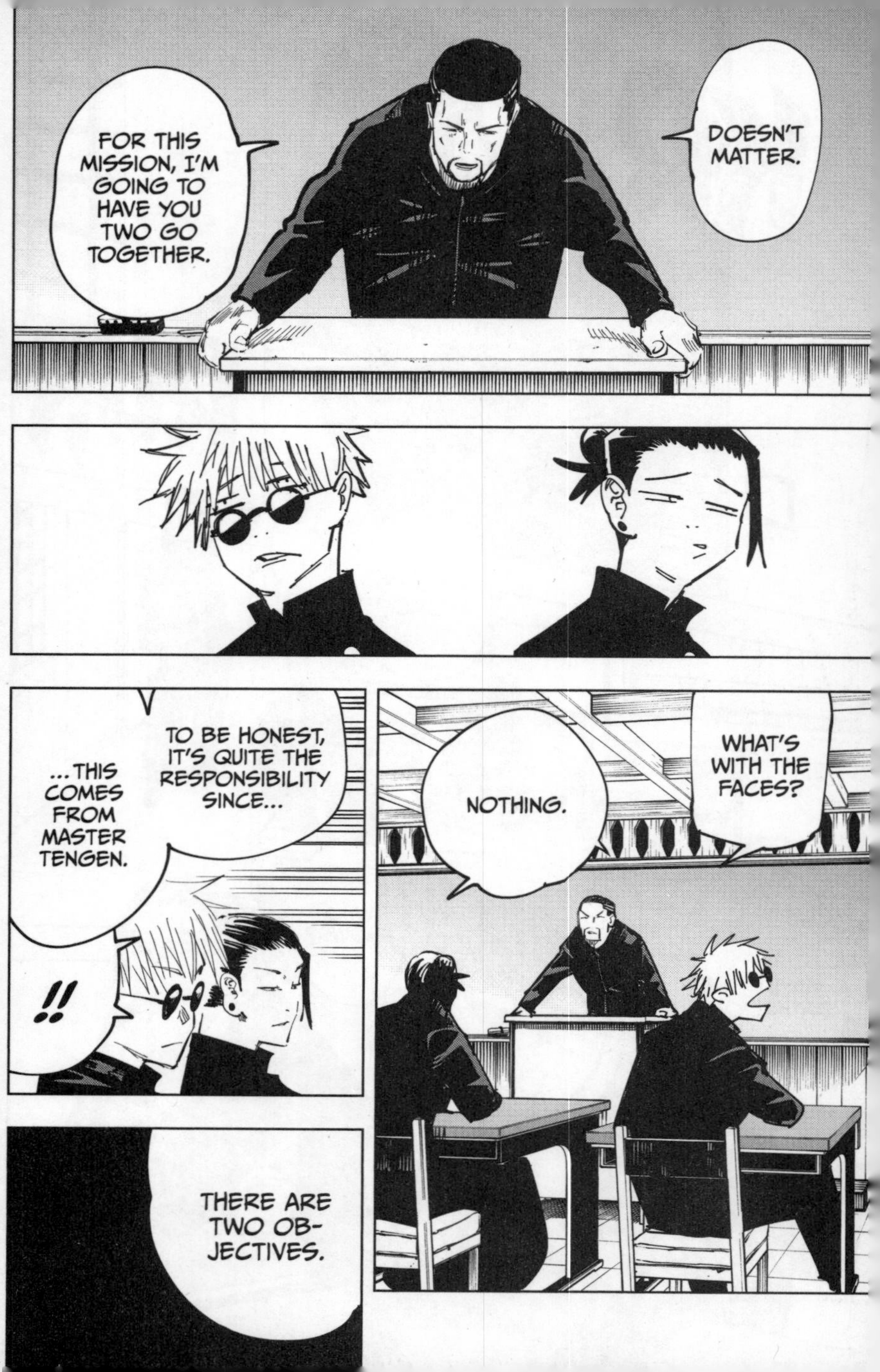
DOESN'T MATTER.
FOR THIS MISSION, I'M GOING TO HAVE YOU TWO GO TOGETHER.
WHAT'S WITH THE FACES?
NOTHING.
TO BE HONEST, IT'S QUITE THE RESPONSIBILITY SINCE...
...THIS COMES FROM MASTER TENGEN.
!!
THERE ARE TWO OBJECTIVES.

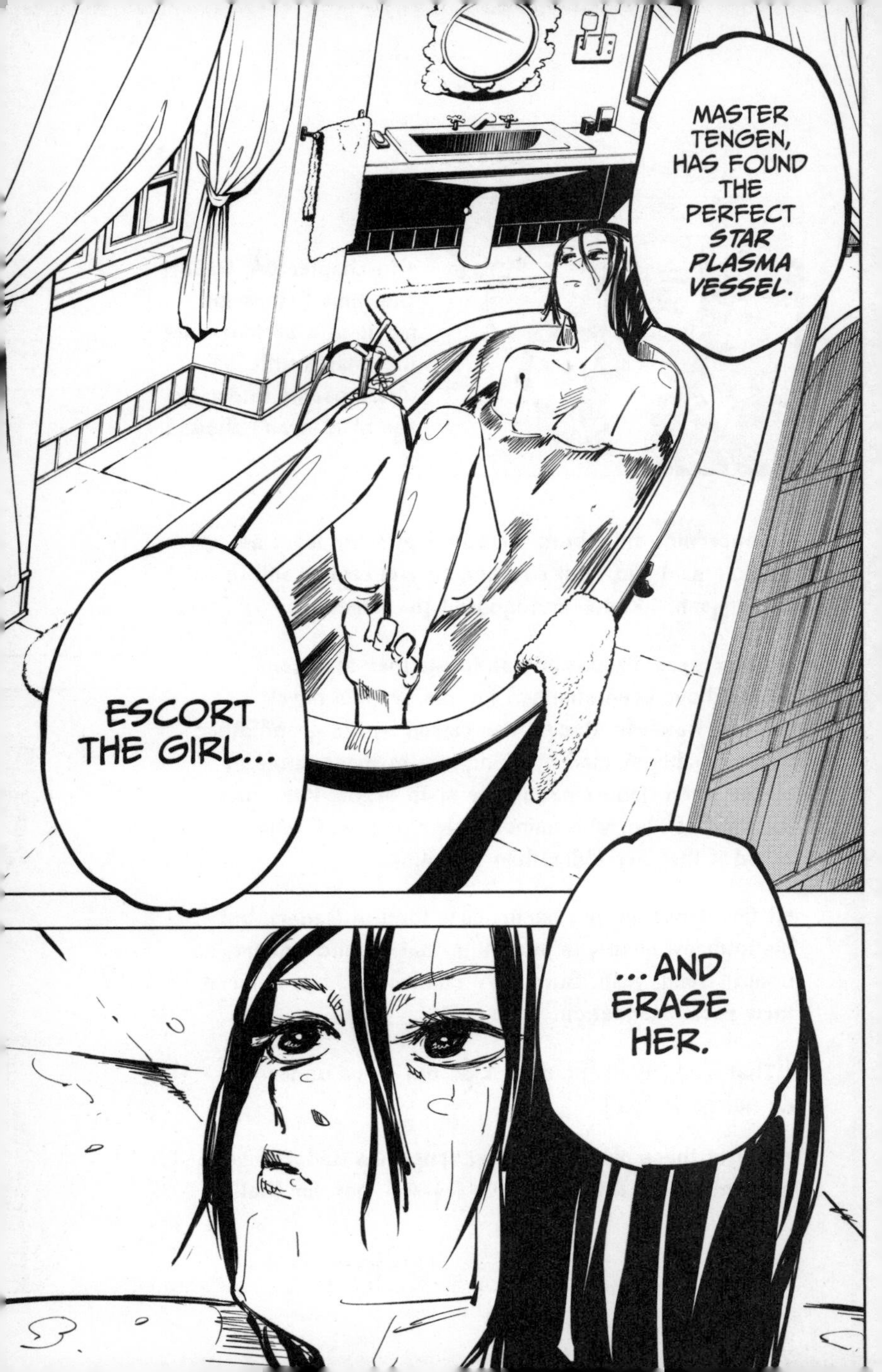
MASTER TENGEN, HAS FOUND THE PERFECT STAR PLASMA VESSEL.
ESCORT THE GIRL...
...AND ERASE HER.

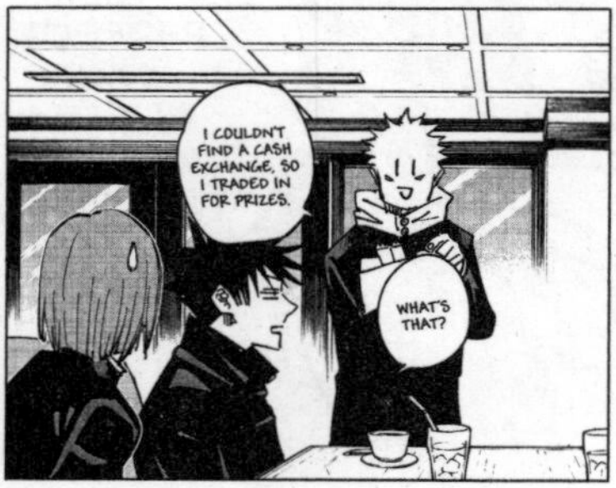
I COULDN'T FIND A CASH EXCHANGE, SO I TRADED IN FOR PRIZES.
WHAT'S THAT?

• In chapter 64, Itadori kills time before the movie at a certain place that starts with "pa" where **people under the age of 18 aren't allowed.**

• Concerning this, both the editor and the team as a whole said "no," but Akutami Sensei replied with a "yeah, yeah, I know" and ignored the warning.

• There were discussions as to whether the scene should have been changed for the graphic novel release. However, Itadori was raised by his grandfather, who probably started bringing him to those kinds of places when Itadori was in the sixth grade. Plus, he's the kind of idiot who immediately clicks "yes" when asked if they are older than 18 online.

• I (Akutami) am not particularly fond of Itadori, but his lowbrow quality is one thing that he and I share, so I said, "Yeah, yeah. Sure, we'll change it..." but ignored their recommendation.

• That said, to all the good kids out there under 18, **do not go to "pa"!**

• But in these places of delinquency lies Itadori's good-natured personality, so please try and look for that!

CHAPTER 66: HIDDEN INVENTORY, PART 2

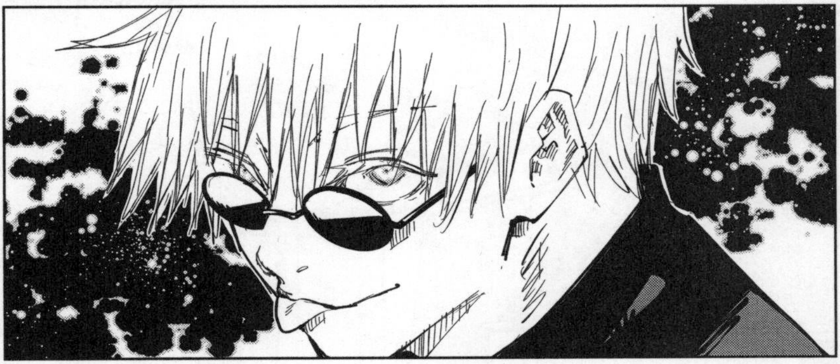

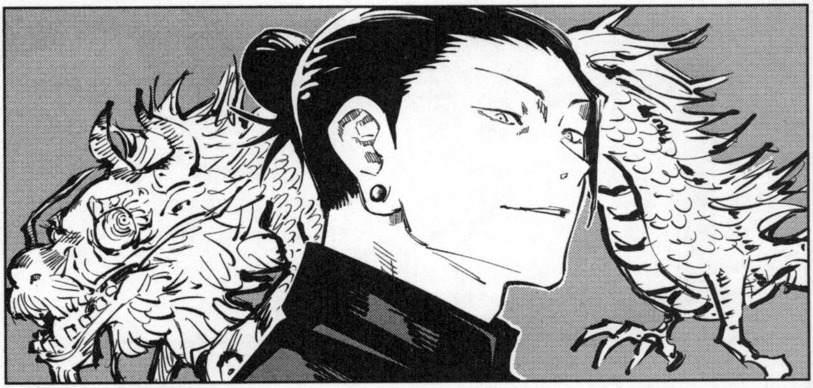

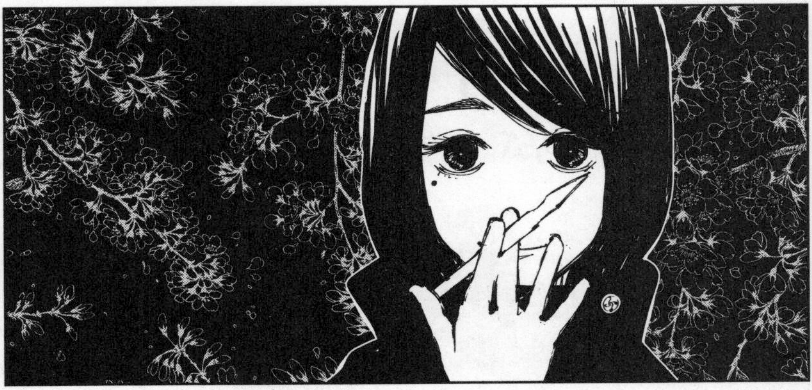

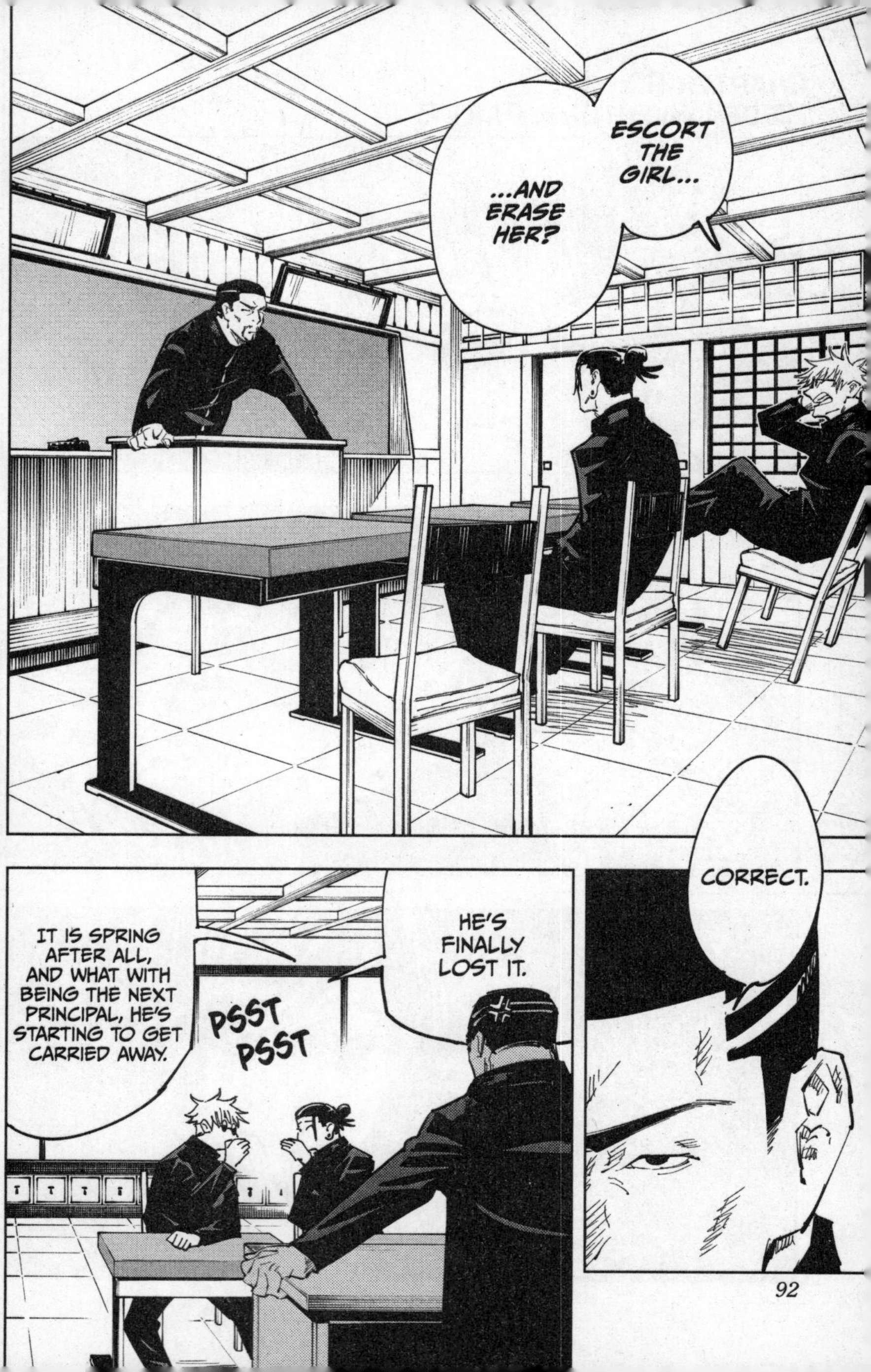
ESCORT THE GIRL...
...AND ERASE HER?
CORRECT.
HE'S FINALLY LOST IT.
IT IS SPRING AFTER ALL, AND WHAT WITH BEING THE NEXT PRINCIPAL, HE'S STARTING TO GET CARRIED AWAY.
PSST PSST

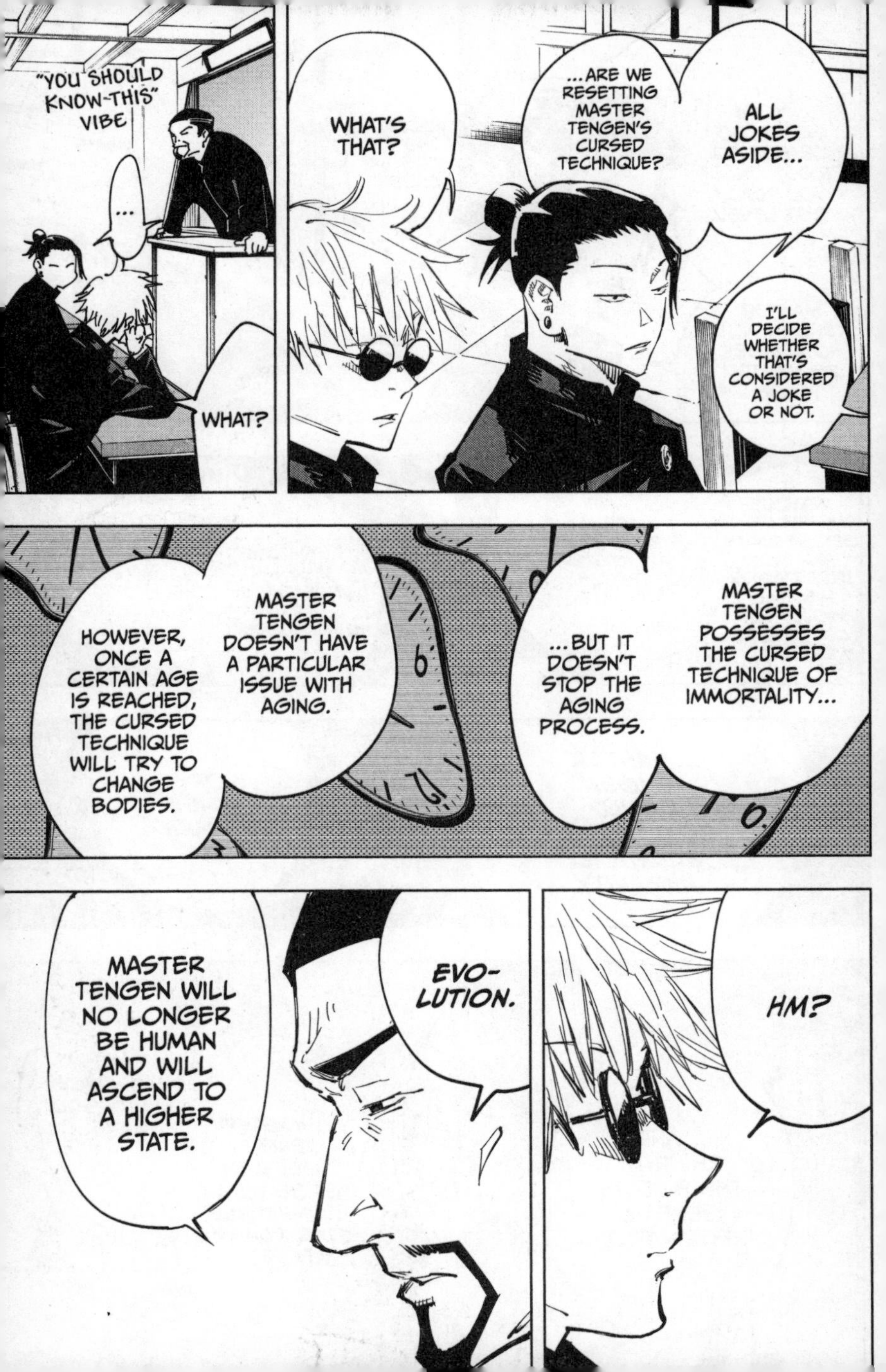
ALL JOKES ASIDE...
...ARE WE RESETTING MASTER TENGEN'S CURSED TECHNIQUE?
WHAT'S THAT?
I'LL DECIDE WHETHER THAT'S CONSIDERED A JOKE OR NOT.
"YOU SHOULD KNOW-THIS" VIBE
...
WHAT?
MASTER TENGEN POSSESSES THE CURSED TECHNIQUE OF IMMORTALITY...
...BUT IT DOESN'T STOP THE AGING PROCESS.
MASTER TENGEN DOESN'T HAVE A PARTICULAR ISSUE WITH AGING.
HOWEVER, ONCE A CERTAIN AGE IS REACHED, THE CURSED TECHNIQUE WILL TRY TO CHANGE BODIES.
HM?
EVO-LUTION.
MASTER TENGEN WILL NO LONGER BE HUMAN AND WILL ASCEND TO A HIGHER STATE.

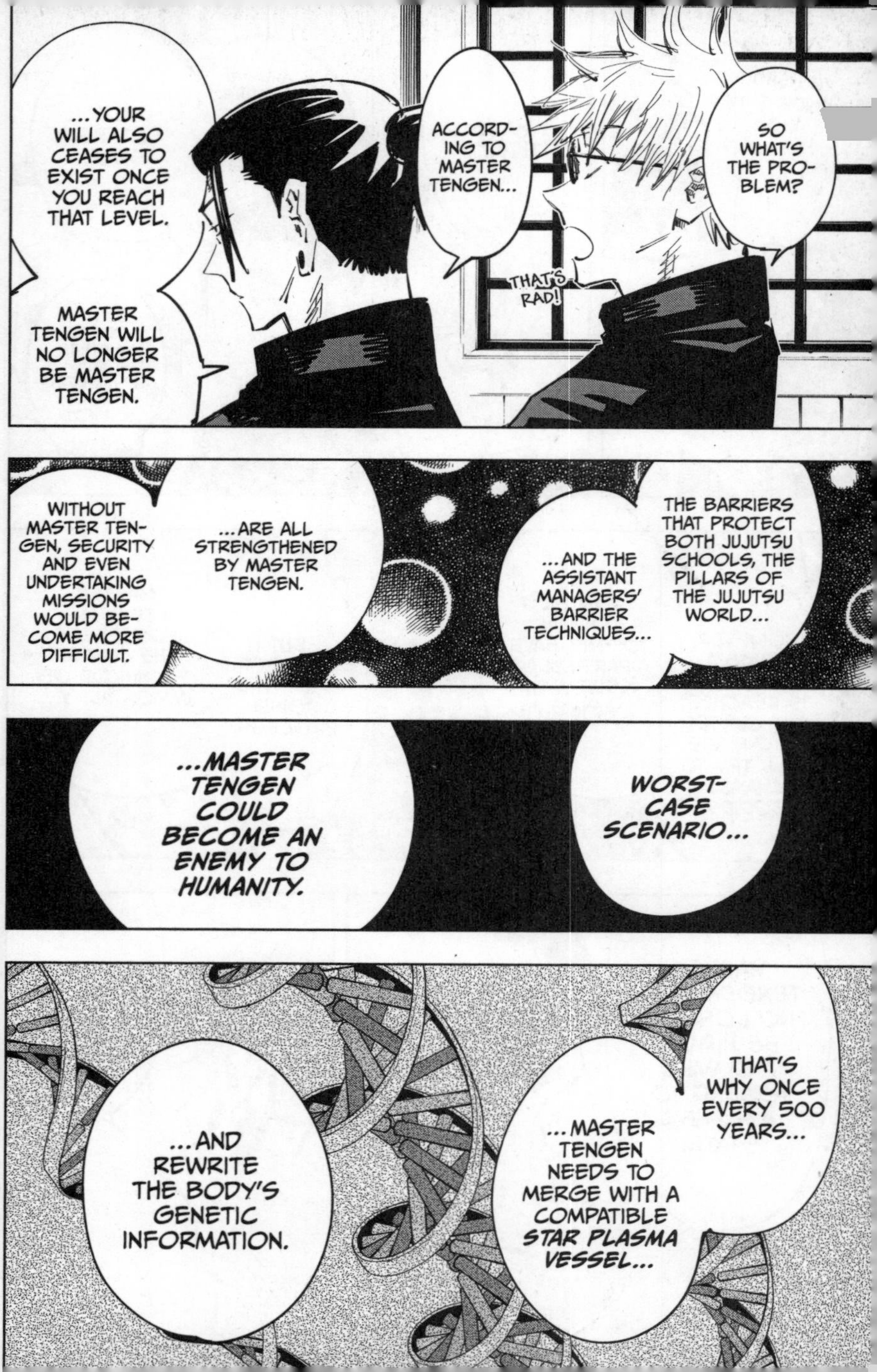
SO WHAT'S THE PRO-BLEM?
ACCORD-ING TO MASTER TENGEN...
THAT'S RAD!
...YOUR WILL ALSO CEASES TO EXIST ONCE YOU REACH THAT LEVEL.
MASTER TENGEN WILL NO LONGER BE MASTER TENGEN.
THE BARRIERS THAT PROTECT BOTH JUJUTSU SCHOOLS, THE PILLARS OF THE JUJUTSU WORLD...
...AND THE ASSISTANT MANAGERS' BARRIER TECHNIQUES...
...ARE ALL STRENGTHENED BY MASTER TENGEN.
WITHOUT MASTER TEN-GEN, SECURITY AND EVEN UNDERTAKING MISSIONS WOULD BE-COME MORE DIFFICULT.
WORST-CASE SCENARIO...
...MASTER TENGEN COULD BECOME AN ENEMY TO HUMANITY.
THAT'S WHY ONCE EVERY 500 YEARS...
...MASTER TENGEN NEEDS TO MERGE WITH A COMPATIBLE STAR PLASMA VESSEL...
...AND REWRITE THE BODY'S GENETIC INFORMATION.

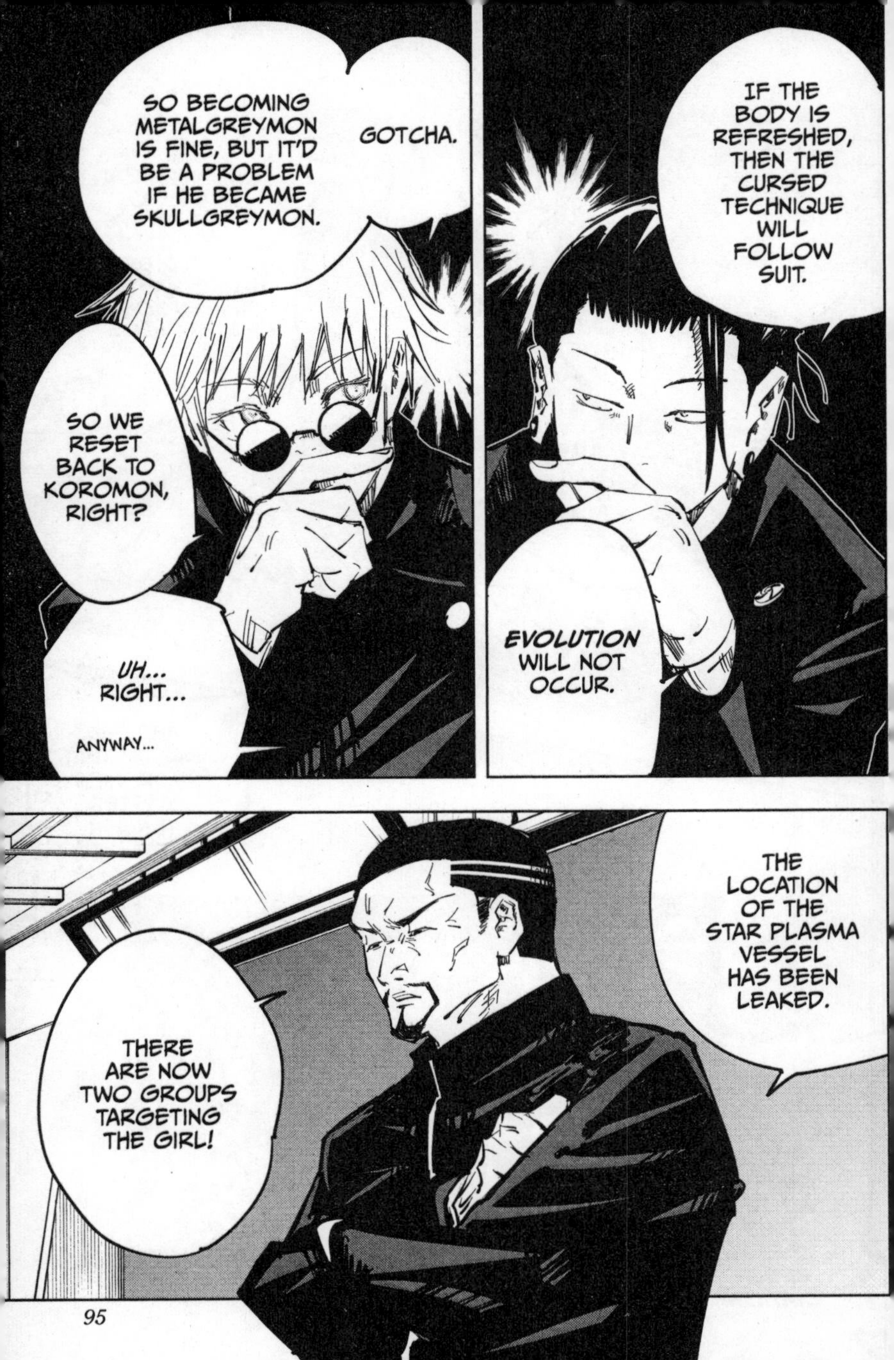
IF THE BODY IS REFRESHED, THEN THE CURSED TECHNIQUE WILL FOLLOW SUIT.
EVOLUTION WILL NOT OCCUR.
GOTCHA.
SO BECOMING METALGREYMON IS FINE, BUT IT'D BE A PROBLEM IF HE BECAME SKULLGREYMON.
SO WE RESET BACK TO KOROMON, RIGHT?
UH... RIGHT...
ANYWAY...
THE LOCATION OF THE STAR PLASMA VESSEL HAS BEEN LEAKED.
THERE ARE NOW TWO GROUPS TARGETING THE GIRL!

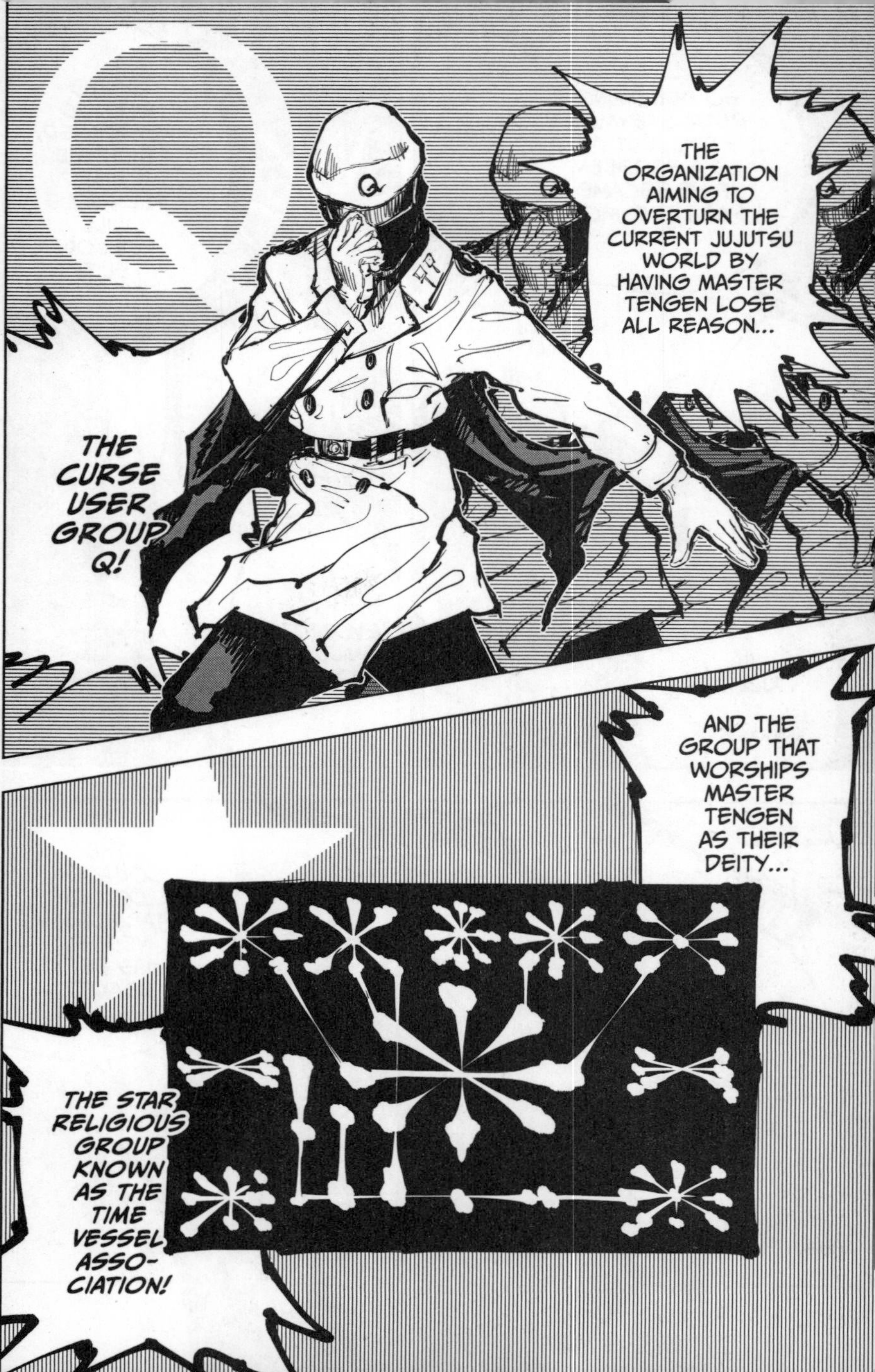
THE ORGANIZATION AIMING TO OVERTURN THE CURRENT JUJUTSU WORLD BY HAVING MASTER TENGEN LOSE ALL REASON...
THE CURSE USER GROUP Q!
AND THE GROUP THAT WORSHIPS MASTER TENGEN AS THEIR DEITY...
THE STAR RELIGIOUS GROUP KNOWN AS THE TIME VESSEL ASSO-CIATION!

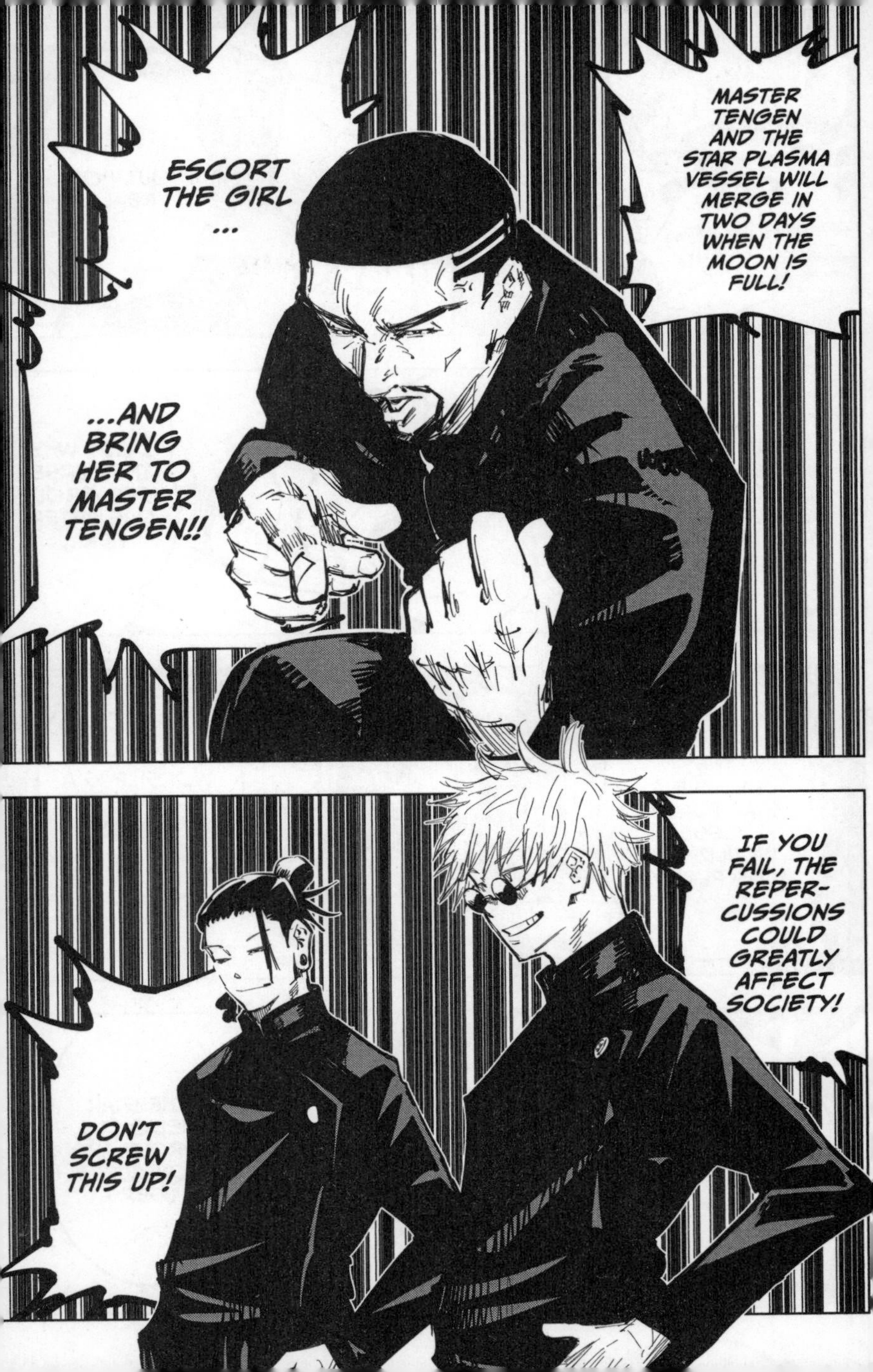
MASTER TENGEN AND THE STAR PLASMA VESSEL WILL MERGE IN TWO DAYS WHEN THE MOON IS FULL!
ESCORT THE GIRL ...
...AND BRING HER TO MASTER TENGEN!!
IF YOU FAIL, THE REPER-CUSSIONS COULD GREATLY AFFECT SOCIETY!
DON'T SCREW THIS UP!

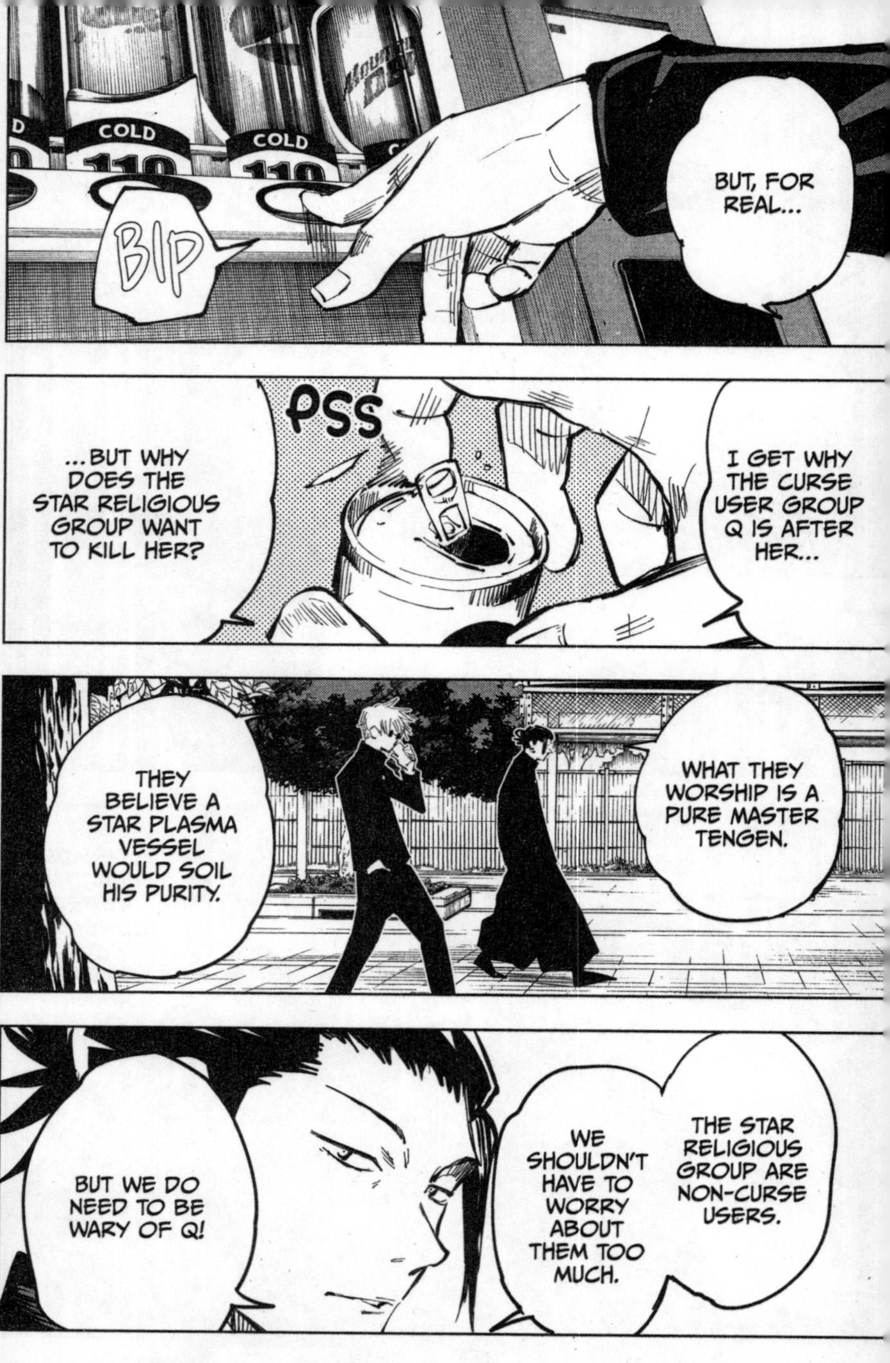
BUT, FOR REAL...
COLD
COLD
BIP
I GET WHY THE CURSE USER GROUP Q IS AFTER HER...
PSS
...BUT WHY DOES THE STAR RELIGIOUS GROUP WANT TO KILL HER?
WHAT THEY WORSHIP IS A PURE MASTER TENGEN.
THEY BELIEVE A STAR PLASMA VESSEL WOULD SOIL HIS PURITY.
THE STAR RELIGIOUS GROUP ARE NON-CURSE USERS.
WE SHOULDN'T HAVE TO WORRY ABOUT THEM TOO MUCH.
BUT WE DO NEED TO BE WARY OF Q!

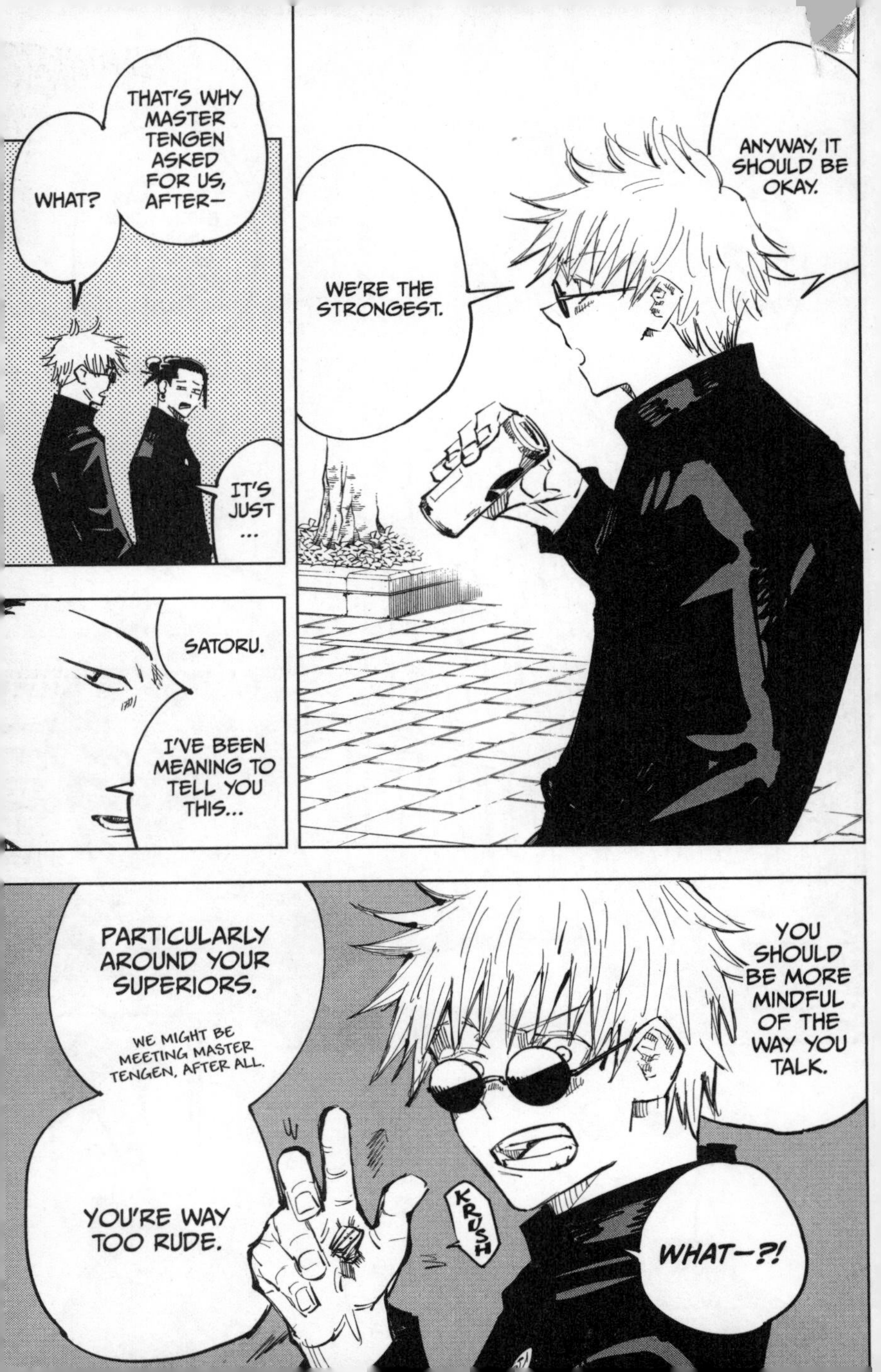
ANYWAY, IT SHOULD BE OKAY.
WE'RE THE STRONGEST.
THAT'S WHY MASTER TENGEN ASKED FOR US, AFTER—
WHAT?
IT'S JUST ...
SATORU.
I'VE BEEN MEANING TO TELL YOU THIS...
YOU SHOULD BE MORE MINDFUL OF THE WAY YOU TALK.
PARTICULARLY AROUND YOUR SUPERIORS.
WE MIGHT BE MEETING MASTER TENGEN, AFTER ALL.
YOU'RE WAY TOO RUDE.
KRUSH
WHAT—?!

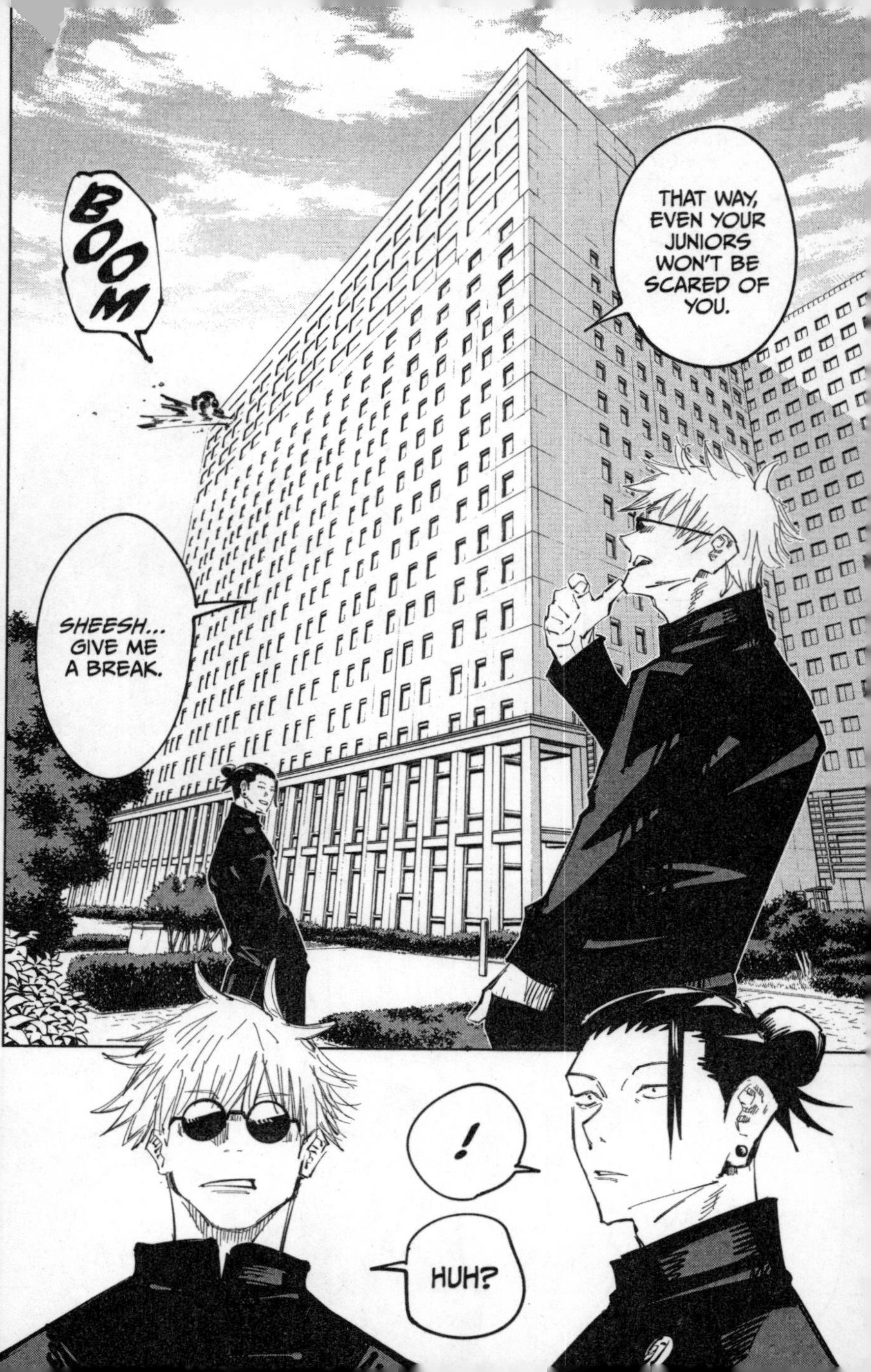
THAT WAY, EVEN YOUR JUNIORS WON'T BE SCARED OF YOU.
BOOM
SHEESH... GIVE ME A BREAK.
!
HUH?

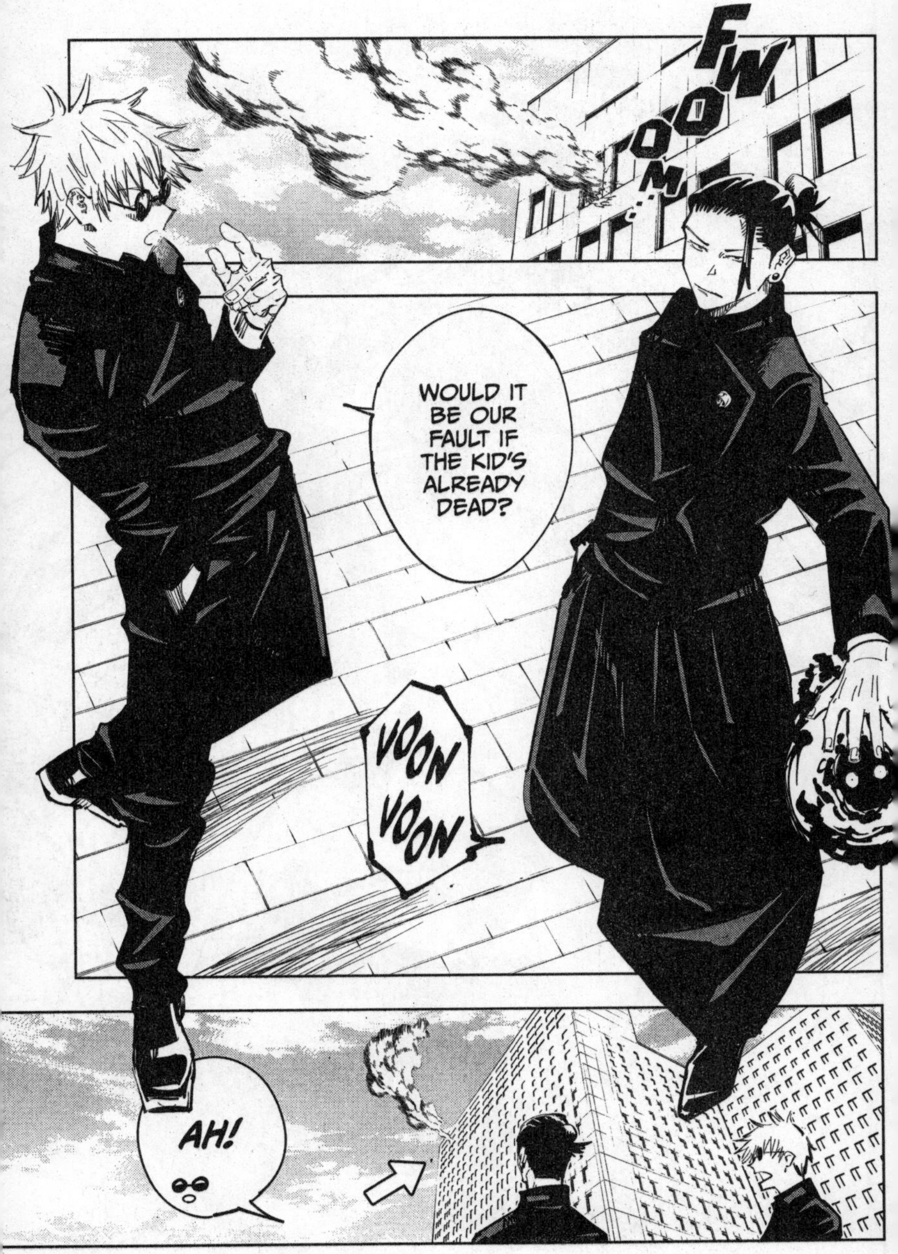
FWOOOM...
WOULD IT BE OUR FAULT IF THE KID'S ALREADY DEAD?
VOON VOON
AH!

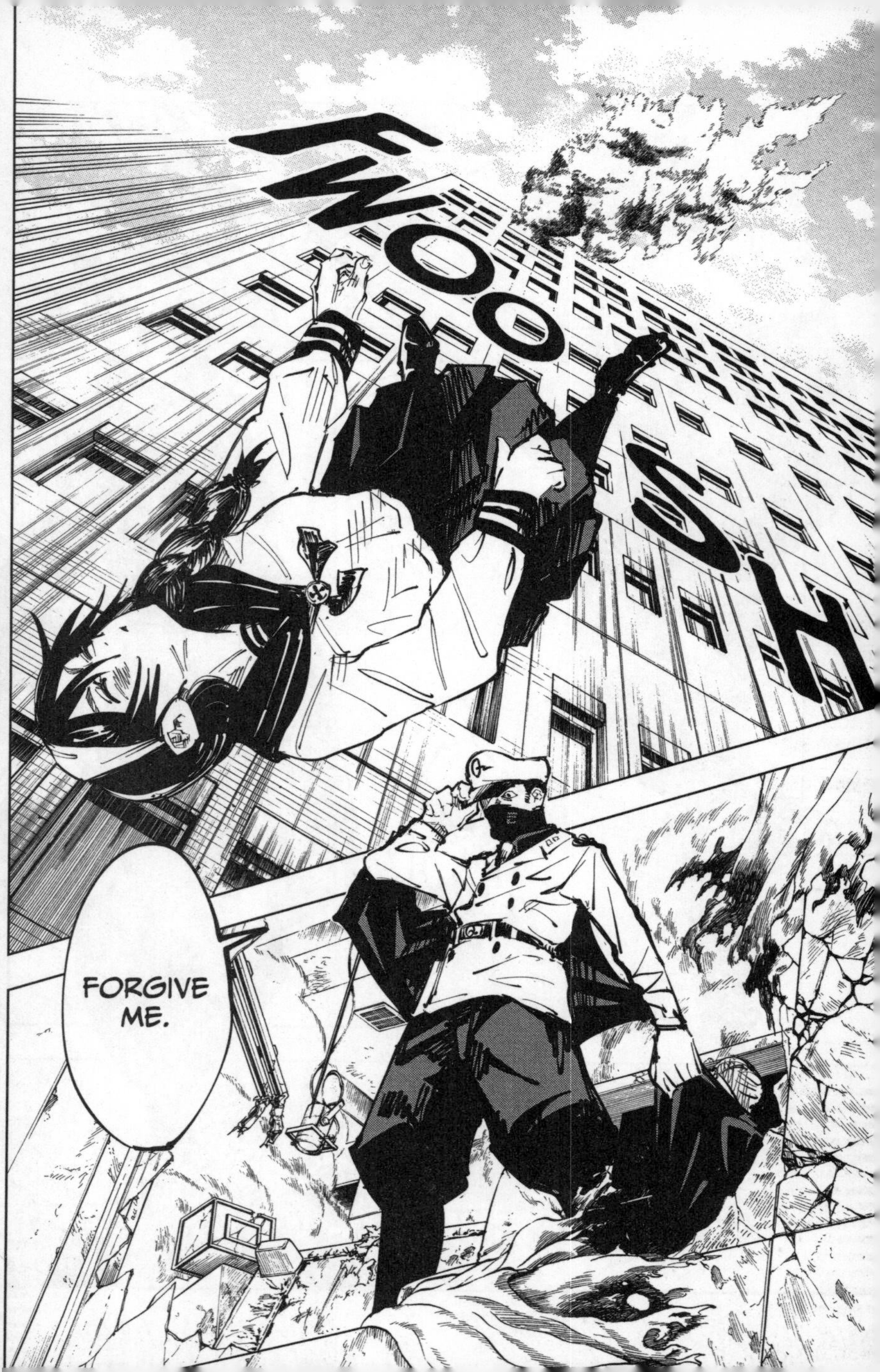
WOOSH
FORGIVE ME.

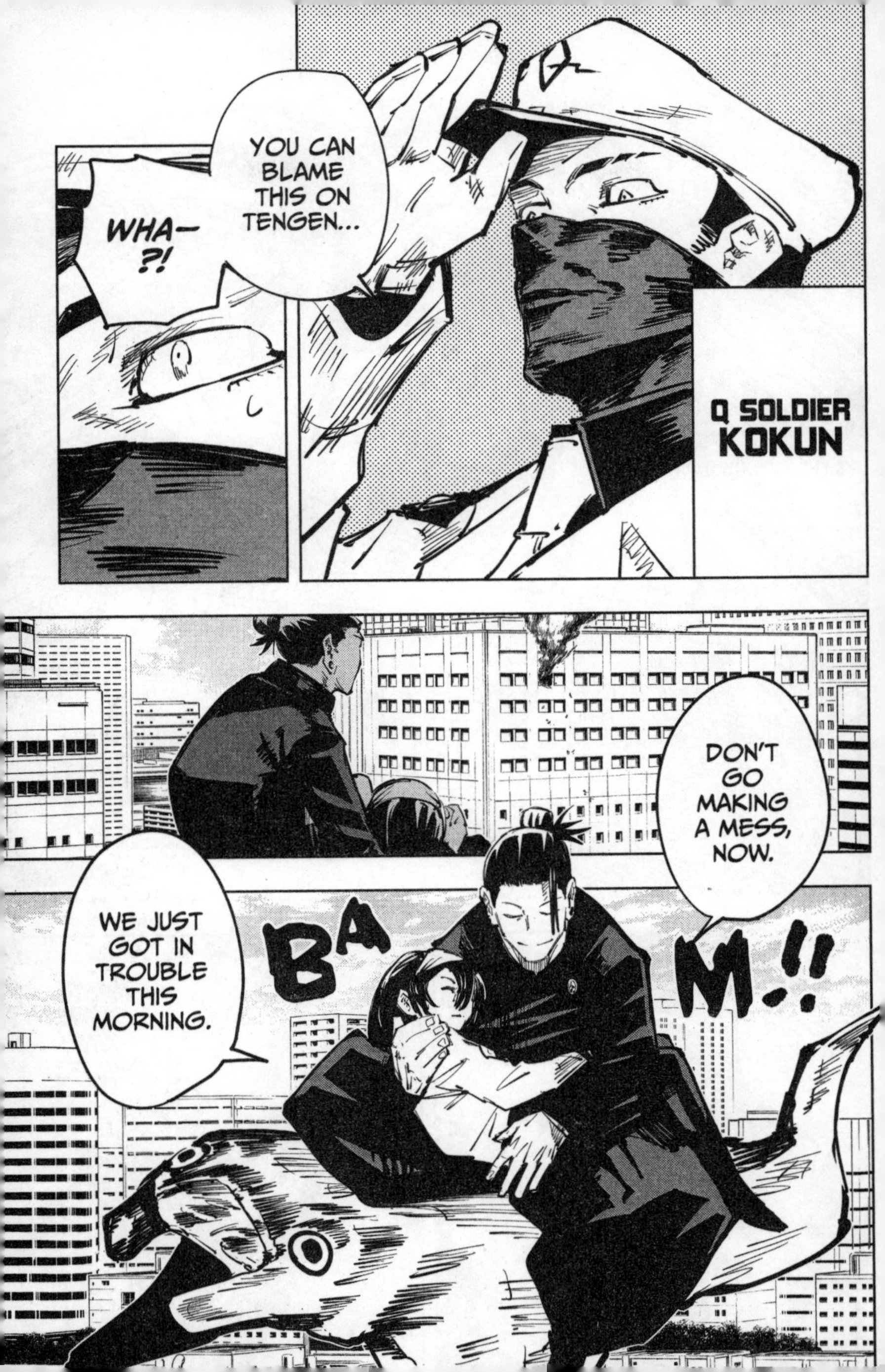
YOU CAN BLAME THIS ON TENGEN...
Q SOLDIER KOKUN
WHA— ?!
DON'T GO MAKING A MESS, NOW.
BAM!!
WE JUST GOT IN TROUBLE THIS MORNING.

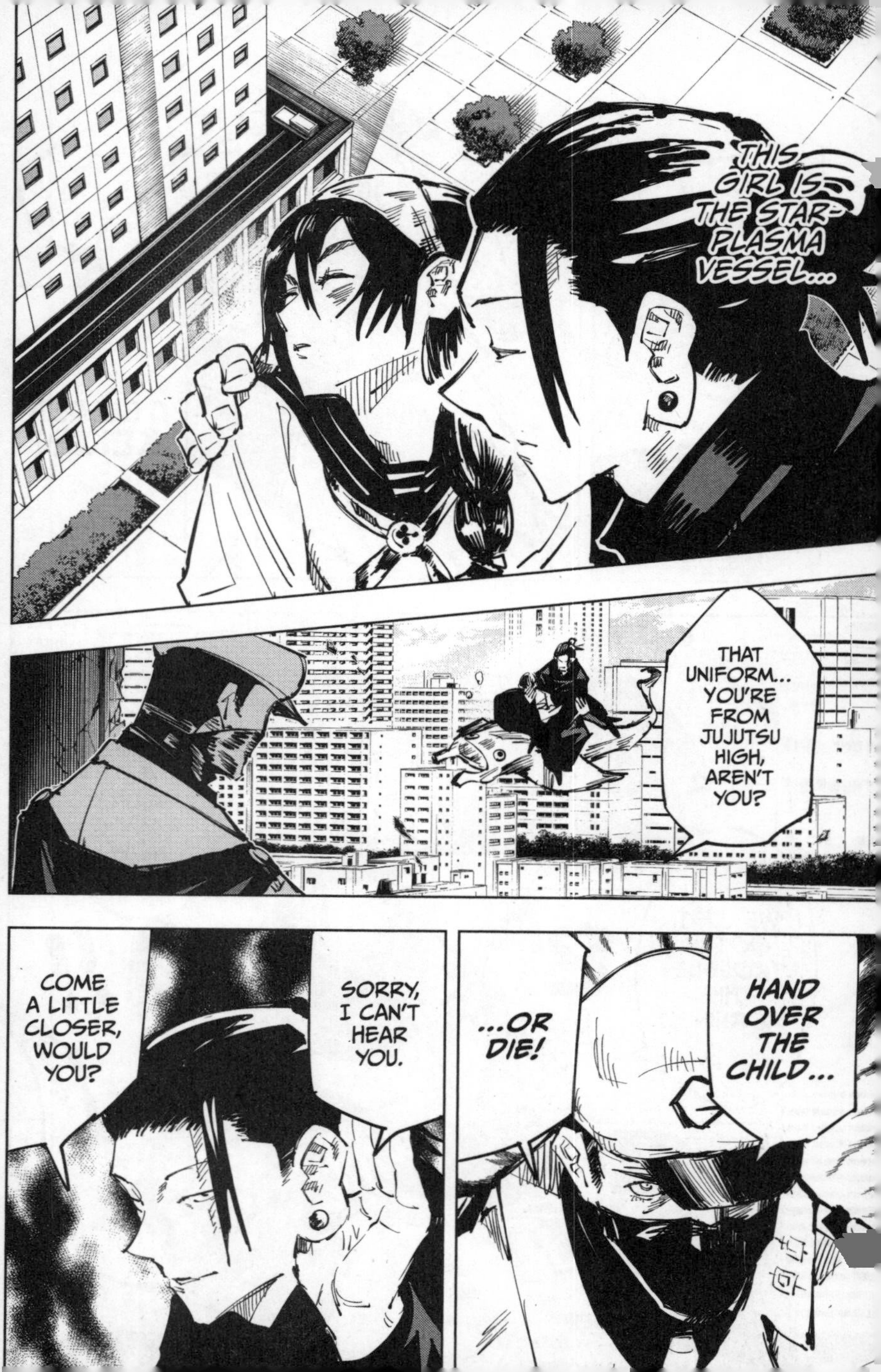
THIS GIRL IS THE STAR-PLASMA VESSEL...
THAT UNIFORM... YOU'RE FROM JUJUTSU HIGH, AREN'T YOU?
HAND OVER THE CHILD...
...OR DIE!
SORRY, I CAN'T HEAR YOU.
COME A LITTLE CLOSER, WOULD YOU?

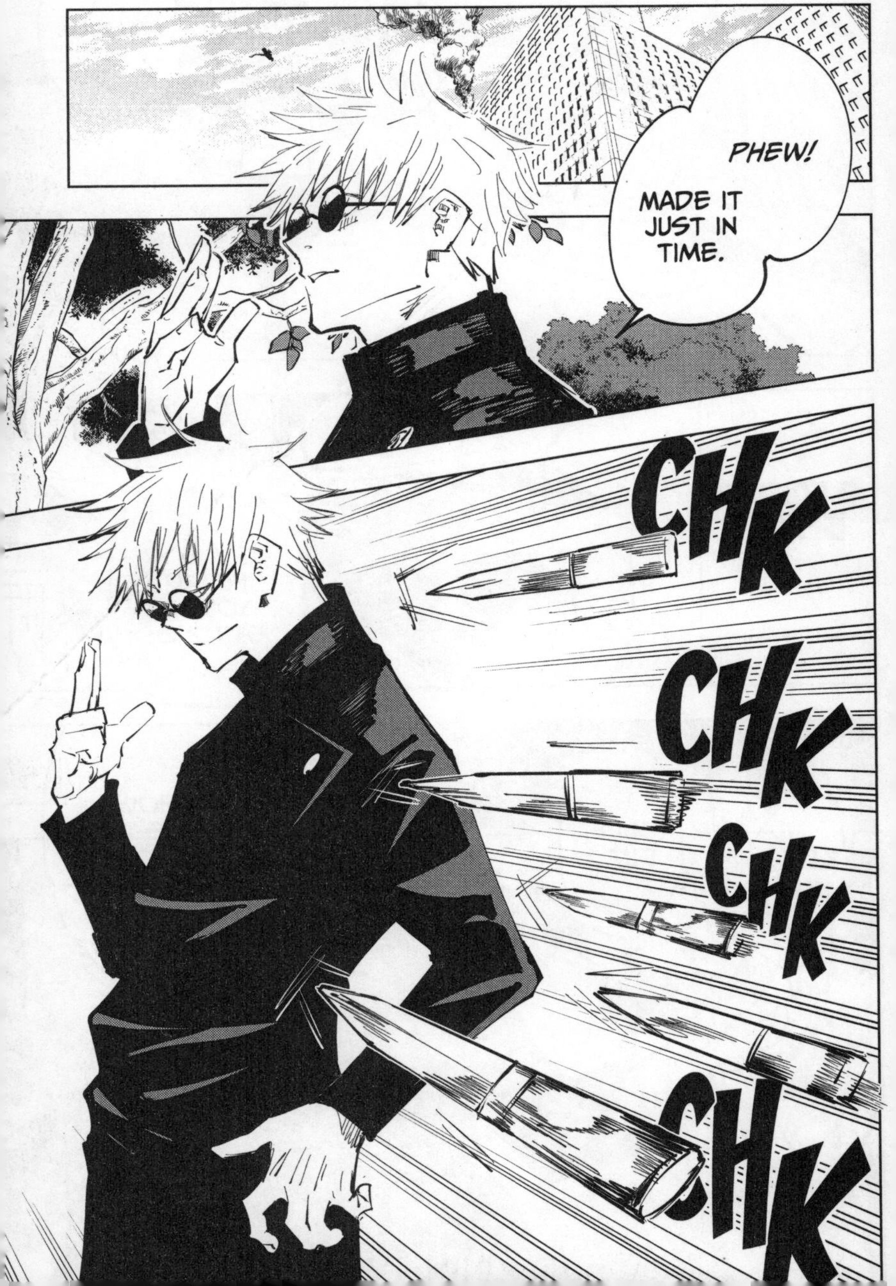
PHEW!
MADE IT JUST IN TIME.
CHK
CHK
CHK
CHK

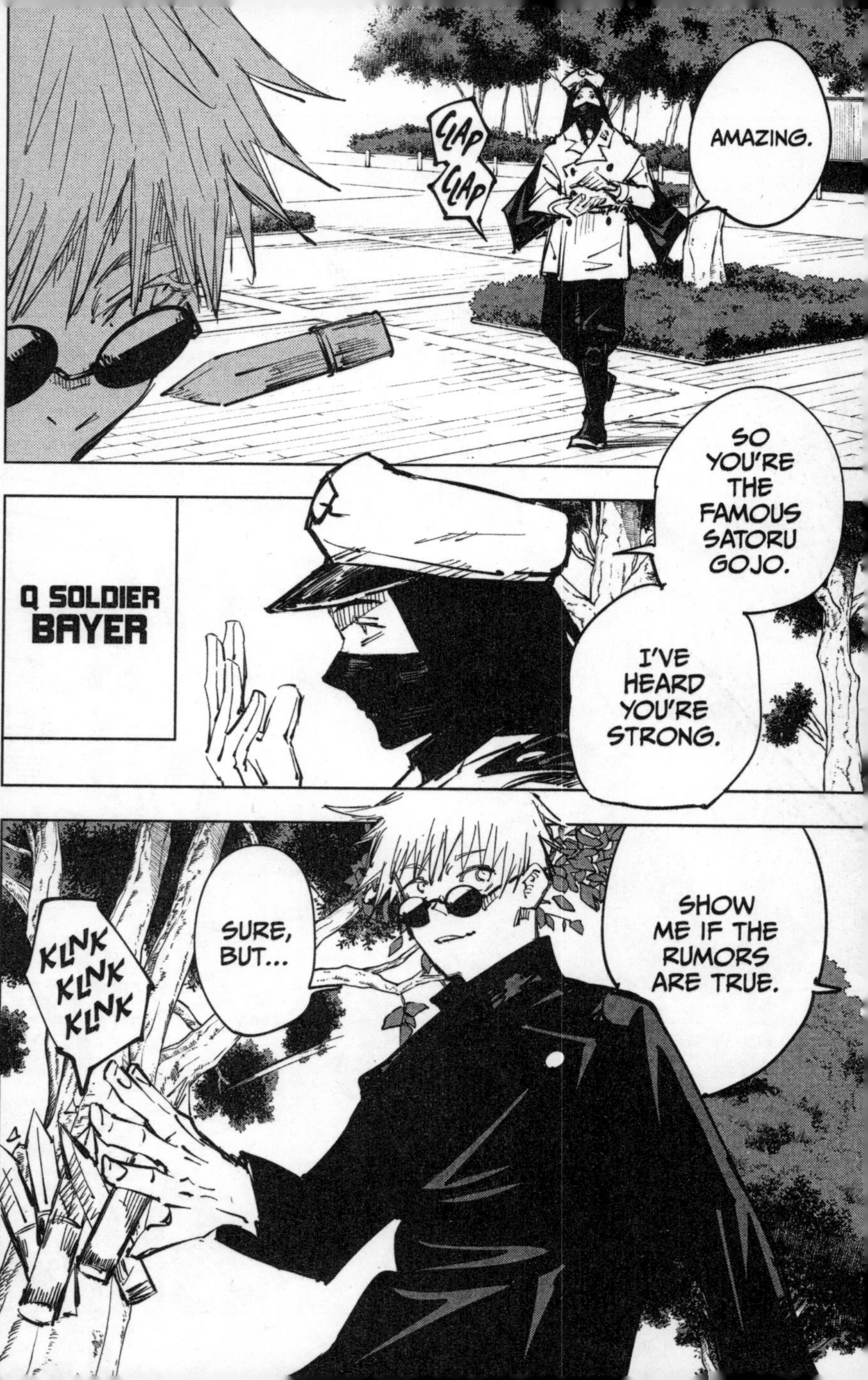
AMAZING.
CLAP CLAP
SO YOU'RE THE FAMOUS SATORU GOJO.
I'VE HEARD YOU'RE STRONG.
Q SOLDIER BAYER
SHOW ME IF THE RUMORS ARE TRUE.
SURE, BUT...
KLINK KLINK KLINK

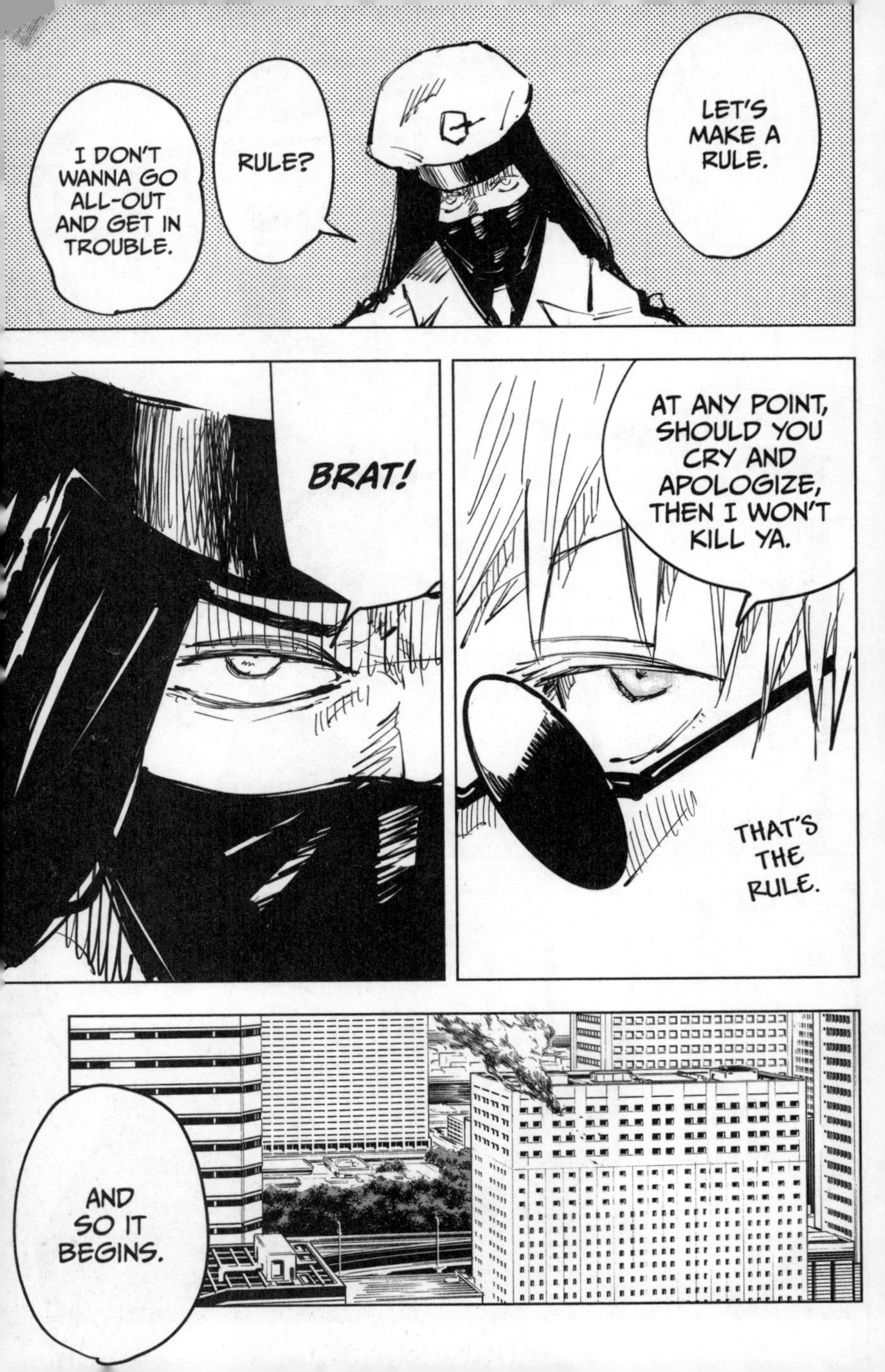
LET'S MAKE A RULE.
RULE?
I DON'T WANNA GO ALL-OUT AND GET IN TROUBLE.
AT ANY POINT, SHOULD YOU CRY AND APOLOGIZE, THEN I WON'T KILL YA.
THAT'S THE RULE.
BRAT!
AND SO IT BEGINS.

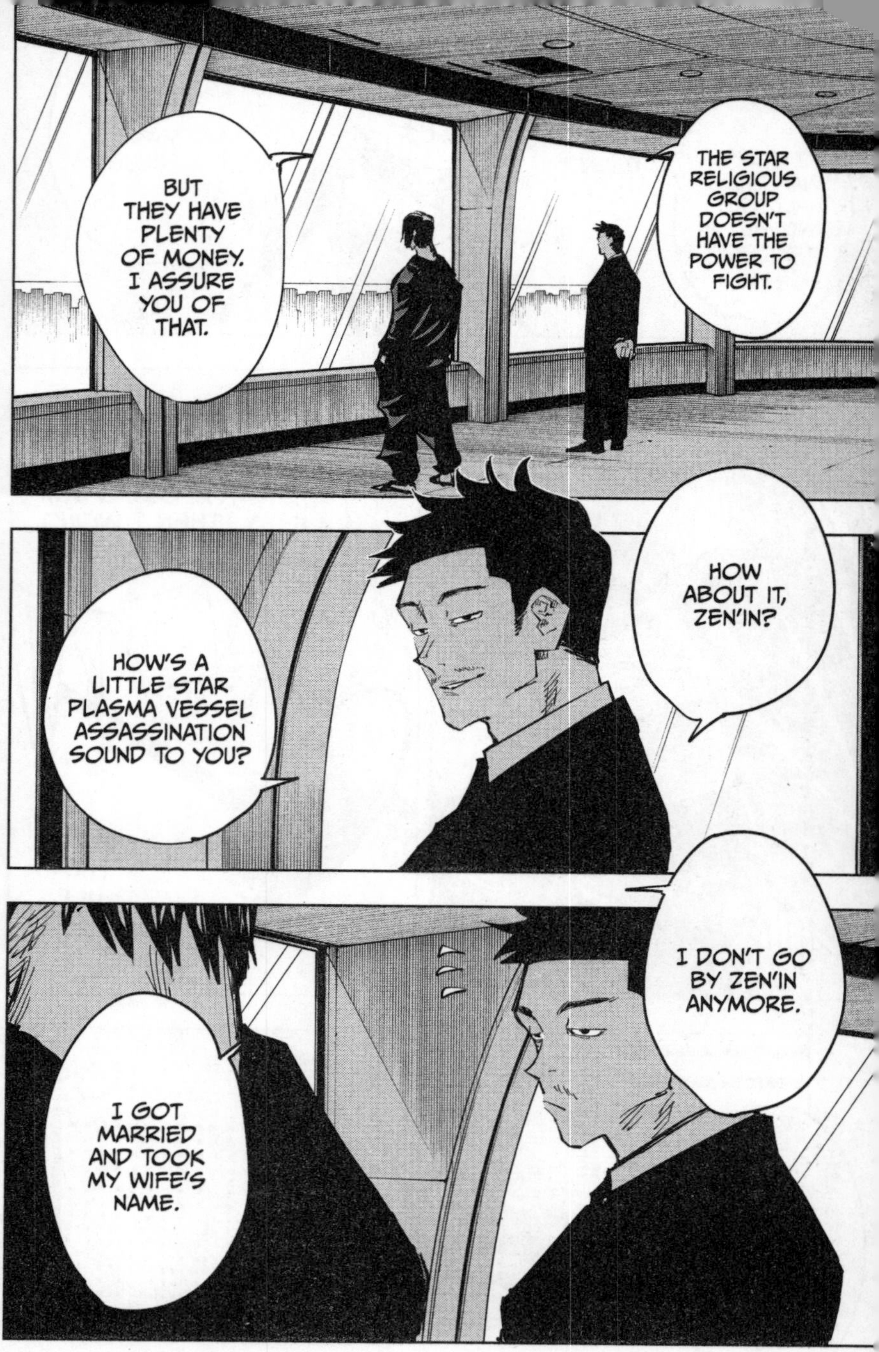
THE STAR RELIGIOUS GROUP DOESN'T HAVE THE POWER TO FIGHT.
BUT THEY HAVE PLENTY OF MONEY. I ASSURE YOU OF THAT.
HOW ABOUT IT, ZEN'IN?
HOW'S A LITTLE STAR PLASMA VESSEL ASSASSINATION SOUND TO YOU?
I DON'T GO BY ZEN'IN ANYMORE.
I GOT MARRIED AND TOOK MY WIFE'S NAME.

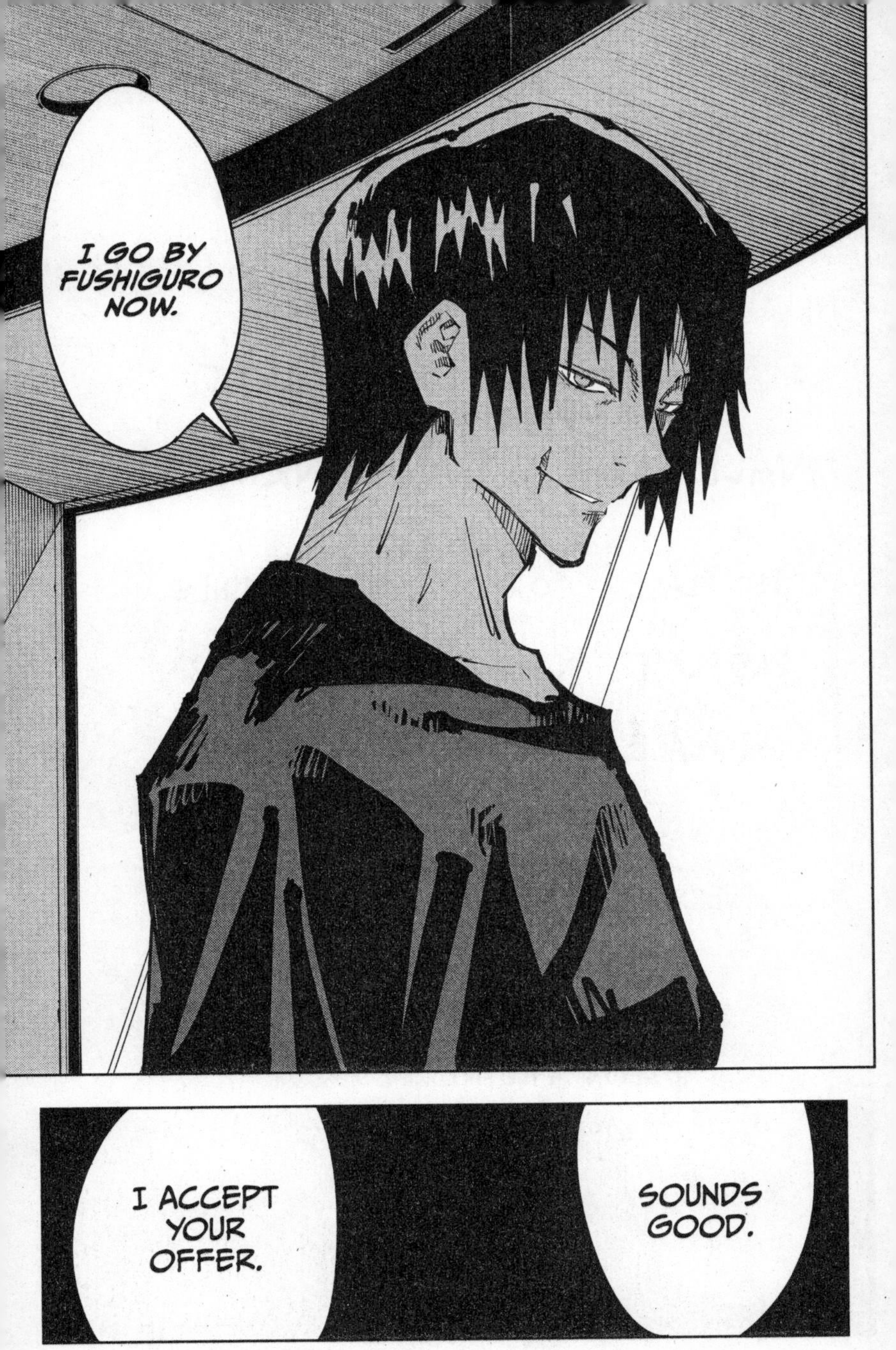
I GO BY FUSHIGURO NOW.
SOUNDS GOOD.
I ACCEPT YOUR OFFER.

I COMPLETELY FORGOT TO REPORT THE 2019 VALENTINE'S DAY RANKINGS!

1ST PLACE	GOJO	12 VALENTINES
2ND PLACE	NANAMI	8 VALENTINES
3RD PLACE	ITADORI	5 VALENTINES

EVERYONE ELSE AVERAGED 1.2 VALENTINES

THE ONE I FOUND THE FUNNIEST WAS ONE SENT
TO GETO WITH THE FOLLOWING MESSAGE:

"A GIFT FROM A MONKEY!♡"

CHAPTER 67: HIDDEN INVENTORY, PART 3

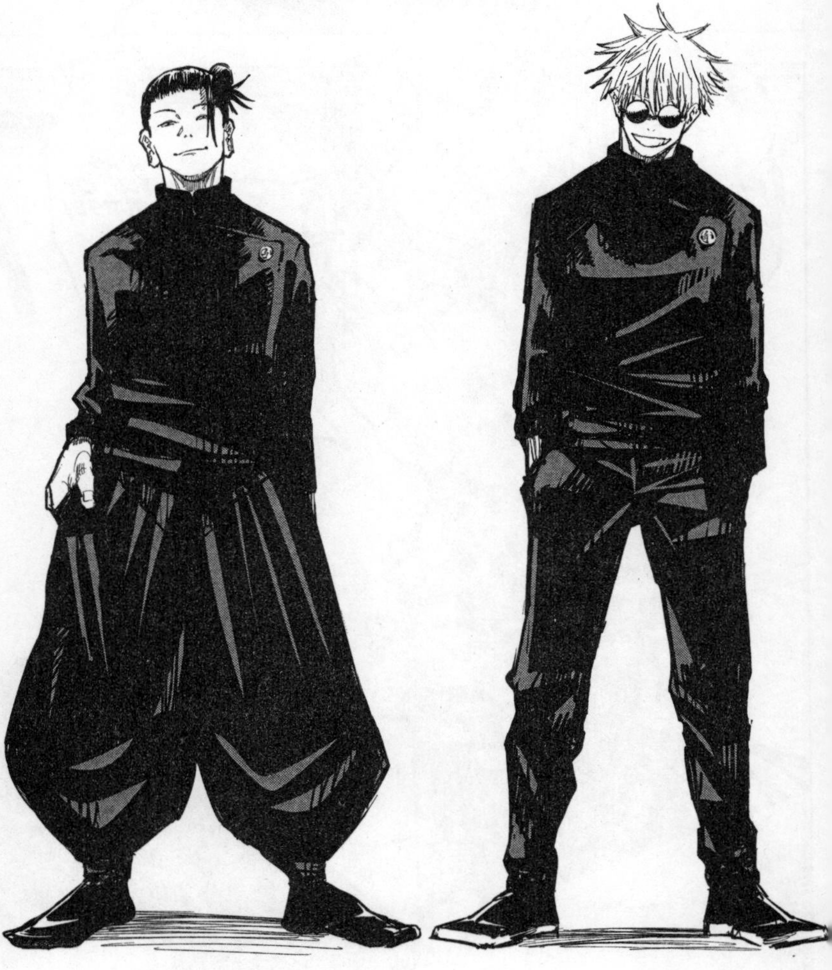

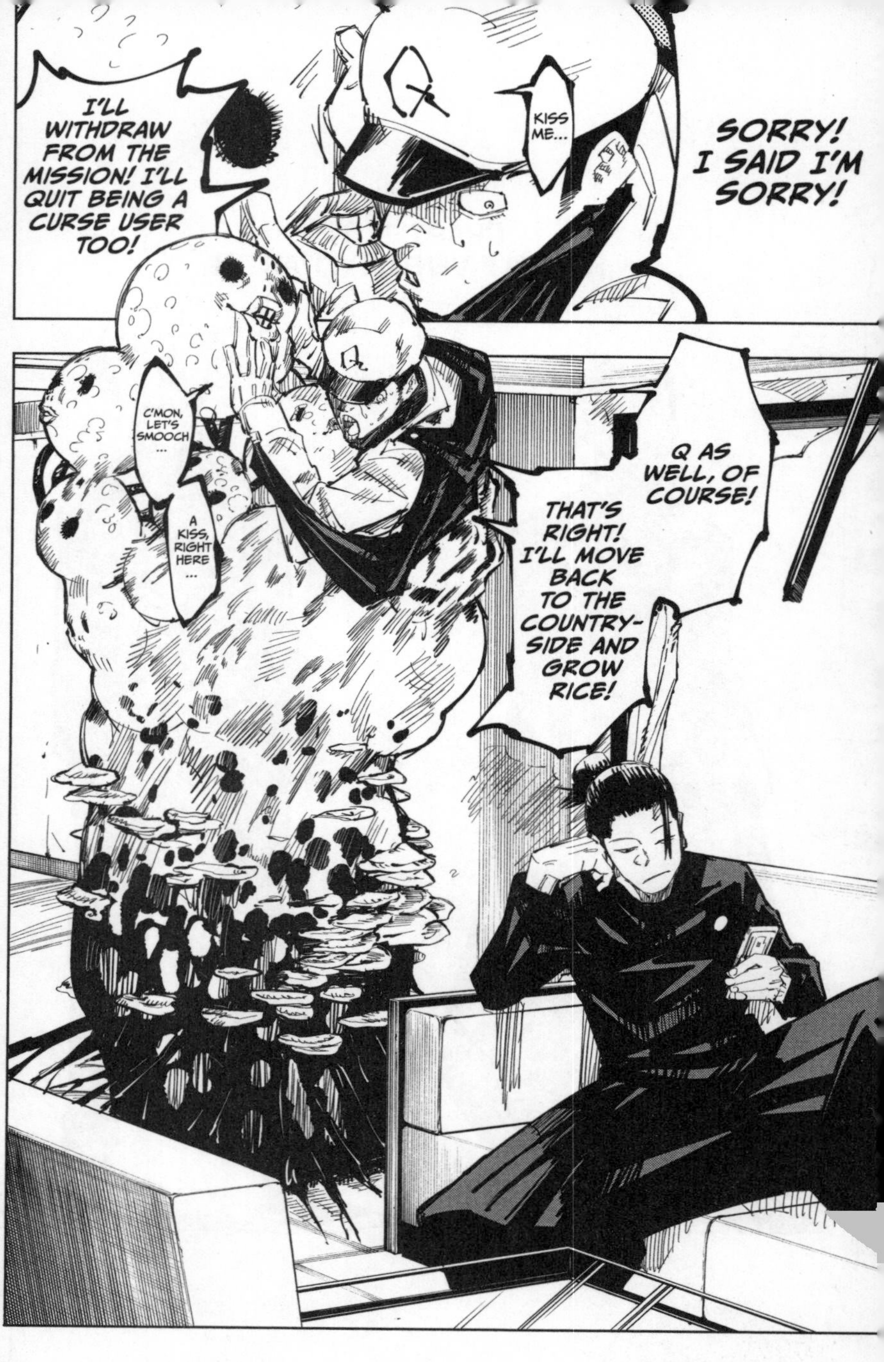
SORRY! I SAID I'M SORRY!
KISS ME...
I'LL WITHDRAW FROM THE MISSION! I'LL QUIT BEING A CURSE USER TOO!
Q AS WELL, OF COURSE!
THAT'S RIGHT! I'LL MOVE BACK TO THE COUNTRY-SIDE AND GROW RICE!
C'MON, LET'S SMOOCH...
A KISS, RIGHT HERE...

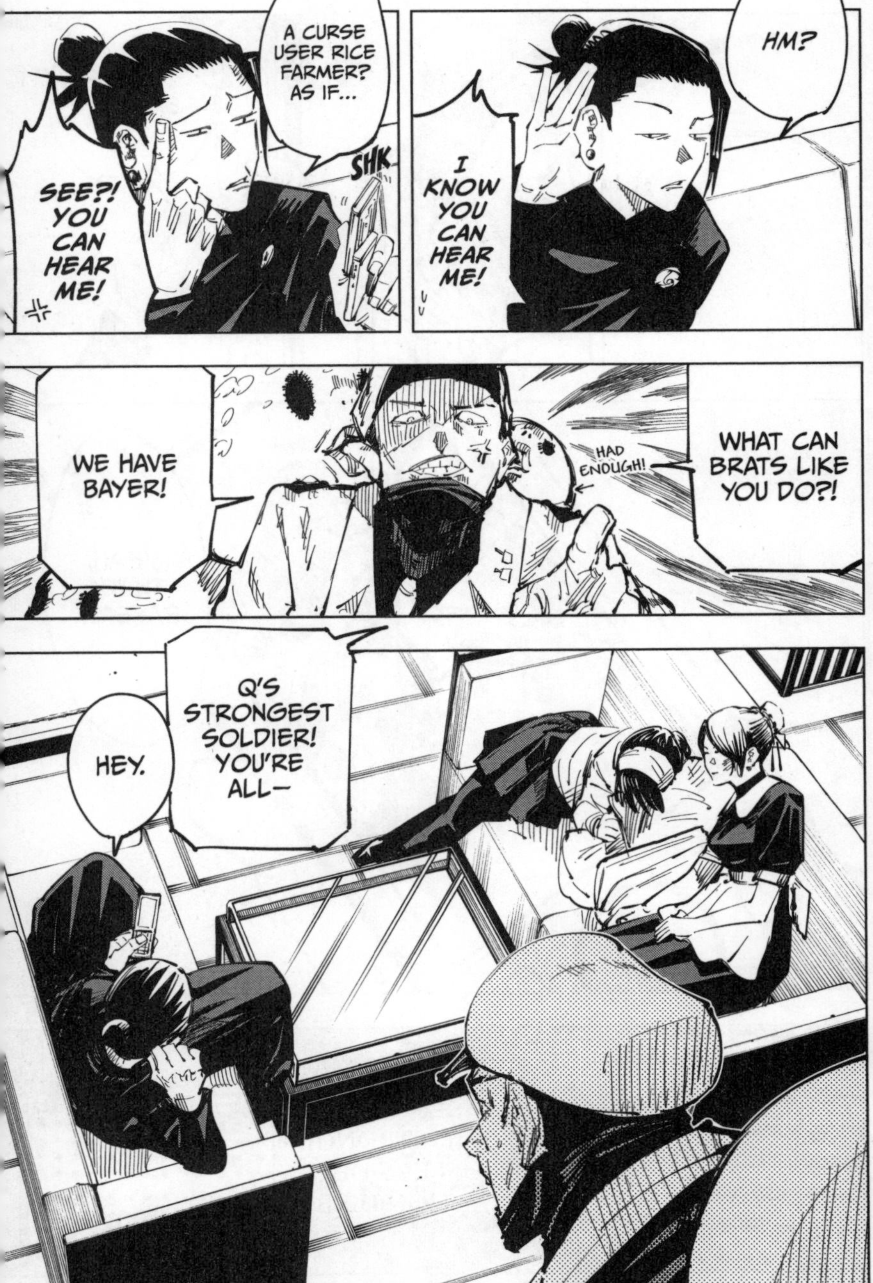
HM?
I KNOW YOU CAN HEAR ME!
A CURSE USER RICE FARMER? AS IF...
SHK
SEE?! YOU CAN HEAR ME!
WHAT CAN BRATS LIKE YOU DO?!
HAD ENOUGH!
WE HAVE BAYER!
Q'S STRONGEST SOLDIER! YOU'RE ALL—
HEY.

IS THIS BAYER?

HUH?

YEAH, THAT'S BAYER...

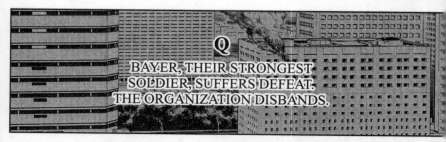

Q
BAYER, THEIR STRONGEST SOLDIER, SUFFERS DEFEAT, THE ORGANIZATION DISBANDS.

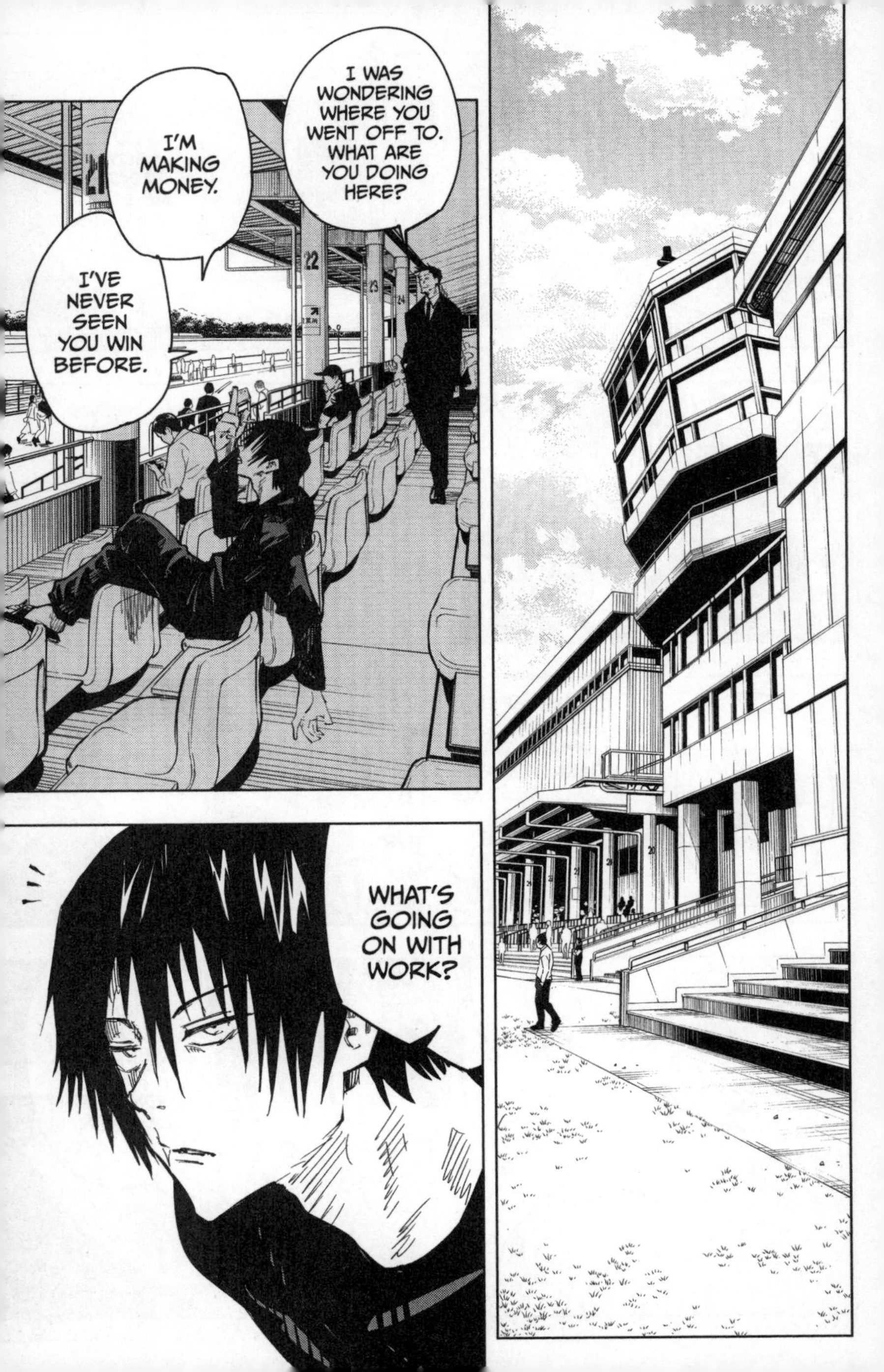
I WAS WONDERING WHERE YOU WENT OFF TO. WHAT ARE YOU DOING HERE?
I'M MAKING MONEY.
I'VE NEVER SEEN YOU WIN BEFORE.
WHAT'S GOING ON WITH WORK?

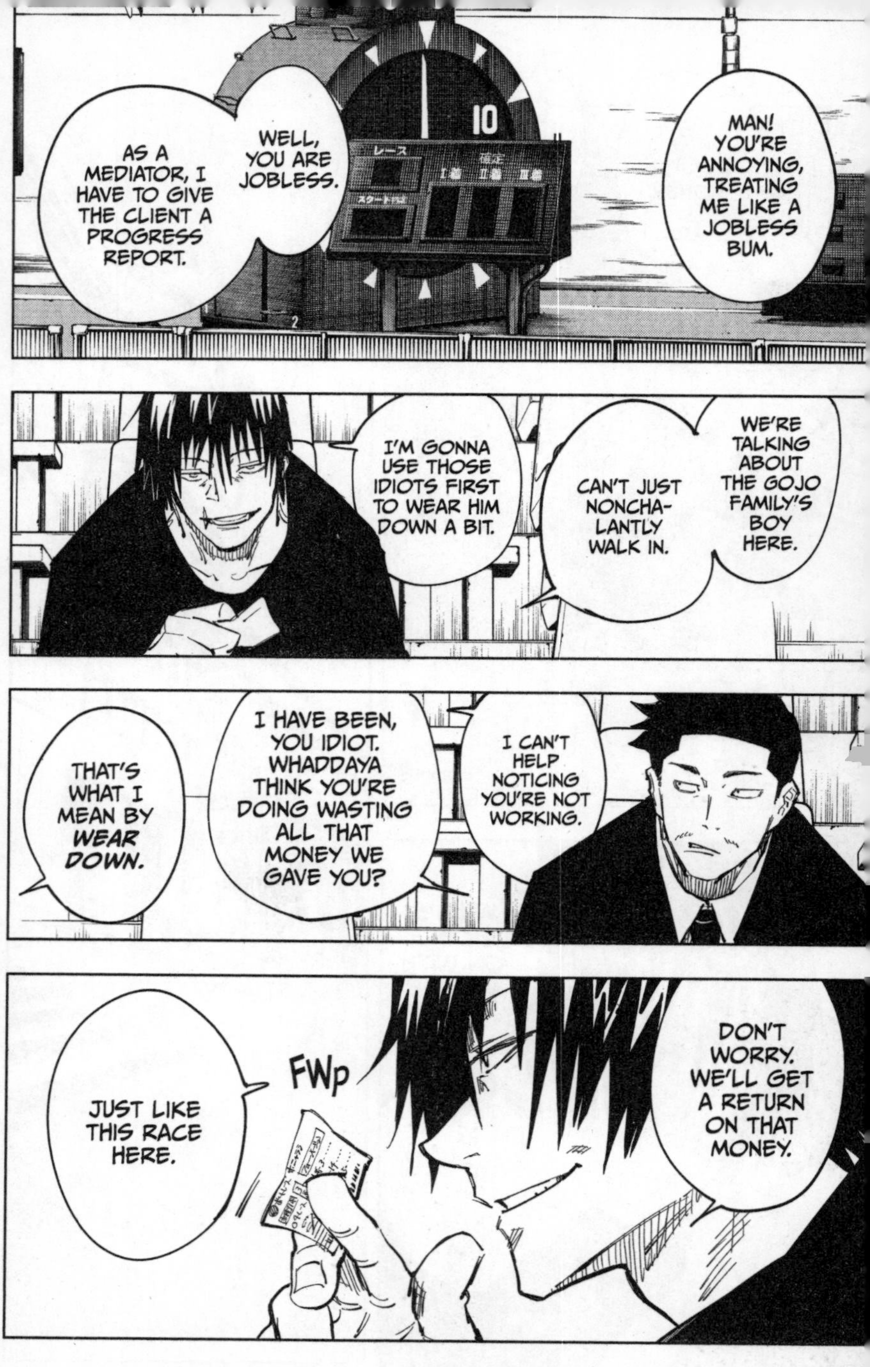
MAN! YOU'RE ANNOYING, TREATING ME LIKE A JOBLESS BUM.
WELL, YOU ARE JOBLESS.
AS A MEDIATOR, I HAVE TO GIVE THE CLIENT A PROGRESS REPORT.
10
WE'RE TALKING ABOUT THE GOJO FAMILY'S BOY HERE.
CAN'T JUST NONCHA-LANTLY WALK IN.
I'M GONNA USE THOSE IDIOTS FIRST TO WEAR HIM DOWN A BIT.
I CAN'T HELP NOTICING YOU'RE NOT WORKING.
I HAVE BEEN, YOU IDIOT. WHADDAYA THINK YOU'RE DOING WASTING ALL THAT MONEY WE GAVE YOU?
THAT'S WHAT I MEAN BY ***WEAR DOWN.***
DON'T WORRY. WE'LL GET A RETURN ON THAT MONEY.
FWp
JUST LIKE THIS RACE HERE.

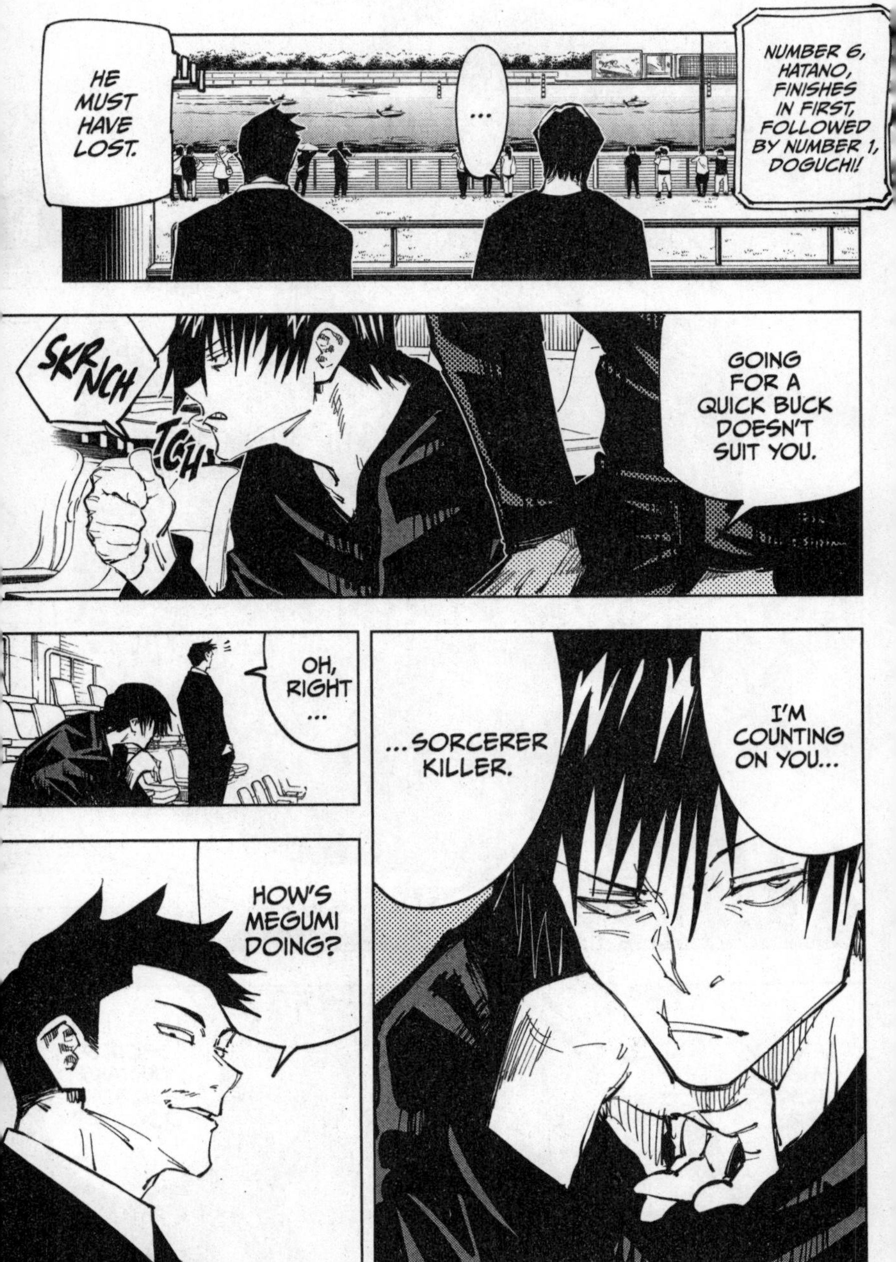
NUMBER 6, HATANO, FINISHES IN FIRST, FOLLOWED BY NUMBER 1, DOGUCHI!
...
HE MUST HAVE LOST.
GOING FOR A QUICK BUCK DOESN'T SUIT YOU.
SKRNCH
TCH
I'M COUNTING ON YOU...
...SORCERER KILLER.
OH, RIGHT ...
HOW'S MEGUMI DOING?

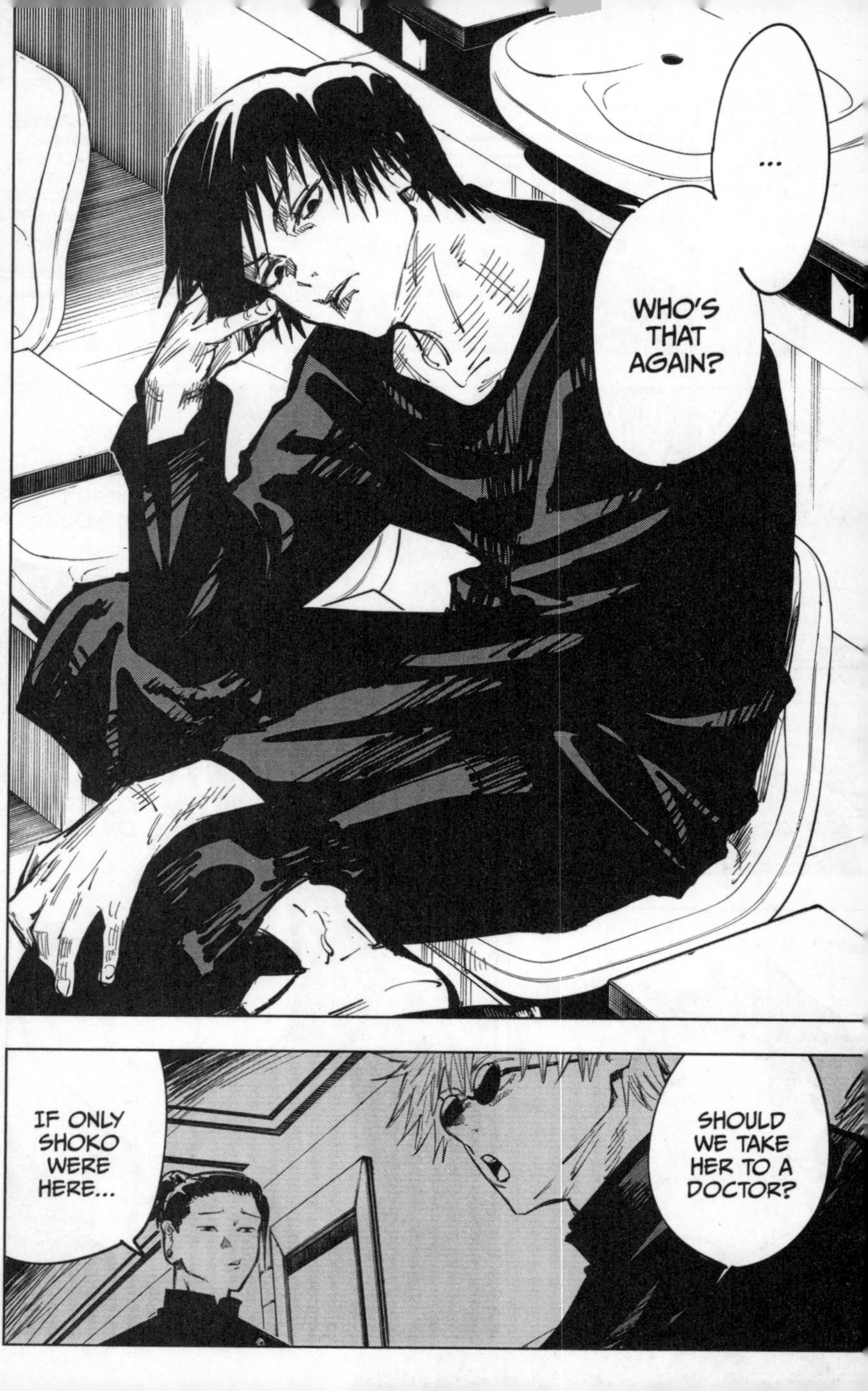
...
WHO'S THAT AGAIN?
SHOULD WE TAKE HER TO A DOCTOR?
IF ONLY SHOKO WERE HERE...

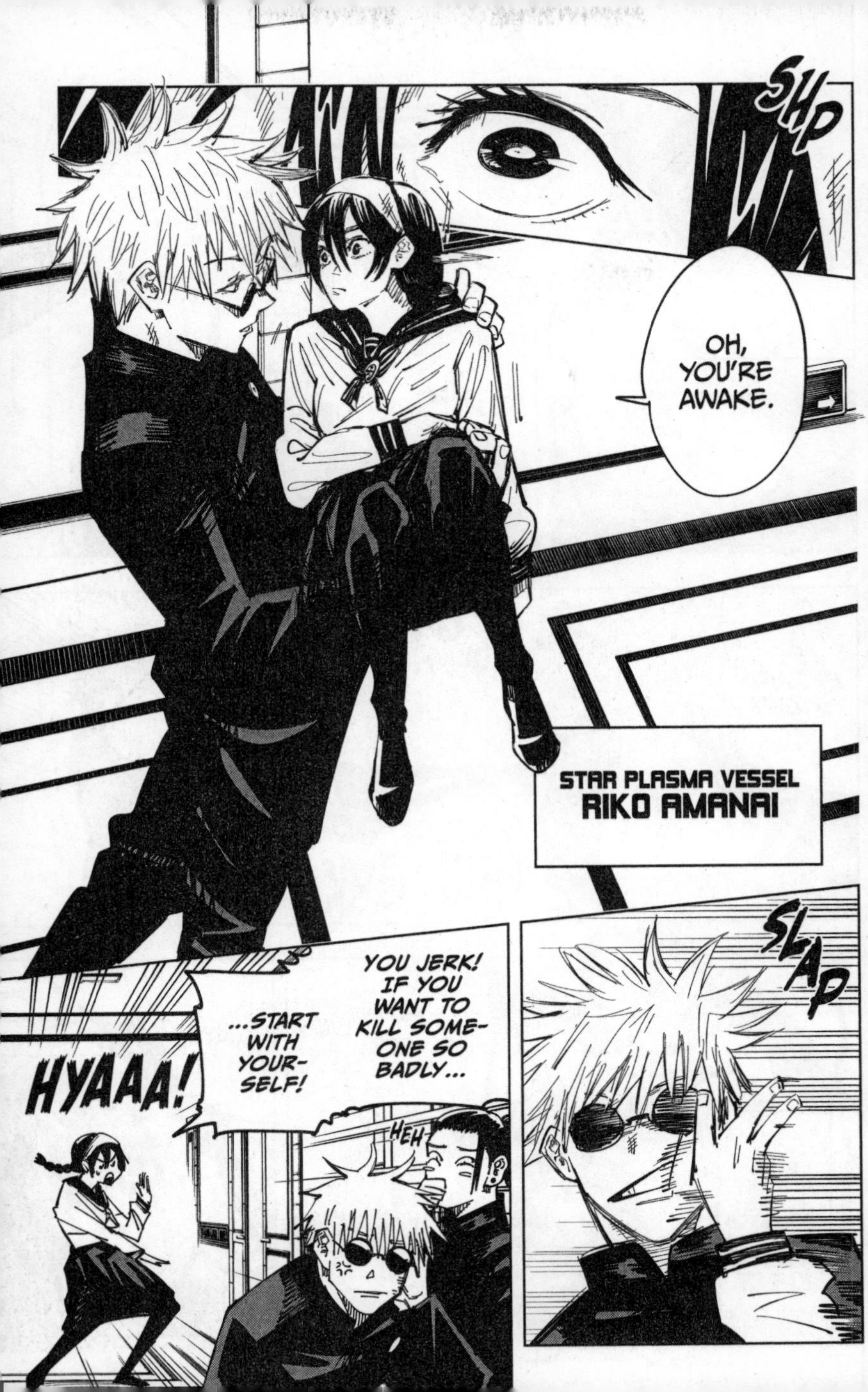
SHP
OH, YOU'RE AWAKE.
STAR PLASMA VESSEL
RIKO AMANAI
SLAP
YOU JERK! IF YOU WANT TO KILL SOME-ONE SO BADLY...
...START WITH YOUR-SELF!
HYAAA!
HEH

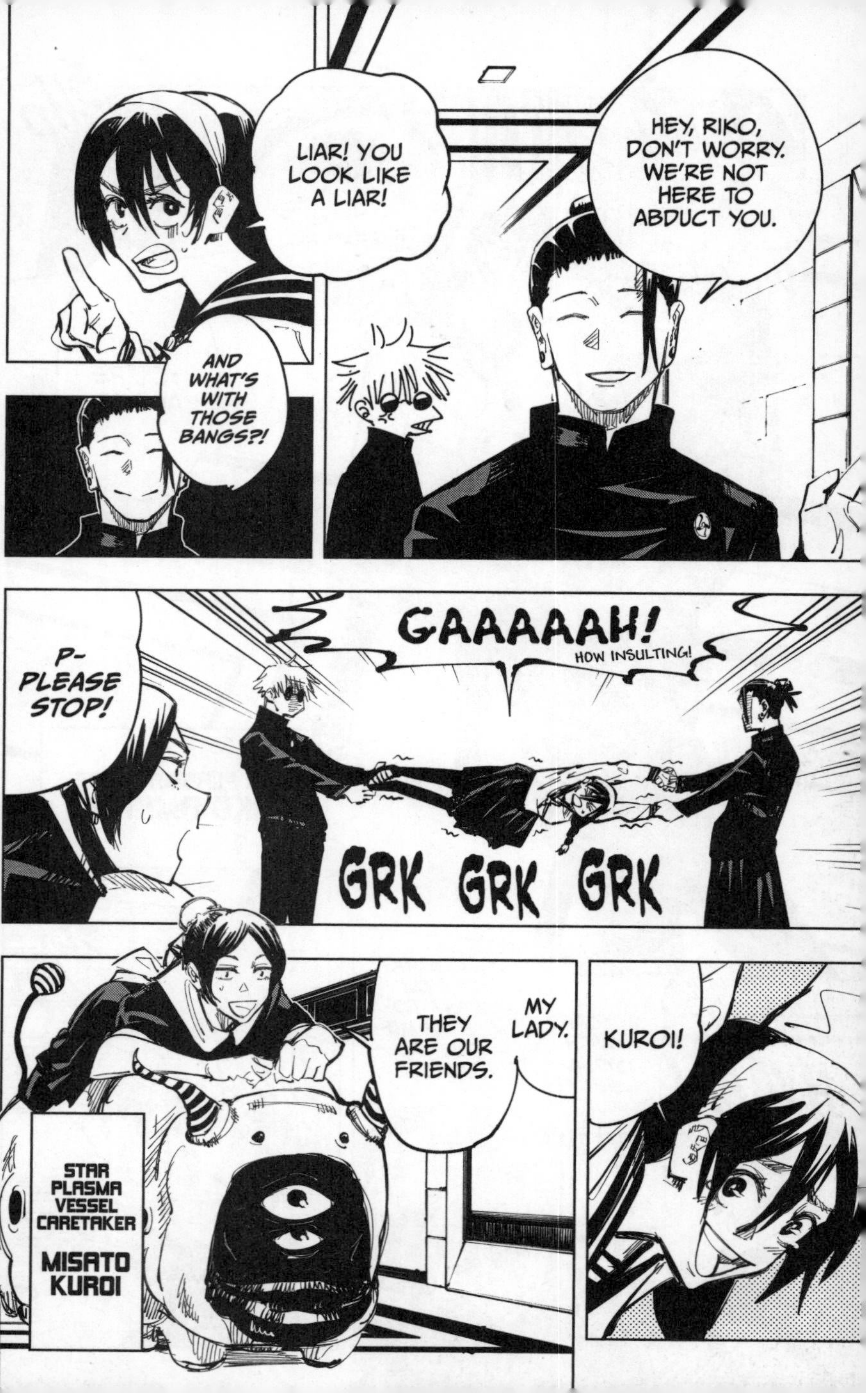
HEY, RIKO, DON'T WORRY. WE'RE NOT HERE TO ABDUCT YOU.
LIAR! YOU LOOK LIKE A LIAR!
AND WHAT'S WITH THOSE BANGS?!
GAAAAAH!
HOW INSULTING!
P-PLEASE STOP!
GRK GRK GRK
KUROI!
MY LADY.
THEY ARE OUR FRIENDS.
STAR PLASMA VESSEL CARETAKER
MISATO KUROI

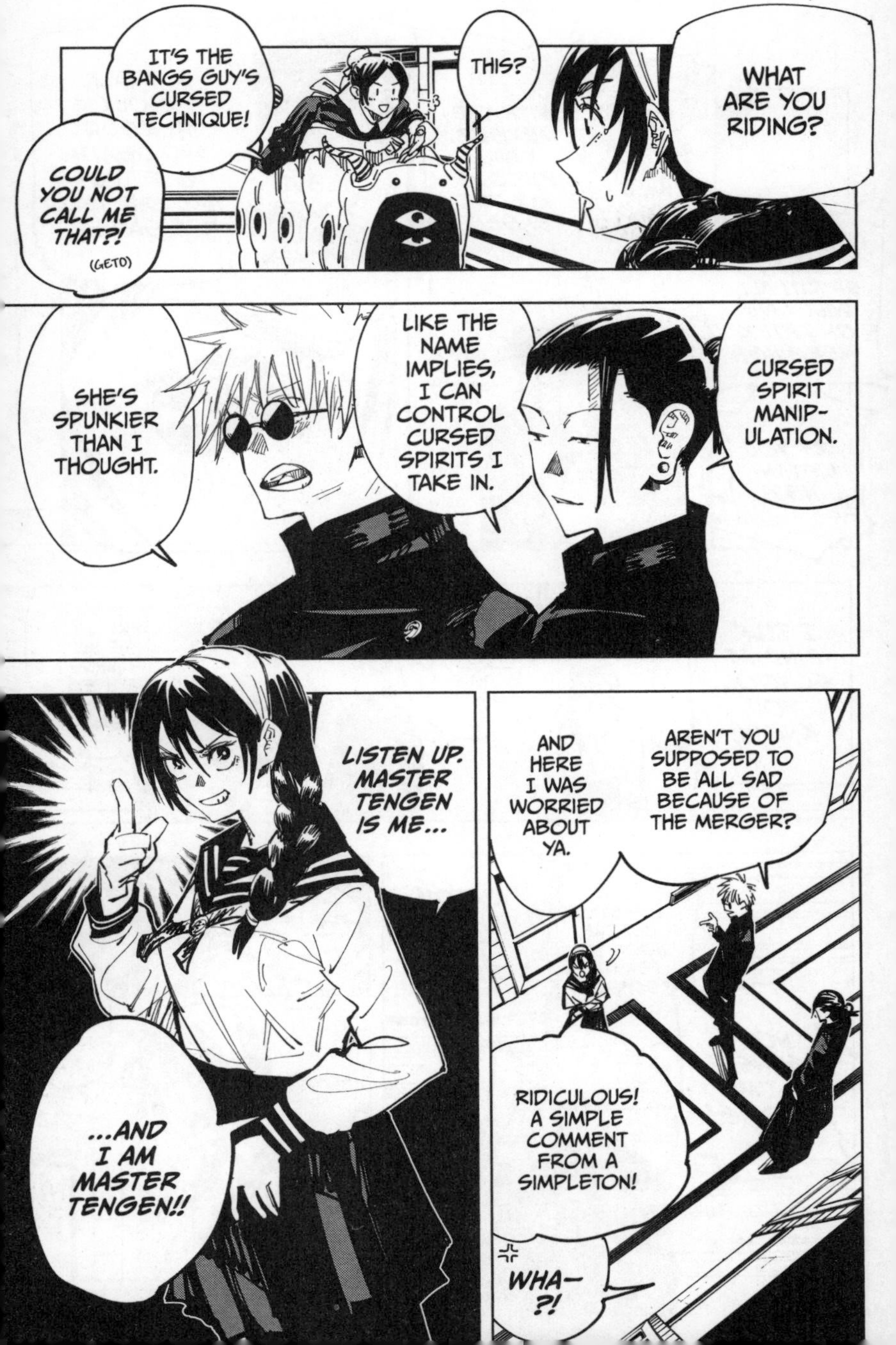
WHAT ARE YOU RIDING?
THIS?
IT'S THE BANGS GUY'S CURSED TECHNIQUE!
COULD YOU NOT CALL ME THAT?!
(GETO)
CURSED SPIRIT MANIP-ULATION.
LIKE THE NAME IMPLIES, I CAN CONTROL CURSED SPIRITS I TAKE IN.
SHE'S SPUNKIER THAN I THOUGHT.
AREN'T YOU SUPPOSED TO BE ALL SAD BECAUSE OF THE MERGER?
AND HERE I WAS WORRIED ABOUT YA.
RIDICULOUS! A SIMPLE COMMENT FROM A SIMPLETON!
WHA—?!
LISTEN UP. MASTER TENGEN IS ME...
...AND I AM MASTER TENGEN!!

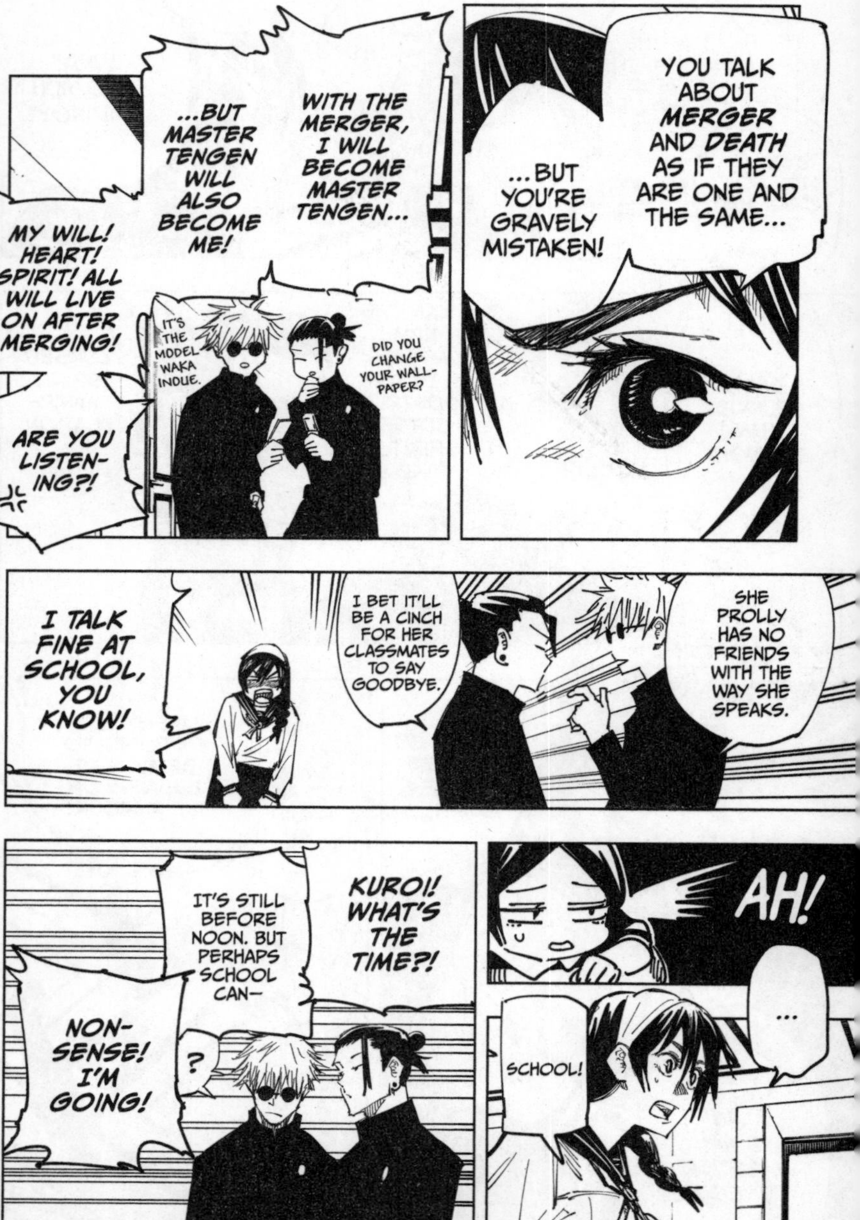
YOU TALK ABOUT MERGER AND DEATH AS IF THEY ARE ONE AND THE SAME...
...BUT YOU'RE GRAVELY MISTAKEN!
WITH THE MERGER, I WILL BECOME MASTER TENGEN...
...BUT MASTER TENGEN WILL ALSO BECOME ME!
MY WILL! HEART! SPIRIT! ALL WILL LIVE ON AFTER MERGING!
DID YOU CHANGE YOUR WALL-PAPER?
IT'S THE MODEL WAKA INDUE.
ARE YOU LISTEN-ING?!
SHE PROLLY HAS NO FRIENDS WITH THE WAY SHE SPEAKS.
I BET IT'LL BE A CINCH FOR HER CLASSMATES TO SAY GOODBYE.
I TALK FINE AT SCHOOL, YOU KNOW!
AH!
...
SCHOOL!
KUROI! WHAT'S THE TIME?!
IT'S STILL BEFORE NOON. BUT PERHAPS SCHOOL CAN—
?
NON-SENSE! I'M GOING!

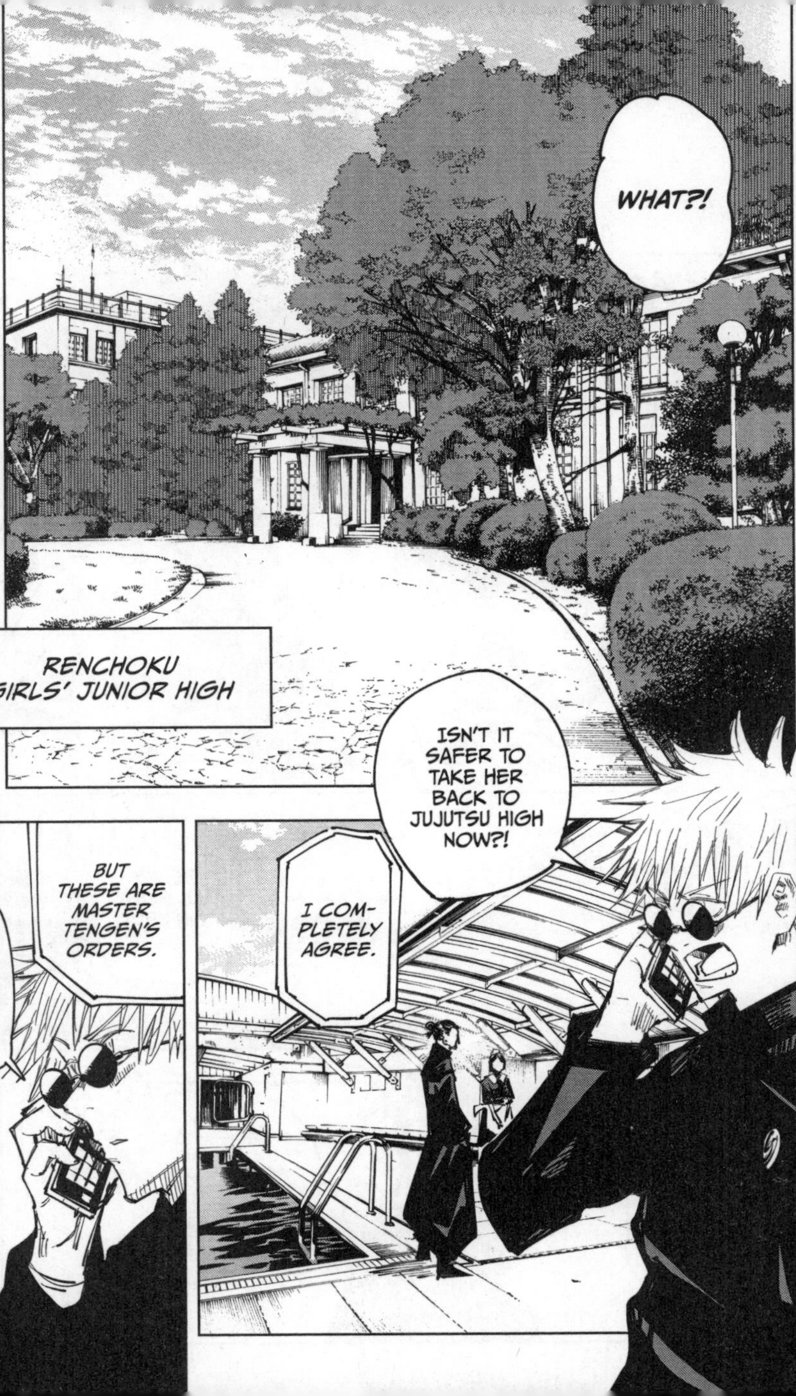
WHAT?!
RENCHOKU GIRLS' JUNIOR HIGH
ISN'T IT SAFER TO TAKE HER BACK TO JUJUTSU HIGH NOW?!
I COM-PLETELY AGREE.
BUT THESE ARE MASTER TENGEN'S ORDERS.
...

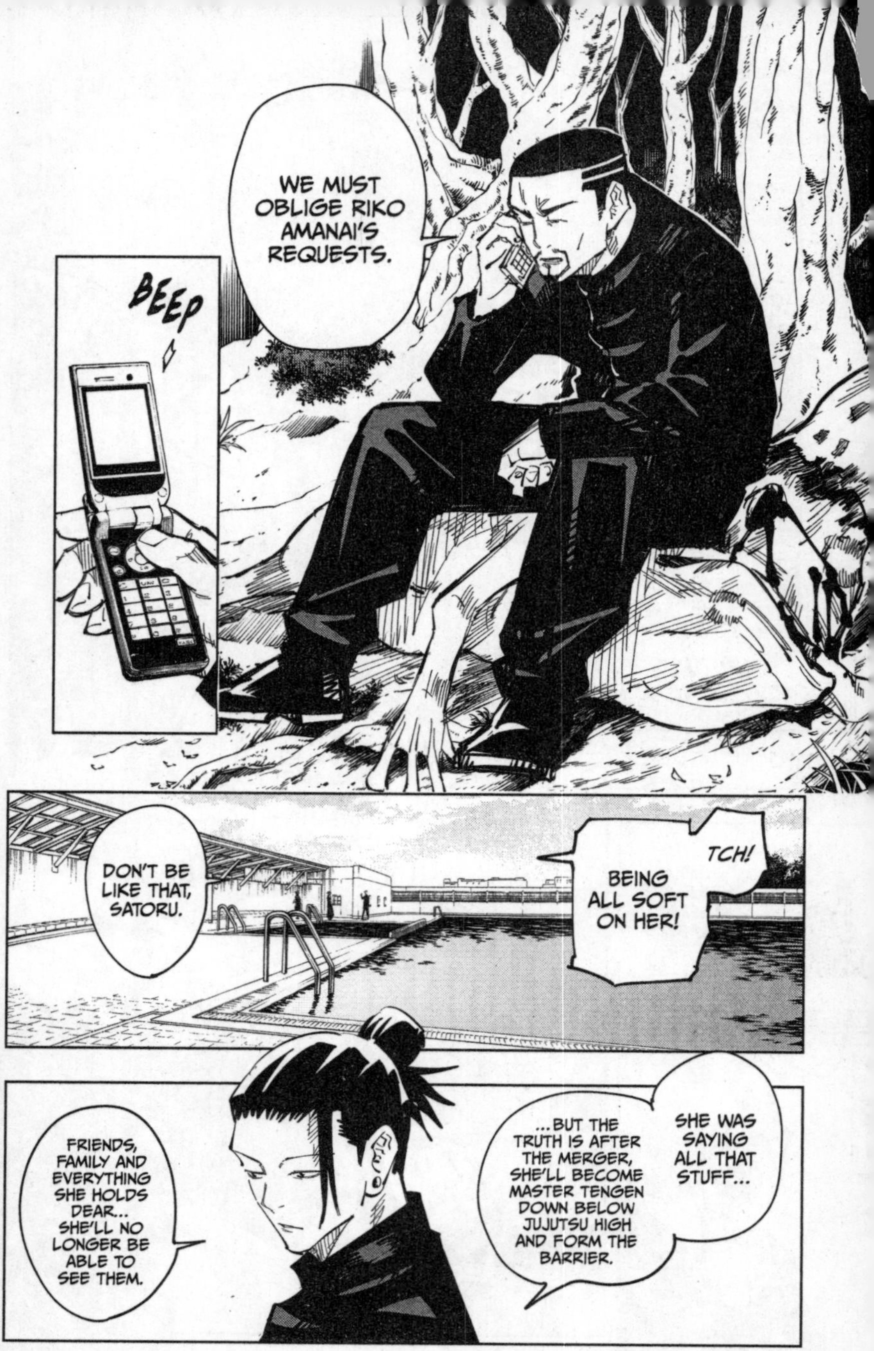
WE MUST OBLIGE RIKO AMANAI'S REQUESTS.
BEEP
TCH!
BEING ALL SOFT ON HER!
DON'T BE LIKE THAT, SATORU.
SHE WAS SAYING ALL THAT STUFF...
...BUT THE TRUTH IS AFTER THE MERGER, SHE'LL BECOME MASTER TENGEN DOWN BELOW JUJUTSU HIGH AND FORM THE BARRIER.
FRIENDS, FAMILY AND EVERYTHING SHE HOLDS DEAR... SHE'LL NO LONGER BE ABLE TO SEE THEM.

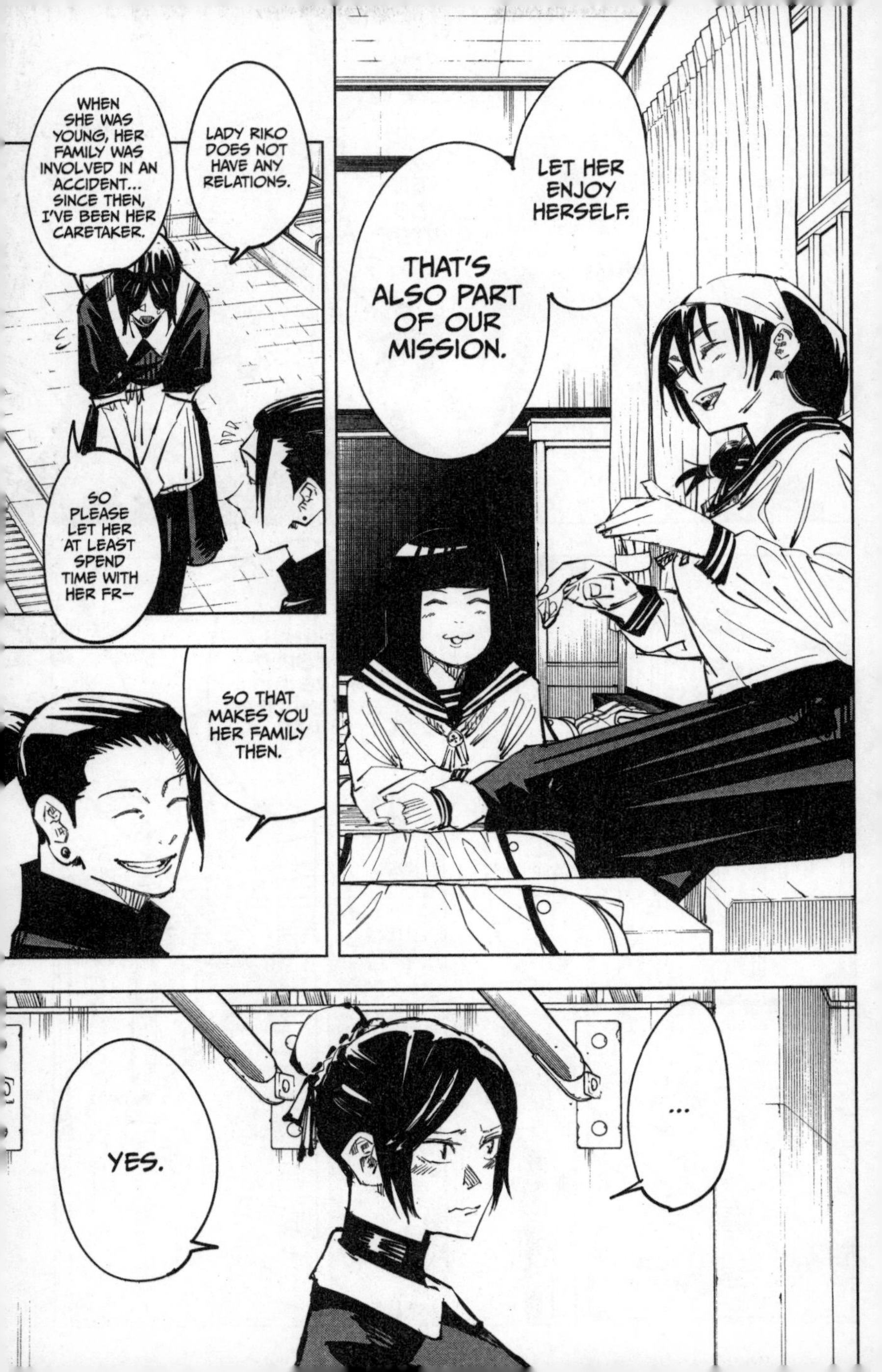
LET HER ENJOY HERSELF.
THAT'S ALSO PART OF OUR MISSION.
LADY RIKO DOES NOT HAVE ANY RELATIONS.
WHEN SHE WAS YOUNG, HER FAMILY WAS INVOLVED IN AN ACCIDENT... SINCE THEN, I'VE BEEN HER CARETAKER.
SO PLEASE LET HER AT LEAST SPEND TIME WITH HER FR–
SO THAT MAKES YOU HER FAMILY THEN.
...
YES.

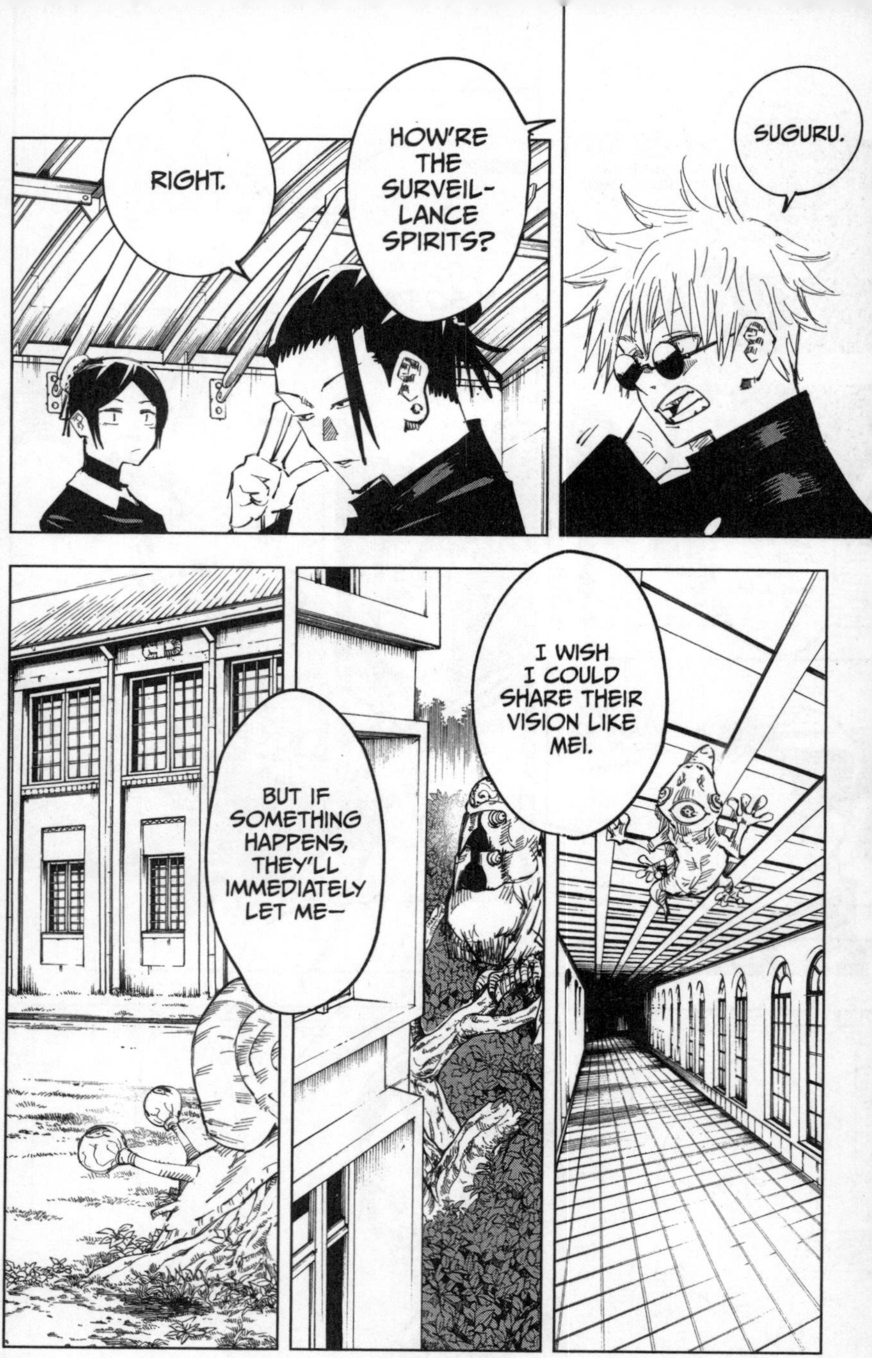
SUGURU.
HOW'RE THE SURVEILLANCE SPIRITS?
RIGHT.
I WISH I COULD SHARE THEIR VISION LIKE MEI.
BUT IF SOMETHING HAPPENS, THEY'LL IMMEDIATELY LET ME—

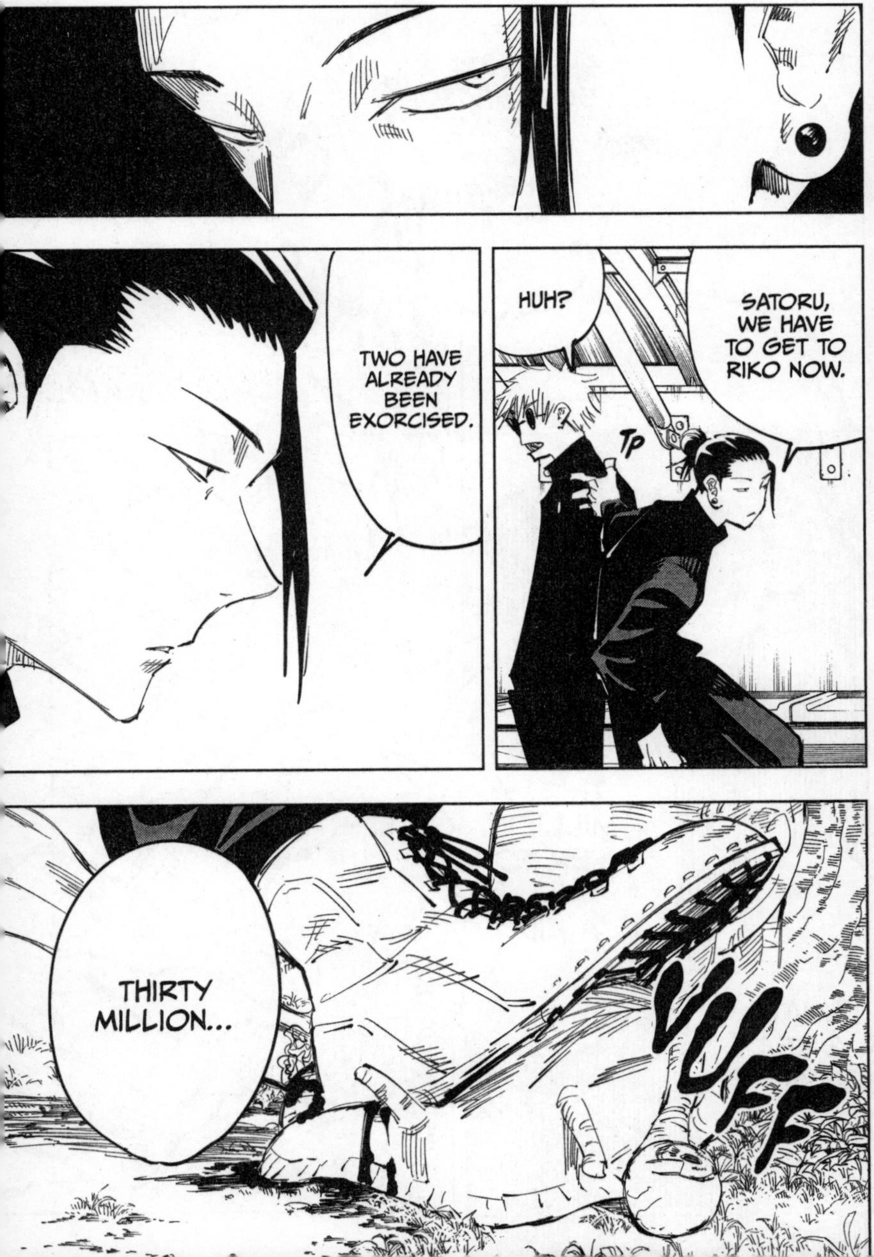
SATORU, WE HAVE TO GET TO RIKO NOW.
HUH?
TP
TWO HAVE ALREADY BEEN EXORCISED.
THIRTY MILLION...

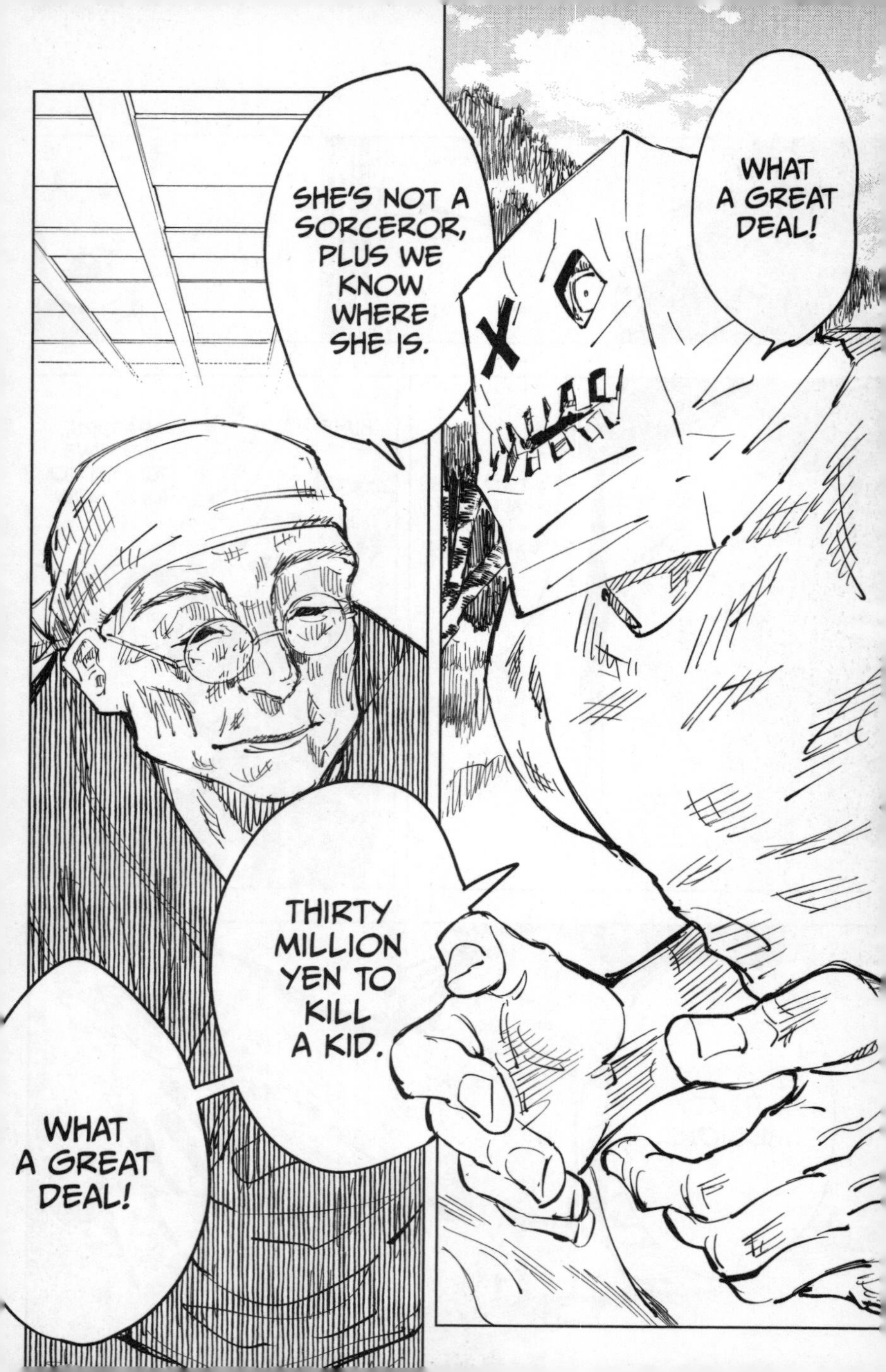
WHAT A GREAT DEAL!
SHE'S NOT A SORCEROR, PLUS WE KNOW WHERE SHE IS.
THIRTY MILLION YEN TO KILL A KID.
WHAT A GREAT DEAL!

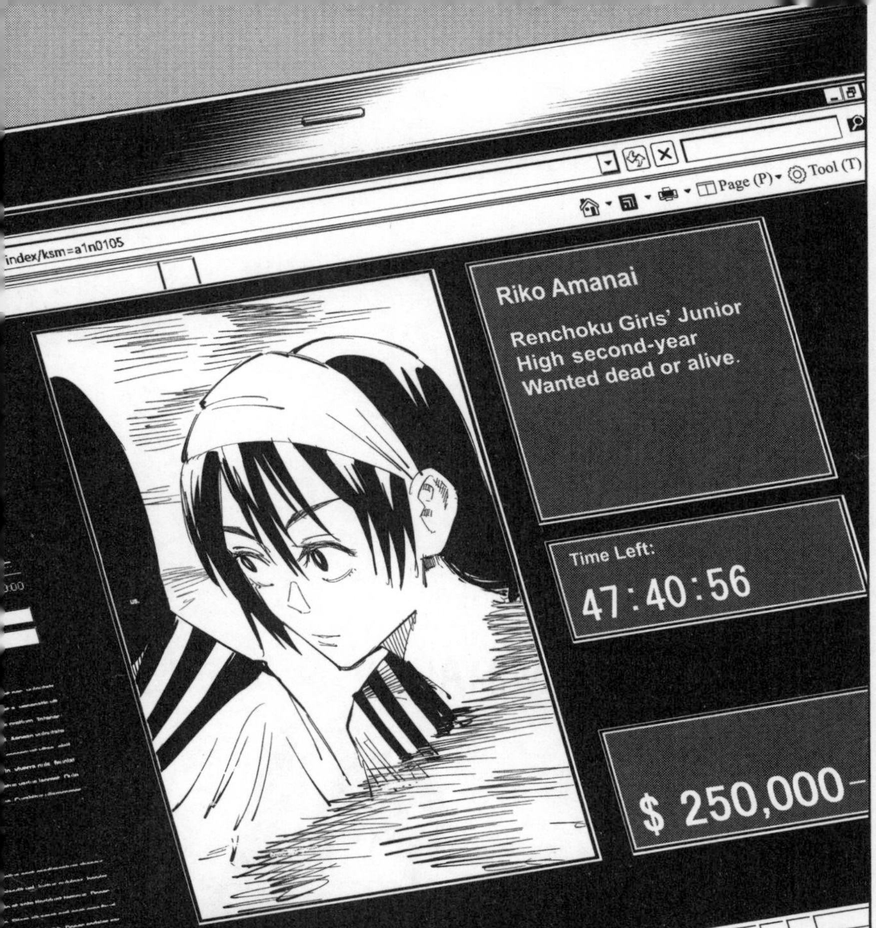
Page (P)
Tool (T)
index/ksm=a1n0105
Riko Amanai
Renchoku Girls' Junior High second-year
Wanted dead or alive.
Time Left:
47:40:56
$ 250,000
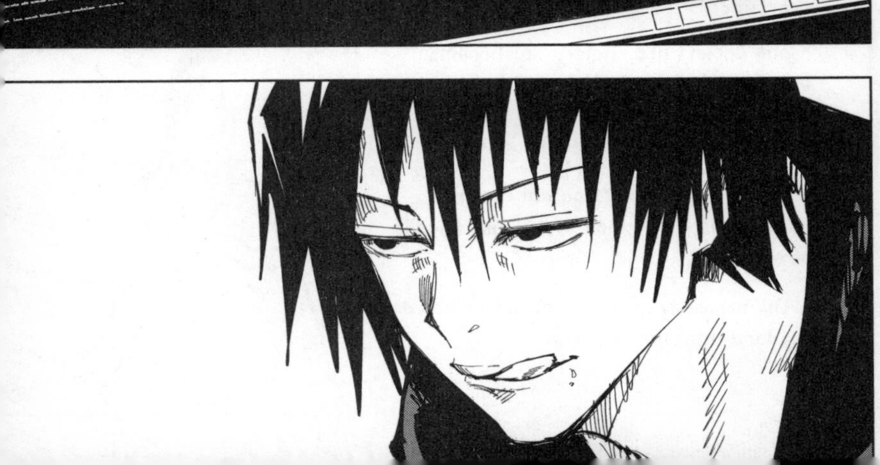

RIKO AMANAI

• Probably a second-year in
Junior High.

• Her parents died in a
car accident when she was
four. She's been with Kuroi
ever since.

• She doesn't like shiitake mushrooms,
but Kuroi has been chopping them up
and secretly mixing them into Riko's
food. She's actually eaten a ton.

• She's not allowed to go out much,
so she's happiest when seeing her friends
at school.

• The necessity of her hairband troubled
Akutami until the very end.

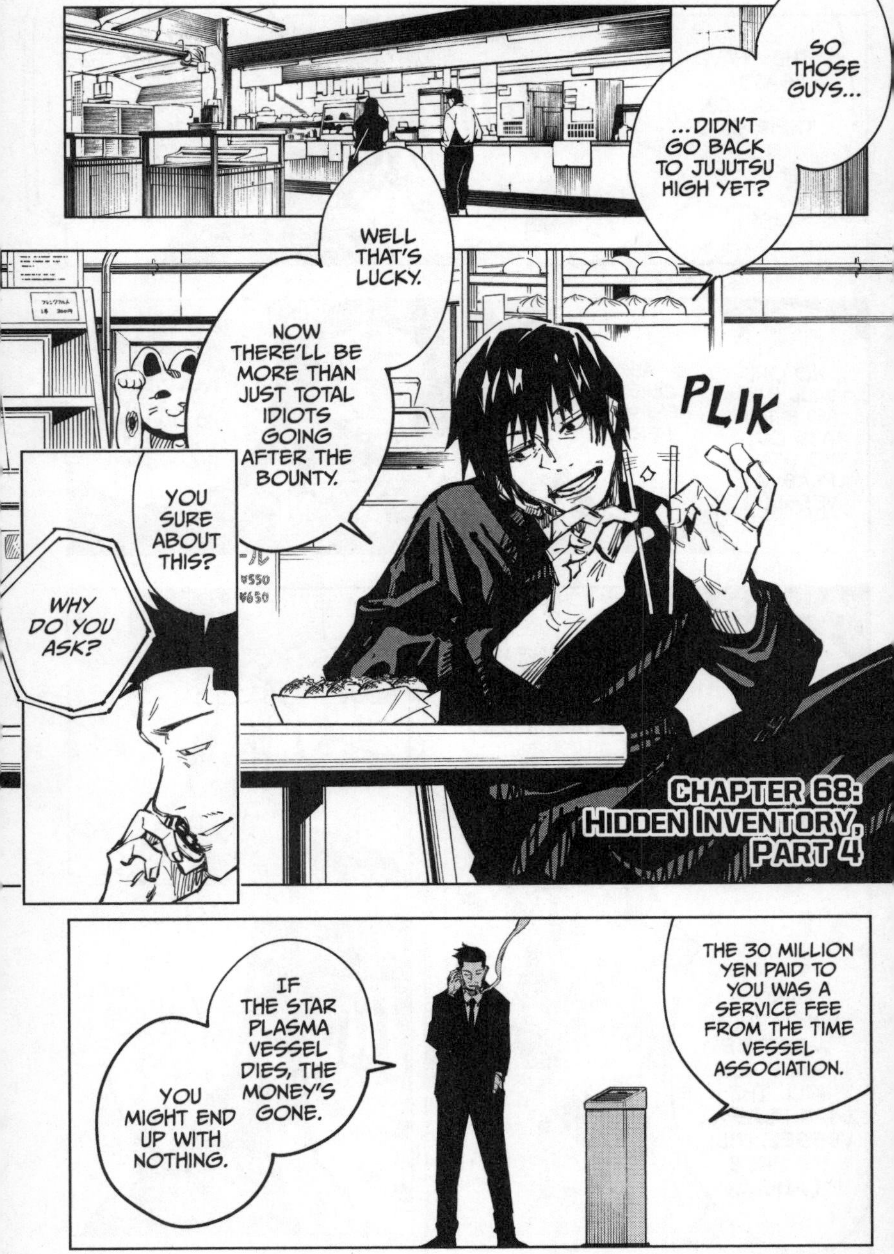
SO THOSE GUYS...
...DIDN'T GO BACK TO JUJUTSU HIGH YET?
WELL THAT'S LUCKY.
NOW THERE'LL BE MORE THAN JUST TOTAL IDIOTS GOING AFTER THE BOUNTY.
PLIK
¥550
¥650
YOU SURE ABOUT THIS?
WHY DO YOU ASK?
CHAPTER 68: HIDDEN INVENTORY, PART 4
THE 30 MILLION YEN PAID TO YOU WAS A SERVICE FEE FROM THE TIME VESSEL ASSOCIATION.
IF THE STAR PLASMA VESSEL DIES, THE MONEY'S GONE.
YOU MIGHT END UP WITH NOTHING.

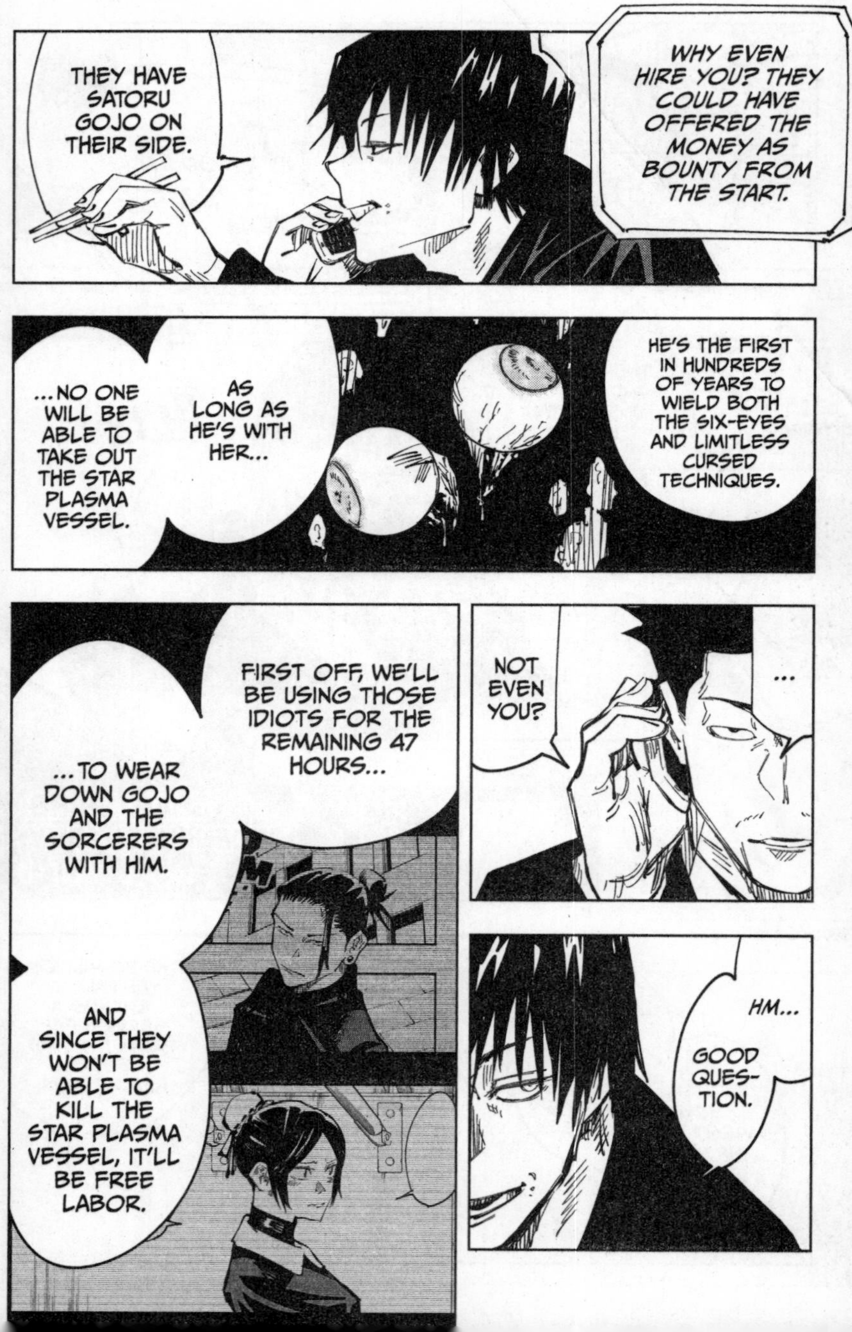
WHY EVEN HIRE YOU? THEY COULD HAVE OFFERED THE MONEY AS BOUNTY FROM THE START.
THEY HAVE SATORU GOJO ON THEIR SIDE.
HE'S THE FIRST IN HUNDREDS OF YEARS TO WIELD BOTH THE SIX-EYES AND LIMITLESS CURSED TECHNIQUES.
AS LONG AS HE'S WITH HER...
...NO ONE WILL BE ABLE TO TAKE OUT THE STAR PLASMA VESSEL.
...
NOT EVEN YOU?
HM...
GOOD QUES-TION.
FIRST OFF, WE'LL BE USING THOSE IDIOTS FOR THE REMAINING 47 HOURS...
...TO WEAR DOWN GOJO AND THE SORCERERS WITH HIM.
AND SINCE THEY WON'T BE ABLE TO KILL THE STAR PLASMA VESSEL, IT'LL BE FREE LABOR.

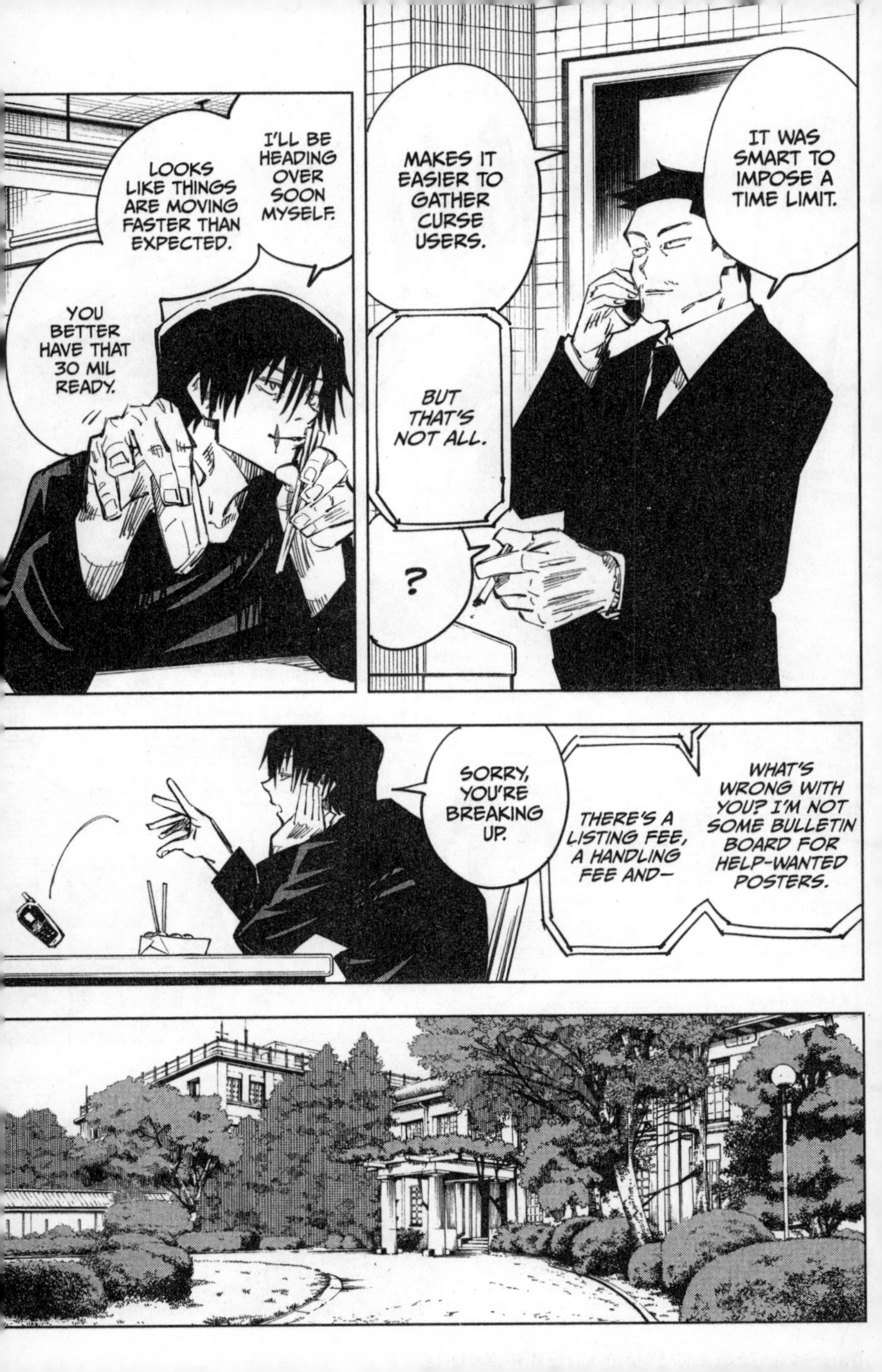
IT WAS SMART TO IMPOSE A TIME LIMIT.
MAKES IT EASIER TO GATHER CURSE USERS.
BUT THAT'S NOT ALL.
?
I'LL BE HEADING OVER SOON MYSELF.
LOOKS LIKE THINGS ARE MOVING FASTER THAN EXPECTED.
YOU BETTER HAVE THAT 30 MIL READY.
WHAT'S WRONG WITH YOU? I'M NOT SOME BULLETIN BOARD FOR HELP-WANTED POSTERS.
THERE'S A LISTING FEE, A HANDLING FEE AND—
SORRY, YOU'RE BREAKING UP.

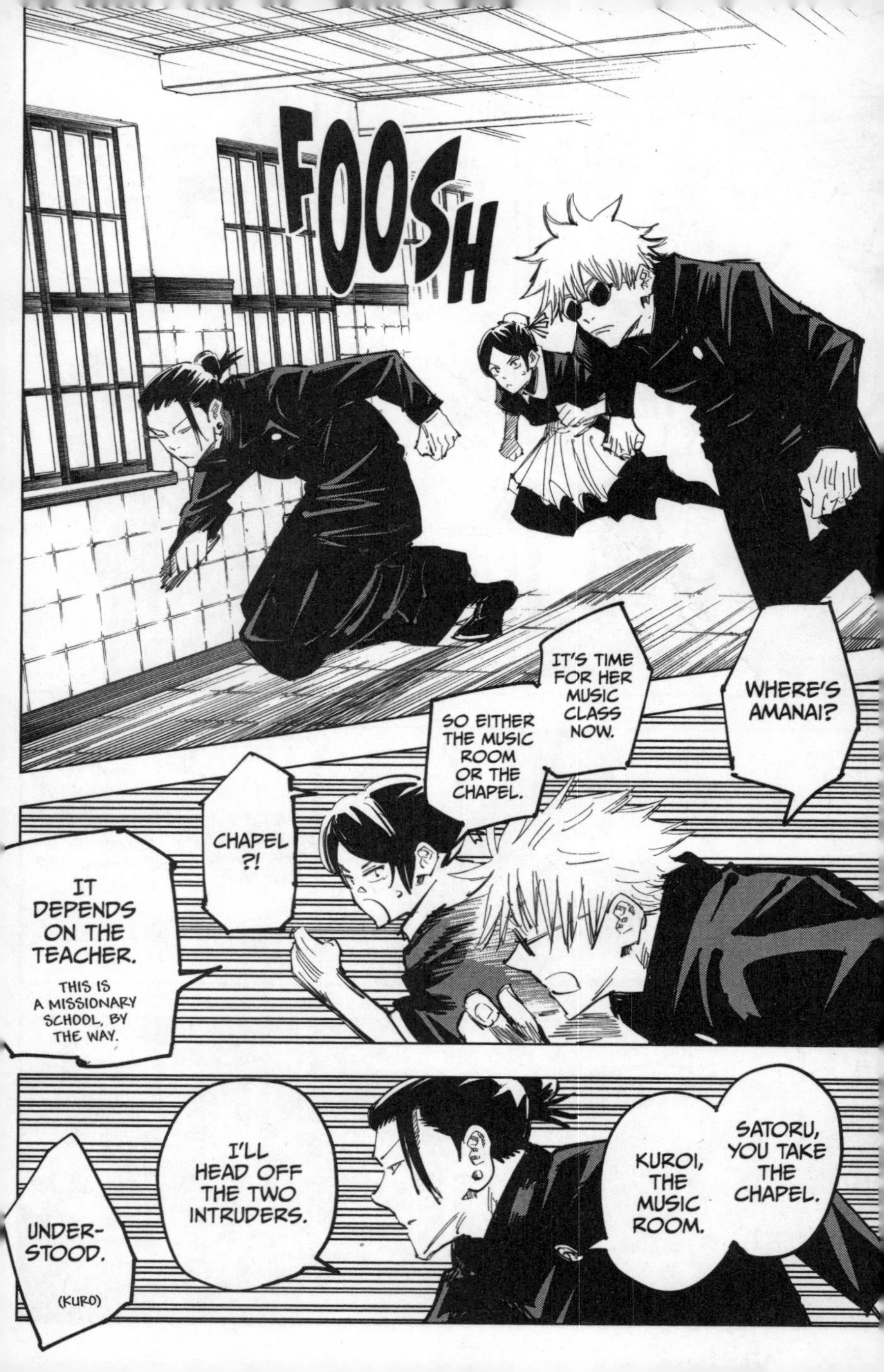
FOOSH
WHERE'S AMANAI?
IT'S TIME FOR HER MUSIC CLASS NOW.
SO EITHER THE MUSIC ROOM OR THE CHAPEL.
CHAPEL ?!
IT DEPENDS ON THE TEACHER.
THIS IS A MISSIONARY SCHOOL, BY THE WAY.
SATORU, YOU TAKE THE CHAPEL.
KUROI, THE MUSIC ROOM.
I'LL HEAD OFF THE TWO INTRUDERS.
UNDER-STOOD.
(KURO)

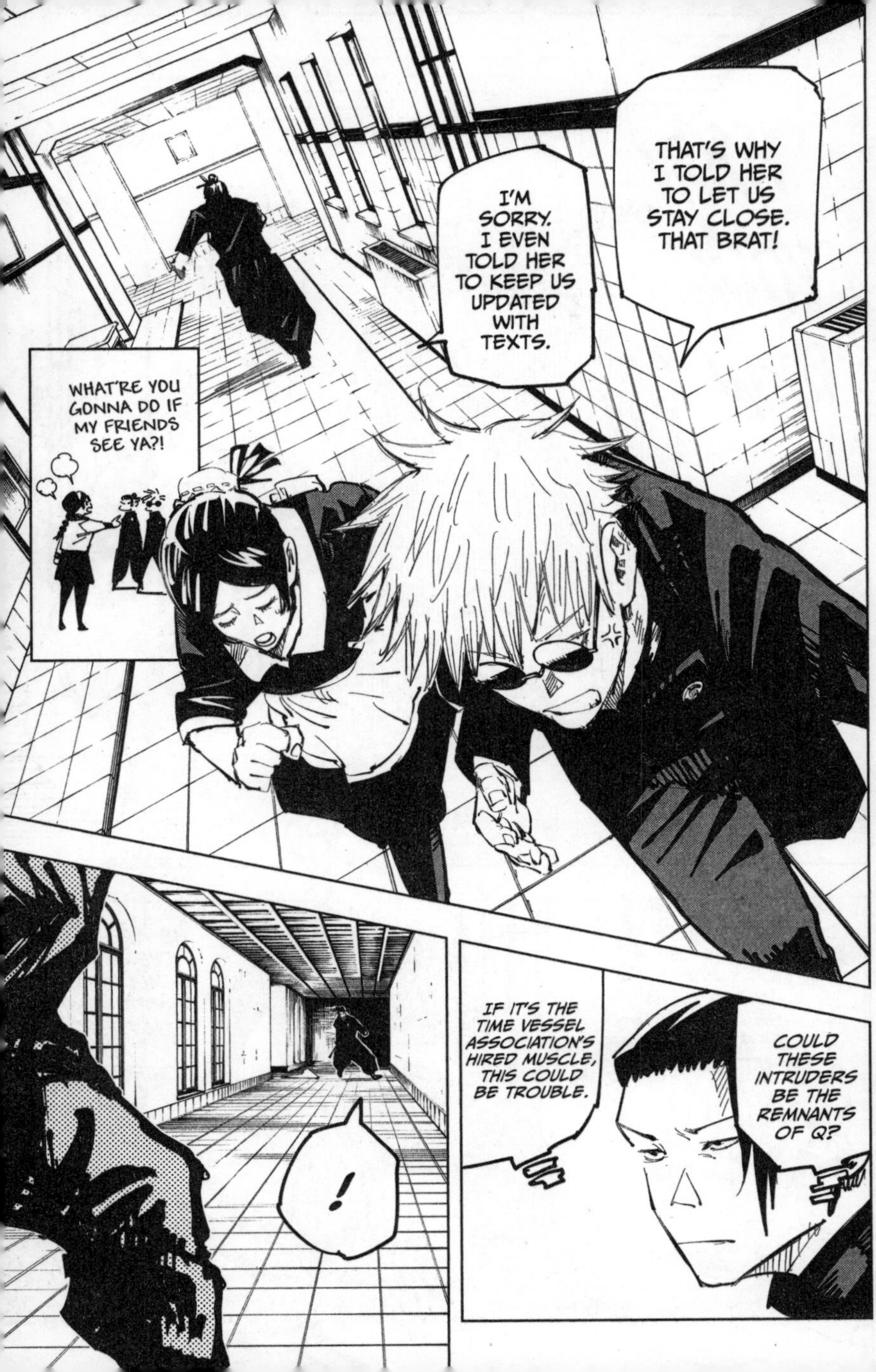
THAT'S WHY I TOLD HER TO LET US STAY CLOSE. THAT BRAT!
I'M SORRY. I EVEN TOLD HER TO KEEP US UPDATED WITH TEXTS.
WHAT'RE YOU GONNA DO IF MY FRIENDS SEE YA?!
COULD THESE INTRUDERS BE THE REMNANTS OF Q?
IF IT'S THE TIME VESSEL ASSOCIATION'S HIRED MUSCLE, THIS COULD BE TROUBLE.
!

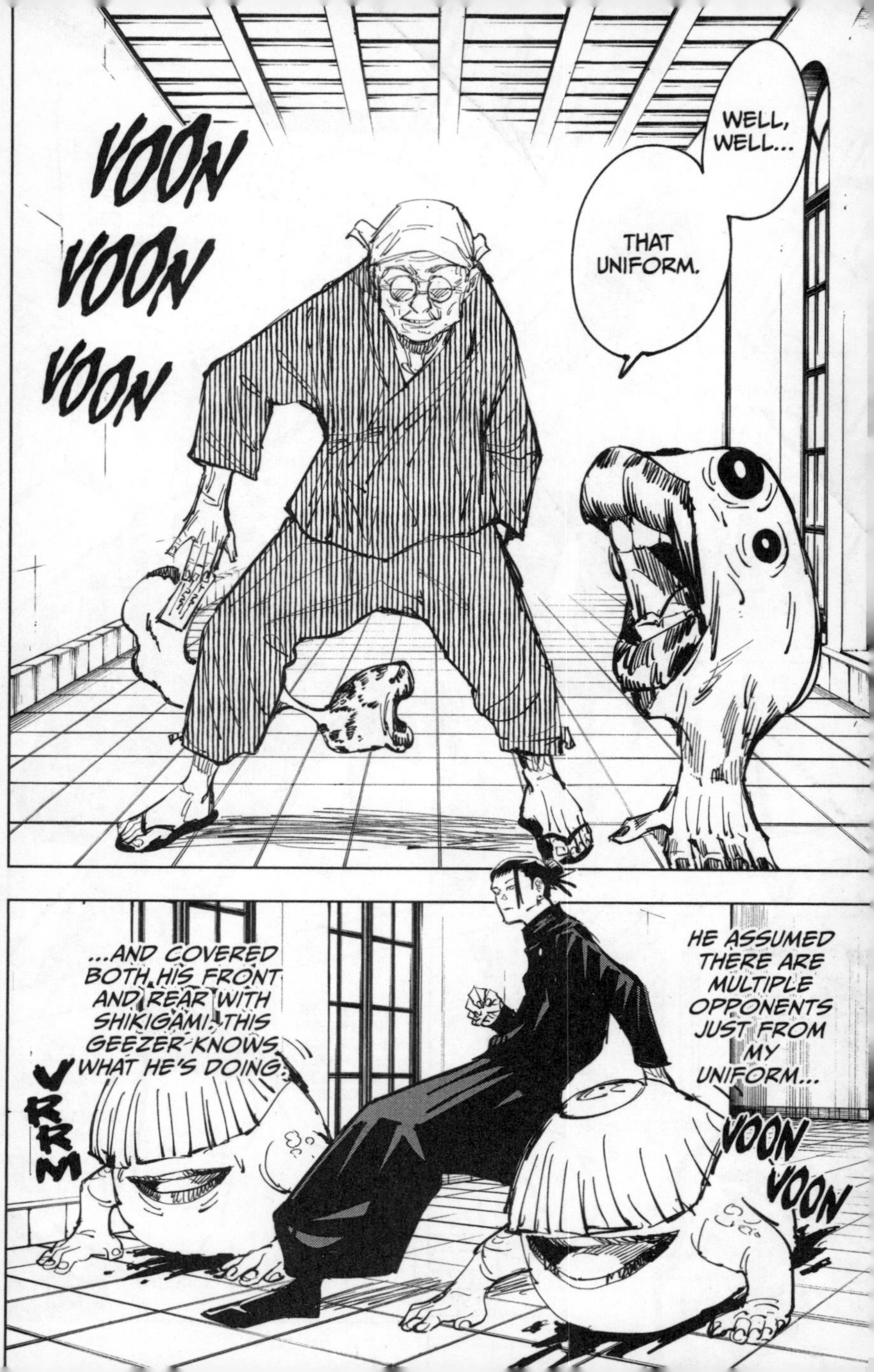
WELL, WELL...
THAT UNIFORM.
VOON VOON VOON
HE ASSUMED THERE ARE MULTIPLE OPPONENTS JUST FROM MY UNIFORM...
...AND COVERED BOTH HIS FRONT AND REAR WITH SHIKIGAMI. THIS GEEZER KNOWS WHAT HE'S DOING.
VOON VOON
VRRM

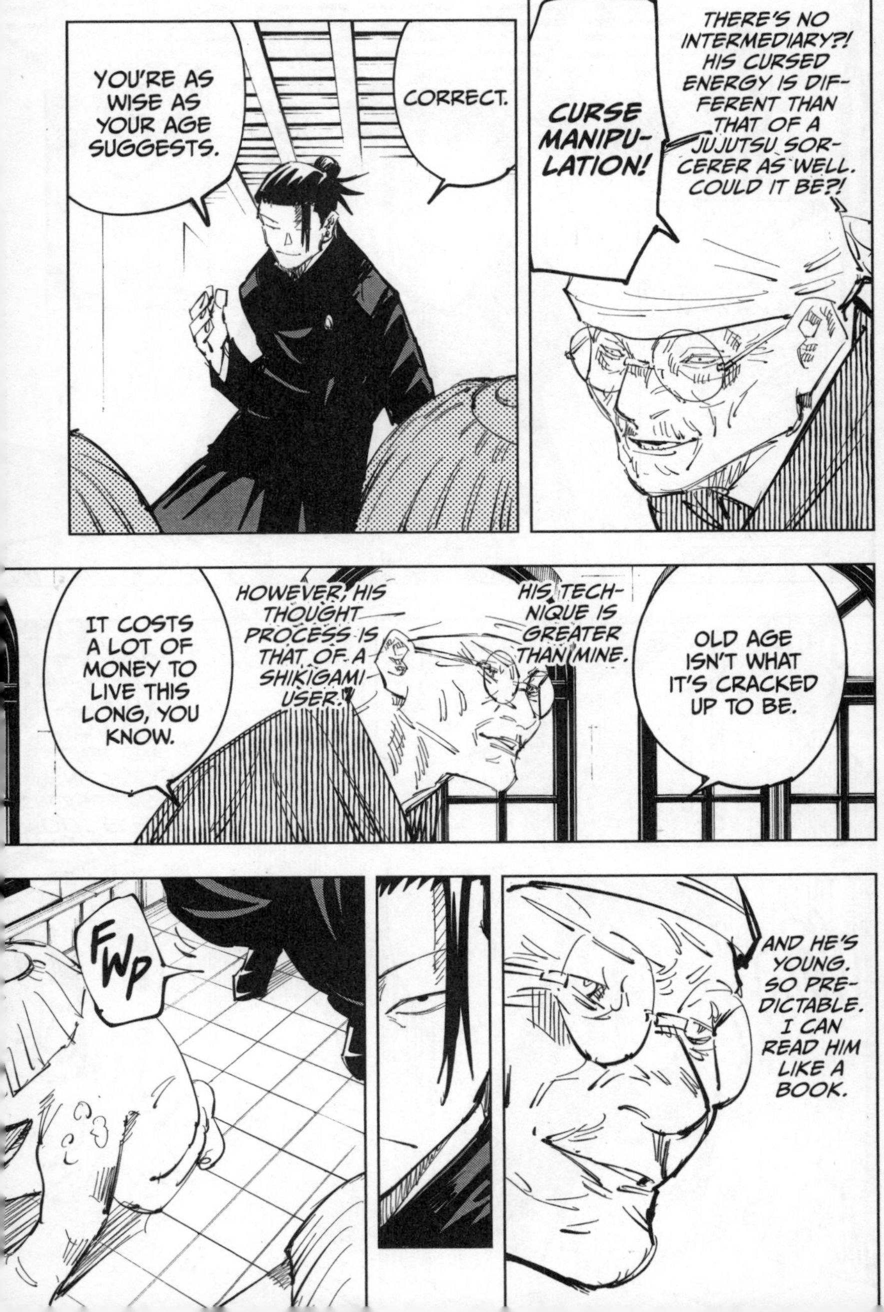
THERE'S NO INTERMEDIARY?! HIS CURSED ENERGY IS DIFFERENT THAN THAT OF A JUJUTSU SORCERER AS WELL. COULD IT BE?!
CURSE MANIPULATION!
CORRECT.
YOU'RE AS WISE AS YOUR AGE SUGGESTS.
OLD AGE ISN'T WHAT IT'S CRACKED UP TO BE.
HIS TECHNIQUE IS GREATER THAN MINE.
HOWEVER, HIS THOUGHT PROCESS IS THAT OF A SHIKIGAMI USER.
IT COSTS A LOT OF MONEY TO LIVE THIS LONG, YOU KNOW.
AND HE'S YOUNG. SO PREDICTABLE. I CAN READ HIM LIKE A BOOK.
FWP

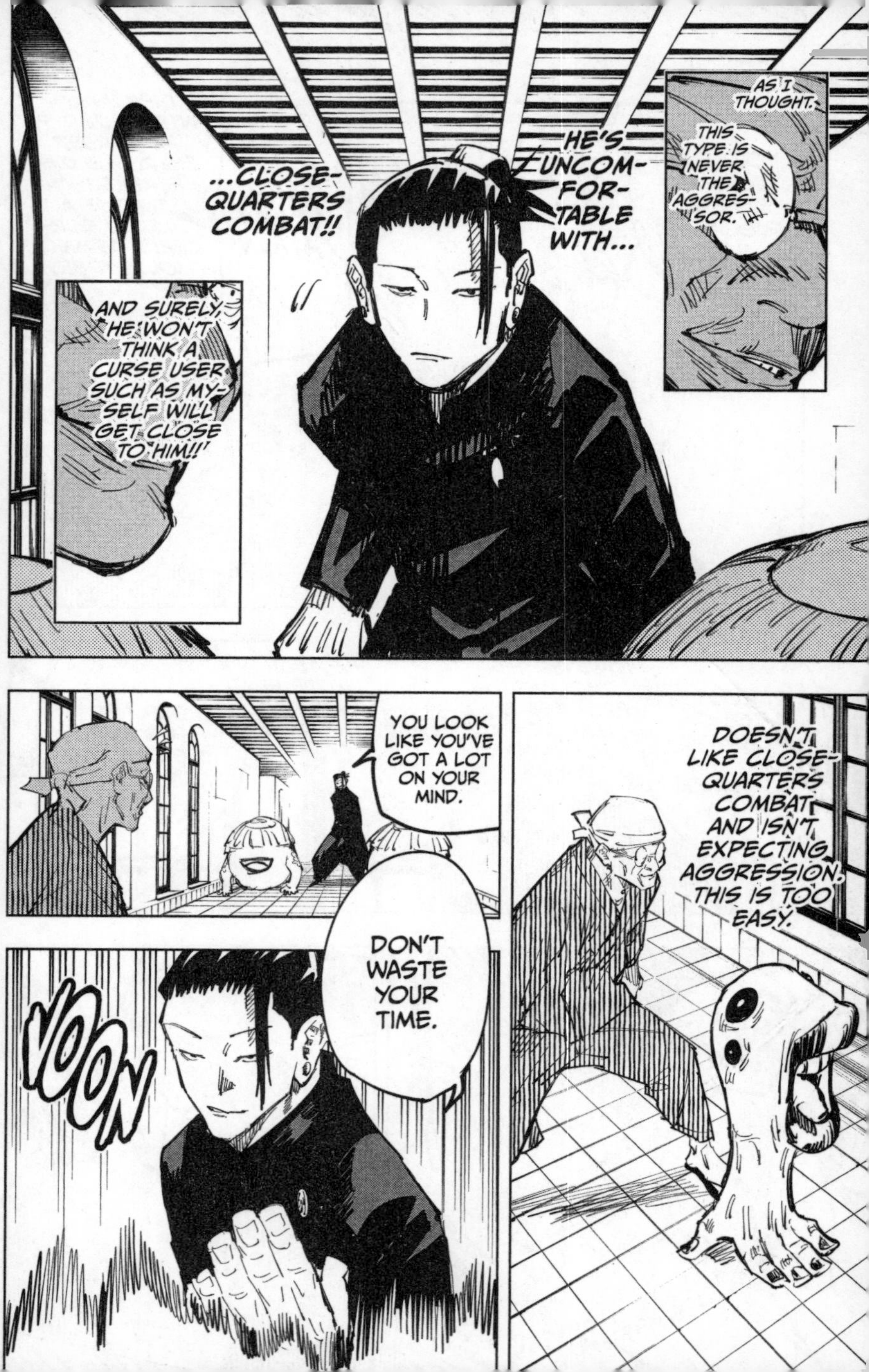
AS I THOUGHT.
THIS TYPE IS NEVER THE AGGRES-SOR.
HE'S UNCOM-FOR-TABLE WITH...
...CLOSE-QUARTERS COMBAT!!
AND SURELY, HE WON'T THINK A CURSE USER SUCH AS MY-SELF WILL GET CLOSE TO HIM!!
DOESN'T LIKE CLOSE-QUARTERS COMBAT AND ISN'T EXPECTING AGGRESSION. THIS IS TOO EASY.
YOU LOOK LIKE YOU'VE GOT A LOT ON YOUR MIND.
DON'T WASTE YOUR TIME.
VOOON

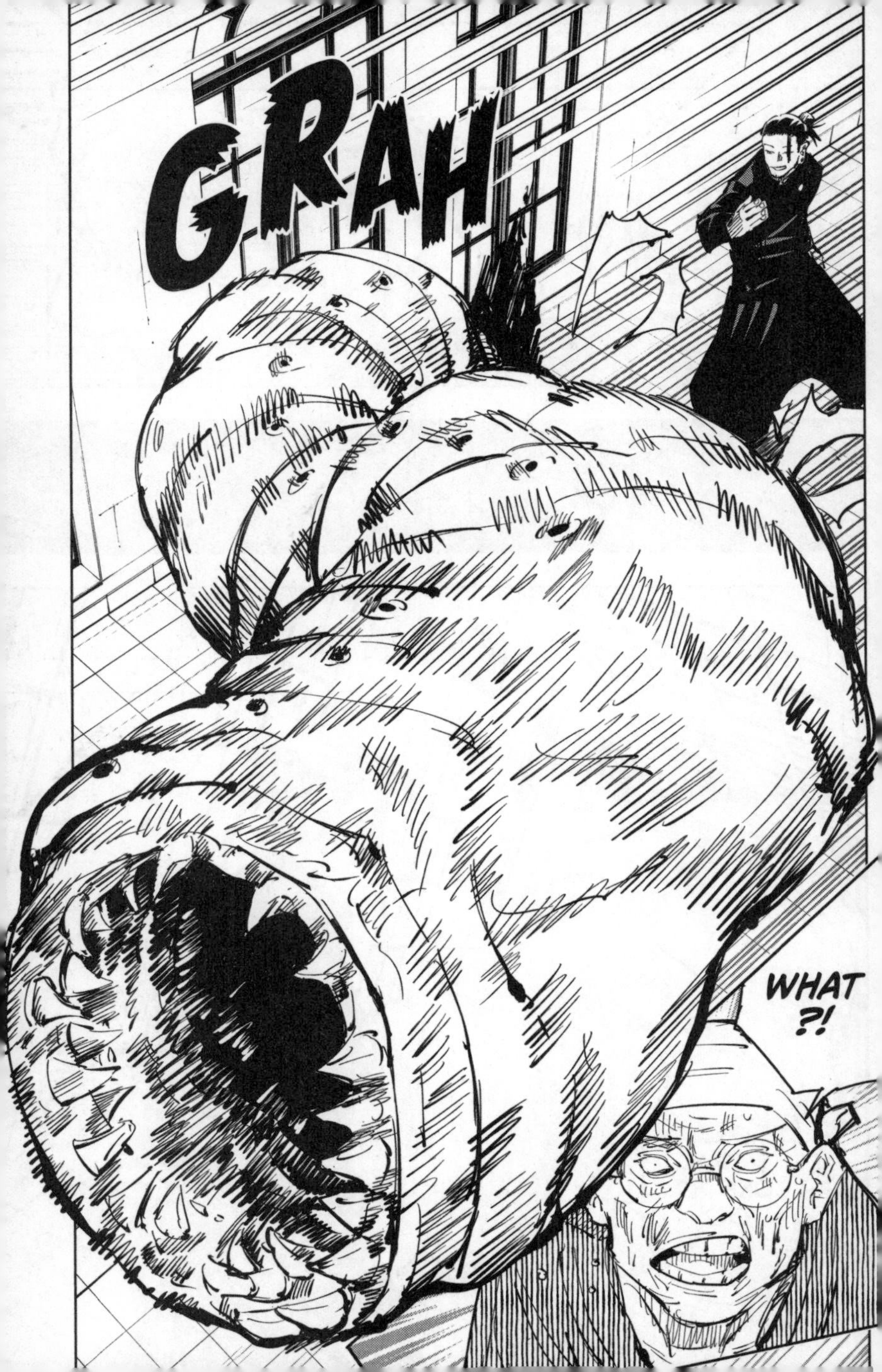
GRAH
WHAT ?!

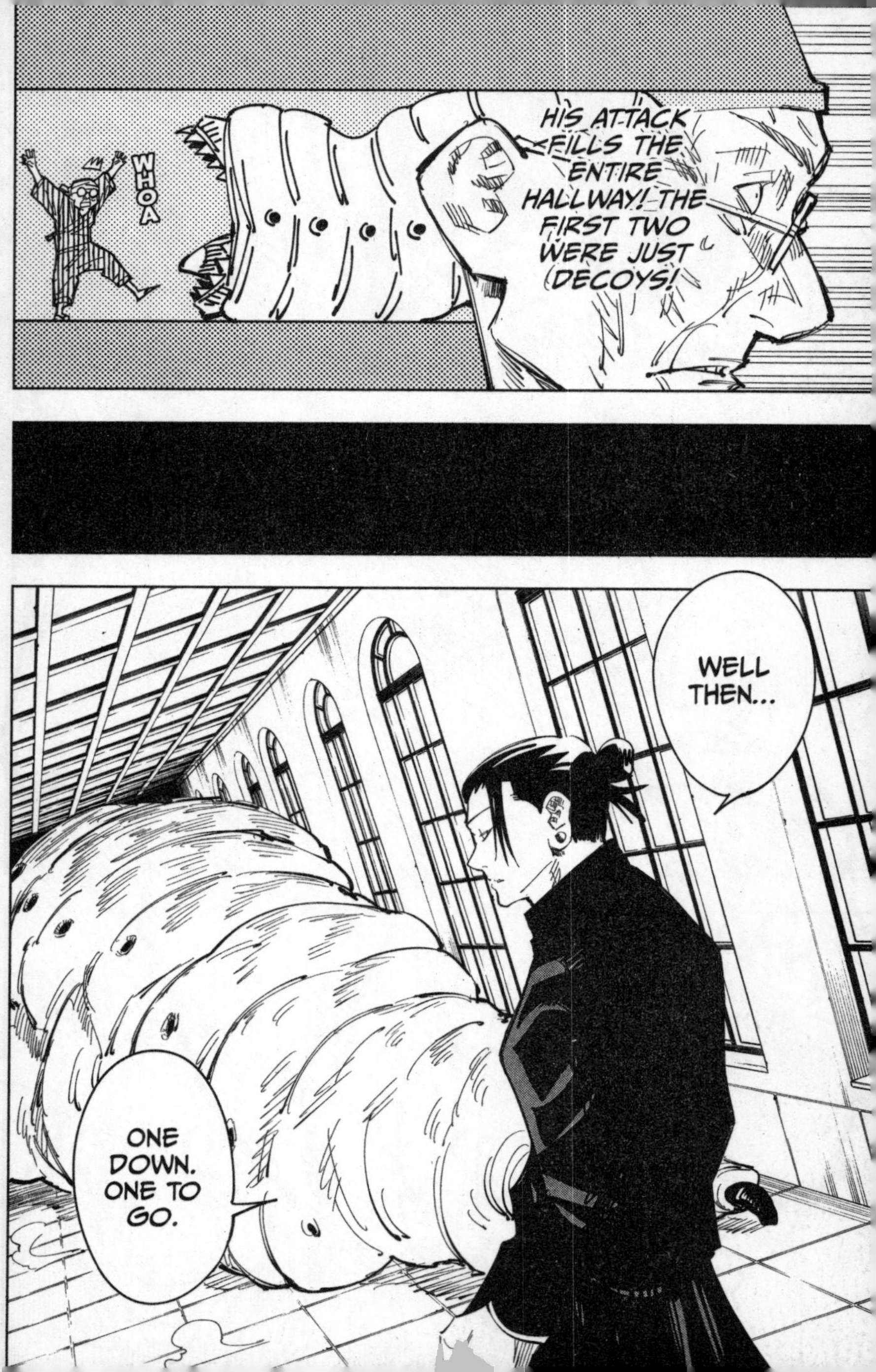
HIS ATTACK FILLS THE ENTIRE HALLWAY! THE FIRST TWO WERE JUST DECOYS!
WHOA
WELL THEN...
ONE DOWN. ONE TO GO.

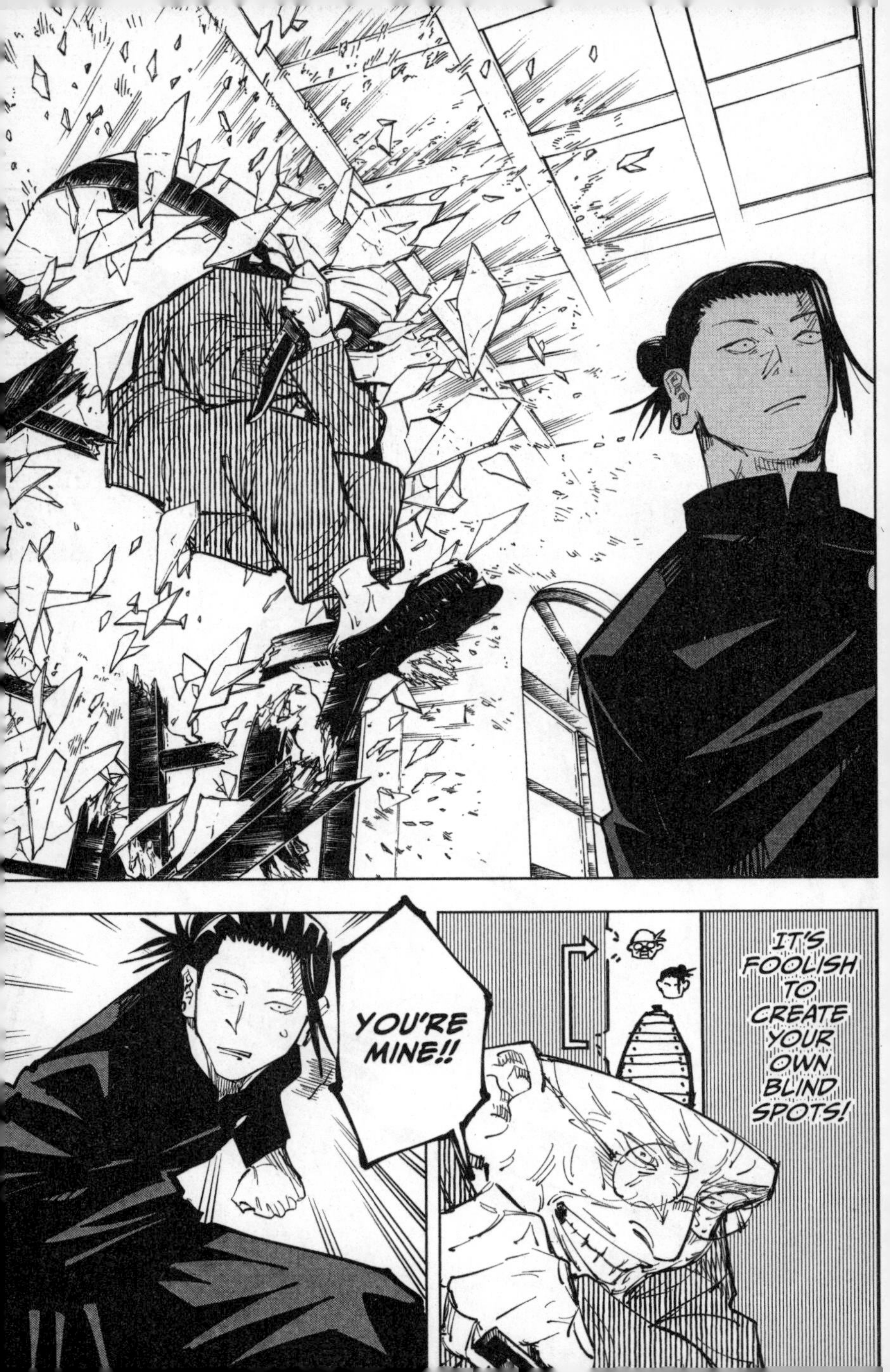
IT'S FOOLISH TO CREATE YOUR OWN BLIND SPOTS!
YOU'RE MINE!!

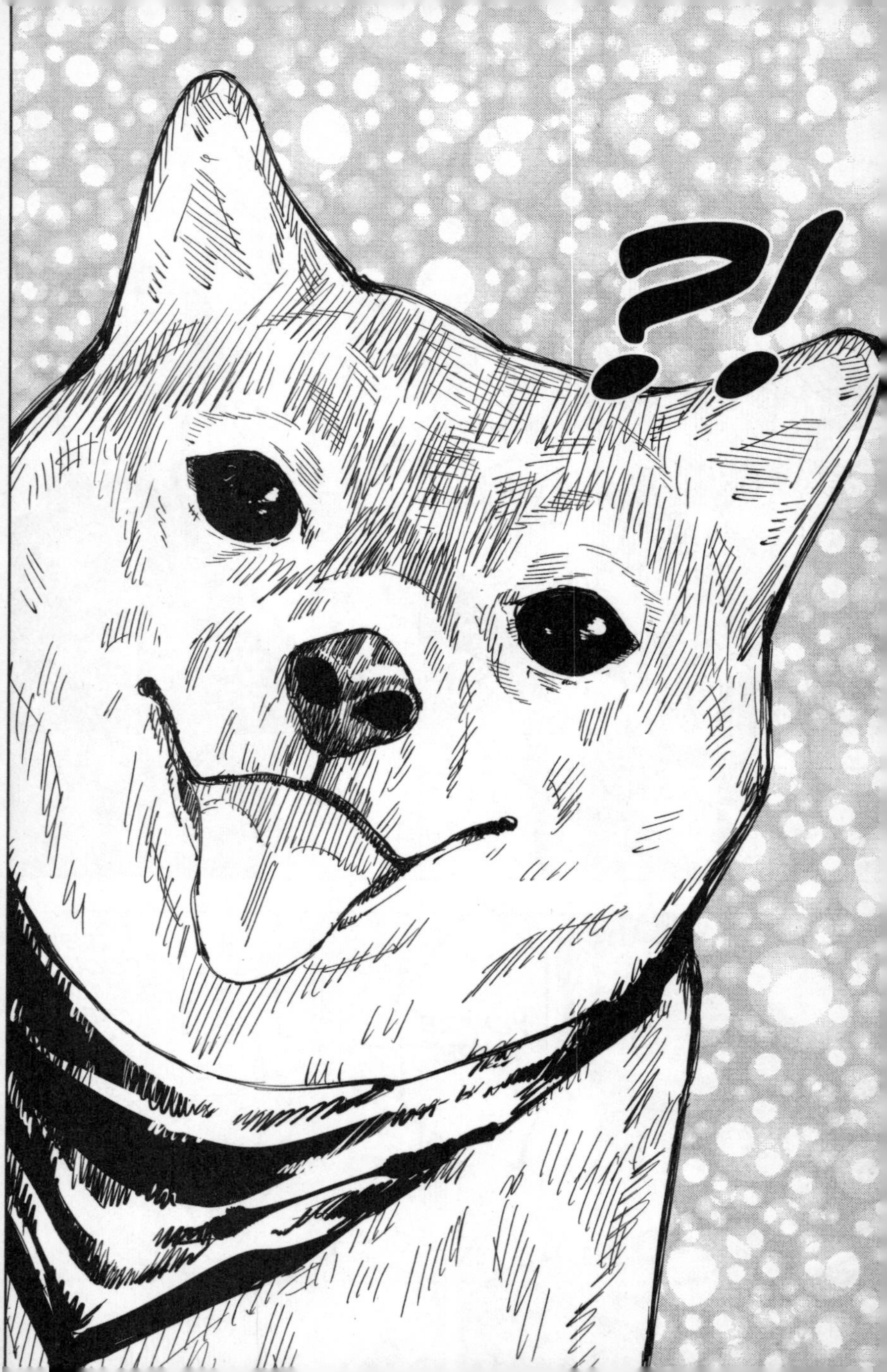
?!

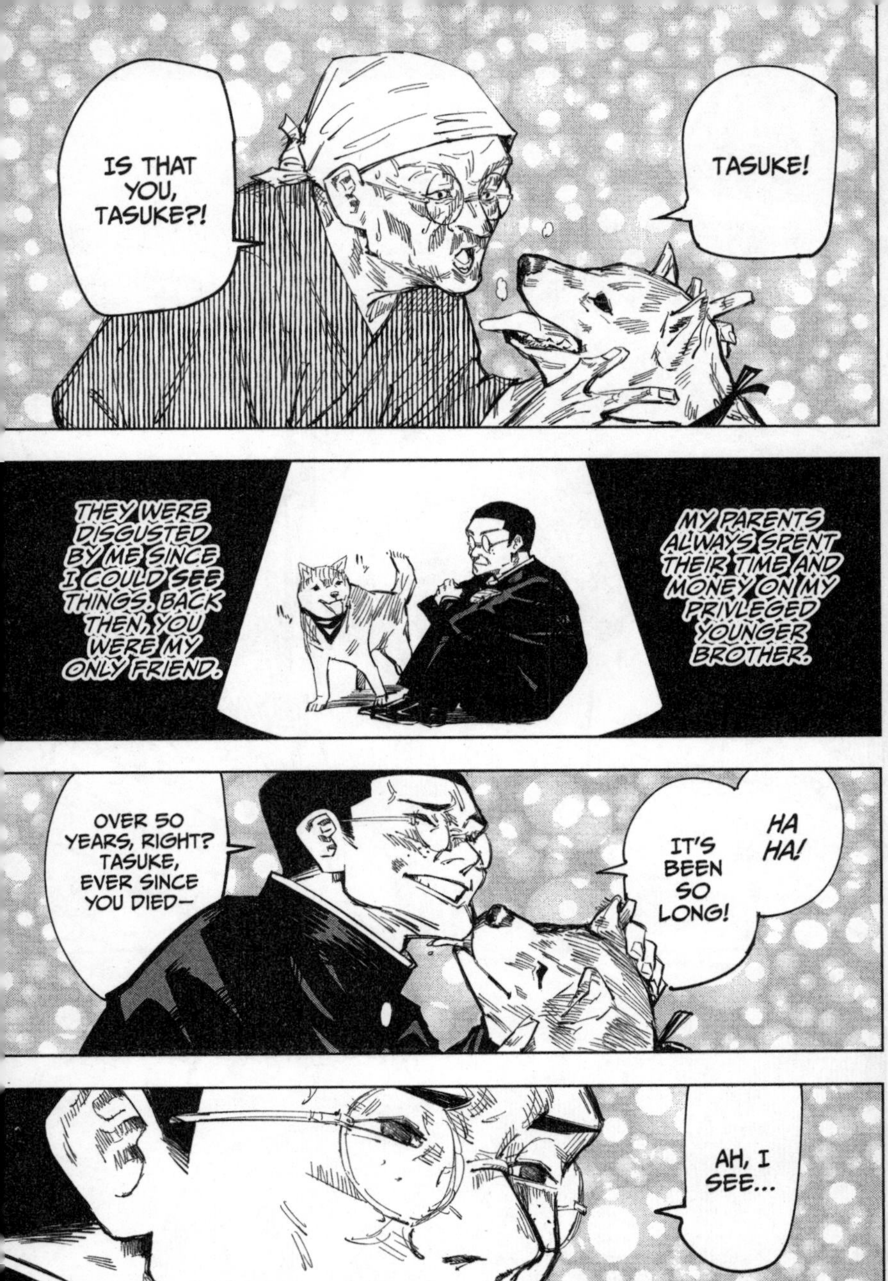
TASUKE!
IS THAT YOU, TASUKE?!
MY PARENTS ALWAYS SPENT THEIR TIME AND MONEY ON MY PRIVLEGED YOUNGER BROTHER.
THEY WERE DISGUSTED BY ME SINCE I COULD SEE THINGS. BACK THEN, YOU WERE MY ONLY FRIEND.
HA HA!
IT'S BEEN SO LONG!
OVER 50 YEARS, RIGHT? TASUKE, EVER SINCE YOU DIED—
AH, I SEE...

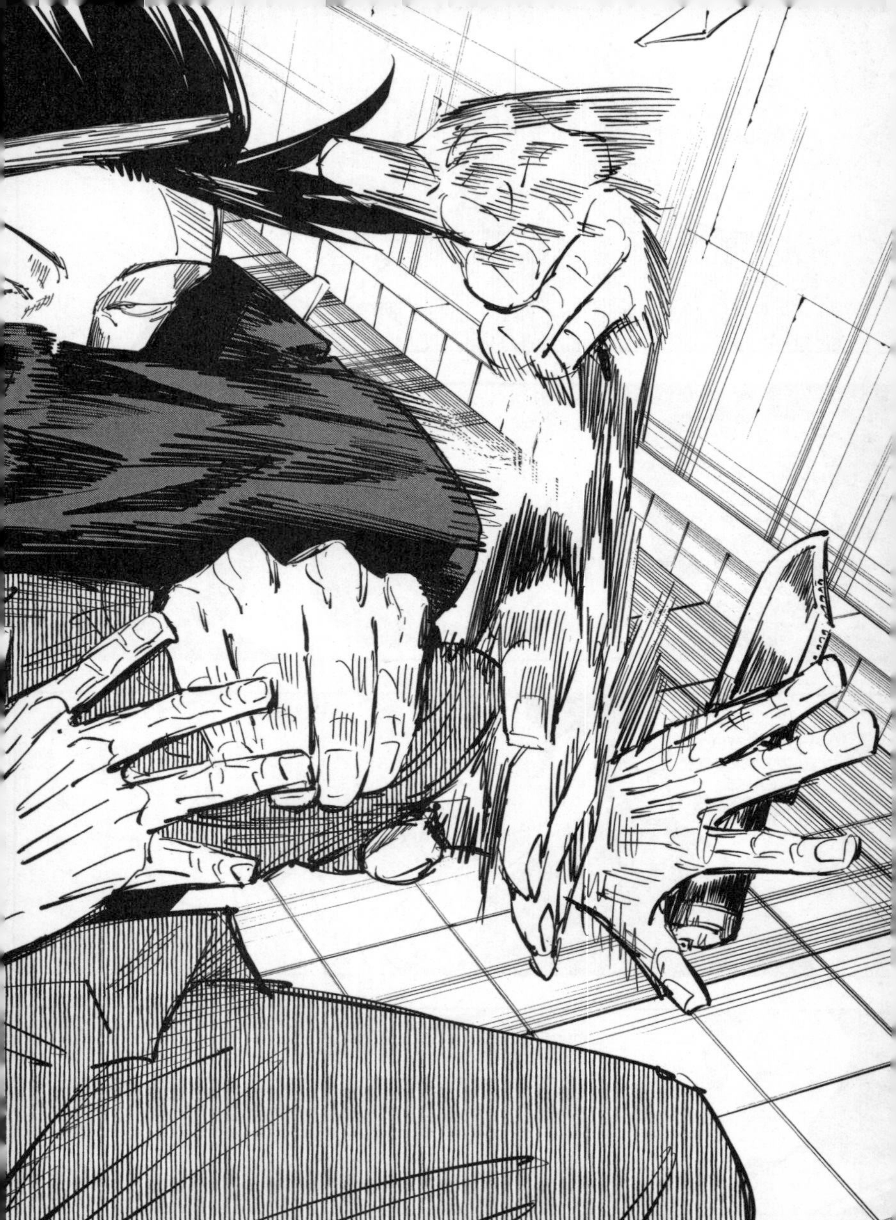

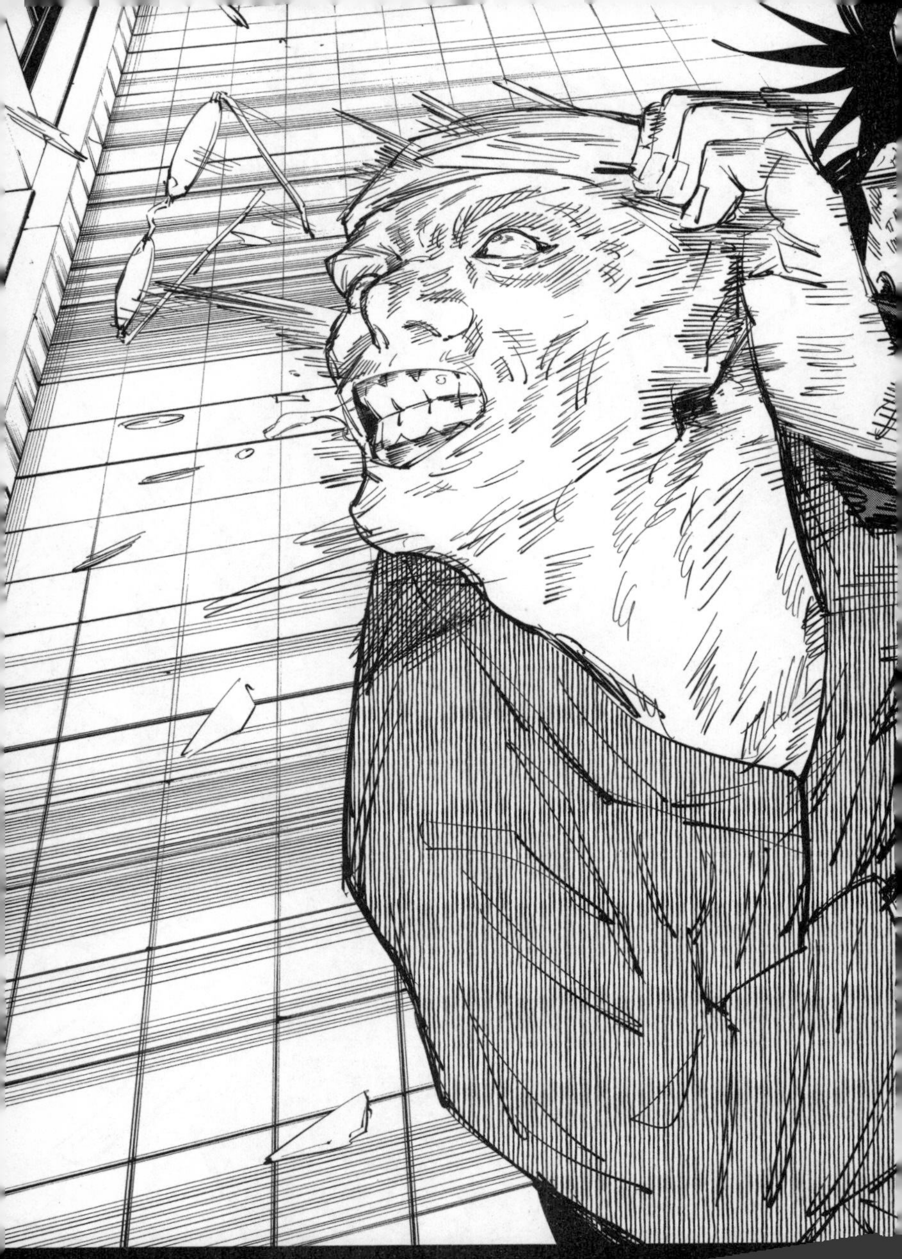

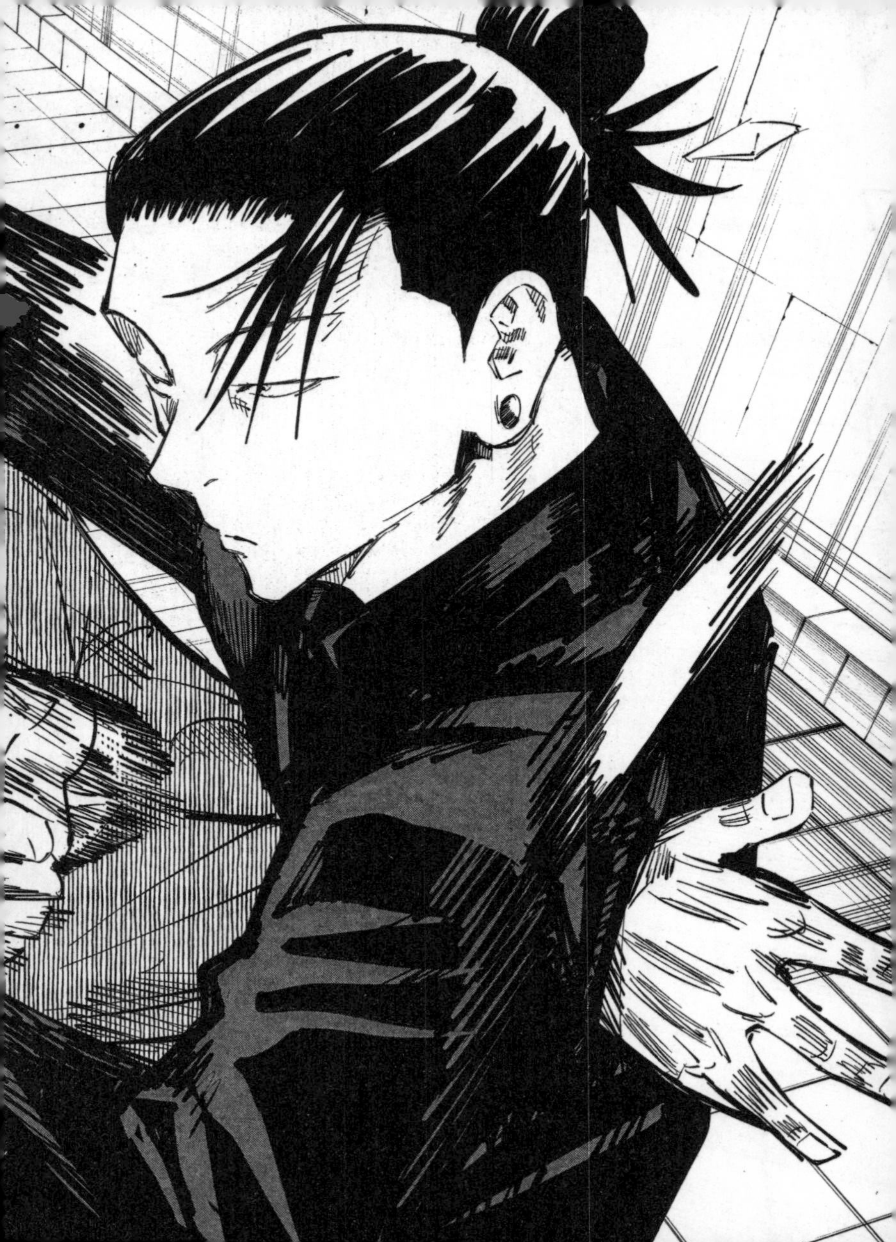

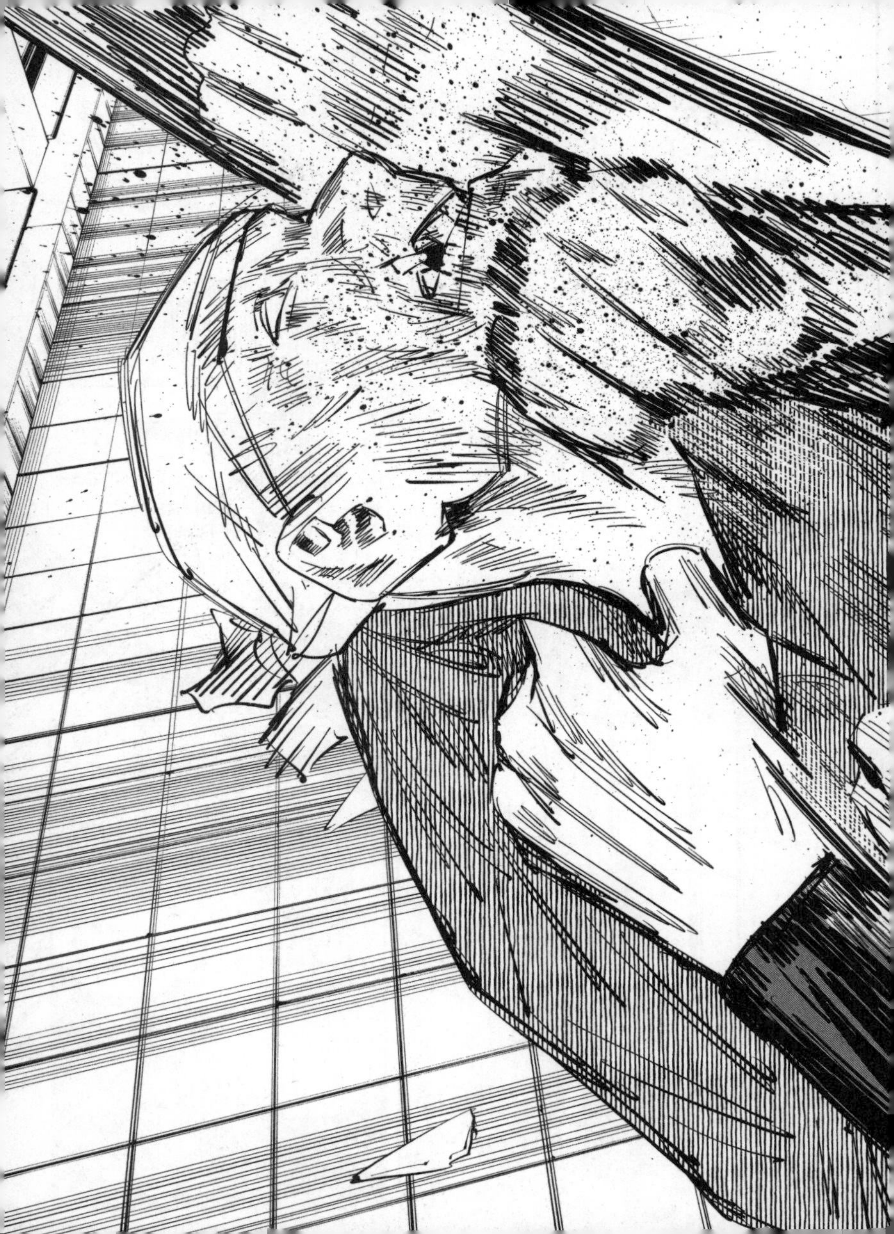

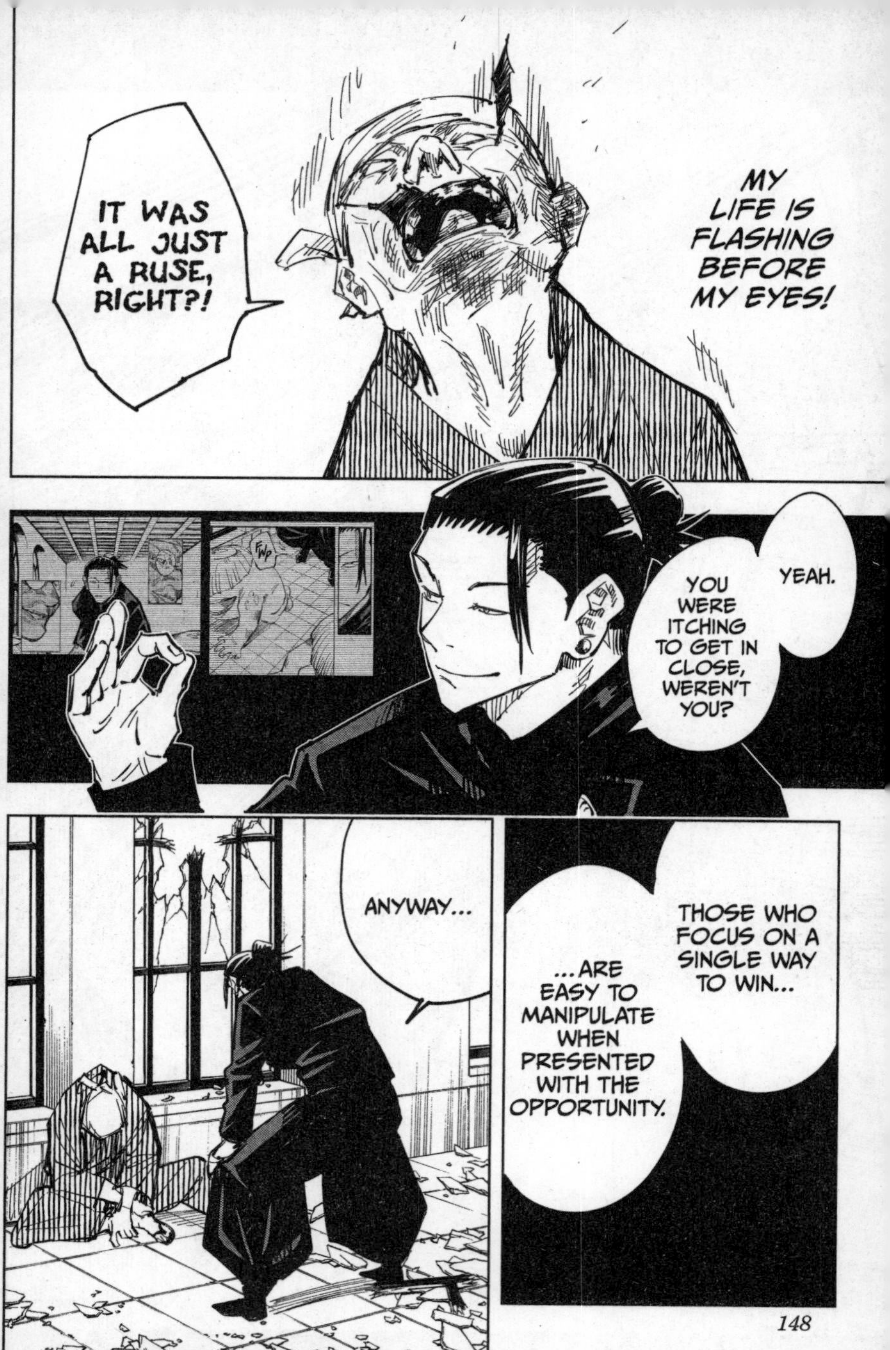
MY LIFE IS FLASHING BEFORE MY EYES!
IT WAS ALL JUST A RUSE, RIGHT?!
YEAH.
YOU WERE ITCHING TO GET IN CLOSE, WEREN'T YOU?
THOSE WHO FOCUS ON A SINGLE WAY TO WIN...
...ARE EASY TO MANIPULATE WHEN PRESENTED WITH THE OPPORTUNITY.
ANYWAY...

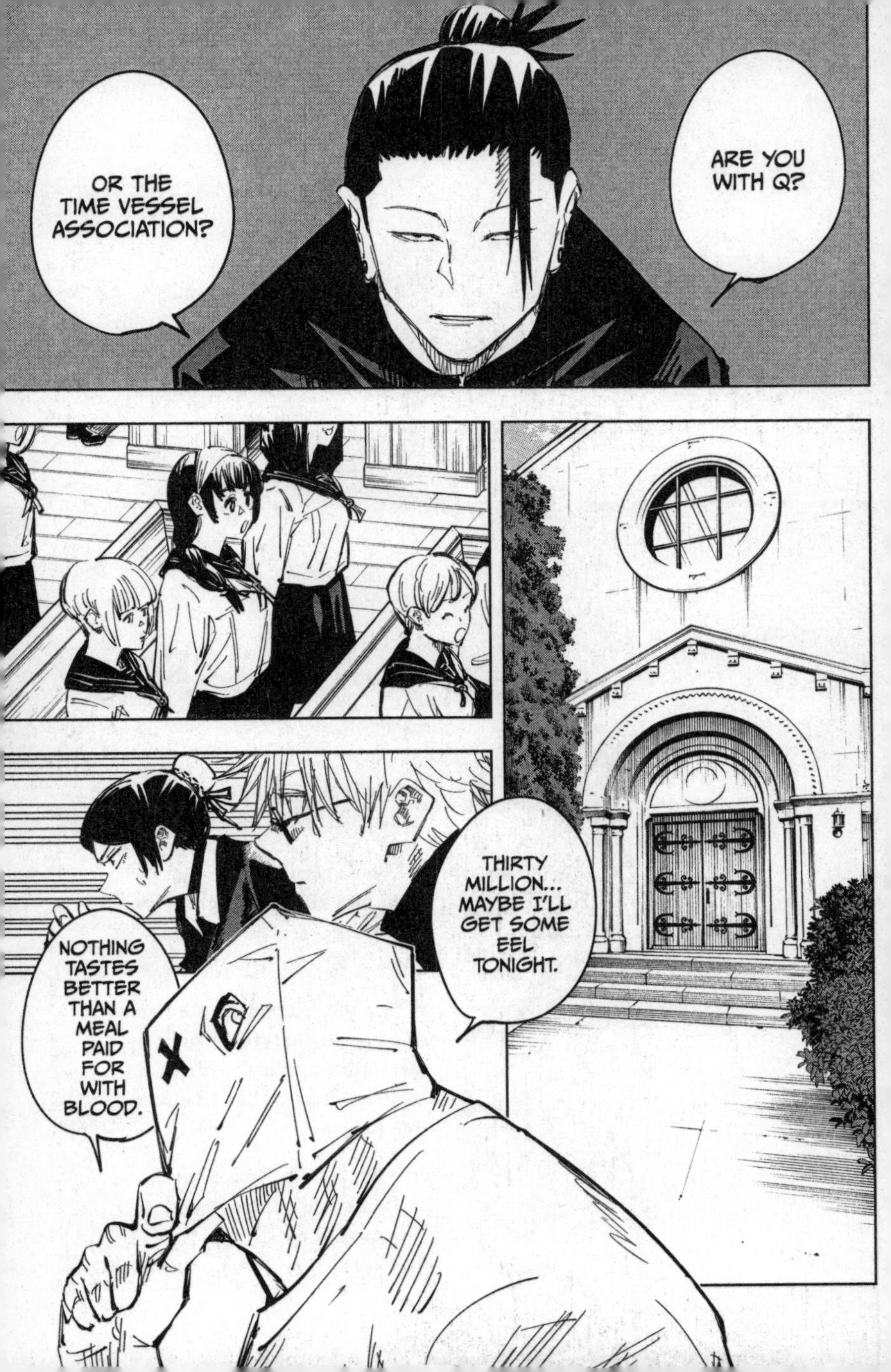
ARE YOU WITH Q?
OR THE TIME VESSEL ASSOCIATION?
THIRTY MILLION... MAYBE I'LL GET SOME EEL TONIGHT.
NOTHING TASTES BETTER THAN A MEAL PAID FOR WITH BLOOD.

MISATO KUROI
(31 YEARS OLD)

• She looks young, so she's often asked if she's a student.

• The Kuroi family is part of a long line of aides to the Star Plasma Vessel. In defiance, Misato left for a junior college.

• She was planning on entering the civilian workforce but was drawn back into the life of an aide because of her fondness for Riko.

• Plays with Riko a lot at home and is supergood at *Mario Kart*.

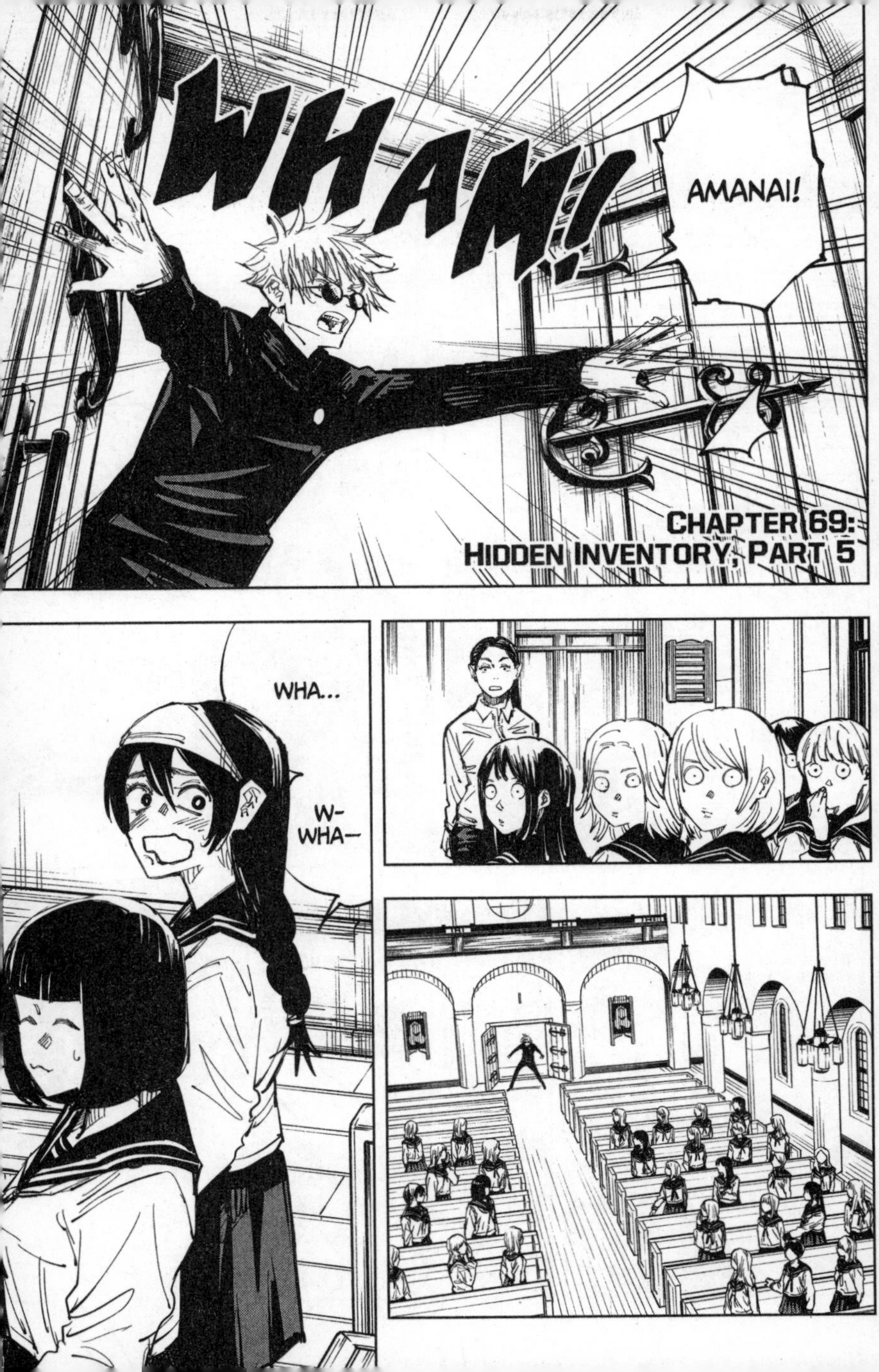
WHAM!!
AMANAI!
CHAPTER 69:
HIDDEN INVENTORY, PART 5
WHA...
W-
WHA—

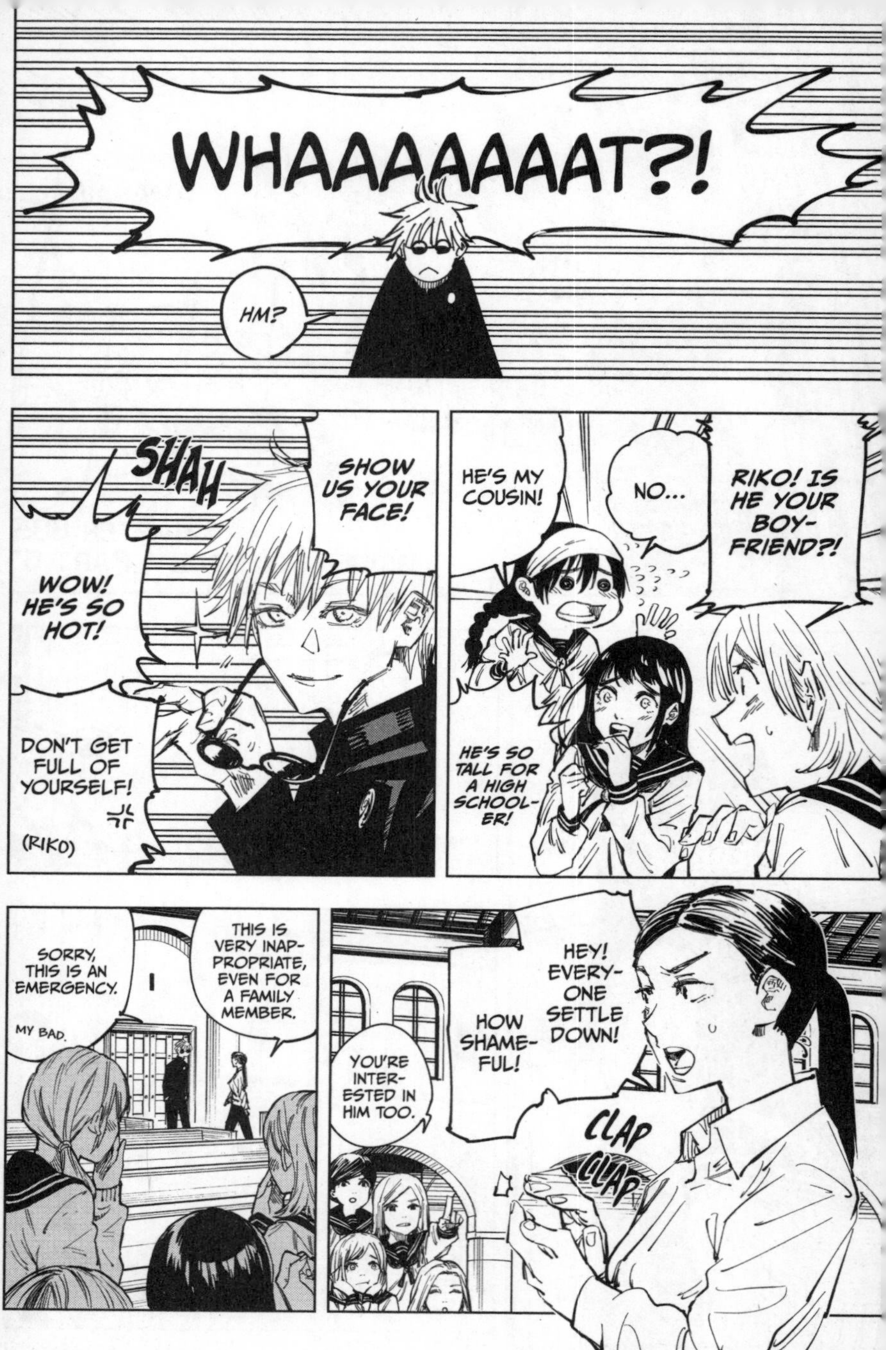
WHAAAAAAAT?!
HM?
RIKO! IS HE YOUR BOY-FRIEND?!
NO...
HE'S MY COUSIN!
HE'S SO TALL FOR A HIGH SCHOOL-ER!
SHAH
SHOW US YOUR FACE!
WOW! HE'S SO HOT!
DON'T GET FULL OF YOURSELF!
(RIKO)
HEY! EVERY-ONE SETTLE DOWN!
HOW SHAME-FUL!
YOU'RE INTER-ESTED IN HIM TOO.
CLAP
CLAP
THIS IS VERY INAP-PROPRIATE, EVEN FOR A FAMILY MEMBER.
SORRY, THIS IS AN EMERGENCY.
MY BAD.

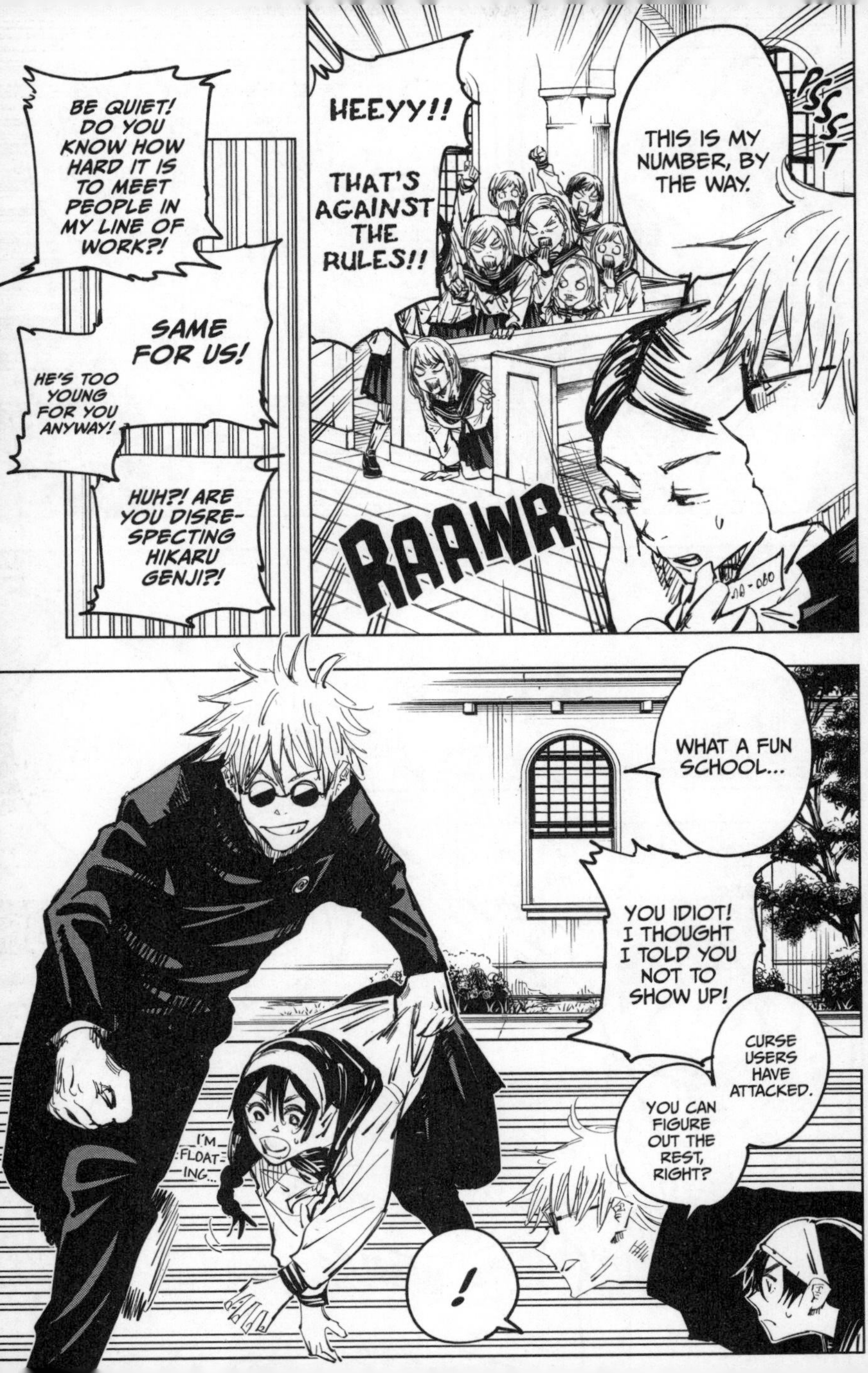
PSSST
THIS IS MY NUMBER, BY THE WAY.
HEEYY!!
THAT'S AGAINST THE RULES!!
RAAWR
BE QUIET! DO YOU KNOW HOW HARD IT IS TO MEET PEOPLE IN MY LINE OF WORK?!
SAME FOR US!
HE'S TOO YOUNG FOR YOU ANYWAY!
HUH?! ARE YOU DISRESPECTING HIKARU GENJI?!
WHAT A FUN SCHOOL...
YOU IDIOT! I THOUGHT I TOLD YOU NOT TO SHOW UP!
CURSE USERS HAVE ATTACKED.
YOU CAN FIGURE OUT THE REST, RIGHT?
!
I'M FLOATING...

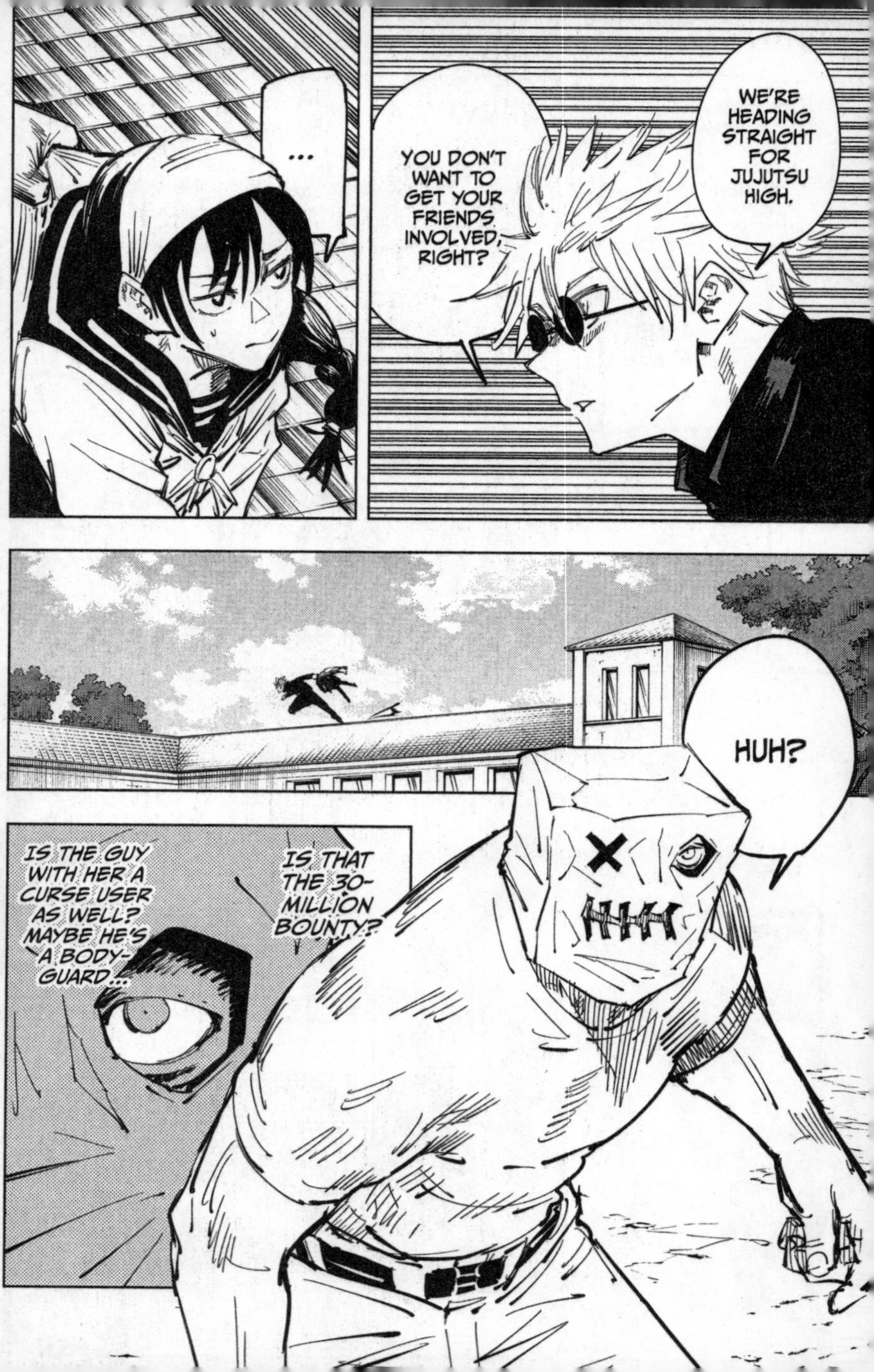
WE'RE HEADING STRAIGHT FOR JUJUTSU HIGH.
YOU DON'T WANT TO GET YOUR FRIENDS INVOLVED, RIGHT?
...
HUH?
IS THAT THE 30-MILLION BOUNTY?
IS THE GUY WITH HER A CURSE USER AS WELL? MAYBE HE'S A BODY-GUARD...

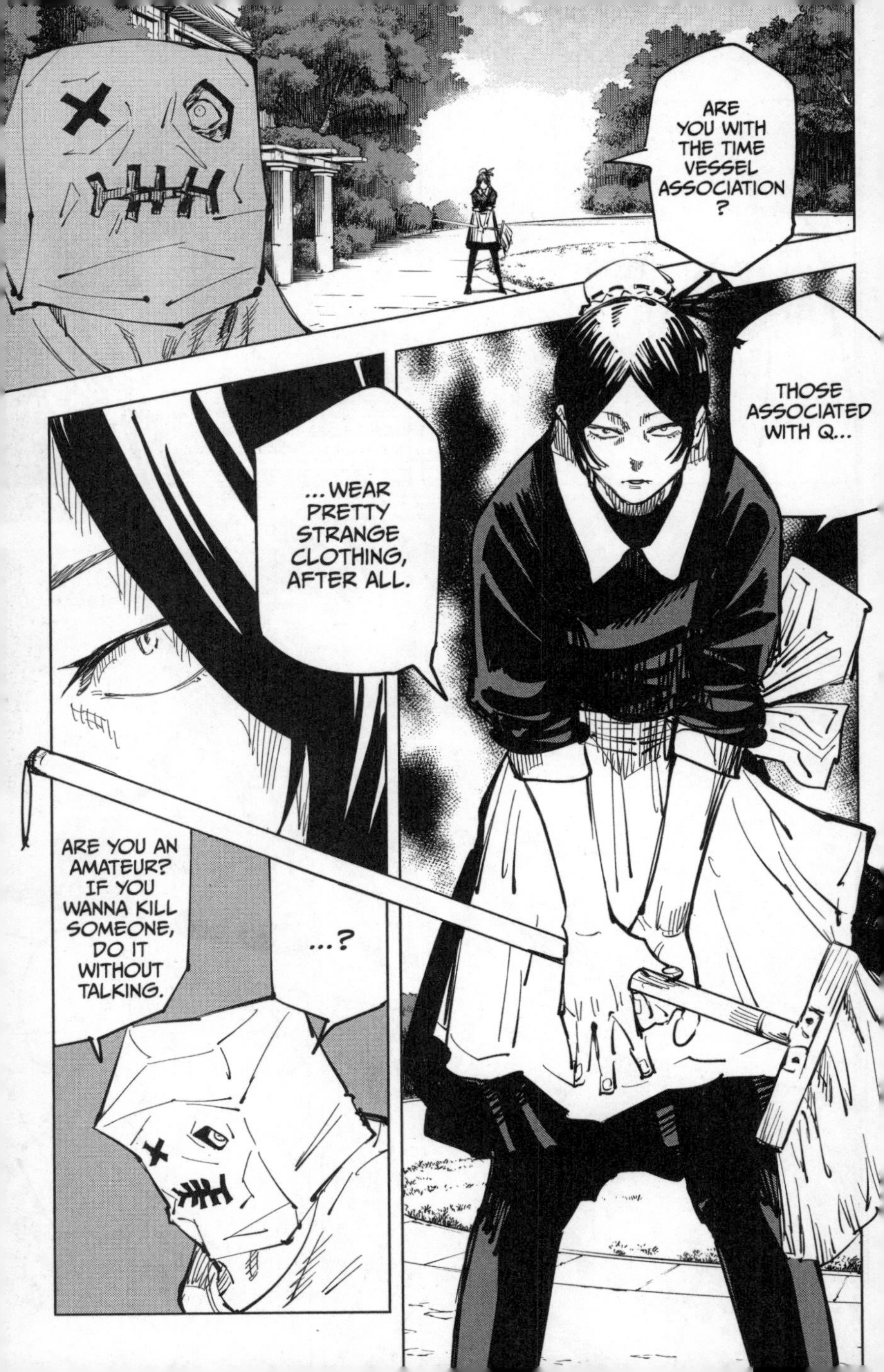
ARE YOU WITH THE TIME VESSEL ASSOCIATION ?
THOSE ASSOCIATED WITH Q...
...WEAR PRETTY STRANGE CLOTHING, AFTER ALL.
...?
ARE YOU AN AMATEUR? IF YOU WANNA KILL SOMEONE, DO IT WITHOUT TALKING.

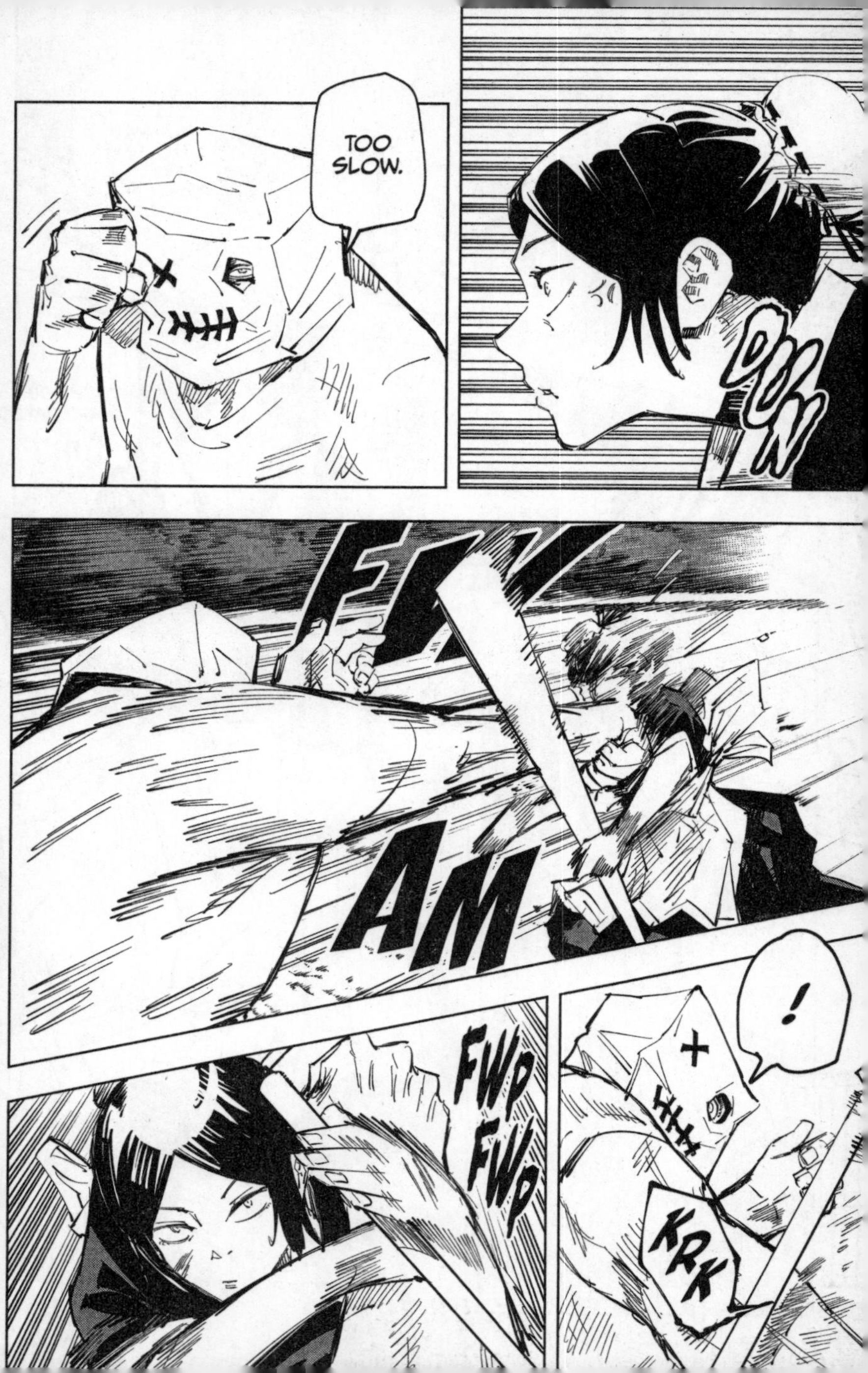
DUN
TOO SLOW.
AM
!
KRK
FWP FWP

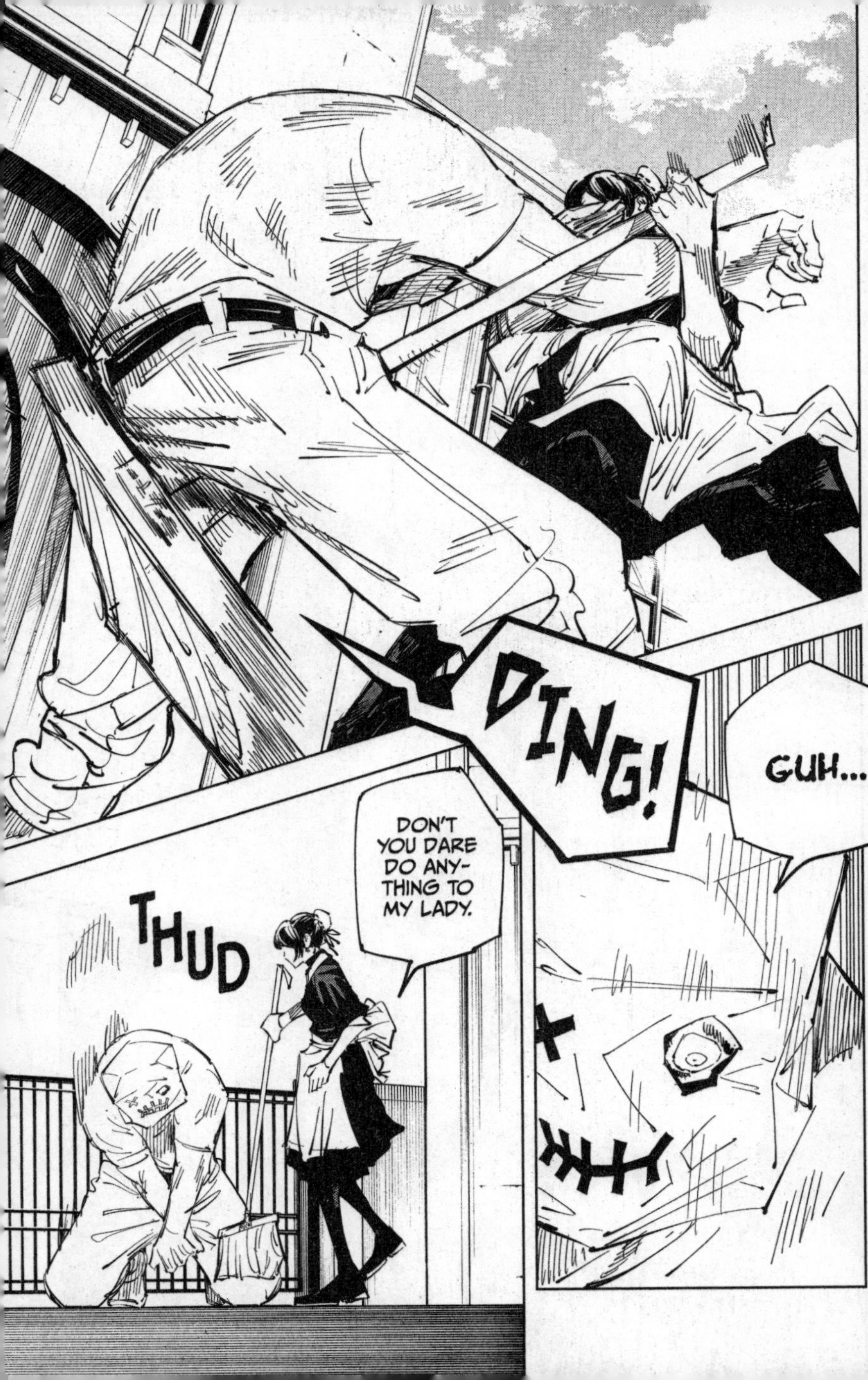
DING!
GUH...
DON'T YOU DARE DO ANY-THING TO MY LADY.
THUD

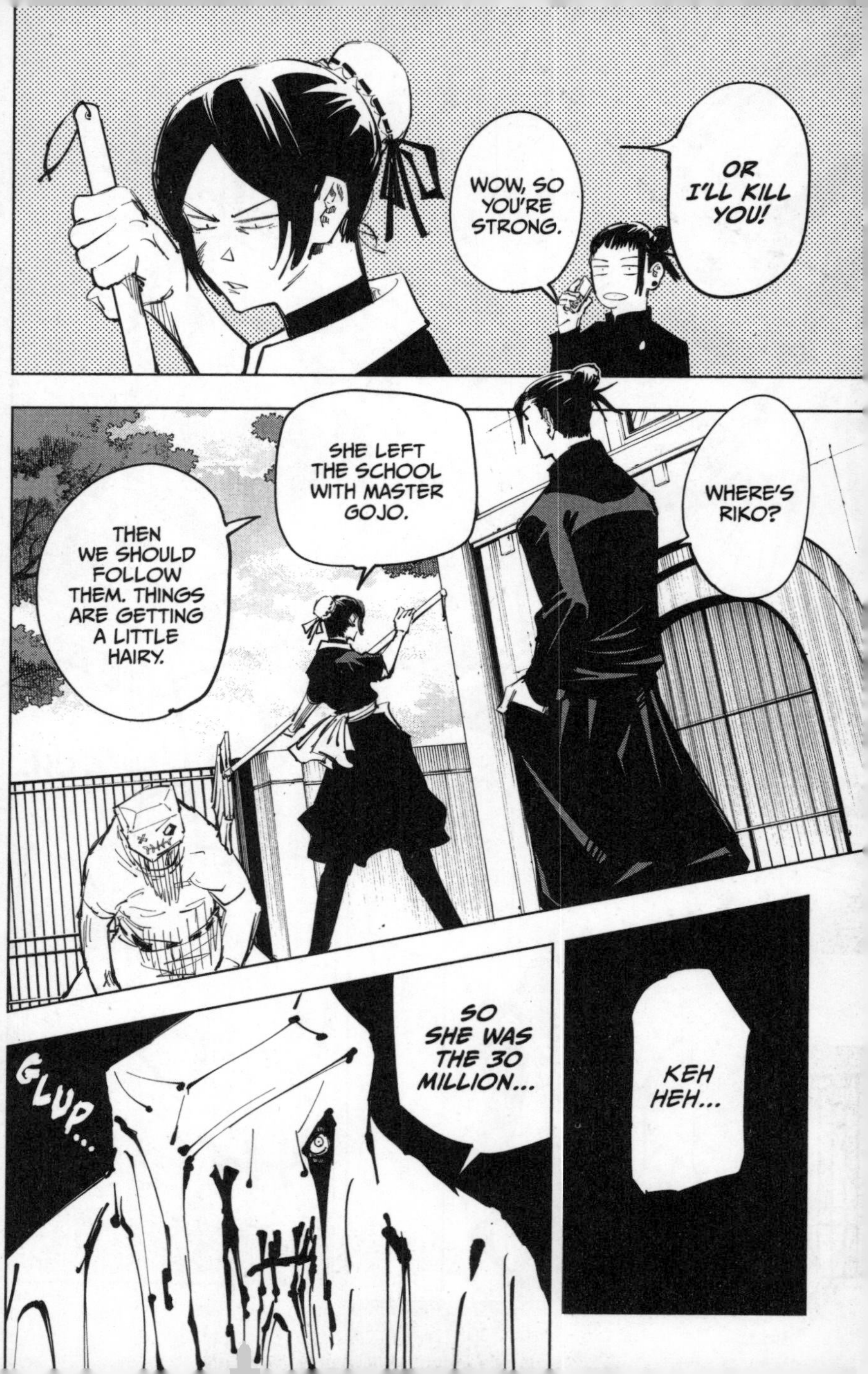
OR I'LL KILL YOU!
WOW, SO YOU'RE STRONG.
WHERE'S RIKO?
SHE LEFT THE SCHOOL WITH MASTER GOJO.
THEN WE SHOULD FOLLOW THEM. THINGS ARE GETTING A LITTLE HAIRY.
KEH HEH...
SO SHE WAS THE 30 MILLION...
GLUP...

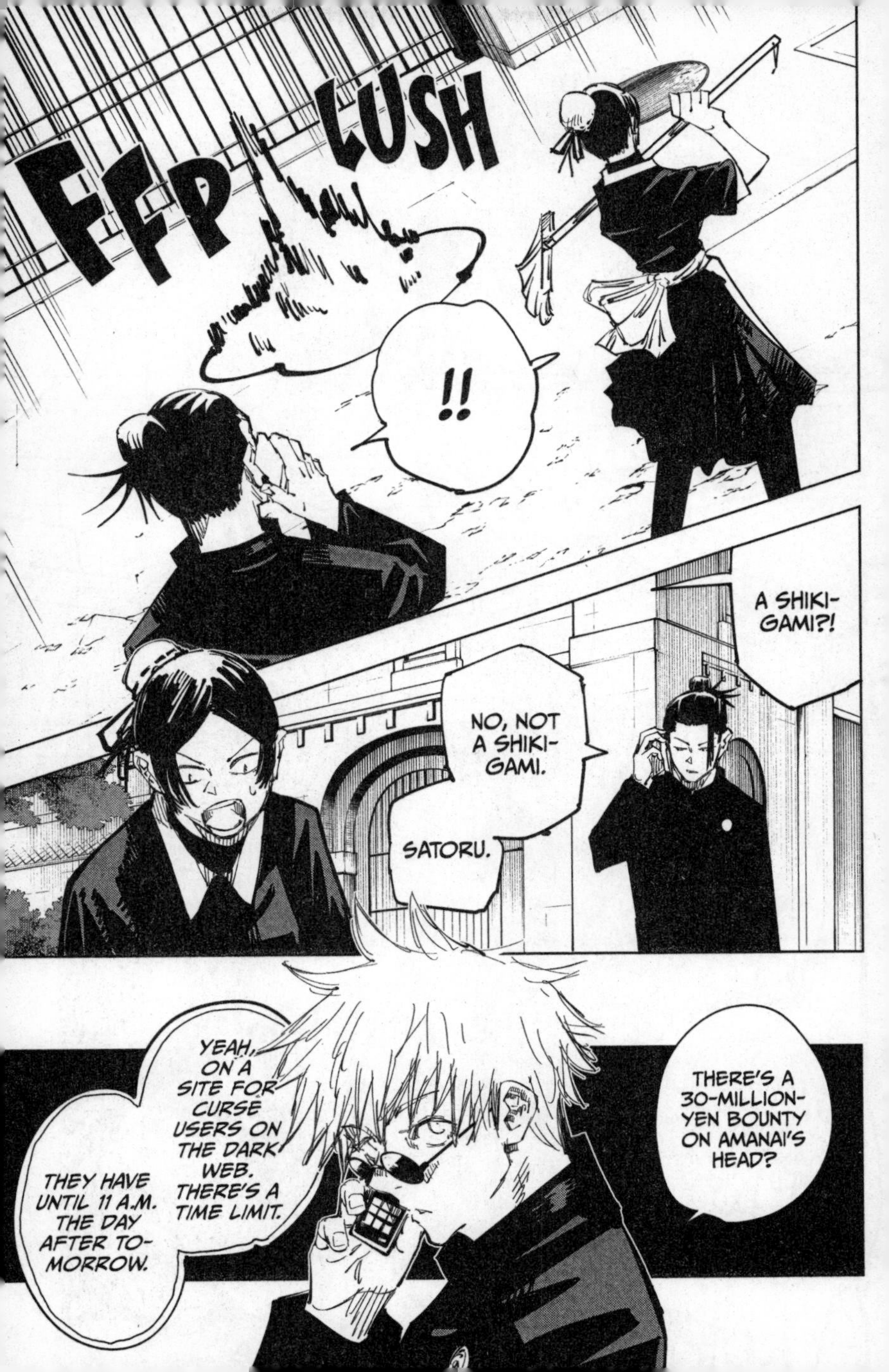
FFFLUSH
!!
A SHIKI-GAMI?!
NO, NOT A SHIKI-GAMI.
SATORU.
THERE'S A 30-MILLION-YEN BOUNTY ON AMANAI'S HEAD?
YEAH, ON A SITE FOR CURSE USERS ON THE DARK WEB. THERE'S A TIME LIMIT.
THEY HAVE UNTIL 11 A.M. THE DAY AFTER TO-MORROW.

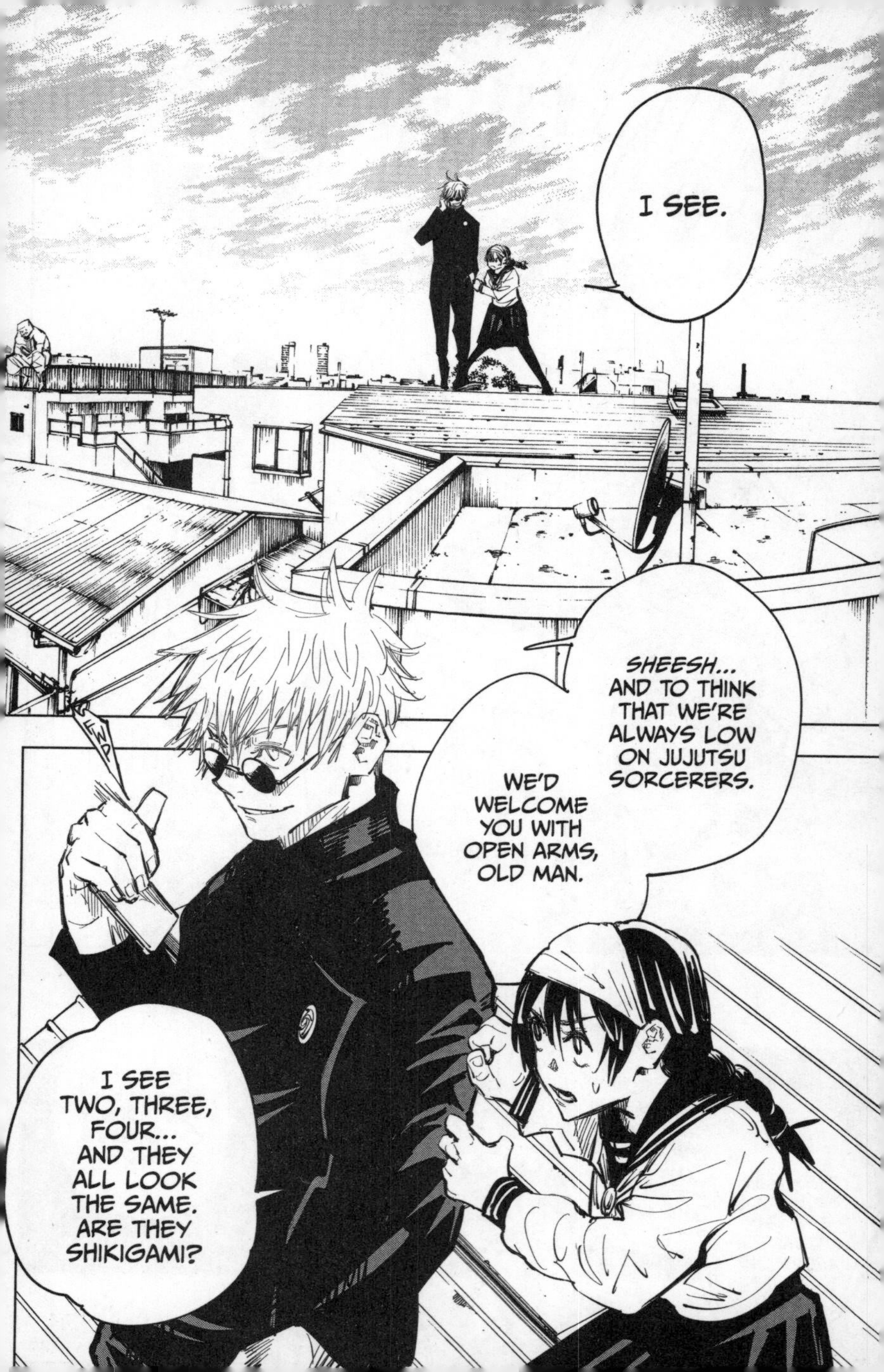
I SEE.
SHEESH... AND TO THINK THAT WE'RE ALWAYS LOW ON JUJUTSU SORCERERS.
WE'D WELCOME YOU WITH OPEN ARMS, OLD MAN.
FWP
I SEE TWO, THREE, FOUR... AND THEY ALL LOOK THE SAME. ARE THEY SHIKIGAMI?

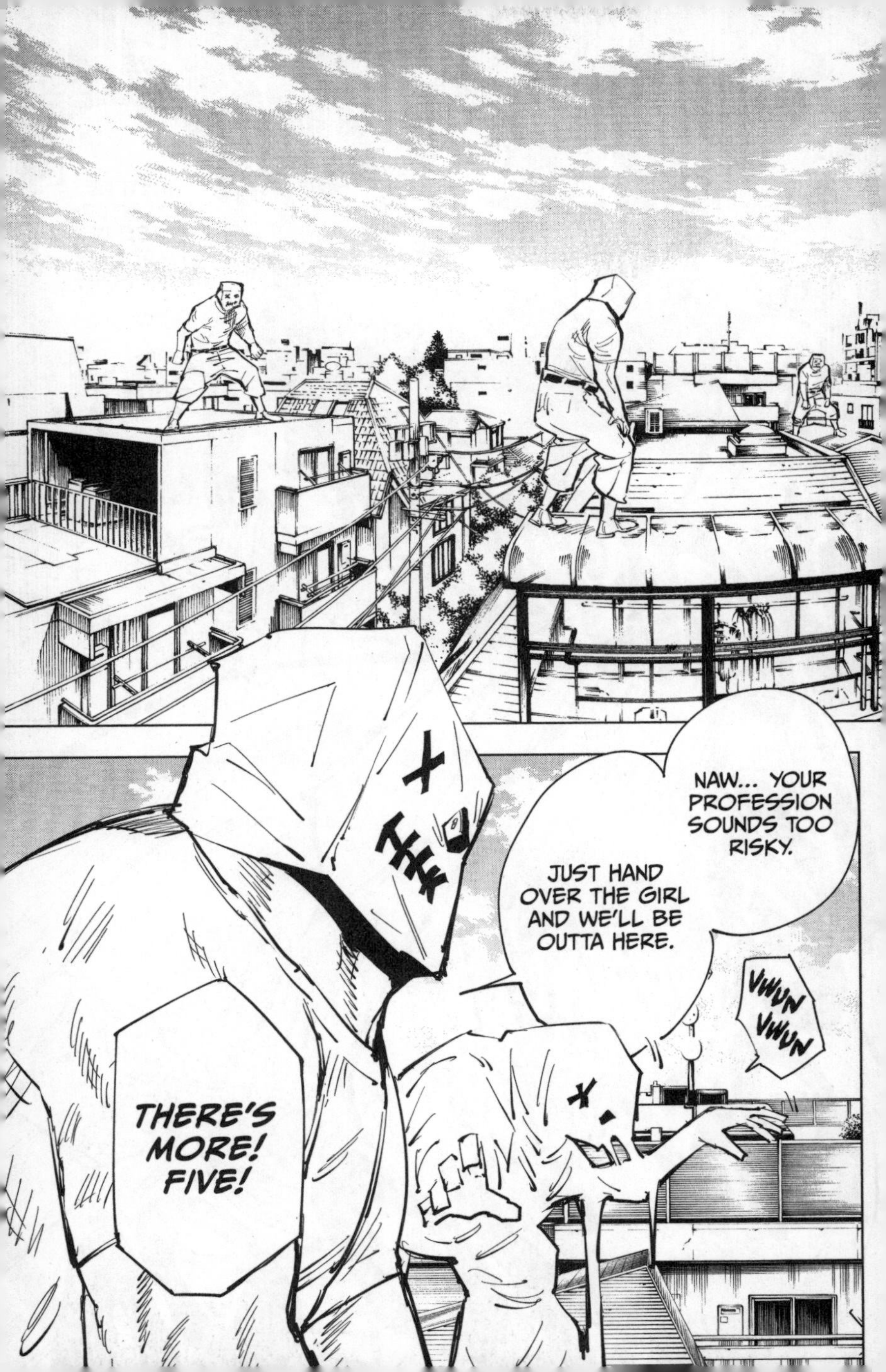
NAW... YOUR PROFESSION SOUNDS TOO RISKY.
JUST HAND OVER THE GIRL AND WE'LL BE OUTTA HERE.
VWUN VWUN
THERE'S MORE! FIVE!

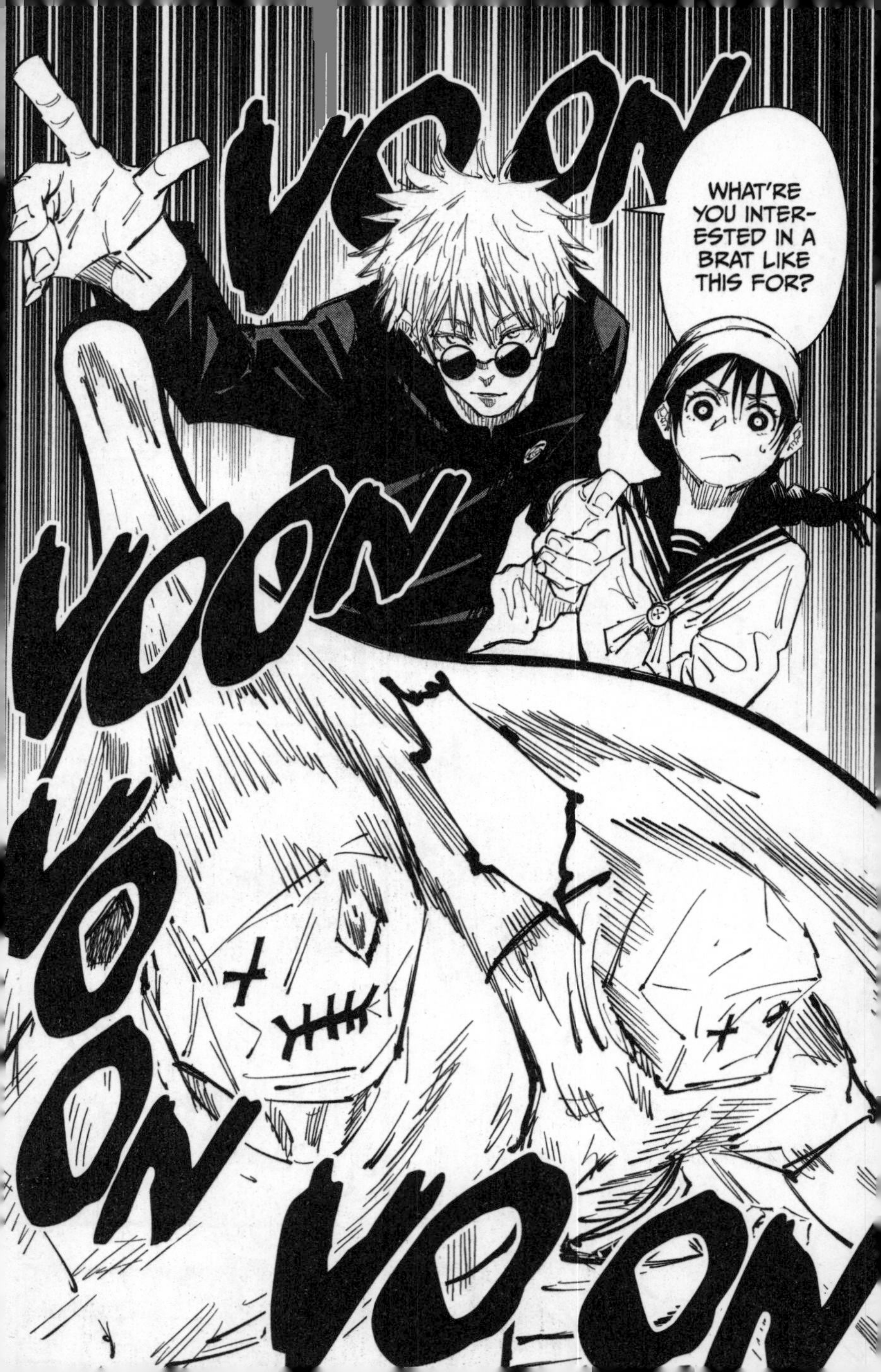
WHAT'RE YOU INTER-ESTED IN A BRAT LIKE THIS FOR?

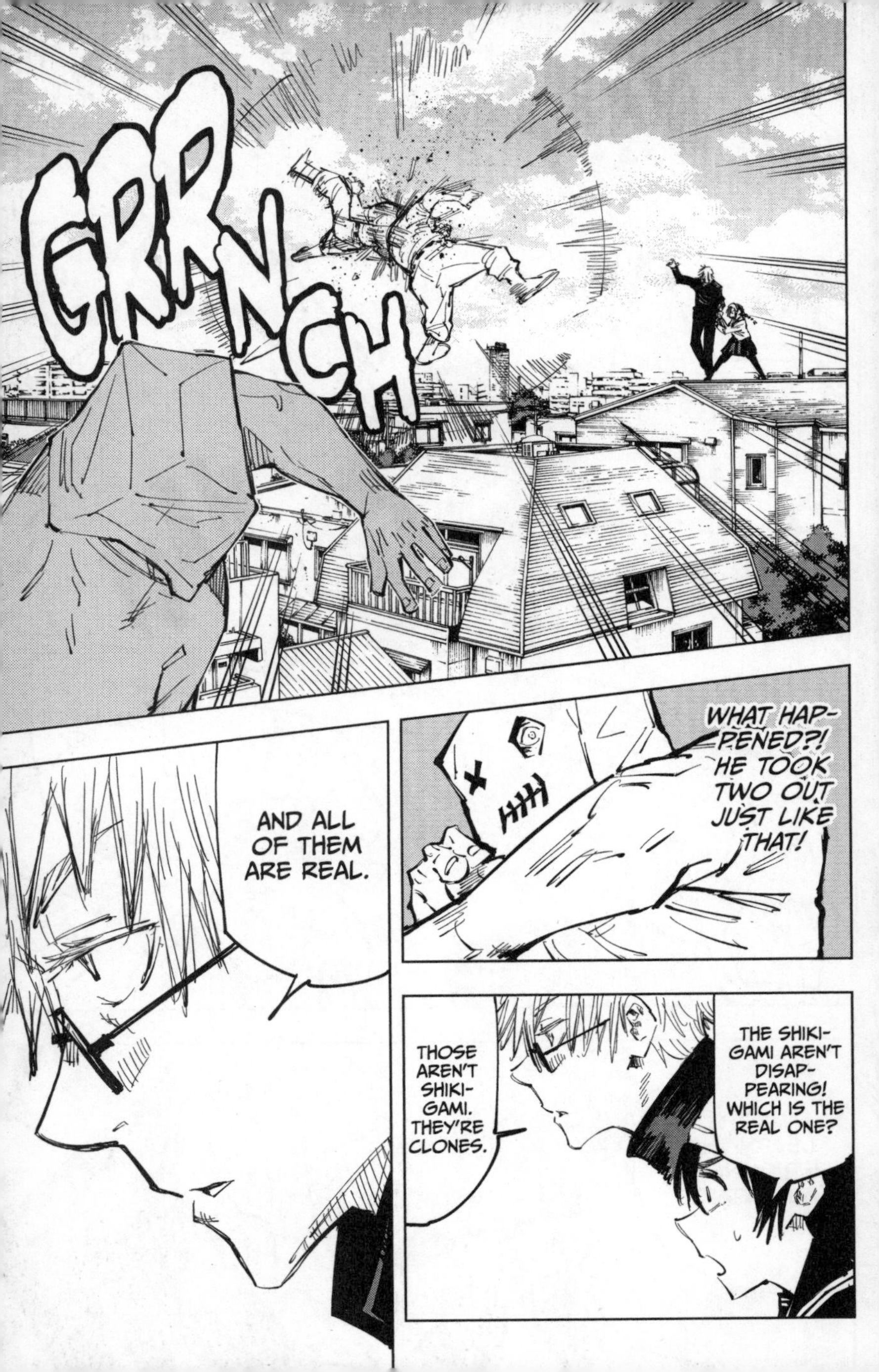
GRRNCH
WHAT HAPPENED?! HE TOOK TWO OUT JUST LIKE THAT!
THE SHIKIGAMI AREN'T DISAPPEARING! WHICH IS THE REAL ONE?
THOSE AREN'T SHIKIGAMI. THEY'RE CLONES.
AND ALL OF THEM ARE REAL.

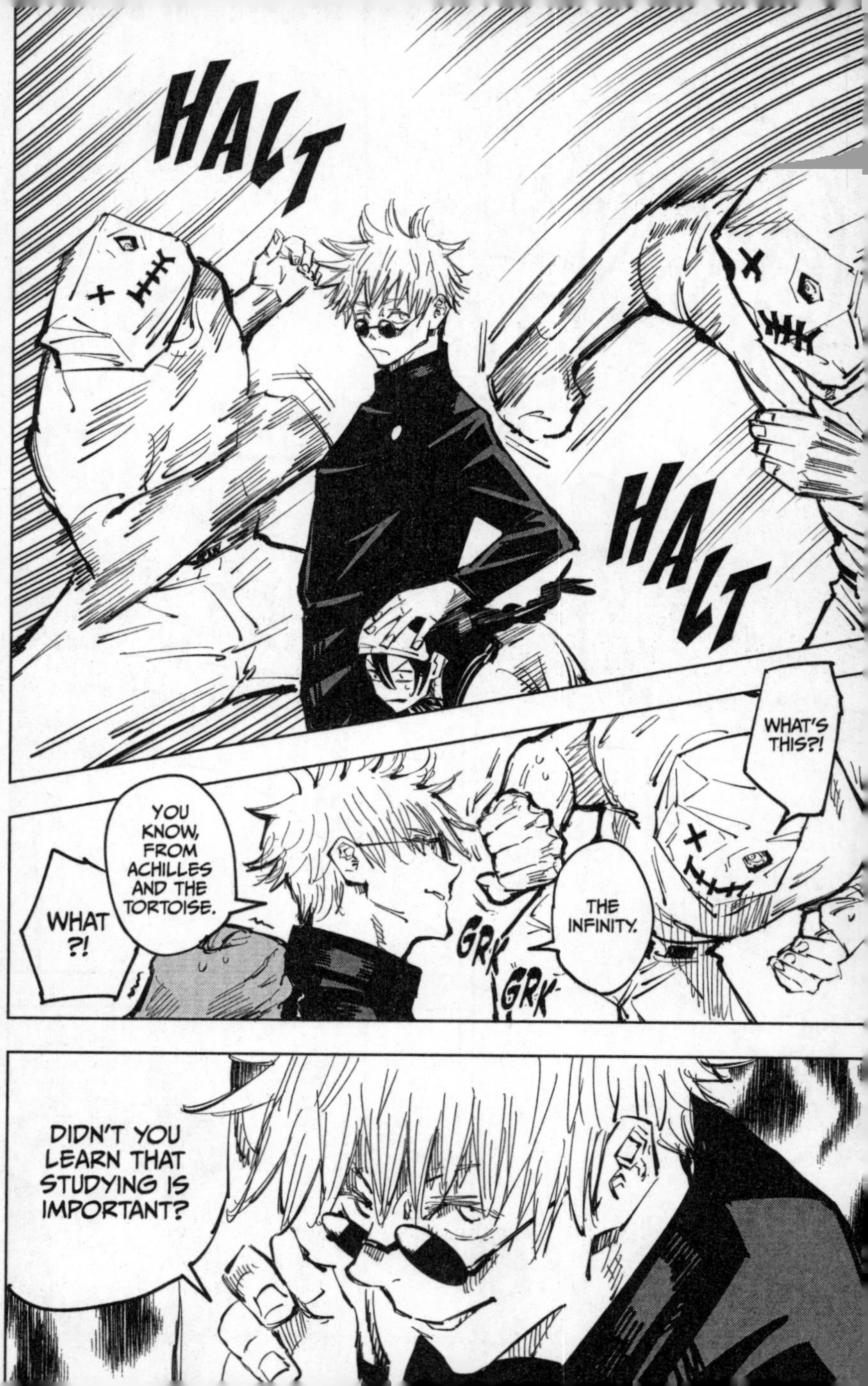
HALT
HALT
WHAT'S THIS?!
THE INFINITY.
GRK GRK
YOU KNOW, FROM ACHILLES AND THE TORTOISE.
WHAT ?!
DIDN'T YOU LEARN THAT STUDYING IS IMPORTANT?

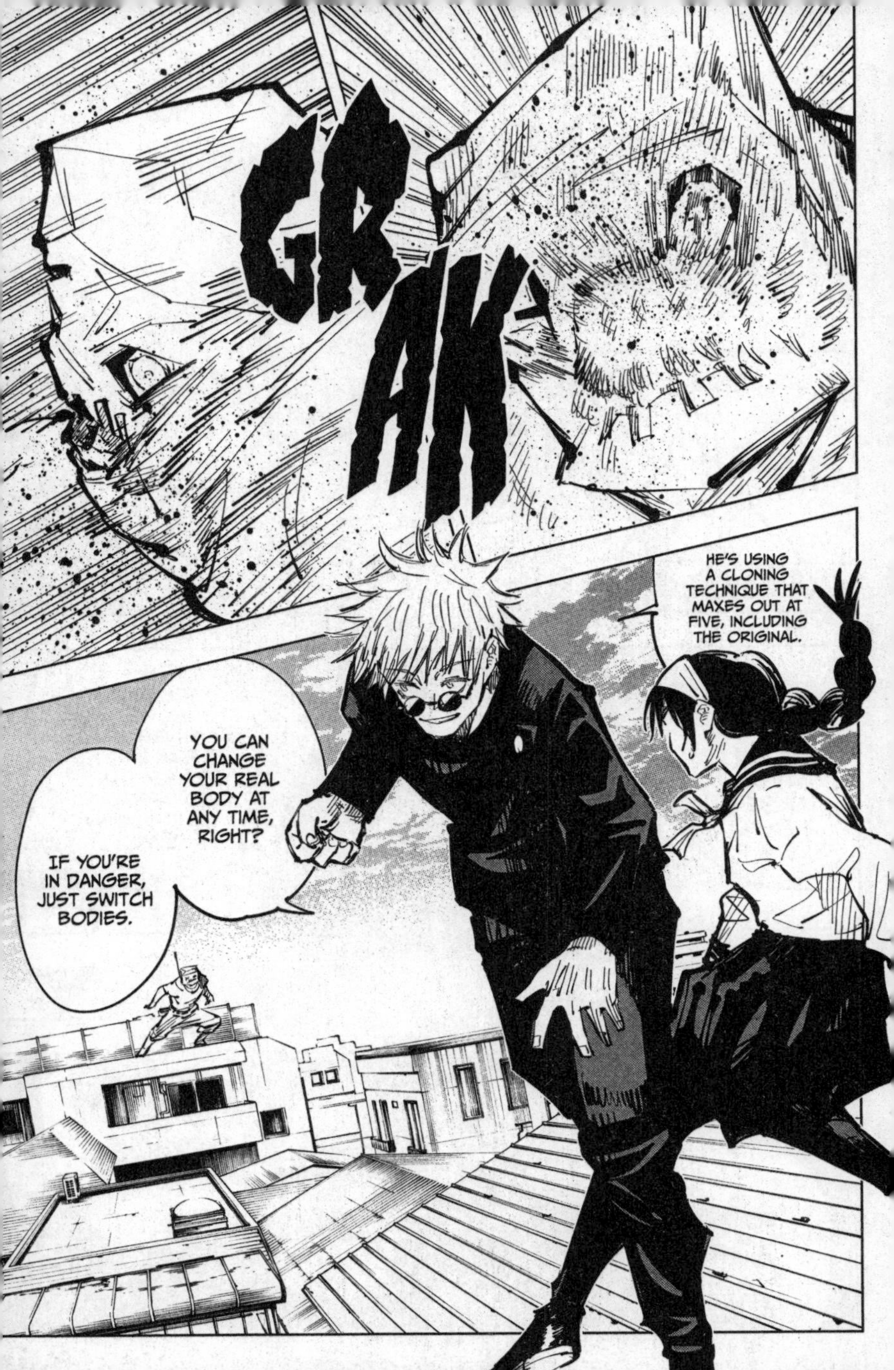
GRAK
HE'S USING A CLONING TECHNIQUE THAT MAXES OUT AT FIVE, INCLUDING THE ORIGINAL.
YOU CAN CHANGE YOUR REAL BODY AT ANY TIME, RIGHT?
IF YOU'RE IN DANGER, JUST SWITCH BODIES.

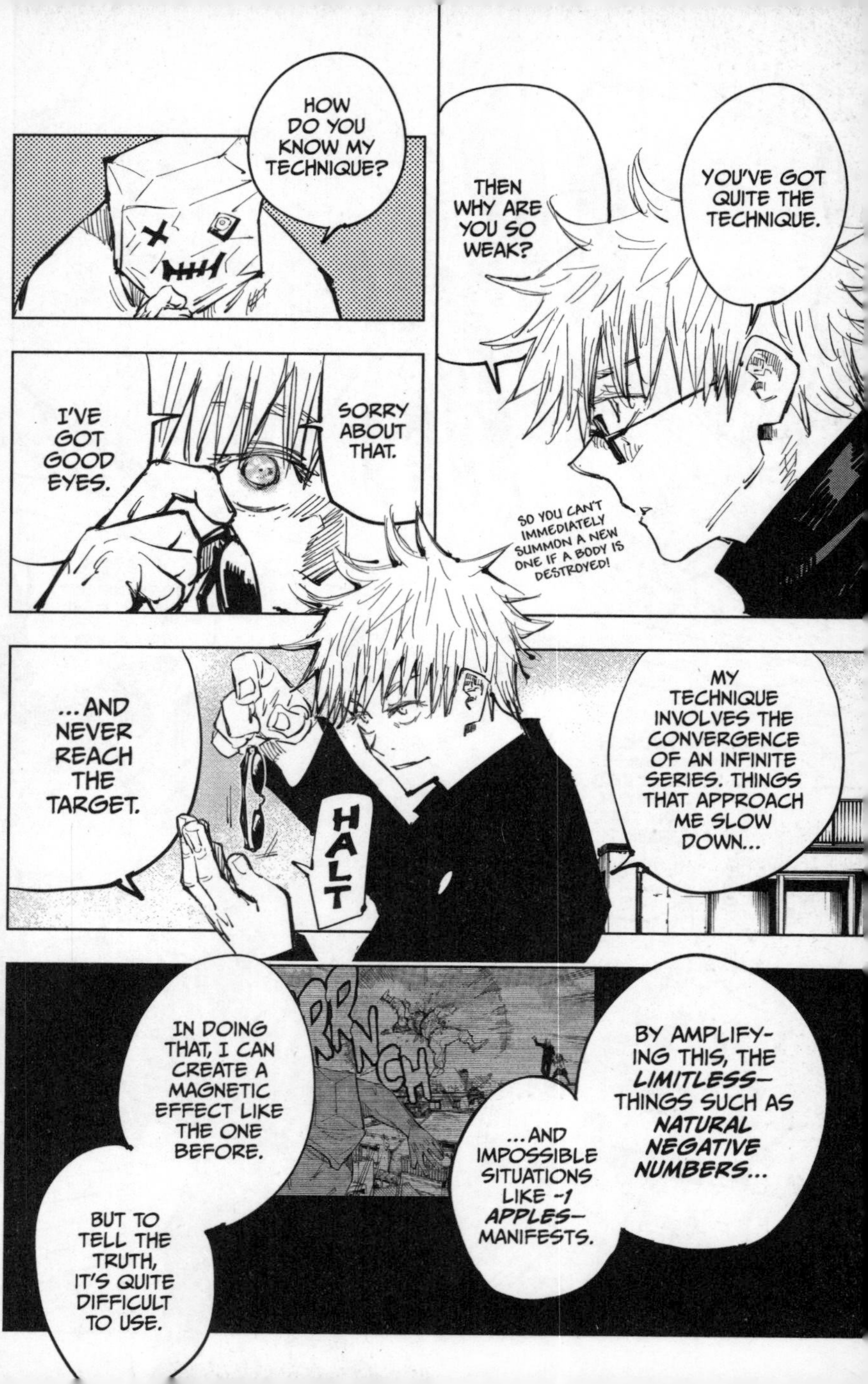
YOU'VE GOT QUITE THE TECHNIQUE.
THEN WHY ARE YOU SO WEAK?
SO YOU CAN'T IMMEDIATELY SUMMON A NEW ONE IF A BODY IS DESTROYED!
HOW DO YOU KNOW MY TECHNIQUE?
SORRY ABOUT THAT.
I'VE GOT GOOD EYES.
MY TECHNIQUE INVOLVES THE CONVERGENCE OF AN INFINITE SERIES. THINGS THAT APPROACH ME SLOW DOWN...
...AND NEVER REACH THE TARGET.
HALT
BY AMPLIFYING THIS, THE *LIMITLESS*—THINGS SUCH AS *NATURAL NEGATIVE NUMBERS*...
...AND IMPOSSIBLE SITUATIONS LIKE *-1 APPLES*—MANIFESTS.
IN DOING THAT, I CAN CREATE A MAGNETIC EFFECT LIKE THE ONE BEFORE.
BUT TO TELL THE TRUTH, IT'S QUITE DIFFICULT TO USE.

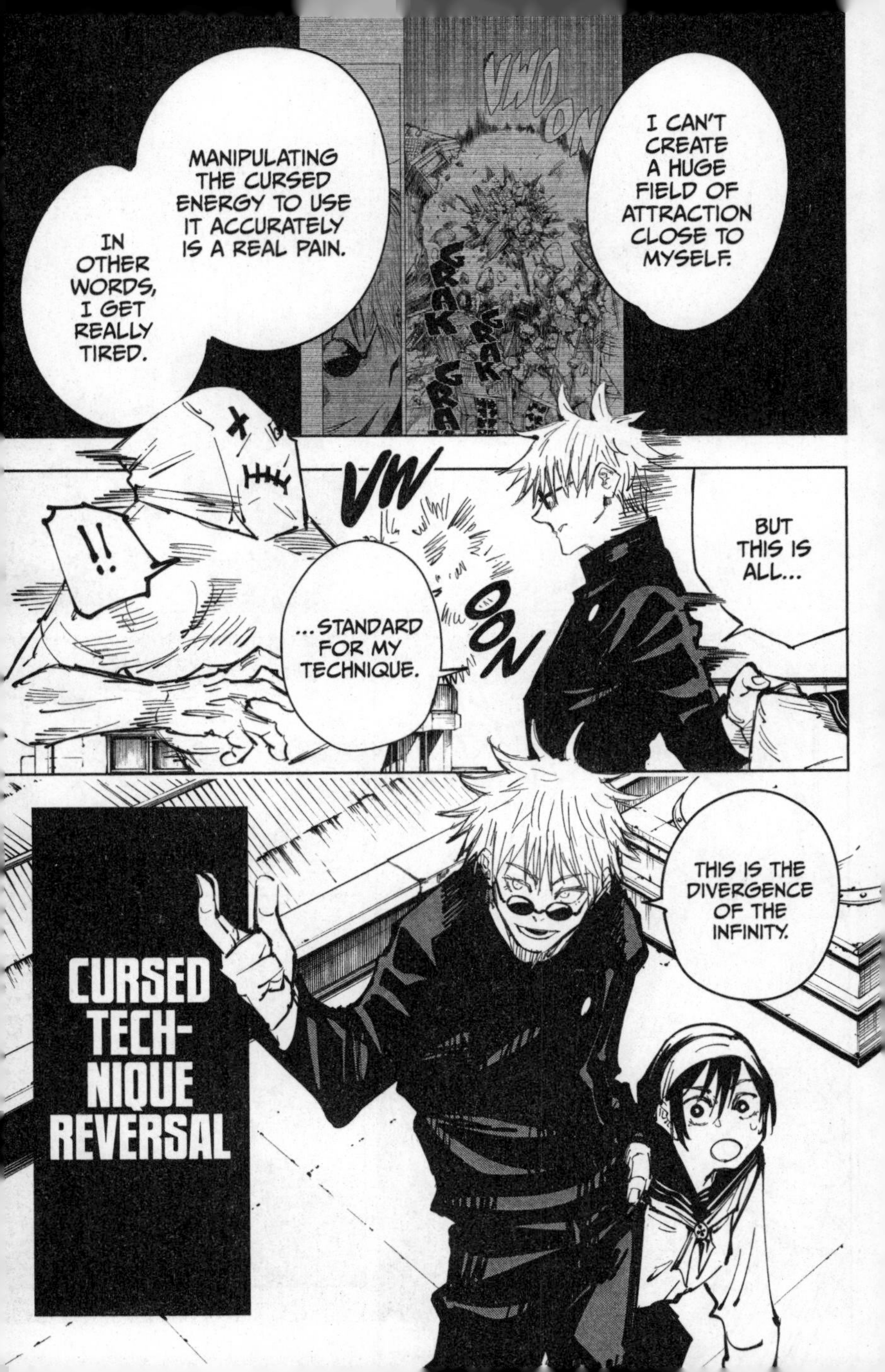
I CAN'T CREATE A HUGE FIELD OF ATTRACTION CLOSE TO MYSELF.
GRAK GRAK
MANIPULATING THE CURSED ENERGY TO USE IT ACCURATELY IS A REAL PAIN.
IN OTHER WORDS, I GET REALLY TIRED.
BUT THIS IS ALL...
VW
OON
...STANDARD FOR MY TECHNIQUE.
!!
THIS IS THE DIVERGENCE OF THE INFINITY.
CURSED TECH-NIQUE REVERSAL

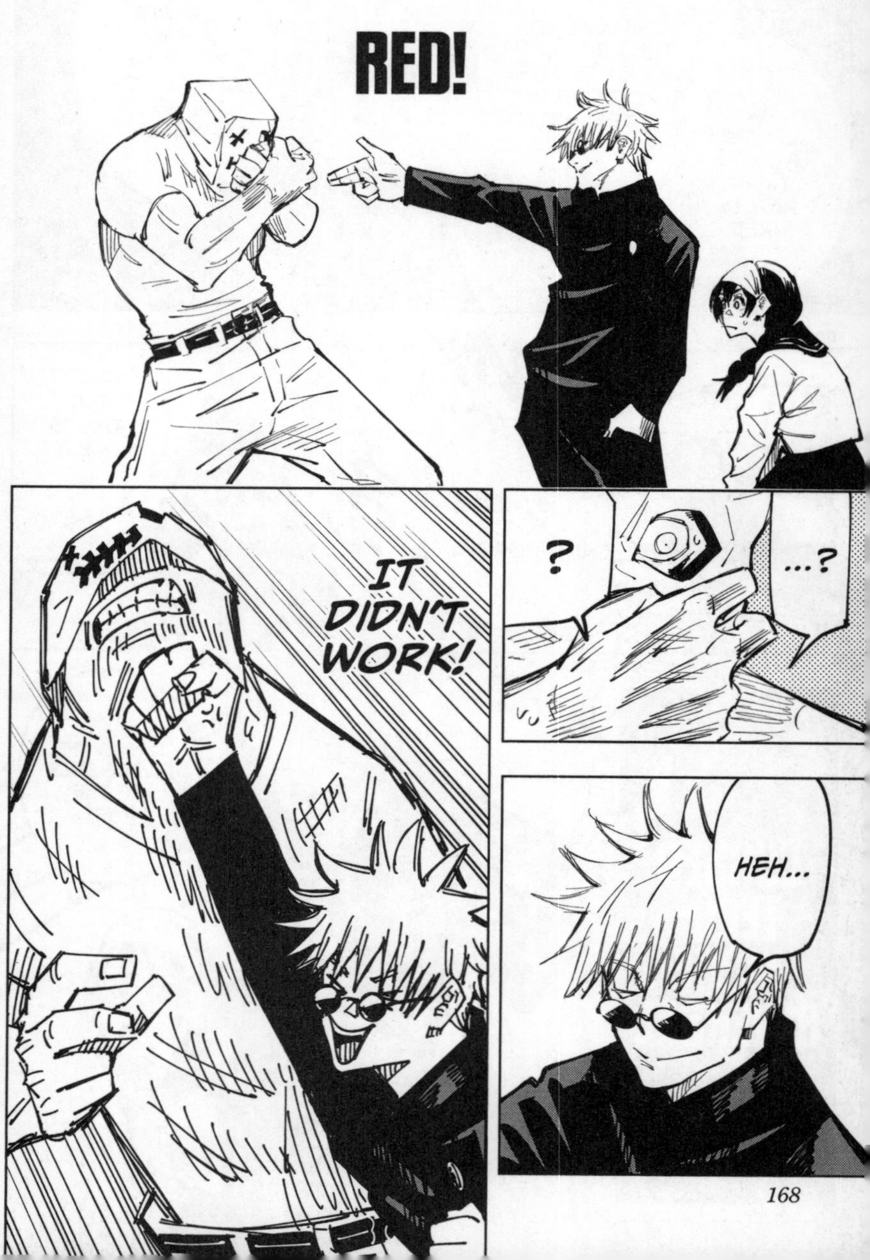
RED!
...?
?
HEH...
IT DIDN'T WORK!

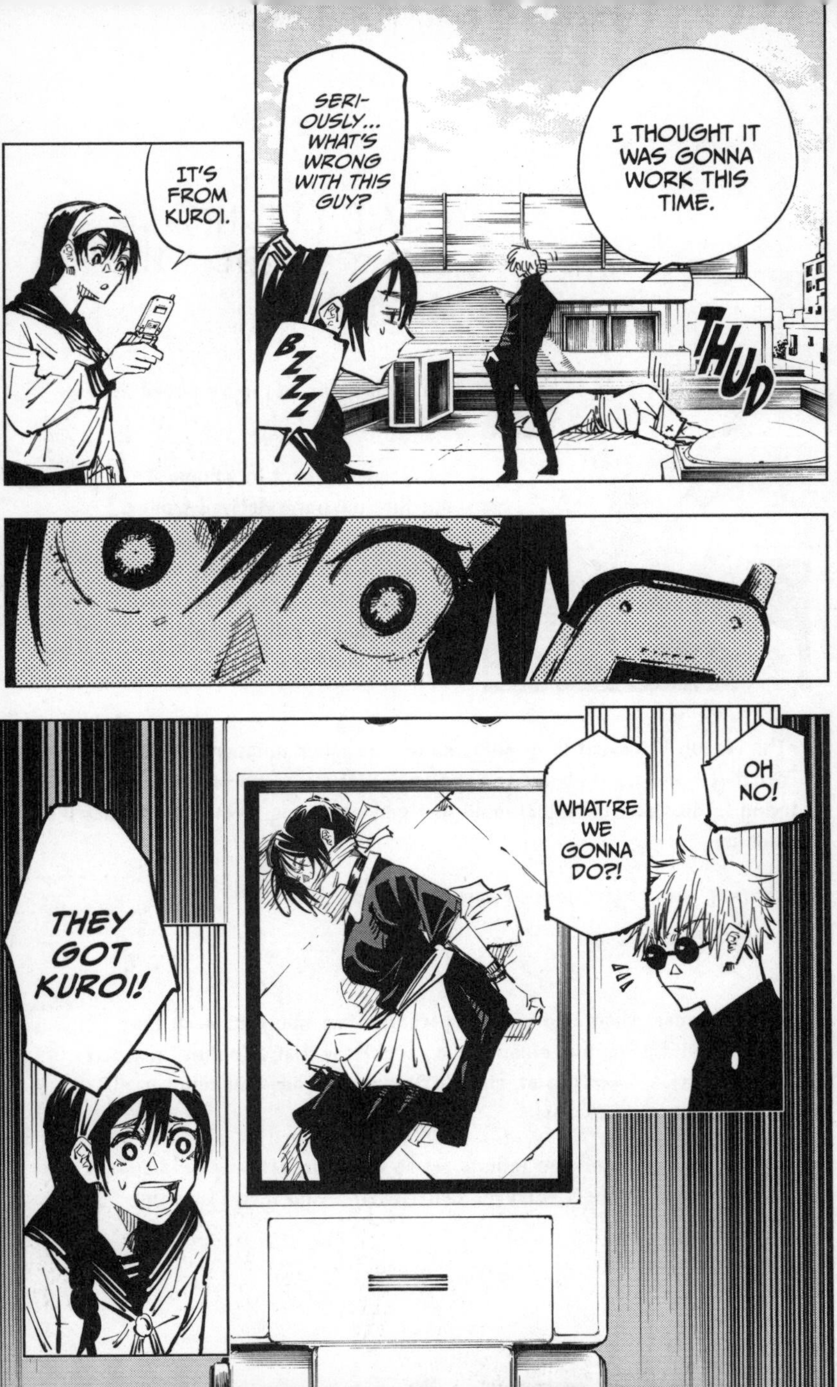
I THOUGHT IT WAS GONNA WORK THIS TIME.
SERI-OUSLY... WHAT'S WRONG WITH THIS GUY?
THUD
BZZZ
IT'S FROM KUROI.
OH NO!
WHAT'RE WE GONNA DO?!
THEY GOT KUROI!

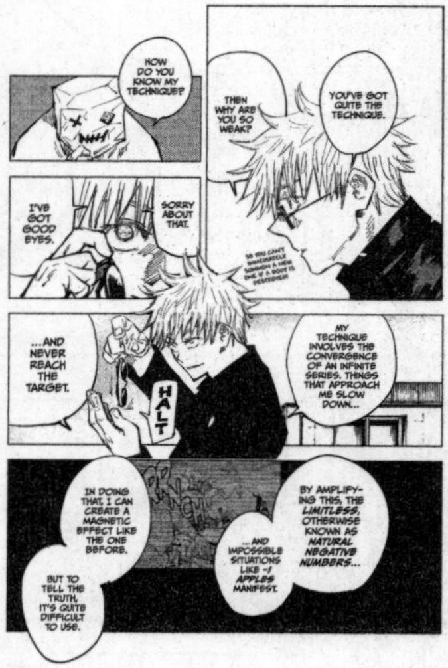
YOU'VE GOT QUITE THE TECHNIQUE.
THEN WHY ARE YOU SO WEAK?
SO YOU CAN'T IMMEDIATELY SUMMON A NEW ONE IF A BODY IS DESTROYED?
HOW DO YOU KNOW MY TECHNIQUE?
SORRY ABOUT THAT.
I'VE GOT GOOD EYES.
MY TECHNIQUE INVOLVES THE CONVERGENCE OF AN INFINITE SERIES. THINGS THAT APPROACH ME SLOW DOWN...
HALT
...AND NEVER REACH THE TARGET.
BY AMPLIFYING THIS, THE *LIMITLESS*, OTHERWISE KNOWN AS *NATURAL NEGATIVE NUMBERS*...
...AND IMPOSSIBLE SITUATIONS LIKE -1 *APPLES* MANIFEST.
IN DOING THAT, I CAN CREATE A MAGNETIC EFFECT LIKE THE ONE BEFORE.
BUT TO TELL THE TRUTH, IT'S QUITE DIFFICULT TO USE.

I SAID I DIDN'T WANT TO DO THIS ANYMORE...

An explanation of Gojo's power in the last panel:

• I glossed over it in volume 2, but the "unknown derived from 0" is included in the limitless cursed technique but theoretically not part of the infinite series. I mustered the courage to call it "natural negative numbers."

•The reason I decided to go with "natural negative numbers" instead of "negative numbers" is because ~~I can explain it away with excuses~~ anyone trying to discredit the logic would just end up saying, "Whatever!" since it's made up.

• Anyway, with regard to my excuse reasoning...

$$S = 1/2 + 1/4 + 1/8...$$

In this manner, when counting, no person exists who can reach the "end." (Right?!) For this reason, one cannot say that a "natural negative number" series doesn't exist, right?! Because nobody can count it all out!! It's that sorta excuse!

• By the way, apparently an infinite series does theoretically have an end, so I find myself asking, "What the hell?! Why?!" And then I give up.

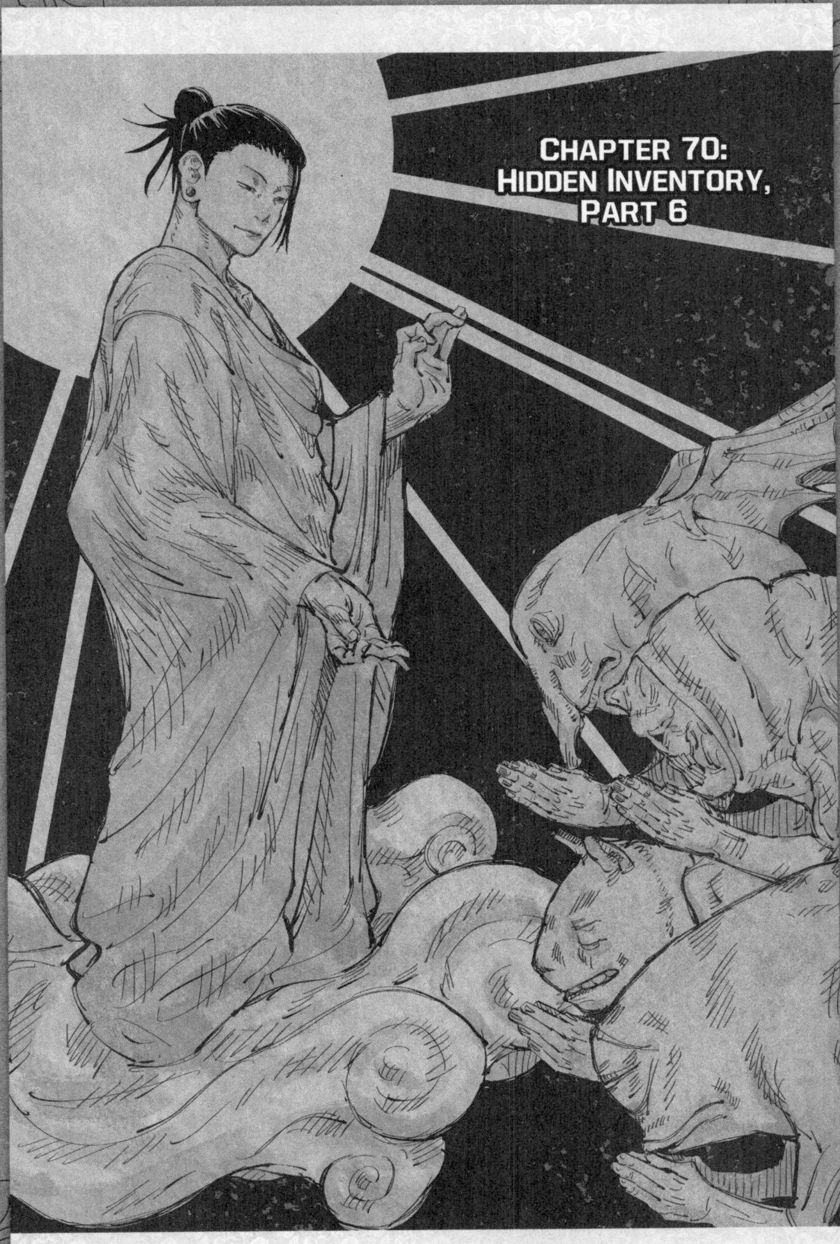
CHAPTER 70:
HIDDEN INVENTORY,
PART 6

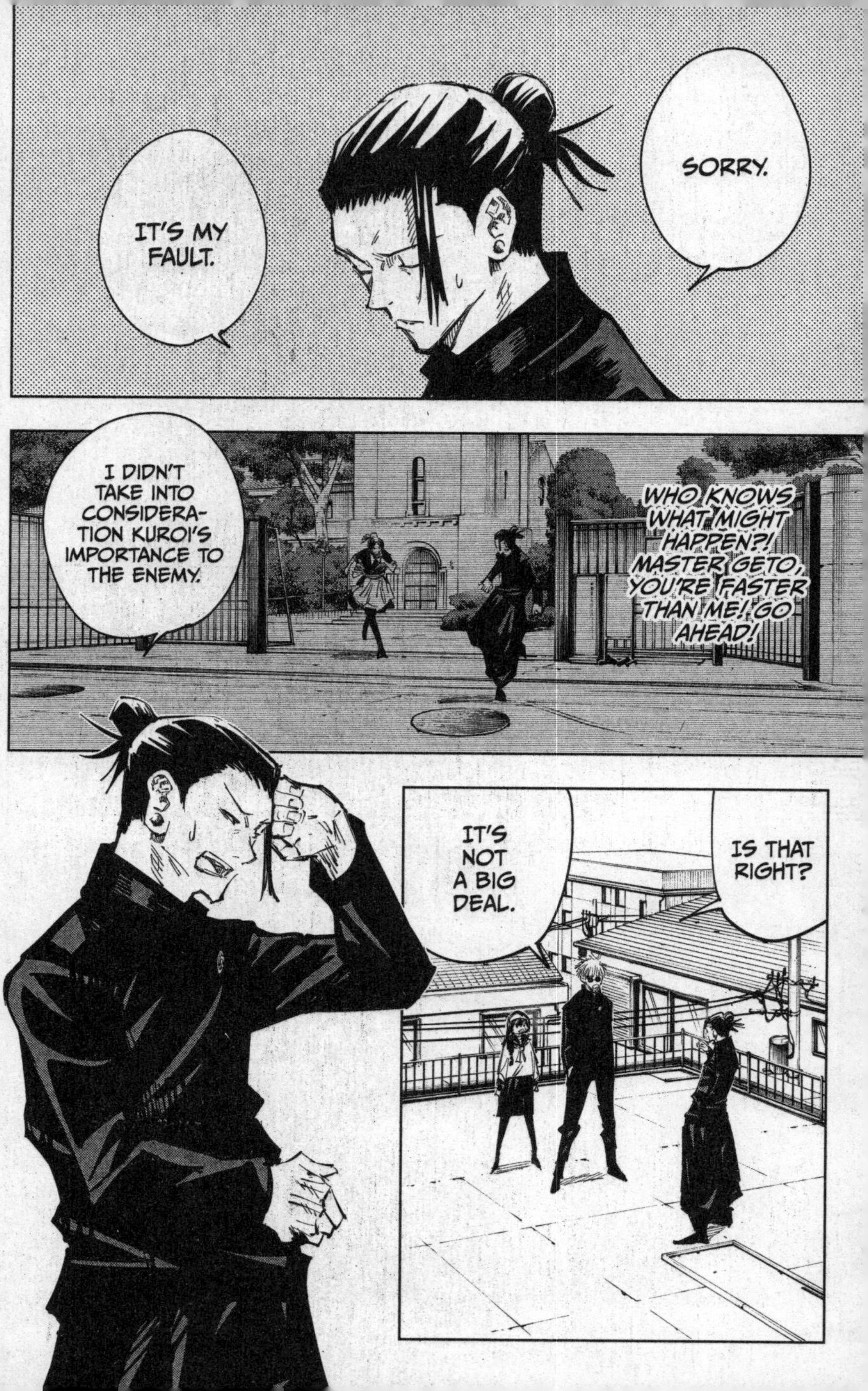
SORRY.
IT'S MY FAULT.
WHO KNOWS WHAT MIGHT HAPPEN?! MASTER GETO, YOU'RE FASTER THAN ME! GO AHEAD!
I DIDN'T TAKE INTO CONSIDERA-TION KUROI'S IMPORTANCE TO THE ENEMY.
IS THAT RIGHT?
IT'S NOT A BIG DEAL.

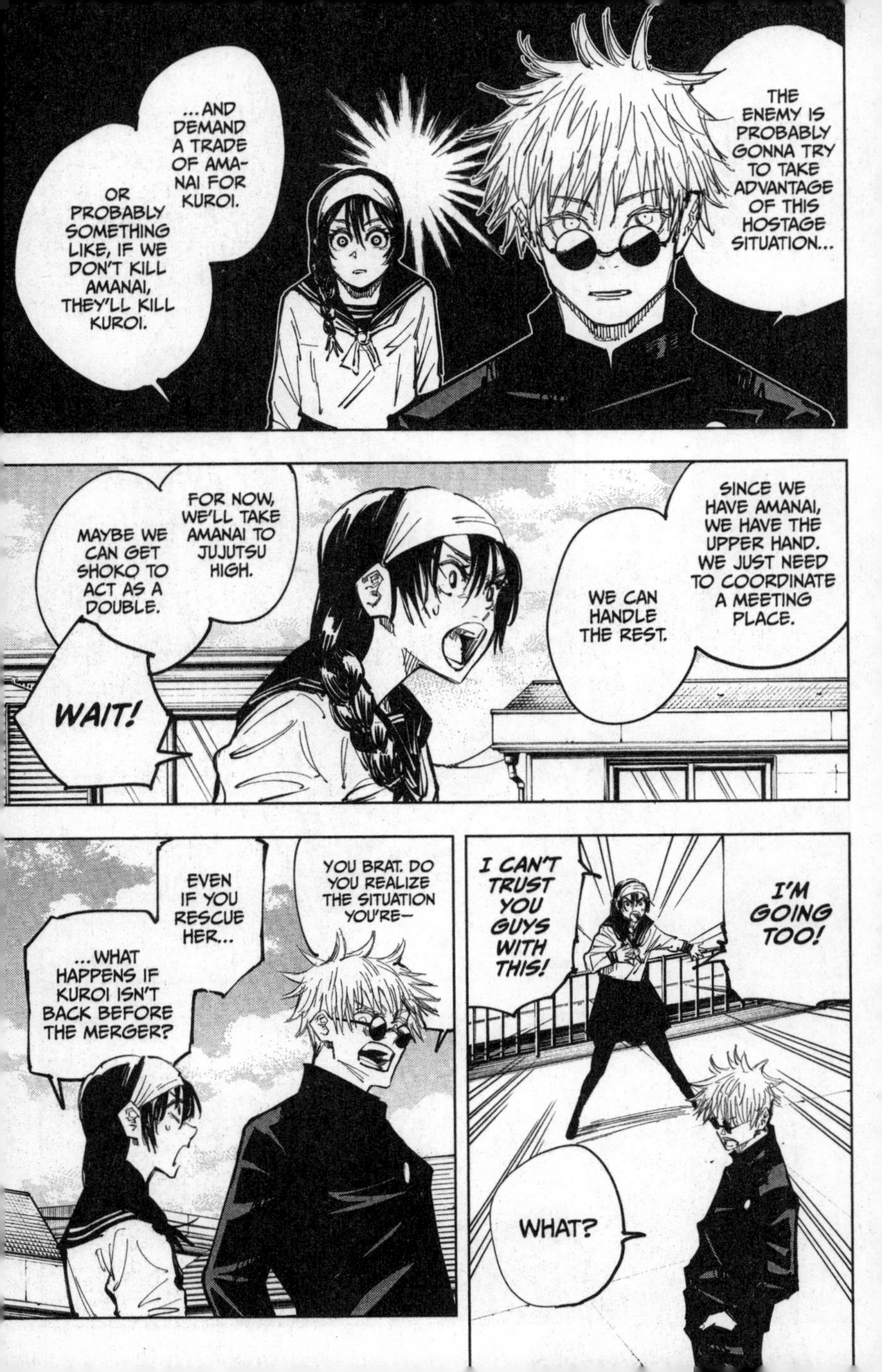
THE ENEMY IS PROBABLY GONNA TRY TO TAKE ADVANTAGE OF THIS HOSTAGE SITUATION...
...AND DEMAND A TRADE OF AMA-NAI FOR KUROI.
OR PROBABLY SOMETHING LIKE, IF WE DON'T KILL AMANAI, THEY'LL KILL KUROI.
SINCE WE HAVE AMANAI, WE HAVE THE UPPER HAND. WE JUST NEED TO COORDINATE A MEETING PLACE.
WE CAN HANDLE THE REST.
FOR NOW, WE'LL TAKE AMANAI TO JUJUTSU HIGH.
MAYBE WE CAN GET SHOKO TO ACT AS A DOUBLE.
WAIT!
I'M GOING TOO!
I CAN'T TRUST YOU GUYS WITH THIS!
WHAT?
YOU BRAT. DO YOU REALIZE THE SITUATION YOU'RE—
EVEN IF YOU RESCUE HER...
...WHAT HAPPENS IF KUROI ISN'T BACK BEFORE THE MERGER?

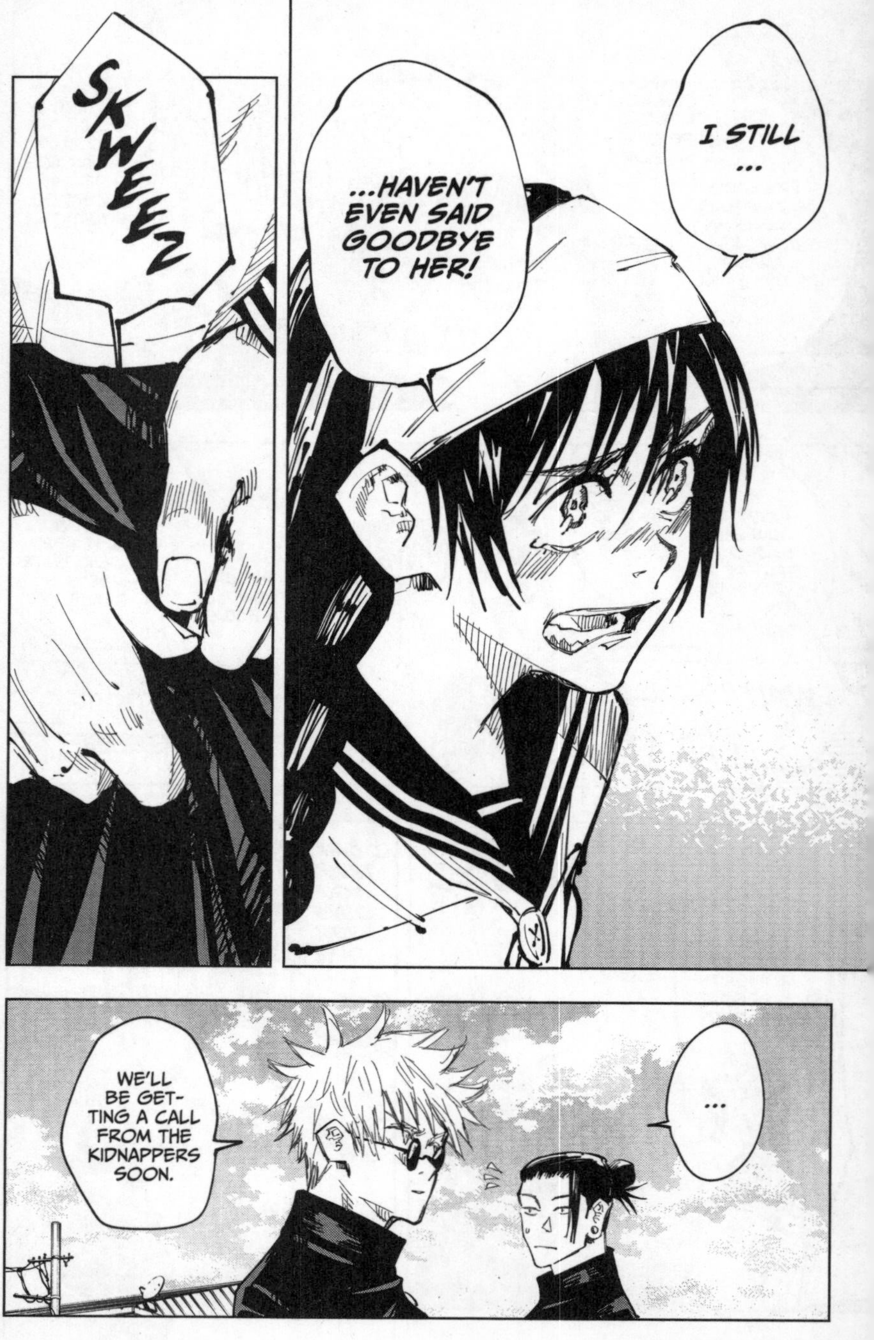
I STILL ...
...HAVEN'T EVEN SAID GOODBYE TO HER!
SKWEEZ
...
WE'LL BE GET- TING A CALL FROM THE KIDNAPPERS SOON.

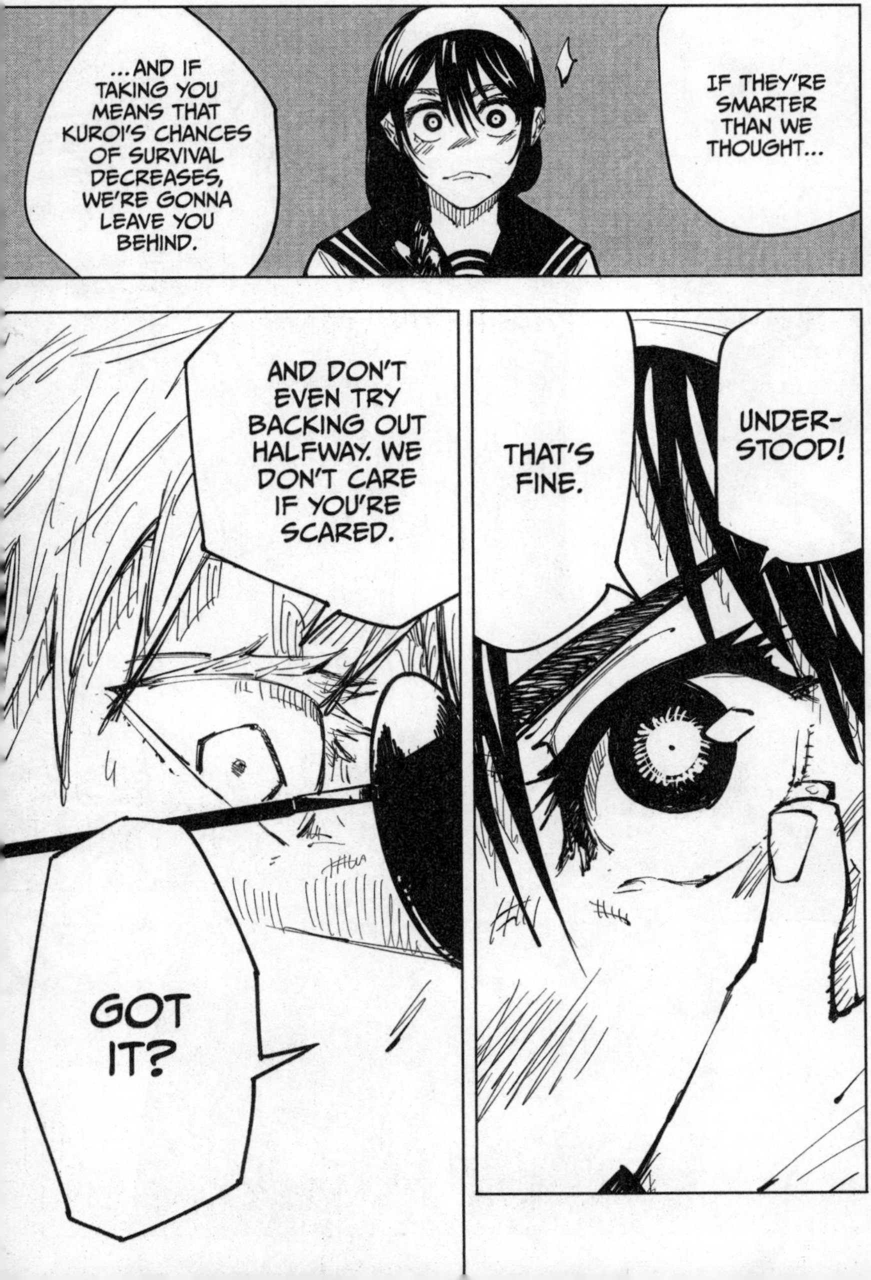
IF THEY'RE SMARTER THAN WE THOUGHT...
...AND IF TAKING YOU MEANS THAT KUROI'S CHANCES OF SURVIVAL DECREASES, WE'RE GONNA LEAVE YOU BEHIND.
UNDER-STOOD!
THAT'S FINE.
AND DON'T EVEN TRY BACKING OUT HALFWAY. WE DON'T CARE IF YOU'RE SCARED.
GOT IT?

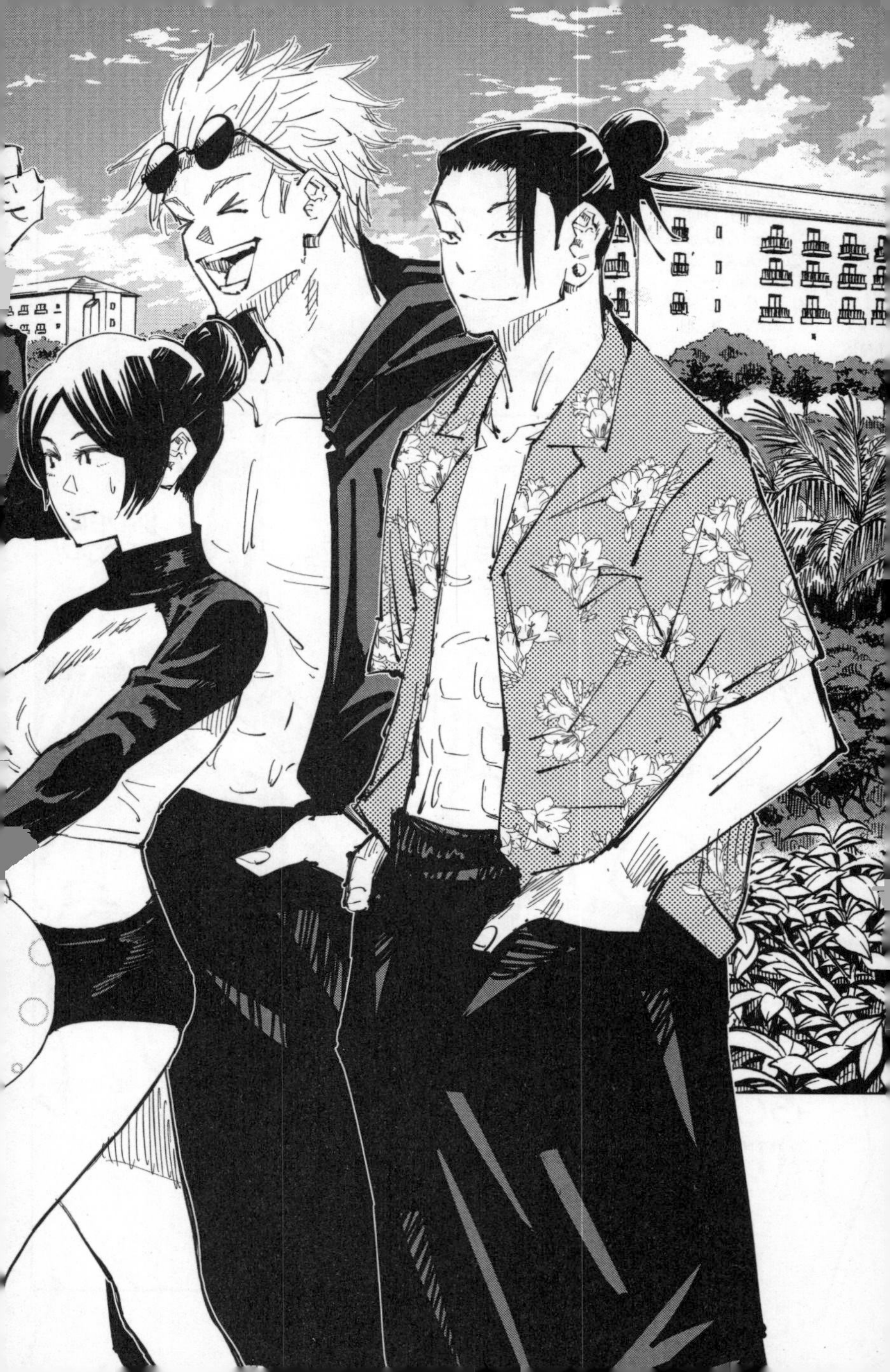

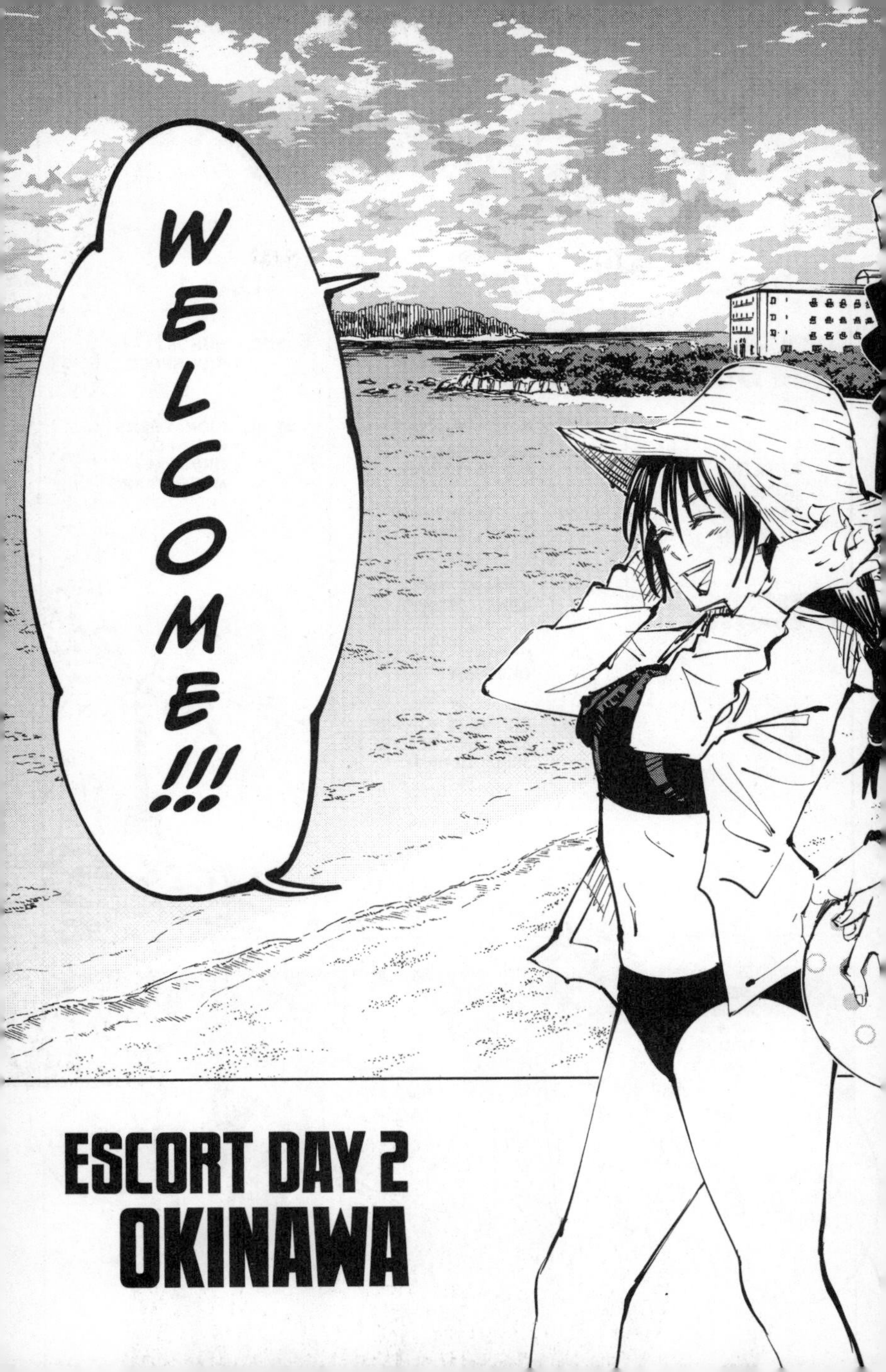
WELCOME!!!
ESCORT DAY 2
OKINAWA

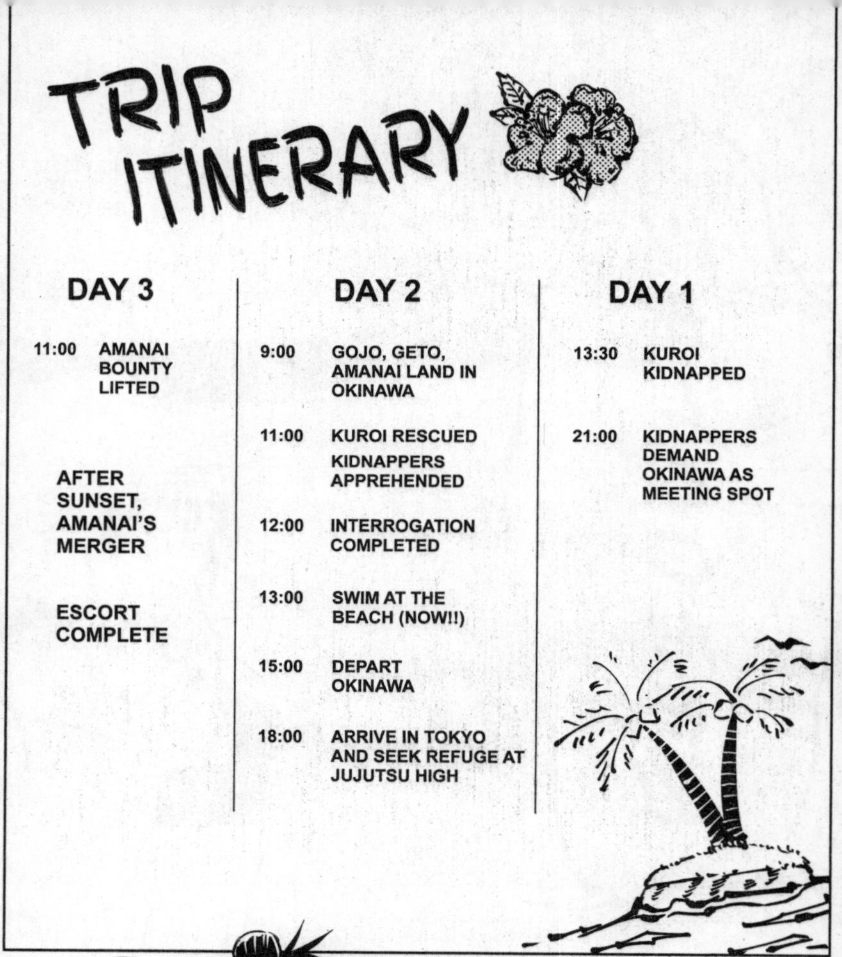

TRIP ITINERARY

DAY 3

11:00	AMANAI BOUNTY LIFTED

AFTER SUNSET, AMANAI'S MERGER

ESCORT COMPLETE

DAY 2

9:00	GOJO, GETO, AMANAI LAND IN OKINAWA
11:00	KUROI RESCUED KIDNAPPERS APPREHENDED
12:00	INTERROGATION COMPLETED
13:00	SWIM AT THE BEACH (NOW!!)
15:00	DEPART OKINAWA
18:00	ARRIVE IN TOKYO AND SEEK REFUGE AT JUJUTSU HIGH

DAY 1

13:30	KUROI KIDNAPPED
21:00	KIDNAPPERS DEMAND OKINAWA AS MEETING SPOT

NO WORRIES, IT WAS A SURPRISE ATTACK.

IT WAS ALSO MY FAULT.

I'M SO EMBARRASSED.

I CAN'T BELIEVE I WAS DEFEATED BY A MEMBER OF THE TIME VESSEL ASSOCIATION. A NON-CURSE USER TOO...

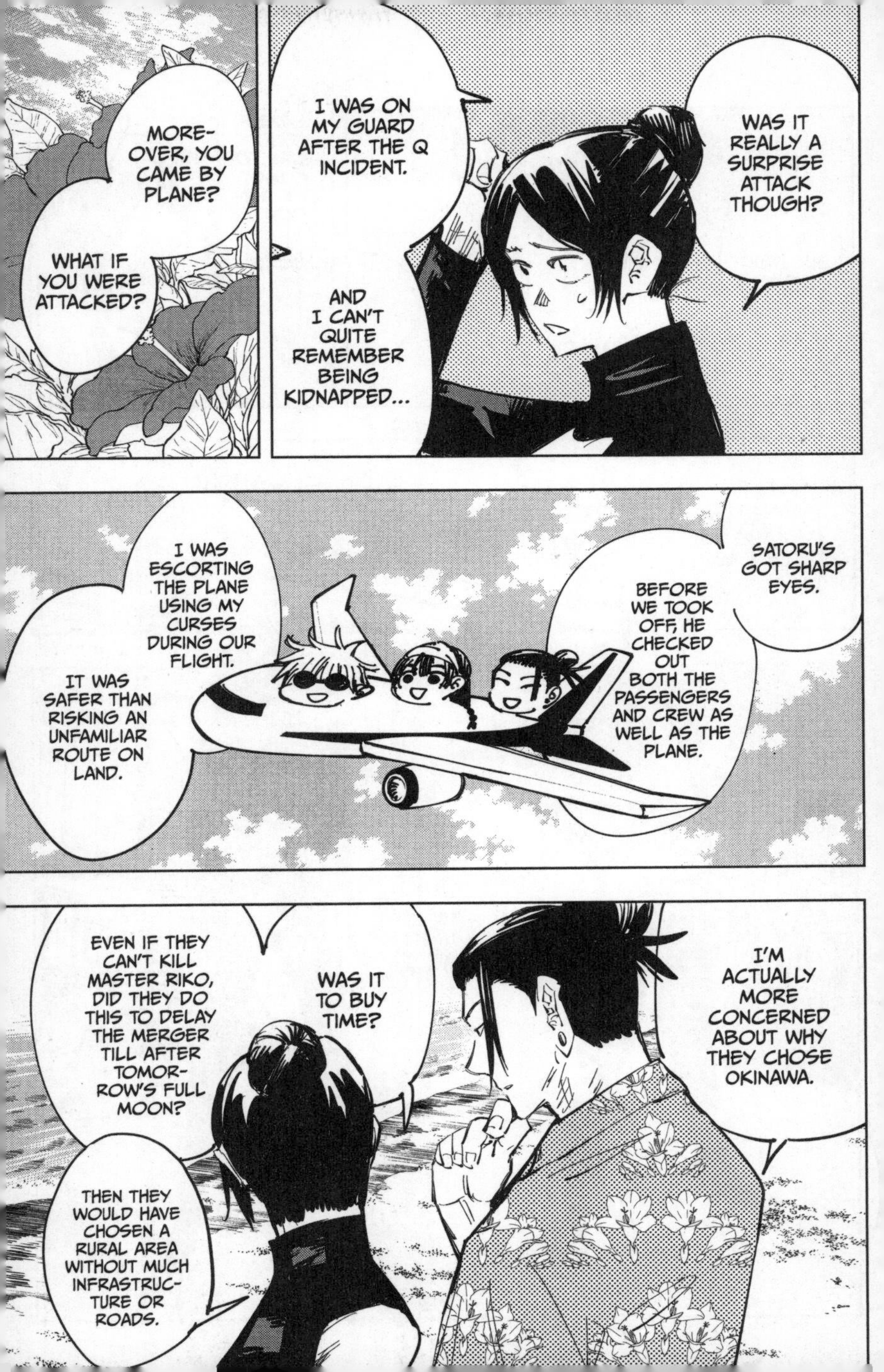
WAS IT REALLY A SURPRISE ATTACK THOUGH?
I WAS ON MY GUARD AFTER THE Q INCIDENT.
AND I CAN'T QUITE REMEMBER BEING KIDNAPPED...
MORE-OVER, YOU CAME BY PLANE?
WHAT IF YOU WERE ATTACKED?
SATORU'S GOT SHARP EYES.
BEFORE WE TOOK OFF, HE CHECKED OUT BOTH THE PASSENGERS AND CREW AS WELL AS THE PLANE.
I WAS ESCORTING THE PLANE USING MY CURSES DURING OUR FLIGHT.
IT WAS SAFER THAN RISKING AN UNFAMILIAR ROUTE ON LAND.
I'M ACTUALLY MORE CONCERNED ABOUT WHY THEY CHOSE OKINAWA.
WAS IT TO BUY TIME?
EVEN IF THEY CAN'T KILL MASTER RIKO, DID THEY DO THIS TO DELAY THE MERGER TILL AFTER TOMOR-ROW'S FULL MOON?
THEN THEY WOULD HAVE CHOSEN A RURAL AREA WITHOUT MUCH INFRASTRUC-TURE OR ROADS.

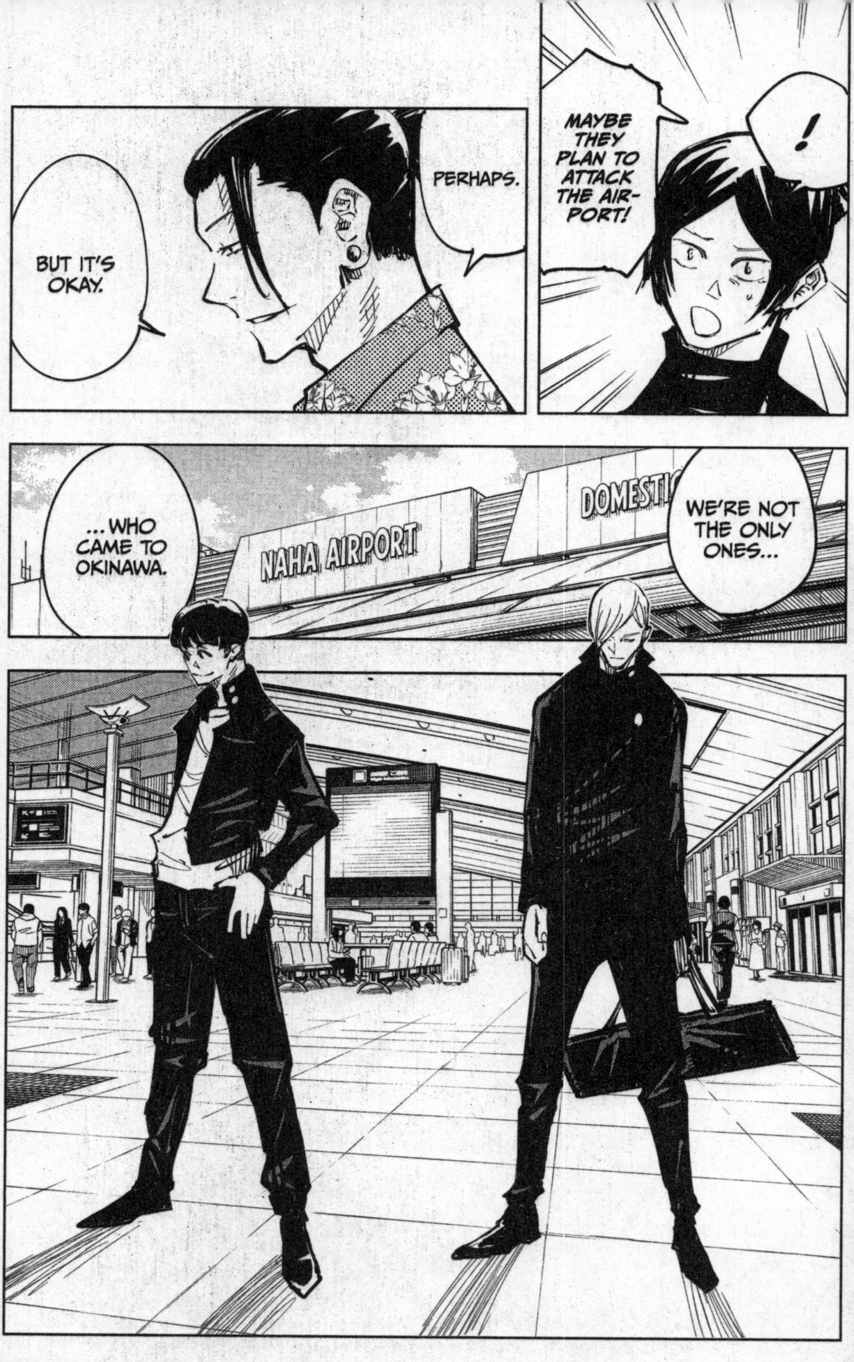
!
MAYBE THEY PLAN TO ATTACK THE AIR-PORT!
PERHAPS.
BUT IT'S OKAY.
DOMESTI
WE'RE NOT THE ONLY ONES...
NAHA AIRPORT
...WHO CAME TO OKINAWA.

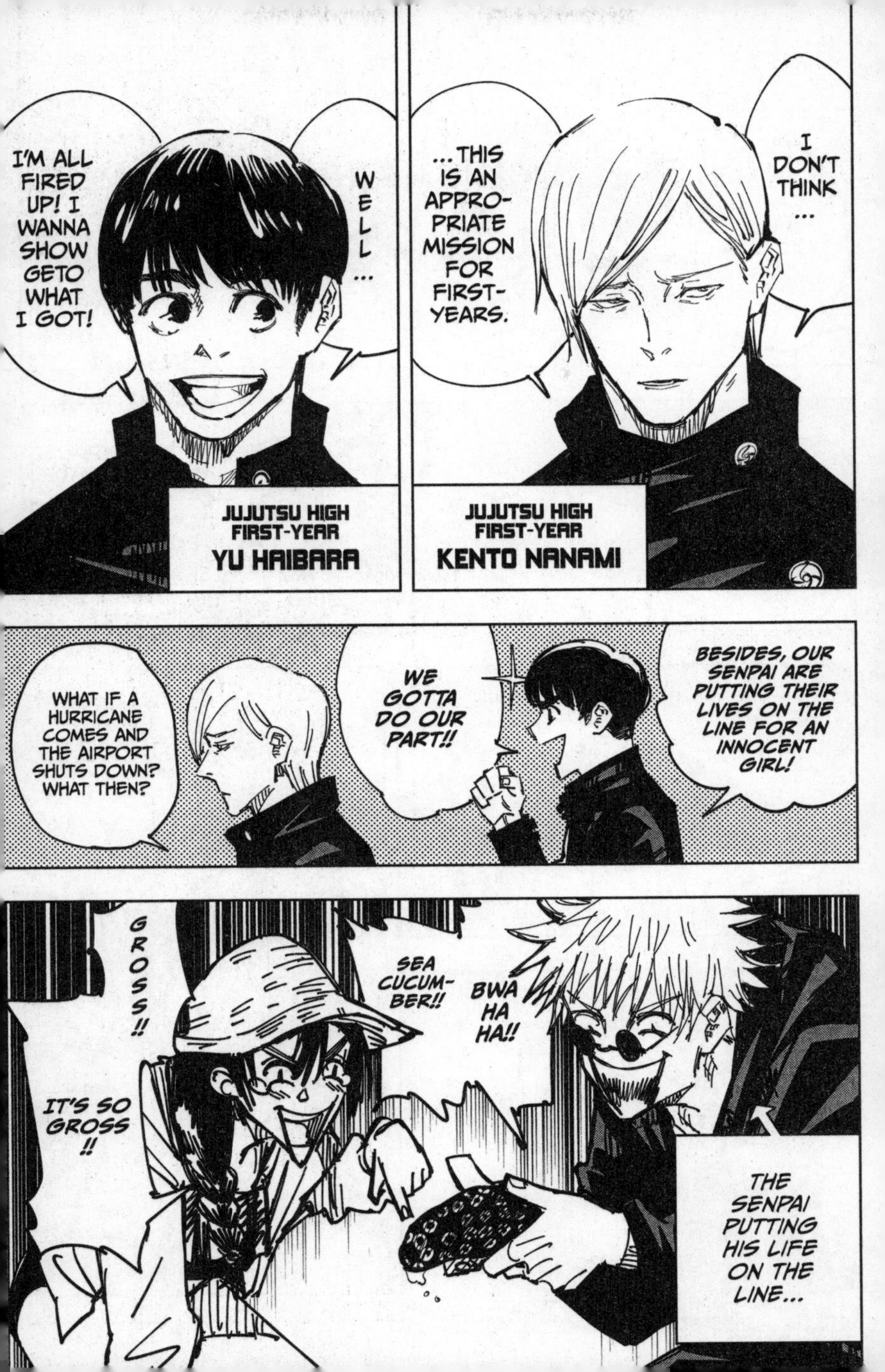
I DON'T THINK...
...THIS IS AN APPROPRIATE MISSION FOR FIRST-YEARS.
JUJUTSU HIGH FIRST-YEAR KENTO NANAMI
WELL...
I'M ALL FIRED UP! I WANNA SHOW GETO WHAT I GOT!
JUJUTSU HIGH FIRST-YEAR YU HAIBARA
BESIDES, OUR SENPAI ARE PUTTING THEIR LIVES ON THE LINE FOR AN INNOCENT GIRL!
WE GOTTA DO OUR PART!!
WHAT IF A HURRICANE COMES AND THE AIRPORT SHUTS DOWN? WHAT THEN?
BWA HA HA!!
SEA CUCUMBER!!
GROSS!!
IT'S SO GROSS!!
THE SENPAI PUTTING HIS LIFE ON THE LINE...

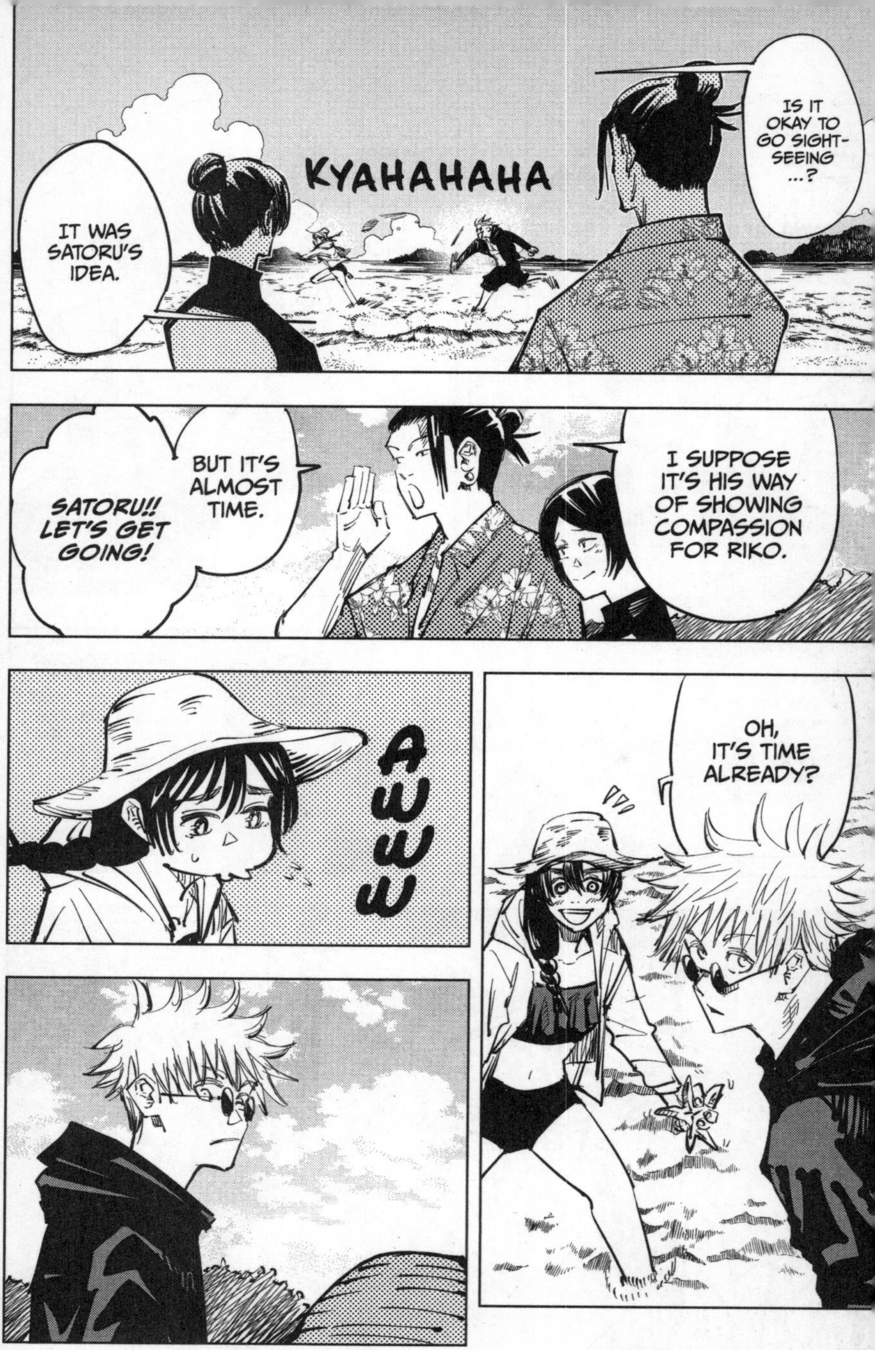
IS IT OKAY TO GO SIGHT-SEEING ...?
KYAHAHAHA
IT WAS SATORU'S IDEA.
I SUPPOSE IT'S HIS WAY OF SHOWING COMPASSION FOR RIKO.
BUT IT'S ALMOST TIME.
SATORU!! LET'S GET GOING!
OH, IT'S TIME ALREADY?
AWWW

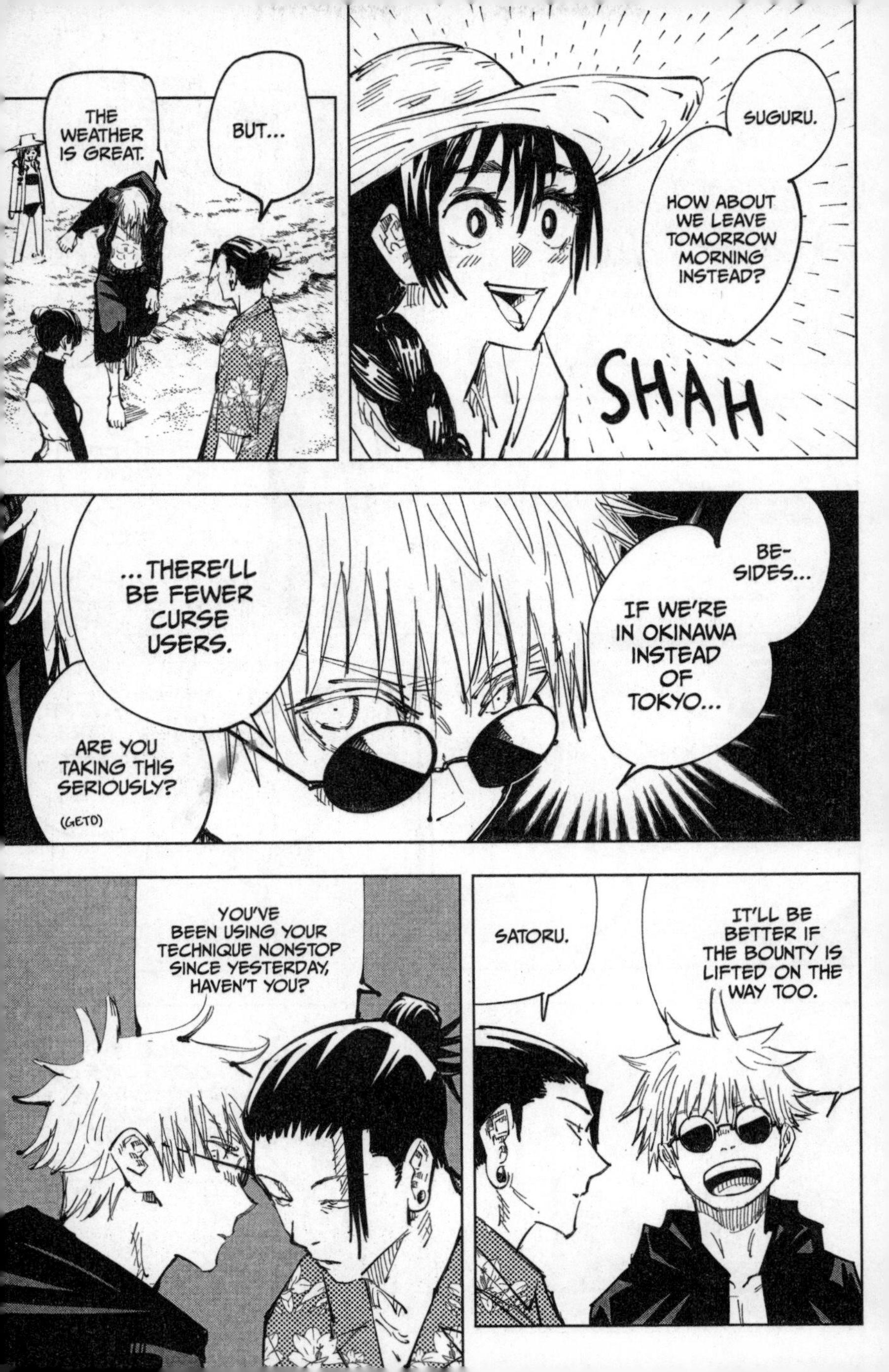
SUGURU.
HOW ABOUT WE LEAVE TOMORROW MORNING INSTEAD?
SHAH
BUT...
THE WEATHER IS GREAT.
BE-SIDES...
IF WE'RE IN OKINAWA INSTEAD OF TOKYO...
...THERE'LL BE FEWER CURSE USERS.
ARE YOU TAKING THIS SERIOUSLY?
(GETO)
IT'LL BE BETTER IF THE BOUNTY IS LIFTED ON THE WAY TOO.
SATORU.
YOU'VE BEEN USING YOUR TECHNIQUE NONSTOP SINCE YESTERDAY, HAVEN'T YOU?

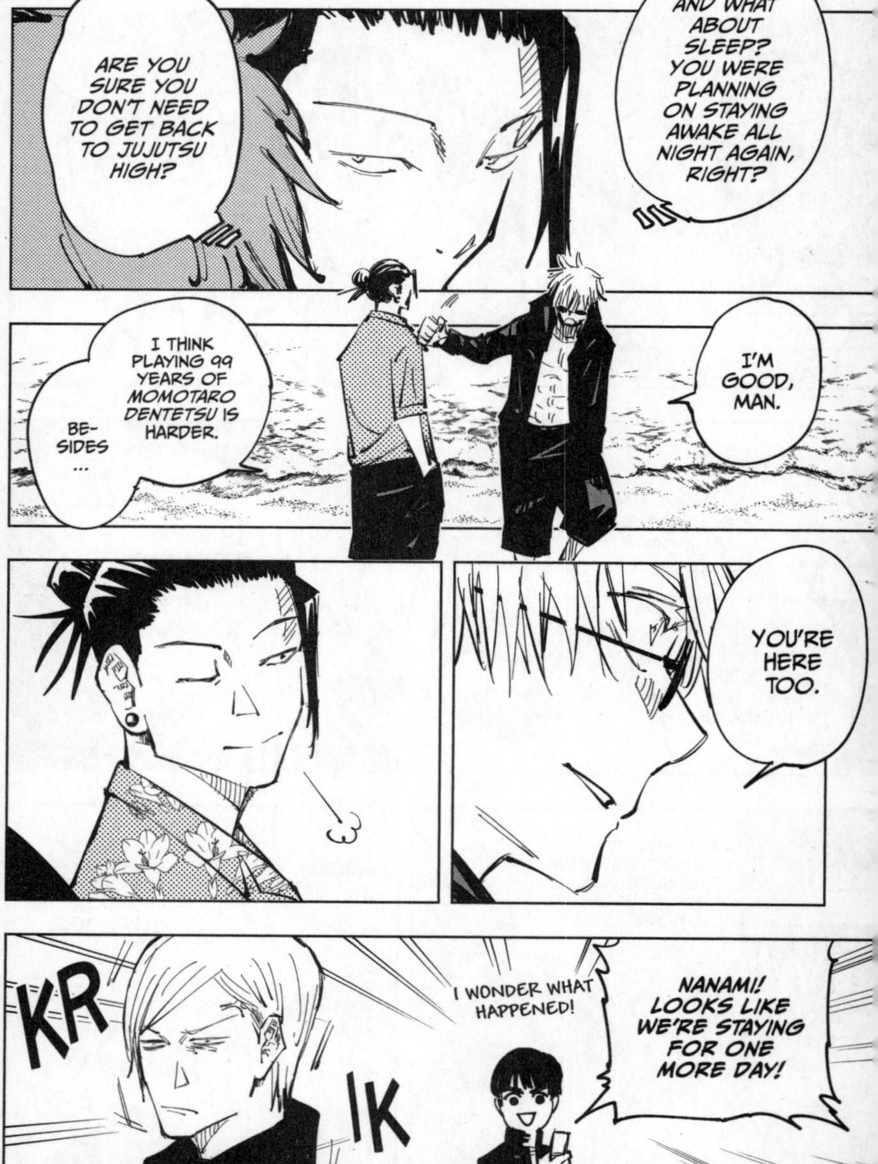
AND WHAT ABOUT SLEEP? YOU WERE PLANNING ON STAYING AWAKE ALL NIGHT AGAIN, RIGHT?
ARE YOU SURE YOU DON'T NEED TO GET BACK TO JUJUTSU HIGH?
I'M GOOD, MAN.
BESIDES...
I THINK PLAYING 99 YEARS OF MOMOTARO DENTETSU IS HARDER.
YOU'RE HERE TOO.
NANAMI! LOOKS LIKE WE'RE STAYING FOR ONE MORE DAY!
I WONDER WHAT HAPPENED!
KR
IK

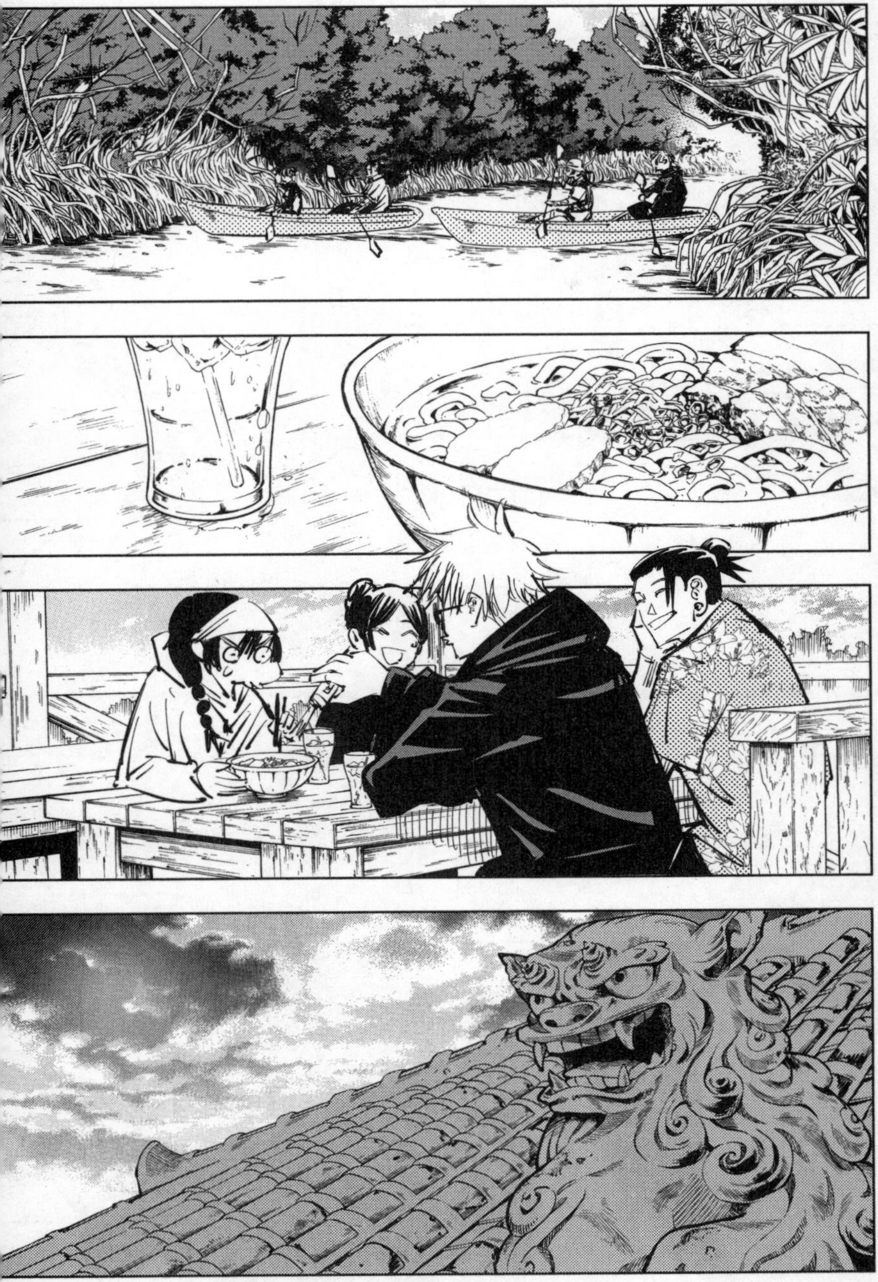

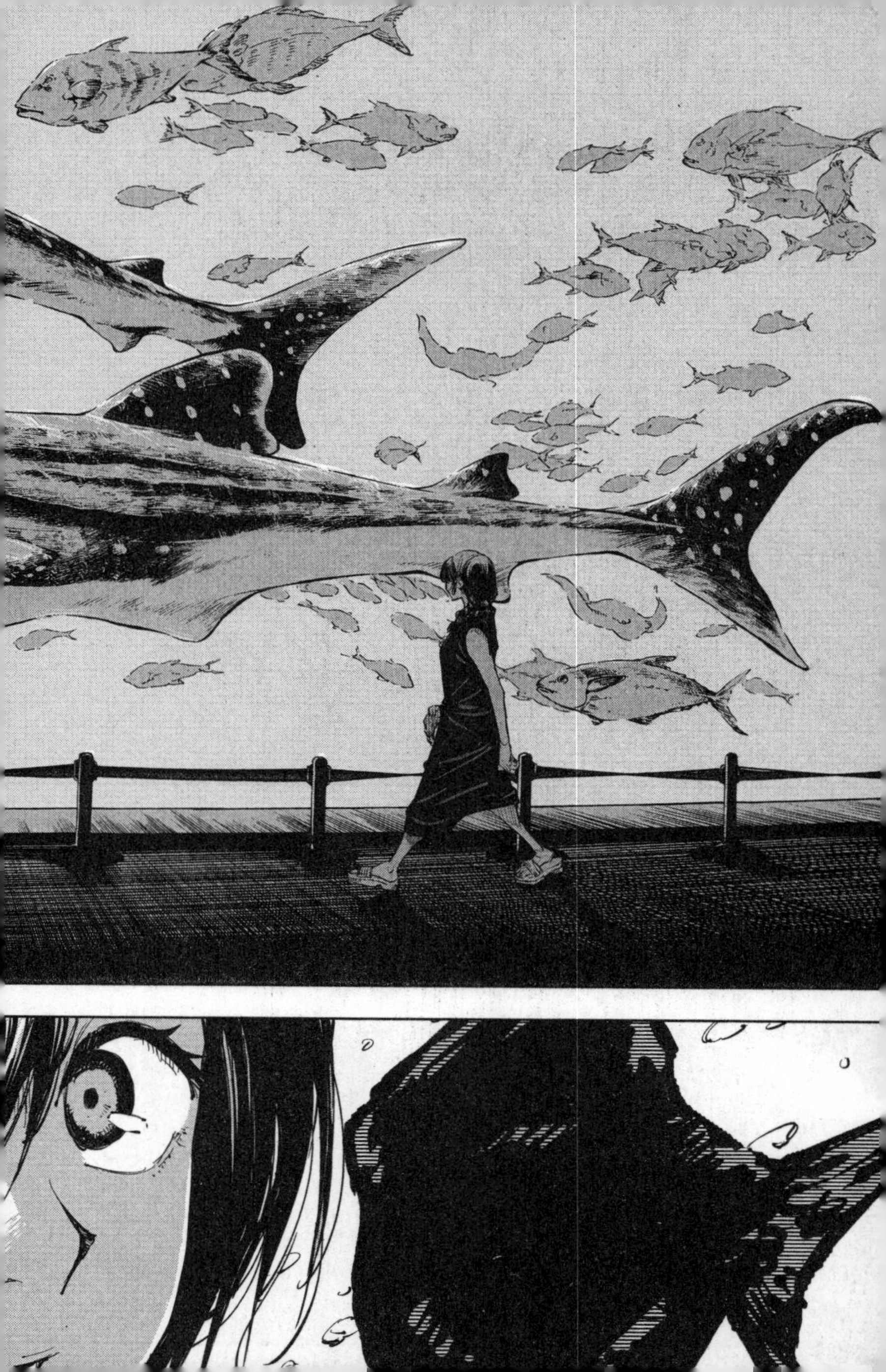

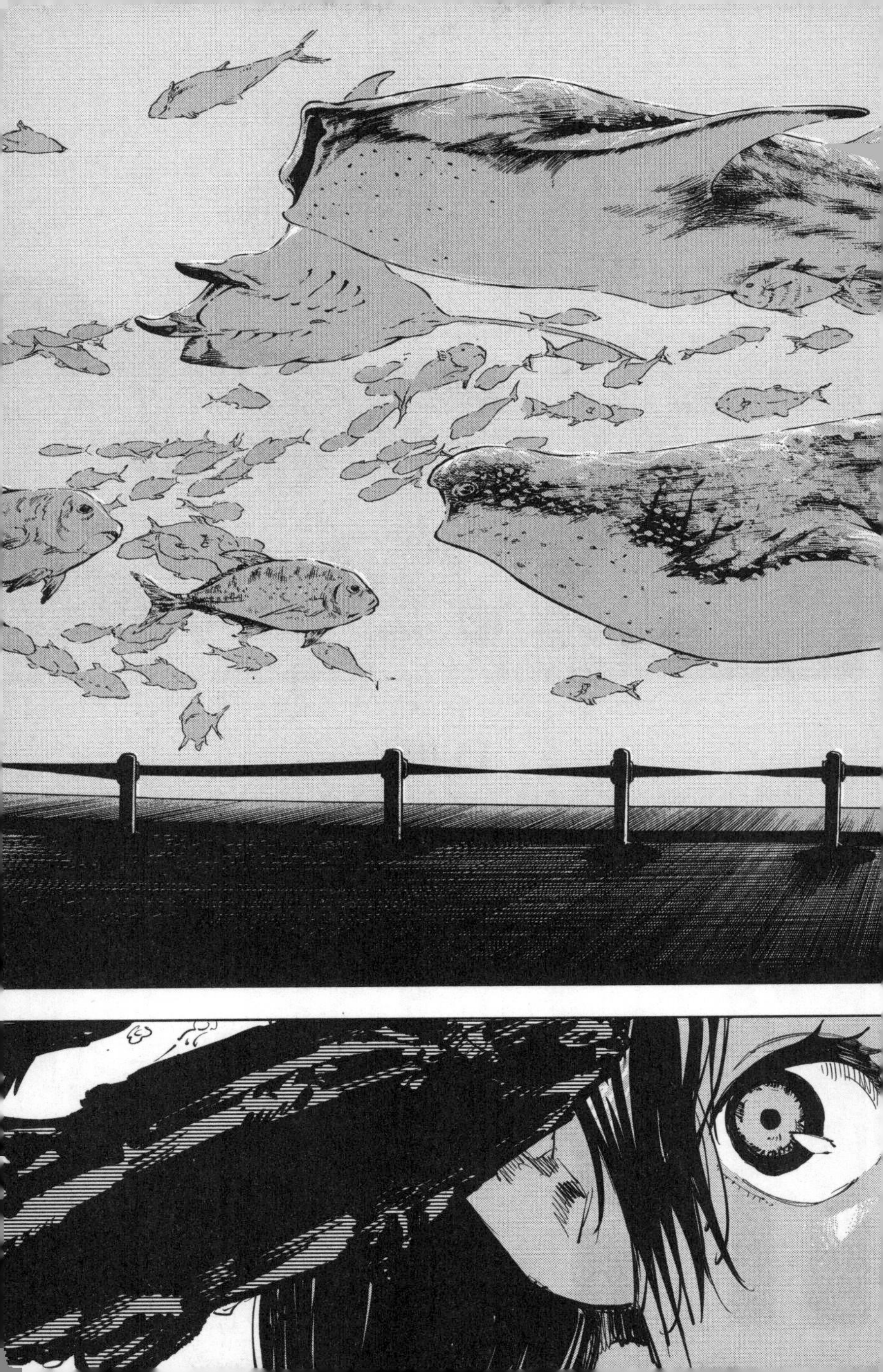

ESCORT DAY 3
(DAY OF THE MERGER)

TOKYO JUJUTSU HIGH IN THE FOOTHILLS OF MOUNT MUSHIRO

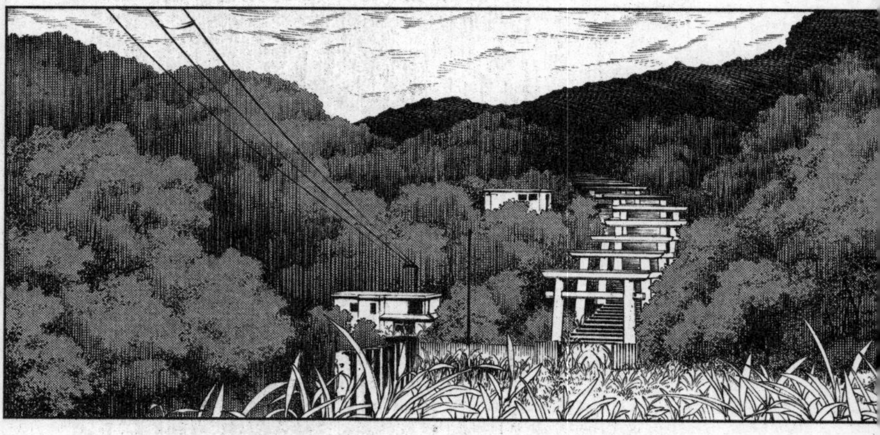

15:00
(FOUR HOURS SINCE RIKO AMANAI'S BOUNTY WAS LIFTED)

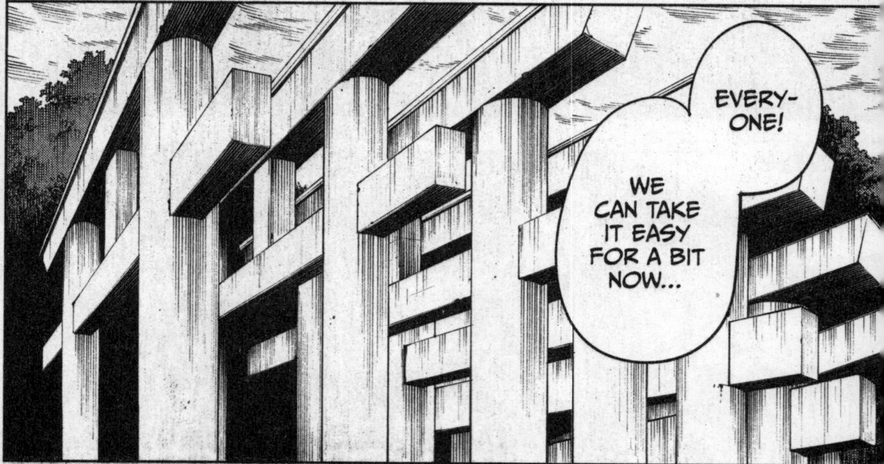
EVERY-ONE!
WE CAN TAKE IT EASY FOR A BIT NOW...

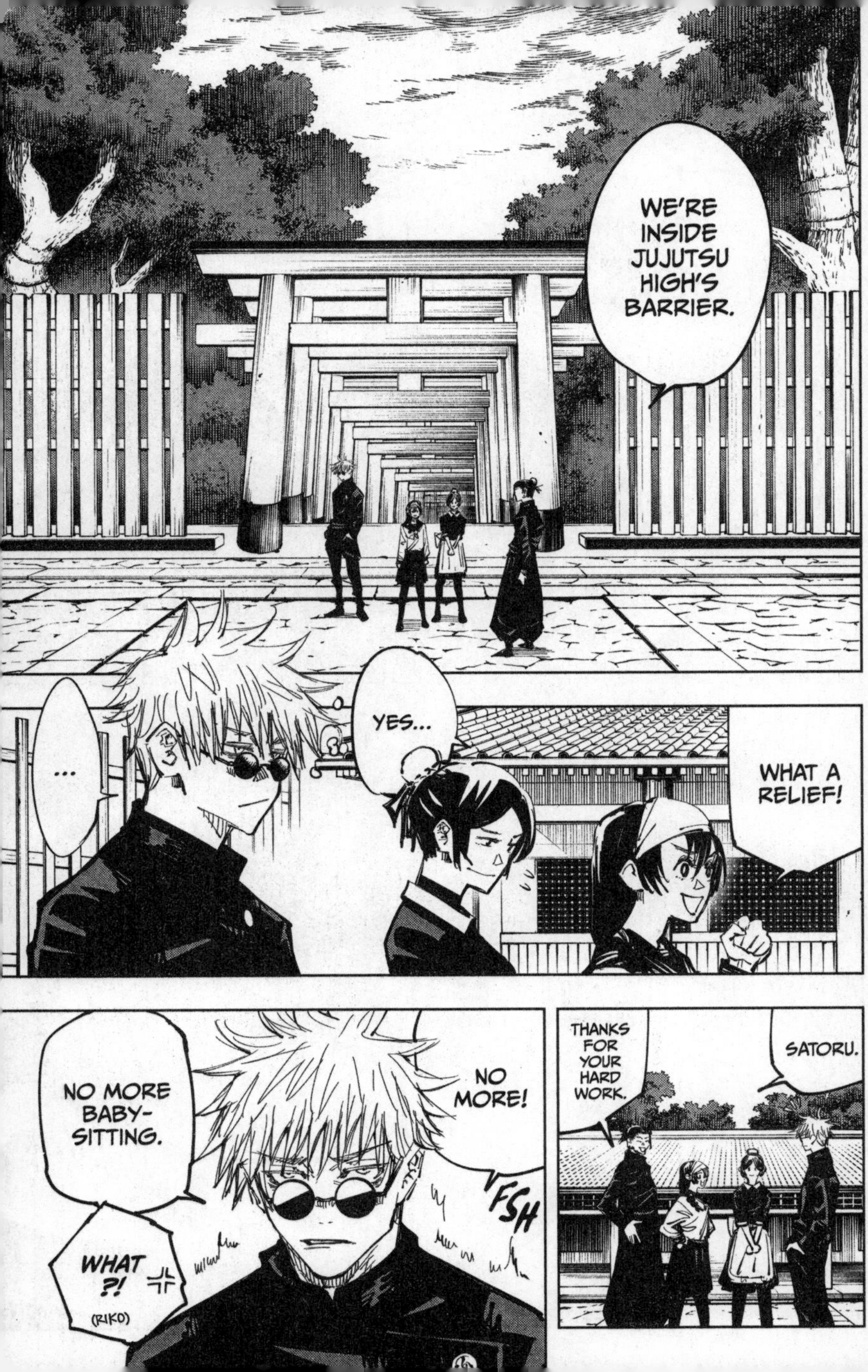
WE'RE INSIDE JUJUTSU HIGH'S BARRIER.
WHAT A RELIEF!
YES...
...
SATORU.
THANKS FOR YOUR HARD WORK.
NO MORE!
NO MORE BABY-SITTING.
FSH
WHAT?!
(RIKO)

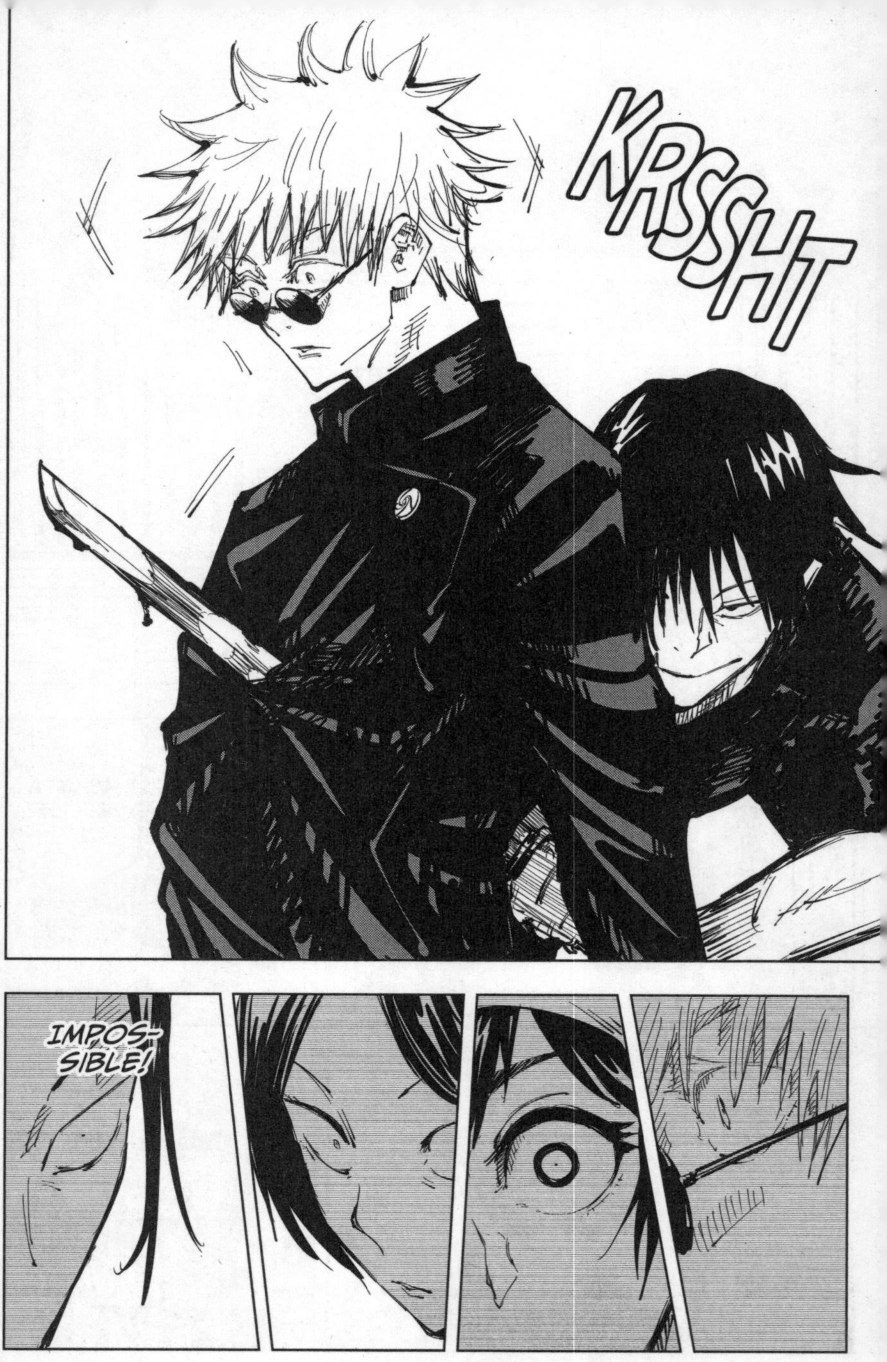
KRSSHT
IMPOS-SIBLE!

THIS IS INSIDE OF JUJUTSU HIGH'S BARRIER!

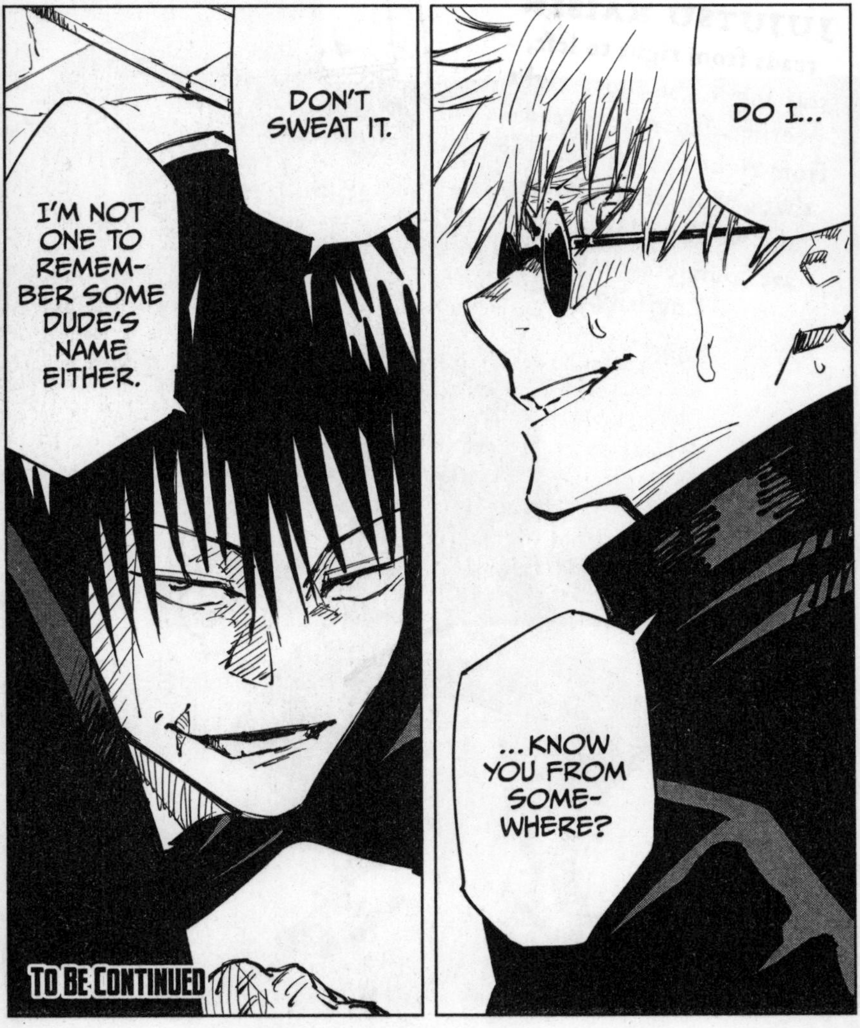
DO I...
...KNOW YOU FROM SOME-WHERE?
DON'T SWEAT IT.
I'M NOT ONE TO REMEM-BER SOME DUDE'S NAME EITHER.
TO BE CONTINUED

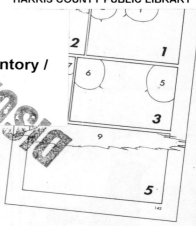

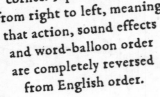
...starting in the upper-right corner. Japanese is read from right to left, meaning that action, sound effects and word-balloon order are completely reversed from English order.